Corrective
and
Remedial
Teaching

Corrective and Remedial Teaching

second edition

Wayne Otto
University of Wisconsin
Richard A. McMenemy
Portland, Oregon, Public Schools
Richard J. Smith
University of Wisconsin

Houghton Mifflin Company • Boston
Atlanta
Dallas
Geneva, Illinois
Hopewell, New Jersey
Palo Alto

Excerpts from the following books and articles have been reprinted by permission of the publishers:

A. D. Bannatyne, The color phonics system, in J. Money (Ed.), *The disabled reader* (Baltimore: Johns Hopkins Press, 1967).

A. Gillingham and B. Stillman, *Remedial training for children with specific disability in reading, spelling and penmanship* (Cambridge, Mass.: Educators Publishing Service, 1968).

D. B. Krathwohl, B. S. Bloom, and B. B. Masia, *Taxonomy of educational objectives, handbook II: Affective domain* (New York: David McKay Co., Inc., 1964).

C. A. Lefevre, *Linguistics, English and the language arts* (Boston: Allyn and Bacon, 1970).

C. C. Fries, R. G. Wilson, and M. K. Rudolph, *Merrill linguistic readers, reader 1—* Teacher's edition (Columbus, Ohio: Charles E. Merrill, 1966).

J. Moffett, *A student-centered language arts curriculum, grades k-6* (Boston: Houghton Mifflin, 1968); *Teaching the universe of discourse* (Boston: Houghton Mifflin, 1968).

J. L. Orton, The Orton-Gillingham approach, in J. Money (Ed.), *The disabled reader* (Baltimore: Johns Hopkins Press, 1967).

W. Otto and R. J. Smith, *Administering the school reading program* (Boston: Houghton Mifflin, 1970).

R. C. Pooley et al., *English language arts in Wisconsin* (Madison, Wis.: Department of Public Instruction, 1967).

C. R. Rogers, *Freedom to learn* (Columbus, Ohio: Charles E. Merrill, 1969).

E. B. Smith, K. S. Goodman, and R. Meredith, *Language and thinking in the elementary school* (New York: Holt, 1970).

Also:

Excerpts from R. G. Nichols and L. A. Stevens, *Are you listening?* Copyright 1957 McGraw-Hill Book Company. Used with permission of McGraw-Hill Book Company.

Reprinted with permission of the publisher: Otto, W., Askov, E., & Cooper, C. Legibility ratings for handwriting samples: A pragmatic approach. *Perceptual and Motor Skills*, 1967, 25, 638.

From the *SRA reading program*—Teaching Guide. © 1964, 1968, 1970, Donald E. Rasmussen and Lenina Goldberg. Reprinted by permission of the publisher, Science Research Associates, Inc.

Adaptation of "Steps in the survey Q3R method" in *Effective study*, 4th Edition, by Francis P. Robinson. Copyright 1941, 1946 by Harper & Row, Publishers, Inc. Copyright © 1961, 1970 by Francis P. Robinson. Reprinted by permission of the publishers.

Lift-off to reading, Cycle I—Teacher's Manual by Myron Woolman. © 1966, Institute of Educational Research. Reprinted by permission of the publisher, Science Research Associates, Inc.

Library of Congress Catalog Card Number: 72-4799

ISBN: 395-12662-2

Human beings have a natural
potentiality to learn.

Carl Rogers
Freedom to Learn

Contents

Preface

Our general purpose in preparing this revised and substantially expanded version of *Corrective and Remedial Teaching* is the same as it was originally:

> This book was written—as were many books before it—in response to a need. In many settings—ranging from brief in-service workshops to courses in remedial education—we have come to know teachers who are concerned about children with learning problems. The great majority of them have expected to continue to work in regular classrooms, some of them have been seeking specialization as full time remedial teachers in school settings, and a few have hoped ultimately to work in clinical settings. Yet, much of what has been written is confined to the specific area of remedial reading and addressed mainly to the latter group. This book is intended for the larger group: teachers who will deal with learning problems in the several basic skill areas in a typical school setting.

The focus remains on the underachiever in any or all of the several basic skill areas and what can be done about solving the underachievement problem in the schools.

In the original edition, we placed at least implicit emphasis on the area of reading. The rationale was that problems in reading are justifiably the cause for the greatest concern in most schools and among most teachers. In this revision the emphasis on reading is quite explicit. We frankly believe that reading is the most basic of the several basic skills; consequently, we have given reading a disproportionate share of the coverage. Two new chapters on reading have been added, for a total of five. One deals with the problem of placing remedial instruction in reading within a framework that includes affective as well as cognitive development in reading. The other presents a careful consideration of the strengths and limitations of a variety of specific approaches that are being advocated for tackling reading problems.

A third new chapter has to do with the development of listening skills. Listening is an important source of information and a vital contributor to language development. As such, it merits consideration among the essential skill areas. Each of the chapters devoted to other skill areas—spelling, arithmetic, handwriting, and oral and written expression—has been revised in view of current trends and developments and of perceptions that have changed on the basis of our experience. The focus of the chapter on oral and written expression is shifted from the pursuit of standards to total language development. Spelling is placed in historical as well as total language development perspective. Specific approaches to the development of handwriting skills are given more attention. The focus on fundamentals remains in the arithmetic chapter, but certain new developments are considered.

The remaining chapters—Chapters 1 through 4 and 15—have to do with the general framework for corrective and remedial teaching, and each has been revised and expanded to reflect new perceptions and procedures. Chapter 2 includes among other additions a section devoted to the concept of dyslexia and a more comprehensive treatment of visual problems. Important additions to Chapter 4 include sections on the potential role of behavioral objectives and behavior modification techniques in corrective and remedial teaching. A brief case study form for use in the classroom is new in Chapter 4. In Chapter 15 principles for facilitating learning, a framework for organizing instruction, and a consideration of compensatory education have been added.

We have deleted the discussion questions of the original edition and substituted "Thoughts for Discussion." More often than not the questions that can be raised relative to corrective and remedial teaching have no definitive answers. Instead there are issues to be confronted, myths to be examined, and stands to be taken. Rather than continue to appear to be demanding arbitrary answers to arbitrary questions, we have decided that an invitation to discussion may be closer to what we wanted in the first place. We have chosen the thoughts for discussion that are included at the ends of chapters because we think they invite discussion, not because we agree, disagree, endorse, or condemn.

Corrective and Remedial Teaching includes the substance of a general course on remedial education, and it is intended to serve as the basic text for such a course. The focus on reading also makes it suitable for use as the primary text for the remedial reading course. The chapters devoted to other skills put reading into a curriculum context that is too often ignored when remedial reading becomes the sole focus of attention. Aside from its principal use as a course text, the book should continue to serve as a guidebook for teachers as they work with underachievers and for faculty groups as they consider ways and means for meeting the challenge of underachievement.

Certain biases of the authors will be apparent throughout the book. Each of us comes from a unique background of training and experience and our perceptions and inclinations are not always the same. We make no apology for this, for what we hope to have achieved is balance in the total coverage.

We owe special thanks to the following people for specific contributions to the preparation of this book:

Robert C. Fredricks, Counselor, Portland Community College

Leonard Z. Friedman, O.D., Optometrist, Portland, Oregon

Judith Brown, Remedial Specialist, Portland Public Schools

And we are again indebted to the usual people—students, colleagues, secretaries, wives, and miscellaneous relatives and friends—for their ideas, criticisms, encouragement, and typing.

Wayne Otto
Richard A. McMenemy
Richard J. Smith

Chapter 1

Introduction

THE PROBLEM OF UNDERACHIEVEMENT

Estimates of the magnitude of the problem of underachievement tend to vary, depending on *how* "underachievement" is defined and *who* is included in the population under consideration. Nevertheless, there is no questioning the fact that the problem is vast and that it is not confined to any particular segment of the general population. Consider some excerpts from a report on reading disorders sponsored by the Department of Health, Education and Welfare (Report of the Secretary's National Advisory Committee on Dyslexia and Related Reading Disorders):

> Despite the efforts of dedicated teachers and ever-increasing expenditures for education, vast numbers of American children are falling behind in school every year. With promotion policies subject to local control and variation, every year from two to ten percent of children become nonpromotion statistics. The most frequent cause is reading failure. (P. 21) [*This book, too, is based on the underlying assumption that the most potent cause for general underachievement is failure in reading. The assumption is discussed in detail later in this chapter and throughout the book. Here the point is that a focus on reading disorders amounts, to a large extent, to a focus on the problem of underachievement.*]
>
> . . . these figures do not divulge the actual magnitude of the problem. Many children with severe reading disorders are promoted with their classmates even though they have difficulty keeping up. Many of these children drop out of school and later fail in society. . . . Various studies . . . lead to the conclusion that reading disorders affect about 15 percent of the children in school today. An exact figure is difficult to determine because of the various ways of defining reading disorders. (P. 21)
>
> . . . Children of adequate intelligence but retarded in reading often perform adequately in nonreading school work during the early grades. However, as the years of reading failure build up feelings of their own inadequacy and dissatisfaction with school, their overall academic work is severely affected. . . . the 15 percent figure, based on measurement of reading performance without reference to mental ability, is well beyond the range to be expected on the basis of normal human variability. . . . That the problem is nationwide is indicated by the fact that such studies have come from every part of the country. (Pp. 22–23)
>
> Although there are few adequate incidence studies of reading disorders among urban, nonwhite, bilingual, and disadvantaged populations, some studies, as

well as reliable estimates from a variety of sources, indicate that the incidence is higher than 15 percent among these population groups. (P. 27)

We shall return to some recommendations of the Secretary's Committee in the final chapter of this book. In the present context the excerpts from the Committee's report serve to demonstrate both the magnitude and complexity of the underachievement problem. But perhaps statistics and committee reports are superfluous. Everyone who has had school experience, either as a teacher or student, is likely to be aware not only of the general problem of underachievement but also of the very specific and very personal problems of underachievers.

There are many causes for underachievement. Some children fail to achieve because their limited ability does not permit them to keep up with their classmates; others fail apparently because they are bored with the too slow pace of instruction; still others fail for a wide variety of reasons ranging from physical and psychological problems to too limited experiential backgrounds. Thus, it is not possible to generalize very broadly about underachievement and underachievers because the learning problems that cause the difficulty are likely to differ from case to case.

We have, however, identified six general categories in which children with achievement problems tend to be classified. The categories are by no means mutually exclusive nor do they amount to well defined clusters of causal factors. Certain physiological and/or psychological factors would, for example, be found in common among the individuals in all six categories. The categories serve mainly to demonstrate the scope of the underachievement problem.

1. *Underachievers with Average Capacity* On the basis of their capacity to learn, children with average intelligence are usually expected to achieve approximately at their chronological grade-placement level; those who do not are underachievers. Any of a wide variety of learning difficulties may be responsible for failure to achieve. The problem is complicated by the fact that in many cases failure leads to frustration and frustration leads to— or complicates existing—emotional problems, which in turn interfere with further attempts to learn and create still more frustration. Thus, the difficulty may become chronic, and as failure begets failure a severe learning problem is created. Such cases often become candidates for remedial programs.

It should be made explicit here that "average" pupils can be expected to score only *approximately* at grade level on achievement tests. In practice, half of the pupils in a particular grade would be expected to score above grade level and half would be expected to score below; "grade level" is simply the midpoint on a distribution of scores attained on a test by pupils in the norming group for the test. As a rule of thumb, it would usually be appropriate to say that pupils who score six months to a year above or below actual grade placement are within the range of expected achievement for pupils with average intelligence.

2. *Slow Learners* Children with IQ's between 80 and 90 are often called slow learners. Because of their limited capacities they cannot realistically be expected to achieve at their chronological grade level. While a child with an average IQ (90–110) is probably an underachiever if he fails to work successfully at about grade level, a slow learner who is achieving substantially below grade level may very well be achieving to the limit of his capacity. All children who are achieving below grade level are not necessarily underachievers. Yet, many schools have special programs, ostensibly for underachievers, that are designed to include all pupils who score below grade level on achievement tests. Such programs are often established under pressure from critics who apparently believe that all pupils can achieve at grade level if they are given special help.

Of course, some slow learners are likely to be underachievers in that they are achieving not only below grade level but also below the expected level of their limited capacity. It is all too common for slow learners to get off to a bad start toward mastering the basic skills because at the time they are enrolled in first grade they have not yet reached a level of mental maturity that enables them to respond successfully to typical beginning instruction. When a child is "ready too late" he is likely to get caught up in the cycle of failure-frustration-more-failure-greater-frustration that leads to both underachievement and severe learning problems. As we shall point out later, slow learners in general are likely to respond best to teaching that is adapted to their level and rate of learning. Only slow learners who have difficulties that interfere with their working up to their capacity level should be given remedial help. The point to be stressed here is that not all slow learners are underachievers nor are they all likely to respond to remedial teaching.

3. *Bright Underachievers* It is good to have the point clearly in mind that some children who *are achieving at grade level* are underachievers. Children with high IQ's have intellectual capacities that make them potentially able to achieve above the level of their chronological grade placement; when they do not, they are clearly underachievers despite the fact that they may produce fairly competent work at grade level. Bright children fairly commonly respond to a lack of challenge in their day-to-day school experience by withdrawing from the learning situation; as a result, they bog down and fail to realize their potential. At best, they continue to produce enough to get by at grade level, but often the lack of challenge results in such complete withdrawal that they finally acquire learning problems of varying degrees of severity. In practice, it is the bright underachiever who is most routinely ignored by the schools. We are so prone to strive to get as many children as possible "up to grade level" that we lose sight of the fact that many children should be substantially above grade level in achievement.

4. *Reluctant Learners* Some children are able to attain adequate scores on achievement tests but fail to function in the classroom at a level con-

sistent with their test scores and abilities. Such children are not likely to be located by screening attempts that are confined to comparisons of formal test scores. It is important, then, to go beyond test scores to the observations and recommendations of classroom teachers in order to do an adequate job of locating and, subsequently, helping these underachievers. Reluctant learners are commonly lacking in motivation. Often they can be reached by teaching that is designed to stimulate and to develop interests. Occasionally they require instruction that is, essentially, individualized remedial help before they can make optimum use of the skills and abilities they possess.

5. *Children with Limited Experiential Backgrounds*   Many children still, in an age of mass communication, come to school from homes that are barren of common cultural advantages and/or essential language experiences. A common mistake is to label such children "dull" when they fail to respond to instruction that is, in fact, alien to most of their previous experiences. Unless these children get the special help they need early in their school experience, most of them are likely to emerge as underachievers in the early grades. When no help is provided, the vicious cycle of failure-frustration-failure becomes operant almost immediately and more complicated learning problems often result.

6. *Children with Limited Language Development*   Language development is inextricably related, of course, to experiential background. Nevertheless, language development per se has been receiving considerable attention from many workers, and there is no questioning that lack of adequate language development can be a seriously delimiting factor in children's achievement (Bush and Giles, 1969; Horn, 1970; Smith, Goodman, and Meredith, 1970). In the present context, we shall do little more than acknowledge the problem, for we feel that at this time the most productive approach is to handle language development as a *prior* concern rather than as a *remedial* concern as the concept of remediation is developed in this book.

We do wish to acknowledge what we consider two particularly sensible and significant approaches to the problem. First, Rohwer and Ammons (1971) have reported on a research project concerned simultaneously with assessing and improving learning skills in culturally disadvantaged children *and* assessing and improving language abilities in children drawn from the same population. While the task of integrating the two thrusts remains for the future, the dual thrust appears clearly to be a step in the right direction. Second, the staff of the Language and Thinking Program at CEMREL (Central Midwestern Regional Educational Laboratory) is developing an instructional package that is designed to ". . . train children to cope with and use language oriented concepts at an early stage in their school experience so that they will be more cognitively competent later in school" (Willis, 1971). In each case, the intent is to provide children with the basic tool concepts they need to respond adequately to the instruction they are receiving—or will receive—in school.

The main point to be made here is that children from widely different backgrounds and with markedly different characteristics may share a common need for special help if they are to break out of the failure-frustration pattern that is so often associated with lack of achievement. Yet the existence of a common need must not suggest that there is a common or routine approach to meeting the need. Unique individuals are still involved. What is suggested is that we must take care not to exclude from corrective and remedial teaching bright underachievers, reluctant learners, or experientially limited children because of a too great tendency to label them "lazy" or "dull."

PURPOSE AND SCOPE OF THE BOOK

The threefold purpose of the second edition of *Corrective and Remedial Teaching* is the same as that of the original edition: to present a résumé of techniques and materials that have been found useful in dealing with many of the problems associated with underachievement, to suggest means for organizing corrective and remedial teaching, and to consider an orientation toward working with underachievers. The book is intended primarily for beginning teachers and experienced teachers who are seeking approaches to dealing with the learning problems of children in their classrooms. Our hope is that teachers with experience in corrective and remedial teaching will also find the book useful both as a source of new ideas and, perhaps more important, as a means for focusing and organizing their thinking. One fact should be quite clear: the emphasis throughout is on corrective and remedial teaching in the school setting. The depth of coverage required for the clinical diagnosis and treatment of extreme learning problems is not provided. In fact, the intensive coverage required to do justice to the latter is probably beyond the scope of any single book.

Since our aim is to present an overview of corrective and remedial teaching, we have attempted to take an eclectic approach and to avoid emphasis of any particular point of view. Readers are referred to the list of references at the end of each chapter if they wish to go beyond the discussion presented. Many, if not most, of the ideas presented here are not new; to the contrary, it has been our purpose to gather together existing ideas from a wide variety of sources and to integrate them into what we hope will be a useful guidebook. The approach is pragmatic: the techniques and materials have been tried and found to be useful.

While corrective and remedial teaching in the several basic skill areas is discussed, emphasis has deliberately been placed upon reading. We feel that reading is the most basic of the basic skills and that it is, therefore, entitled to primary emphasis. Typically, school administrators, parents, and students themselves are more concerned with failure in reading than with failure in arithmetic, spelling, handwriting, or language usage. There is good reason for this, for in a large measure success in all academic areas is directly dependent upon reading ability. Frequently, too, failure in other basic skills is accompanied by failure in reading, although this is not necessarily so. Finally, much more research has been done with reading problems and more techniques and materials have been developed than with the other skill areas. The intent, then, is not to belittle problems in skills other than reading, but to give reading the coverage it demands.

ORGANIZATION OF THE BOOK

The presentation of materials is organized to move from general background and orientation to specific techniques and materials. Common causes of learning difficulties are discussed in Chapter 2. Learning difficulties may be caused by a multitude of factors that are often complicated by being interrelated; and difficulty in one basic skill area is often closely related to, or the result of, difficulty in one or more of the other basic skills. Chapter 3 introduces general diagnostic procedures that can be useful in discovering the causal factors in individual cases and continues with some fundamentals of remedial teaching. The case study approach, which is probably the most effective method for identifying the causal factors involved in the more severe disability cases, is discussed in Chapter 4.

Chapters 5 through 14 deal with the specifics of diagnostic and remedial teaching in the several skill areas. Five chapters, 5 through 9, are devoted to the area of reading. Two new chapters on reading have been added to this second edition. Chapter 6 represents an attempt to put corrective and remedial efforts in perspective. In our experience, attempts to deal with reading problems tend too often to deteriorate into a manipulation of bits and pieces—skills and materials—with both teacher and pupil losing sight of the total act of reading. The intent in Chapter 6, then, is to present a global view that will assist teachers in putting the bits and pieces together as they help children move toward maturity in reading. Chapter 9 is devoted to a discussion of the strengths and limitations of several rather specific remedial approaches that have gained popularity in some circles. The general purpose is to consider the usefulness of each approach in the regular classroom. Taken together, the chapters on reading deal with the skill development, cognitive, and affective aspects of reading. Single chapters are devoted to spelling, arithmetic, listening, handwriting, and oral and written expression. While the several skill areas are dealt with as separate entities, a theme of overall language development runs through the language related chapters. Our hope is that the interrelatedness of the several areas will be clear and that this interrelationship will be reflected in instruction.

The final chapter, Chapter 15, is addressed personally to the teacher. It amounts to an invitation to consider the responsibility for and orientations toward remedial teaching.

REFERENCES

Bush, W. J., and Giles, M. T. *Aids to psycholinguistic teaching.* Columbus, Ohio: Charles E. Merrill, 1969.

Horn, T. D. (Ed.) *Reading for the disadavantaged.* New York: Harcourt, 1970.

Rohwer, W. D., Jr., and Ammons, P. R. The assessment and improvement of learning and language skills in four and five year old culturally disadvantaged children. Final Report, Office of Economic Opportunity, Contract No. B99-4776, June, 1971.

Secretary's (HEW) National Advisory Committee on Dyslexia and Related Reading Disorders. Reading disorders in the United States. Washington, D.C.: Department of Health, Education and Welfare, 1969.

Smith, B. E., Goodman, K. S., and Meredith, R. *Language and thinking in the elementary school.* New York: Holt, 1970.

Willis, H. D. Description, language and thinking: New directions, a curriculum in language and reasoning skills. Report of the Instructional Systems Program, CEMREL, July, 1971.

Chapter 2

Correlates of Learning Disability

The correlates of learning disability are varied and complex. Seldom is only one factor responsible for the learning deficit; more often a variety of factors is involved. This is not to say that every youngster with reading difficulties has a complex problem. Sometimes, if the pupil has been exposed to limited or poor quality teaching, or if he simply was not ready to learn when he first received instruction, or if his learning was arrested by some personal problem, the teaching task can be relatively simple. A rule of thumb among remedial teachers is that if a case is uncomplicated and diagnosis suggests that straightforward skill development will overcome the problem, the case is a corrective one, not a remedial one. On the other hand, if diagnosis determines that lack of basic skills is only part of the problem and that it has been complicated by biological, psychological, or environmental deficits, it is a remedial case and the pupil needs a considerably different program. In the latter type of case it would seem wise to use as many resources as possible in diagnosis of the problem. Classroom teachers are not helpless in the face of multiple problems. To the contrary, the vast majority of disabled learners can be taught successfully by the professionally adequate teacher, and only the extreme cases need be referred outside the classroom. However, probably the greatest single factor operating against classroom remediation is the high pupil-teacher ratio in many school situations. Regardless of the causal factors, proper use of diagnostic tests and remedial procedures is likely to consume more teacher time than the routine evaluation and instruction normal for the average classroom program. A plan for attacking this problem by establishing working relationships within the school is discussed in Chapter 3.

The drawing (fig. 1) below represents an attempt to illustrate not only the wide range of factors that coexist with learning problems but also, as indicated by the broken lines, the possibility of interrelatedness among the three major categories. Remember, though, that correlations mean only that two or more factors coexist; a cause-effect relationship cannot necessarily be inferred.

Although the correlates of learning disability are numerous and diverse, they may be classified into three general categories: biological, psychological, and environmental. The biological factors include vision and hearing dis-

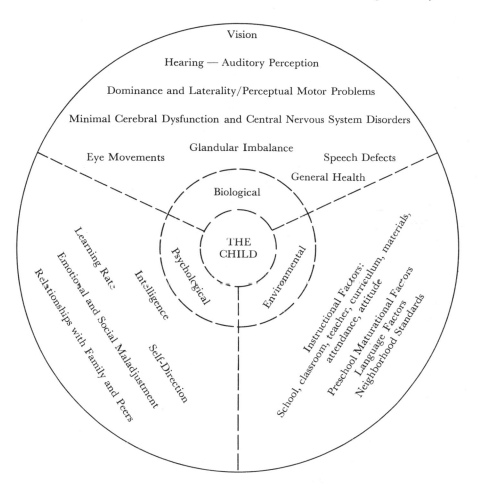

FIG. 1   Correlates of Learning Disability

orders, glandular dysfunction, dominance and/or laterality confusion, disorders of the central nervous system, and many other physical problems, some of which are so esoteric as to be beyond the scope of this introductory book. The environmental category includes such factors as instructional inadequacies, cultural deprivation, and preschool experiences. Intelligence poses a special problem. Certainly intelligence is physically based, but the influence of environment upon its development is great. We have, perhaps arbitrarily, classed it as a psychological factor.

There is one important area of learning disability, however, that does not fit neatly into any one of the three categories. This is the syndrome of disabilities commonly designated as "dyslexia." Because of the overlap and some of the related problems, "dyslexia" will be discussed first, as a separate major category.

DYSLEXIA

In recent years the term *dyslexia* has come into wide usage to describe a certain type of severe reading disability. Yet the fact remains that there is a substantial disagreement about the meaning of the term among educators, psychologists, physicians, neurologists, ophthalmologists, and others who recognize and attempt to deal with cases of severe reading disability. Cruickshank (in Keeney and Keeney, 1968) described one of the major stumbling blocks in pinning down a definition when he said:

> First, there is confusion in defining dyslexia. If the child diagnosed as dyslexic in Philadelphia moved to Bucks County, 10 miles north, he would be called a child with a language disorder. In Montgomery County, Maryland, a few miles south, he would be called a child with special or specific reading problems. In Michigan, he would be called a child with perceptual disturbances. In California, he would be called either a child with educational handicaps or a neurologically handicapped child. In Florida and New York State, he would be classified as having minimal brain dysfunction. (P. 69)

Whether a consensual definition will ever be reached remains to be seen. Meanwhile, the fact is that consensual definition or not, children who display severe reading problems continue to exist and the great need for remedial methods and materials does not diminish. The brief discussion that follows brings together some of the current thinking on the syndrome known as *dyslexia* in some circles. Because the concept turns out to be so nebulous, we prefer generally to avoid using the term.

To *avoid* the welter of terms that have been used in the literature to describe severe reading problems—Cruickshank (in Keeney and Keeney, 1969, p. 84) says forty-three in the last fifteen years!—a scheme for classifying and distinguishing between severely disabled (dyslexic) and less seriously disabled readers has been advanced by Rabinovitch (1962), Kolson and Kaluger (1963), and others. The scheme amounts to separating reading disability into two categories: *primary* and *secondary* reading disability. The lists that follow serve to differentiate between the two in terms of related problems and characteristics.

PRIMARY READING DISABILITY

Factors are endogenous; that is, they are internally based.

Pupils have adequate intelligence.

Spelling and arithmetic skills as well as reading skills are poor.

Auditory and visual discrimination are poor. Symbolization—translating letters into meaningful words—is the deficient aspect. Blending is also difficult.

Poor visual memory and great difficulty learning sight words.

Mixed dominance. Confused or mixed handedness, eyedness, or footedness. (There is, however, considerable disagreement about the significance of this factor.)

Reversals or rotations, e.g., "was" for "saw," "on" for "no," "b" for "d," "p" for "q," etc. in reading and/or writing.

Transpositions, e.g., "gril" for "girl," "mazagine" for "magazine."

Mirror writing, e.g.,   A wolloy pob.

Faulty body image and poor coordination. (Here again there is disagreement about the significance of the factor.)

Familial, or, to use other terminology, genetically determined defects.

Emotional problems, but not as a primary causal factor.

No gross physical or ophthalmologic defects.

Record of possible birth trauma or head injury.

SECONDARY READING DISABILITY

Factors are exogenous; e.g., environmental, educational, emotional, societal. Secondary disability may be as severe as primary disability in terms of degree of the deficiency in norm-referenced performance, but the problem appears to be externally caused.

Lack of motivation.

Limited intellectual ability.

Emotional problems (anxiety and/or depression) as a cause for the learning problem.

Complexity of the problem is not as great as in primary disability. In general, if the pupil responds to well planned remedial teaching directed at correcting skill deficiencies, the problem is judged *secondary*. (Note, then, that a diagnosis of primary disability may come by default.)

As in any complex area, it is not possible to draw a neat line between primary and secondary disability. The fact is that all neurologists, pediatricians, psychologists, learning specialists and others would not agree on all the points in the above lists. This is, of course, to be expected, because much research remains to be done and many issues remain to be resolved. Diagnosticians appear to agree, too, that there may be overlapping between the two categories, for they not infrequently conclude ". . . secondary reading disability with evidence of some aspects of primary symptoms."

There are many who suggest that attempting to differentiate between primary and secondary learning disability is unproductive. (Another way to put it is that setting apart some problems as cases of *dyslexia* is making a distinction that has no practical value.) Their point is that differences in treatment are hard to identify: in either case the aim is to teach the pupil as straightforwardly as possible. We tend to agree. Nevertheless, the hassle is likely to be with us for some time, so the reader is well advised to at least be aware of some of the terms.

BIOLOGICAL CORRELATES

Vision

The research concerning the relationship of visual factors and learning problems may seem conflicting and confusing. For example, researchers, such as Edson, Bond, and Cook (1953) and many others, have found little relationship between visual anomalies and reading ability. Other reseachers, such as Eames (1948), Robinson and Huelsman (1953), and others, have found evidence of a relationship between certain kinds of visual defects and inability to read. In studying clinical reading cases, Robinson (1946) found that eleven out of twenty-two cases had visual problems which were considered to be causal factors to the reading disability. This conflict is due not only to the definition of *vision* utilized by the various researchers but also to their conception of the conditions which are generally classified as learning disorders. As an example of the differences existing between optometric and ophthalmological researchers, Friedman (1967) and Keeney and Keeney (1968) fail to agree on what actually constitutes a vision problem. The former appears to be concerned about functional binocular behavior while the latter focus mainly on visual acuity, or the ability to see clearly. Spache (1964) and other researchers agree that these two areas of concern are quite different and cannot be equated.

This is not the place to attempt to resolve the conflict. Here we shall simply identify the visual defects most likely to be of consequence to classroom teachers and describe some screening procedures. The most common disorders which affect visual acuity are: *Astigmatism,* which causes a generalized blurring of the vision and is often the result of irregular corneal curvature; *Myopia,* or nearsightedness, which is a condition where sight is clear at near but blurred at far distances; *Hyperopia,* or farsightedness, where sight is clear at far but blurred at near distances. These conditions, which are due to optical and sometimes anatomical variants, can almost always be improved with corrective spectacle lenses or contact lenses. Roberts and Dyan (1970) found that approximately 25 percent of the children in the 6–11 age group suffer from these conditions.

Amblyopia is a general term for reduction of central visual acuity, usually in one eye. Suspicion that amblyopia exists is often aroused during routine vision screening. The teacher should bear in mind that there may be a simple explanation for a decrease in visual acuity and refrain from a hasty diagnosis of amblyopia, which is not as prevalent as at one time was believed. A professional examination will, of course, provide definite diagnosis. Flom and Neumaier (1966) found that amblyopia, along with other visual difficulties, appears more frequently among children who exhibit extreme learning disorders than among children who are not experiencing learning difficulties.

Other anomalies which are not so common are worth consideration because they fall into the broad category of *binocular* dysfunction. A generalized descriptive term, *Dyschriesopia,* is assigned by Woolf (1969) to these conditions. *Anisekonia* is a rare condition characterized by vast differences between the optical qualities of the two eyes. It can result in unequal image sizes seen by each eye. *Accommodative* dysfunction, an inability to focus the eye's lens, results in a blurring of print after periods of concentrated reading. *Convergence* dysfunction, lack of inturning of the eyes to fix an object or printed material, can result in the inability to maintain a single image while reading; therefore, the child would either see double or suppress the sight in one eye. Usually these two conditions are not constantly present. They tend to appear only after various degrees of near-seeing tasks are encountered. *Strabismus* (deviation of an eye) results in a consistent lack of binocular control; and *Hystagmus* (oscillation of one or both eyes), which is less common, also accounts for vision disorders that affect children. According to Eames (1948) and others, these conditions are frequently seen in children with learning problems. More often than not two or more of the conditions described above are found in combination.

From the description above of types of binocular dysfunction, which by no means represent all of the variations, it is clear that not all visual disorders are accompanied by loss of visual acuity. Therefore, the following description of symptoms that may be indicative of vision problems can be valuable for the classroom teacher:

losing place while reading
avoiding close work
consistent reliance upon a marker—pointing at words
poor sitting position and/or posture while reading
holding reading material closer than would be regarded normal
frowning, blinking, scowling, and other facial distortions while reading
excessive head movement while reading or viewing distant objects
body rigidity while looking at a distant object
excessive eye rubbing
thrusting the head forward while reading or focusing on objects
tension during close work

A knowledgeable teacher will be sensitive to pupils who experience blurred vision after reading for a short period of time or who experience double vision at any time. Many other symptoms may be signals to the teacher. These indicate that a competent professional vision examination is in order. The literature on vision and on perception is replete with examples of children who, regardless of chronological age, are not aware that they see things differently from the way most people see them. These children often do not have the verbal facility to describe their problem.

Whether one accepts or rejects the notion that visual anomalies interfere with learning, wisdom and good judgment suggest that the learner ought to have as little discomfort and distraction as possible if he is to learn efficiently. A substantial share of the apparent confusion in the research regarding the relationship of visual problems to school achievement can also be due to widely different thresholds of pain or discomfort. A given degree of visual discomfort might be accommodated by one child but be debilitating for another.

Rosenbloom (1961) succinctly summarized the importance of visual factors and their influences upon learning disabilities:

> A child with a vision problem may make a variety of adjustments. It is not uncommon to find a child adapting by retreating from the reading act. Not being able to take advantage of the reading instruction, he becomes further and further retarded in reading and reading subjects until he is finally classed as a retarded reader. His comprehension of reading material will often be low because his conscious attention must be directed toward maintaining clear and single vision. He may achieve this, but often at the expense of failing to re-member what he reads. This child will often be found in the failing or border-line failure group. In many instances he may achieve only with repeated tutoring and outside help despite a high learning capacity. If he is highly motivated, he will achieve by spending much more time at his studies than the average child. If he is not a highly motivated child, he will become discouraged. He will announce that he does not like reading and may secretly conclude that he is dumb. He may become resentful of his associates who achieve where he fails, and he may resent the demands of his teachers who seem to require the impos-sible of him. (P. 92)

In such cases the tendency for a specific reading problem to become a gen-eral learning problem is clear.

There is no simple method for determining whether or not a child has visual problems. Diagnosis in the school setting should remain at the screen-ing level. When screening tests indicate that poor vision may be interfering with learning, referral should be made to a vision specialist. The visual screening device most widely used in classrooms is designed to identify loss of visual acuity. It is based upon principles formulated by Hermann Snellen in 1862 and is commonly called the Snellen Test. The test consists of letters or symbols in varied positions and sizes. For young children or persons not familiar with the alphabet, the test is constructed of *E's, C's,* or common pictures constructed in accordance with Snellen's formula. The person being examined stands twenty feet from the chart and names the progressively smaller letters or symbols. It should be clearly understood that the Snellen chart evaluates only central vision acuity. The 20/20 notation means that a person is able to identify appropriate symbols at twenty feet, whereas a 20/40 notation would mean that he sees at twenty feet what a normal per-son would see at forty feet. The same is proportionately true for 20/80, 20/100, or any other value. Convenient charts have also been manufactured according to the Snellen formula for evaluating central visual acuity at the near-seeing distance. The child is asked to hold the test card at the specified distance from his eyes, usually twelve to sixteen inches. Of course the presence of dysfunctions of central visual acuity need not imply the presence of such factors as lack of convergence ability, faulty oculo-musculature control, muscle imbalance, lack of fusion ability, stereopsis, or a host of other visual abnormalities. Furthermore, far-point acuity is generally not crucial to reading a book held twelve to fourteen inches from the eyes. However, it can conceivably affect the learner in other ways, for we must consider both the near environment (reading books, charts, etc.) and the distant environment (chalkboard, movies, demonstrations, etc.) with which the child may be involved.

There are other optical devices which measure central visual acuity, muscle imbalance, fusion, stereopsis, color vision, and other visual skills. They have in common the characteristic of compressing the twenty-foot testing distance into a small box approximately twenty inches long. Illumination is standardized. Some of the available instruments are: the Ortho-Rater (Bausch & Lomb); the Keystone Telebinocular (Keystone View Company); the Titmus Screener (Titmus Optical Company); and the Sight Screener (American Optical Company).

A modified clinical technique utilizing optometrists and opthalmologists would be the most reliable, and it would amount to an improvement over employing teachers and/or parents, with or without screening instruments, to evaluate the visual status of children. The general screening devices described above can be useful but they are *all* that should be utilized by a classroom or remedial teacher. Professional evaluation by an optometrist or ophthalmologist is certain to be more competent.

Hearing

Hearing loss and learning problems are often presumed to be interrelated, but substantiating studies are relatively scarce. Yet, the scarcity of objective evidence does not negate the fact that much of the instruction a youngster receives in elementary school is on an oral-aural basis. For example, Bond and Tinker (1957) report a study by Bond wherein hard-of-hearing children were found to be at a disadvantage when a phonics approach to reading was used; and Robinson (1946) and others have found that children unable to hear at high frequencies are often poor readers. If a pupil needs to strain to hear, or can only partially hear, it is likely his attention will wander and he will probably receive less than the maximum benefit of the teacher's presentation. This would be especially true when an instructional method is used that demands fine auditory discrimination, as most phonics instruction does.

Audiometric testing done by a qualified person is undoubtedly the most accurate means of testing hearing. Many state departments of education provide this type of testing on a scheduled state-wide basis so that no child with a severe hearing loss goes undetected for any length of time. If such a service is not available, it may be necessary to seek testing on a private basis.

An alert teacher who is aware of his pupils' habits will suspect that hearing may be impaired when the following conditions occur:

earache
faulty pronunciation
tendency to favor one ear
breathing through the mouth
complaints of head noises or dizziness
unnatural pitch of voice
inattention or poor scholastic achievement
frequent rubbing of the ear
blank expression when directions are given

It is probably safe to say that if these symptoms are observed, a child should be referred for professional evaluation and treatment. If the school district has the services of a speech therapist, this would probably be the referral starting point.

In any event, a classroom teacher needs to consider special seating placement for a child who has a hearing difficulty. Depending upon which ear is affected and the nature of the hearing loss, a pupil might be seated at the front of the classroom, with his right or left ear (as the case may be) toward the focal point of conversation or, in some cases, be allowed to move about as the focal point of the conversation changes.

Auditory Perception

Many poor readers are deficient in the ability to discriminate between speech sounds in words. Ample evidence has been provided by Durrell (1958) and others to substantiate the importance of auditory perception as a most necessary skill in beginning or remedial instruction in reading if a phonics approach is being taught. A key point to be made here is that auditory perception is different from hearing acuity. Hearing acuity refers to the ability of the individual to receive sounds in the frequency range of spoken language at the intensity level used in normal speaking situations; auditory perception refers to the ability to make the fine discriminations often needed to identify speech sounds that are, for some pupils, somewhat alike. Every remedial teacher is aware of certain pupils who find difficulty in hearing the differences in the short *e* and short *i* sound, for example. Some children have difficulty discriminating between the sounds of *f* and *v*, and words such as *very* and *fairy* cause problems in both speech and reading; other examples will occur to most experienced teachers. Simply stated, poor auditory perception is somewhat similar to being tone deaf in music. Luckily the problem is easier to correct than tone deafness through practice in careful listening together with diligent, corrective training with troublesome sounds.

A screening test that enables the teacher to determine a child's ability to recognize fine differences between sounds in English words, i.e., that measures the ability to hear accurately, has been devised by Joesph Wepman. This test, or one similar to it, should be available to remedial teachers as a diagnostic instrument to be used when auditory discrimination appears to be a problem.

Neurological Considerations

In regard to the role of neurological function in cases of reading disability most attention has been given to the area of cerebral dominance. Otto and Smith (1970) have summarized the results of investigations in this area as follows:

A. J. Harris (1961) captured the general mood when he wrote, "One of the most puzzling and most controversial issues in the whole field of reading is the significance of lateral dominance" (P. 249). In the simplest terms, cerebral (or lateral) dominance amounts to the preference of use and dominance of function of one side of the body over the other. Many workers have contended that children who are not right-dominant—that is, those who have either a consistent left-side preference or a mixed or converted dominance—are disposed to reading disability. While the results of studies have tended to be somewhat inconsistent, the fact is—at least with clinical groups—that groups of poor readers tend generally to include disproportionately many individuals with dominance problems. That all poorly lateralized children are not poor readers has been the source of some embarrassment to certain investigators, but Zangwill (1962) has suggested that perhaps poorly developed laterality results in reading difficulty only in combination with another factor (e.g., cerebral lesion, constitutional weakness in maturation, extreme anxiety).

After a thorough review of the literature Zangwill concluded, "It is difficult to arrive at a very clear-cut conclusion. . . . [However] fuller understanding of reading and its disorders must presuppose fuller understanding of the ways in which asymmetrical functions become established in the human brain" (P. 113). With regard to present approaches to the treatment of reading disability on the basis of current knowledge of cerebral dominance (e.g., Delacato, 1959), Money (1962) concluded in 1962 that "Scientifically speaking, it is far too premature to be applying hypotheses of cerebral dominance to methods of treatment. What these hypotheses need, above all else, is to be tested experimentally, and in controlled observation, for validity" (P. 28). No support has been forthcoming, and Robbins (1967) is only representative of those who have issued further indictments. For the practitioner with more concern for persons than panaceas, the message seems to be: Proceed with caution. (Pp. 19–20)

Frank brain injury has also received attention as a possible causal factor in reading disability. Otto and Smith have commented upon this concern as follows:

> There seems to be little doubt that children with significant impairment are likely to have learning problems, but the specifics of causality are by no means clear. Exactly what constitutes *"significant* impairment" is not precisely known: There is no straightforward relationship between amount or locus of damage and ultimate academic achievement. Furthermore, neurological examinations are not always sensitive enough to pick up subtle but significant dysfunctions (Thelander *et al.*, 1958); and dysfunction may become critical only at higher levels of skill development in basic academic areas like reading, writing, and spelling (Pasamanick and Knobloch, 1960).
>
> The issue is further clouded by the tendency of some workers to lump together "brain injury," "minimal cerebral dysfunction," "diffuse brain damage," "word blindness," "dyslexia," "strephosymbolia," and "specific reading disability" as if they all meant the same thing. Since the designations can and often do— depending, apparently, upon the investigator's fancy—describe quite different conditions, confusion is rampant. The reader is referred to two excellent books edited by John Money (1962, 1966) for clarification. A point essential to consideration of the person has been suggested by Eisenberg (1966, P. 14): Some children with sufficient brain damage to result in moderate mental deficiency are able, in the elementary grades, to attain better than average fluency in oral reading, but they can comprehend little of what they read. That this is the case serves both to demonstrate a subtle manifestation of brain damage and to underscore the need for careful reading diagnosis in conjunction with an adequate physical examination. (P. 20)

A word of caution needs to be added here in connection with the problems of hyperactivity and central nervous system disorders. The existing research concerning these rather common contributing factors in learning disability affords no clear-cut conclusions. While the researchers cited in the preceding paragraphs, and many others too numerous to be cited, have found a syndrome of disorders such as poor motor coordination, perceptual and orientational difficulties, minor speech disorders and hyperactivity common to many children with learning problems, they are almost universally unwilling to state categorically that this syndrome is directly the result of brain damage or central nervous system disorder. Workers in the field of medicine, and particularly those in the field of neurology (which is considered by many to be the most sophisticated of all medical fields) are quick to state that thus far their findings in this area are still only in the hypothesis stage; present knowledge and technology is insufficient to enable them to be certain. It would seem clear, then, that lay diagnosticians should be *extremely cautious* in using this terminology in their diagnosis or in their conferences with parents.

Within very recent years a great many pediatricians have resorted to prescribing medication to alleviate or control hyperactivity. While the writers would not question the right and the duty of medical practitioners to prescribe whatever they have found safe and effective, a remedial text would be remiss if it did not make teachers aware of some of the educational problems connected with such an approach. Almost invariably the hyperactivity and the extreme learning problem are discovered by a classroom teacher and often the parent is advised by the teacher to seek medical help before a thorough and competent educational diagnosis is made. When this is the case, medical practitioners may be making a diagnosis on the basis of faulty or incomplete information. The physician is blameless because he has the right to expect that all the educational aspects and remedial methods have been explored by professional people and that the problem defies solution by more conventional means. Too often this is not the case. Some factors that may lead to hyperactivity are discussed under the "Psychological Correlates" and "Environmental Correlates" sections that follow. In the opinion of the writers, possibilities in each of these areas should be assessed before looking to the physician to solve the problem.

In appropriate instances, the teacher needs to have some firm plans for remedial teaching if and when medical therapy is successful. The medication, at best, will only *allow* the child to learn, it will not *teach* him; the child will need to make up the months, or in some cases years, of educational achievement he has failed to attain. Only a sound, intensive remedial program can remedy the deficit.

Perceptual-Motor Considerations

Some investigators have addressed themselves to the effects of perceptual-motor training on reading ability. The work of two of these investigators (Frostig, 1964, and Kephart, 1960) has been highly touted in some areas and indeed perceptual-motor training programs have been implemented on a wide scale in some school districts. By and large the results of these training programs have not appeared to directly affect reading ability. The desired transfer effects from work with nonletter forms and from motor activities, such as hopping and walking balance beams, to reading have not occurred. Karlin (1971) sums up the situation well when he says,

> It seems that ability to discriminate among letter and word forms has a greater influence upon the ability to recognize words than the ability to see differences and similarities among nonverbal forms. If children are weak in recognizing letters, it would seem appropriate to provide training in letter forms; if they are weak in discriminating between words, then training with words ought to be provided. Experiences directly related to tasks children are expected to perform should be more productive than experiences which might have some tangential relation to the task. (P. 81)

Speech Defects

Faulty speech patterns, particularly articulation defects, have often been found to be associated with reading disability, especially when oral reading is one of the measures of reading success. Bond (1935), for example, long ago found that oral reading is affected by defective speech, but the relationship is negligible when only silent reading skill is involved. Probably a more significant fact is that as age increases such disorders may result in nonacceptance or ridicule by peer groups and may create a social handicap. When this is true, emotional and learning difficulties can result. Some support for this notion is inherent in the fact that in school systems having both speech therapy and remedial programs many of the same children are enrolled in both programs. In the absence of research, however, this could be attributed simply to the fact that some children have multiple problems which may not be specifically related.

Eye Movements

Whether or not inefficiency of eye movement and rate of perception have any direct bearing upon learning problems has not been clearly established. Generally speaking, inefficient eye movements are more often considered symptoms of poor reading rather than causes. It is safe to say, however, that every experienced classroom teacher has seen youngsters who are so painfully slow in reading that to finish any reading task in the normal time allotted is impossible. This may not present as much of a problem at the elementary level as it does at the junior high and high school levels, where scheduling is arbitrary and the work load is likely to be considerably greater.

As a result of eye-movement photography a great deal of objective evidence has been accumulated on how we read and the exact physical movements the eye makes during the reading process. The eye-movement camera has shown that when we read our eyes do not move steadily along the line of print but progress in a series of quick, jerky movements. The pauses between these movements are called *fixations*. Even though these fixations are of minute fractions of a second, the eyes actually see only during the fixation. The following norms from Taylor, Frackenpohl, and Pettee (1960) indicate when rate of reading deviates sufficiently to constitute a problem.

	Grades								
	1	*2*	*3*	*4*	*5*	*6*	*7*	*High School*	*College*
Words per minute	80	115	138	158	173	185	195	214–250	280

It must be remembered, however, that these figures represent averages only and certainly a deviation of 10 to 25 percent would not be cause for concern. The difficulty level of concepts involved and the vocabulary load in any given piece of reading matter are crucial determinants in all reading rates. Therefore, care must be exercised lest one become concerned with rate of reading when no problem exists.

General Health

Research workers who are concerned with causal factors in learning disability have largely tended to neglect the aspects of general health. This cannot be interpreted to mean, however, that poor general health, inherited or acquired, is not frequently an important contributing factor to the child's learning disability. There can be little doubt that pupils who suffer from chronic health conditions such as sinusitis, asthma, dermatitis (in any of its forms), rheumatic fever, dental health problems, etc., cannot devote their whole attention and energy to the learning process. Often—due to ill health per se, the absence from school which it causes, or an interaction of both—normal progress is delimited and the stage is set for the development of a severe learning problem. Brueckner and Bond (1955) have put it succinctly: "Any condition within the child that lessens his energy, distracts him, or makes him in any way uncomfortable may have deleterious effects upon his learning" (P. 37).

Malnutrition and improper diet may in themselves be causal factors. Teachers in extremely low socioeconomic areas are all too familiar with the problem of the pupil who comes to school without breakfast or the child who has had only a bottle of some carbonated beverage for breakfast. In such instances children cannot be expected to sustain the energy or interest level required for effective learning

A school nurse, a school physician or, in some cases, a school dentist—when they are available—can do a great deal in correcting or alleviating the problems mentioned. In some instances the school or community social worker can help to improve situations where health or diet is part of the problem. The classroom teacher needs to be aware of the kinds of health problems that exist for three reasons: first, she may need to adjust her instructional goals; second, her teaching or remedial method might be affected by her understanding of the physical health factors; and third, she needs to be alert to the possibilities for referral of pupils to proper sources for professional help.

PSYCHOLOGICAL CORRELATES

Psychological correlates are rather clearly divided into the categories of intelligence, and emotional and social maladjustment. There are, however, some considerations that do not clearly fall within these categories. Little conclusive research has been done on them but they appear to be important. Teachers and psychologists have long been aware of their existence, and we feel they should not be ignored when considering the psychological barriers to learning.

Some of the more frequent observations made by psychologists, social workers and remedial diagnosticians are: *(a)* nonlearning is sometimes more rewarding than learning; *(b)* nonlearning and/or hyperactivity is some-times an anxious, driven attempt to overcome the limits imposed by modest mental ability in an intellectually oriented school; *(c)* nonlearning, inat-tention and hyperactivity can be an active defense against depression; *(d)* hyperactivity can indicate a prepsychotic child; *(e)* nonlearning may be an attempt to get punished in school for "crimes" committed at home; *(f)* hyperactivity and frustration over the school tasks together with non-learning have sometimes been the result of an out-of-control alcoholic in the home; and *(g)* sometimes these latter problems are caused by a paranoid child-beating parent in the home. It should be clear to diagnosticians that not only are these factors complex but also more often than not the solu-tion to them lies outside the classroom.

Intelligence

Reading is essentially an intellectual activity, and a person's intelligence will play a major role in the level of reading development which he can attain. Otto and Smith (1970) say:

> . . . intelligence is the single factor most clearly related to reading ability; yet it is equally clear that there is far from a one-to-one relationship between read-ing ability and intelligence as it is now measured. As early as 1933 Durrell (1933) made the point that group intelligence tests that include a large number of reading items should be regarded as reading tests that have been inappropri-ately named; and the point has been made by virtually every writer on the topic since then. Poor readers are bound to do badly on reading-loaded "intelli-gence tests." Equally important, but not so often considered, is the fact that good readers are likely to do exceptionally well on reading-loaded intelligence tests. If the person is truly our concern, we must be as concerned about over-assessment as under-assessment of intelligence, for to err in either direction is to establish the basis for unrealistic expectations regarding ultimate achievement.
>
> In general, correlations between intelligence test scores and reading achieve-ment test scores tend to range between .40 and .60. While these are substantial correlations, as correlations go, it is quite apparent that other factors are very much involved in determining reading achievement. The correlations between individual intelligence test scores and reading scores tend to be lower (on the order of .50) than the correlations between verbal group intelligence test scores and reading scores (often .60 or higher). This finding is as might be expected in view of the fact that group intelligence tests and reading tests measure essen-tially the same thing: ability to read test items. When the purpose is to establish a prognosis (an estimate of rate and ultimate level of growth), the best available measure of intelligence *plus other important factors*—like motivation, experien-tial background, and quantity and quality of instruction—must be considered. Some highly intelligent children fail to learn to read; on the other hand, many slow learners and even moderately retarded children learn to read well enough to get along in a literate society. No person's potential can be described by a single test score. (P. 22)

Emotional and Social Maladjustment

The fact that emotional and/or social maladjustment is common among children with extreme learning problems is axiomatic. This is not to suggest, however, that researchers are agreed on either incidence or cause-effect relationships. Before sampling the research in this area, it may be useful to note that emotional problems are generally thought of as being intrapsychic (within the person), while the problems of social maladjustment are generally visible in the youngster's behavior. Yet there may be considerable overlapping of the two. Generally, these are the major problems exhibited: nervous tension, inadequate self-concept, fear of or antagonism toward learning to read, chronic fear of failure, poor attention span, undue dependence upon approval, anxiety, introversion, malingering, antisocial behavior, irresponsibility, inability to accept blame, and many like reactions and responses.

Harris (1970) feels that close to 100 percent of the children seen in the Queens College Clinic over a fifteen-year period showed maladjustment of some kind, and in more than 50 percent of the cases it was thought to be a causal factor of learning problems. Clinical researchers—such as Robinson (1946) in her classic study—have found less than 50 percent of children with reading difficulties to have emotional difficulties. In general, it is realistic to say that researchers are agreed that the incidence of emotional maladjustment is high.

It is more difficult to say, however, whether these maladjustments are primary or secondary. In this connection, Fernald (1943) felt emotional maladjustment was a result rather than a cause of inability to learn to read. In a study of seventy-eight disabled readers she found only four pupils whom she felt had had an emotional problem before the failure in learning to read occurred. But most authorities feel there can be no categorical statement about the causal relationship between social and emotional adjustment and reading achievement. It seems unlikely, though, that a child could be severely disabled in any or all of the basic skills and not become emotionally involved because of his failure. As pointed out by Harris (1970), children react to feelings of failure in different ways. One may develop inferiority feelings and take little or no part in classroom activities while another may develop into a braggart and attempt to hide his failure behind a facade of unrealistic boasting.

There is little dispute that a reciprocal relationship between emotional problems and learning disability does exist, but it is easier to state the generalization than to explore or explain the relationship. Challman (1939) years ago suggested three categories into which learning/emotional problems may fall; we feel that the third is the most common.

1. An unfavorable learning situation disposes a child toward academic failure with consequent emotional maladjustment.

2. A pre-existing emotional maladjustment creates inner conflict and instability which results in reading failure.

3. Many factors, both pre-existing and acquired, become so intertwined it is virtually impossible to say which came first.

What can classroom or remedial teachers do to alleviate problems of emotional or social maladjustment? Admittedly they are not psychotherapists, and many feel such problems are outside their jurisdiction and competence. For the severe or clinical case, this attitude may be justified. But the authors take the position that teaching is therapy too, and often the most effective therapy is the success experienced by a pupil when he reaches a worthwhile goal. Remedial teachers often see emotional problems diminish or vanish when a pupil is warmly accepted in spite of his learning disability and helped, slowly but surely, to overcome his learning problem. This is not to be construed as a negation of the effectiveness of the efforts of the psychiatrically trained social worker, the psychologist, or the psychiatrist. The extreme cases desperately need the highly skilled and knowledgeable efforts of these professions. Their services should be utilized whenever indicated and available.

ENVIRONMENTAL CORRELATES

We have included, rather arbitrarily, three main clusters of factors in this discussion of environmental correlates. Language factors are discussed here because of the obvious environmental influence on language development. Instructional, or school-related, factors are also included. And finally, preschool maturational—or readiness—factors are discussed. The last cluster of factors does, of course, touch on both biological and psychological as well as strictly environmental factors. We have included them here because the powerful influence of environment is clear.

Language Factors

It is generally agreed that there is a strong relationship between the mastery of spoken language and progress toward successful beginning reading. There is, however, less agreement on how much of a role language development plays in cases of reading disability. Generally, corrective or remedial teaching does not begin in earnest until a pupil is eight or more years old, after he has demonstrated an inability to handle the decoding aspect of reading instruction. The remedial or corrective process has in the past been largely concerned with teaching the decoding skills rather than the broader language skills. For this reason the discussion that follows will only review the most significant and interrelated aspects of language development as a reminder to the remedial teacher that in some cases these factors need to be taken into account when planning a remedial program.

The language development of a child can be said to depend greatly upon the opportunities his environment provides for verbal interactions. The importance of *environment* is attested to by the emphasis on early childhood education that is becoming more prevalent, especially in programs dealing with children who come from deprived and culturally different homes. Wide varieties of experiences and activities are provided to improve or change the course of language development for prereaders in order to help them overcome the influence of their impoverished or different background. Verbal interaction is the key to the development of effective communication abilities. For the corrective and remedial pupil, vocabulary development is a vital area. Sentence structure and clarity of speech are important, but for the older pupil are not usually a major deficit. *Intelligence* is probably the most crucial of all the factors mentioned. It is a commonly observed fact that slow or dull children do not learn to speak as clearly as bright children. It is also a fact that although even mentally retarded children learn to decode, albeit at a slower pace, they never become adept at the comprehension or cognitive aspects of reading. Perhaps teachers must be content to teach decoding skills and face the reality that less able children will never become mature readers in the ultimate sense of the word.

Instructional Factors

While research is sketchy and inconclusive on instructional inadequacies and their importance as causal factors in learning disabilities, there can be little doubt that they loom large as factors to be considered. Ineffective teaching can be an important causal factor, whether it is due to inadequate teacher preparation at the college level; to misdirected emphasis in the curriculum; to lack of attention to individual differences; or, as some administrators put it, to the three *M*'s—marriage, maternity, and moving. Unsatisfactory pupil-teacher relationships and irregular school attendance are also factors that merit consideration.

Inadequate teacher preparation at the college level is not universal, but all too often beginning teachers complain that they were inadequately prepared or that their practice teaching situation was unrealistic or too short. Perhaps the trend toward intern programs will help to eliminate this complaint.

Misdirected emphasis in the curriculum could occur in many forms:

Basic reading skills may be neglected once the child leaves the primary grades.

Sufficient readiness activities may not be provided.

Perhaps too much emphasis is placed on *one* method of teaching reading to the detriment of individuals' learning progress.

There might be too much dependence on "incidental" learning and not enough direct instruction.

Lack of attention to individual differences may also be a causal factor in that many times materials of sufficient range are not provided for the wide span of ability levels. It has also been demonstrated that production-line teaching cannot and does not reach all children. Remedial programs are filled with youngsters who have wide gaps in their overall grasp of certain basic skills. These skills may have been taught, but they are not learned until a remedial teacher adjusts the instruction to the individual's particular rate or best method of learning.

Marriage, maternity, and moving are problems which no doubt affect the large school district more than they do the small one. Teachers who enter the profession and do not remain long enough to develop maturity, skill, experience, or interest in their chosen field sometimes create a learning problem for children who find difficulty in adjusting to changing personalities, methods, and treatment.

Bond and Tinker (1957) indicate the unfortunate results of unsatisfactory pupil-teacher relationships. They feel that any hostility or anxiety on the part of the teacher when a pupil is having difficulty in reading intensifies the child's emotional reactions and feelings of insecurity.

A child's attendance in school may certainly have a bearing upon a learning problem. Very often a gap in basic skills can be traced to a youngster's absence during a period when certain fundamentals were being introduced. For this reason, remedial specialists have found it useful to seek this data in their case studies.

Preschool Developmental Factors

Speech development, perceptual development, motor control, environmental and cultural factors, and mental and physical growth are all important facets of preschool development. Underdevelopment or latency in one or more of these areas can, and often does, predispose a youngster toward learning problems.

Reading readiness can be defined as a state of *general maturity* which allows a child to learn to read successfully. General maturity, of course, involves age, sex, physical health, intelligence, visual and auditory perception, freedom from directional confusion, and adequate emotional and social adjustment; and all are significant factors in readiness for school learning. Some of the above factors are briefly discussed below.

Even with regulations regarding the age at which a pupil may enter school, there may be a considerable difference in the chronological ages of first graders, inasmuch as some children are just under the cut-off date and others have just reached eligible age. Thus, the child who was just under the cut-off date the previous year is almost a full year older when he enters school than the child who has just reached eligible age. Some children are, for this simple reason, less ready for school than others because they are literally less mature. Occasionally, intensive study of a disabled learner seems to reveal that the primary cause for his disability is the fact that he was too immature to respond to beginning instruction. Yet chronological age is often a poor indicator of maturity and the preponderance of evidence seems to indicate that children can be taught certain of the basic skills at almost any age if the method is adapted sufficiently. Thus, it may be possible to say that a specific child is too young for a specific school experience, but our present knowledge does not permit us to generalize very broadly about minimum ages.

The sex factor may be significant in that girls tend to mature earlier than boys and, thus, are usually more ready to begin to tackle school tasks. Many explanations have been advanced for the fact that in almost any remedial program there are more boys than girls. These explanations make use of constitutional, social, and other factors; but certainly simple lack of maturity may have been a contributing factor.

Adequate physical health is an important part of readiness in that a child who is not alert and physically able to take part in learning activities cannot be expected to learn at a normal rate. Absences due to poor health may also be an important factor, particularly when they occur at the crucial beginning stages of any school learning.

Intelligence as a factor in learning ability was discussed earlier in this chapter, but intelligence as a factor of readiness warrants special comment here. The relationship between IQ and chronological age is illustrated by the following:

| | Chronological Age | | | |
	5 yrs., 3 mos.	5 yrs., 9 mos.	6 yrs., 0 mos.	6 yrs., 3 mos.
IQ	MA	MA	MA	MA
80	4–2	4–7	4–9	5–0
90	4–9	5–3	5–6	5–8
100	5–3	5–9	6–0	6–3
110	5–9	6–4	6–6	6–9
120	6–4	6–11	7–2	7–6
130	6–10	7–6	7–10	8–2

It can be seen that a six-year-old child with a 100 IQ has a mental age of 6.0, but a child six years old with an 80 IQ has a mental age of only 4.9. This has important implications in regard to readiness, for it further demonstrates the fact that chronological age alone is a poor indicator of readiness.

Visual and auditory perception are also factors to be considered in readiness. Unless a child has reached a stage of maturity that enables him to perceive figures accurately, to note small details, and to perceive similarities and differences in letters or to hear and perceive the difference in sounds, his ability to respond to instruction is seriously impeded. The nature of perceptual demands is, of course, largely dictated by the particular teaching methods used. This means that, to some extent at least, the details of the instruction to be provided must be considered in assessing readiness. Many things can be done with individual instruction and specially adapted materials that cannot be done with mass instruction and traditional materials. See Chapter 15 for a discussion of "compensatory" education.

In concluding the discussion of correlates in learning disability, it is important to re-emphasize the interrelationships that exist among them. Rarely, if ever, is there a severe learning or reading problem that would not show signs of several of the factors listed. A remedial specialist might, in the course of a case study and diagnostic work-up, find other causal factors as well. The classroom teacher has neither the time nor the training to delve as deeply into a case as the specialist, but in many cases he is expected to solve some extremely complex learning problems. The classroom teacher can take encouragement from the fact that, in the case of most disabled learners, nothing has as salutary an effect upon the learning process as success. In many cases the causal factors tend to become less important once the pupil finds he *can* learn and is shown a method by which he can overcome his handicap.

It should also be stressed that different children react differently to any given handicap, and what is a causal factor for one child may not necessarily be a handicap for another child. Each child is unique and each teacher works best in his own way. If sound remedial methods are applied, if individual differences in children are provided for, if enthusiastic and aggressive teaching techniques are used, progress in learning is likely to follow.

THOUGHTS FOR DISCUSSION

"When a teacher or someone else in a school system finds a child's behavior intolerable and suspects a medical cause, the school system might well follow a different procedure from that for ordinary medical cases and allow only school personnel whose relationship with the child is a strictly professional, confidential one, and who are not in a position to reward or penalize him directly or indirectly, to approach a parent about possible medical treatment." (Ladd, 1970, p. 83)

"The causes of reading failure are many and complex. Almost always a matrix of factors is involved. Good teachers, as a result, must be good detectives. They must be alert to any and all symptoms indicating the presence of factors that are inimical to learning." (Schubert and Torgerson, 1968, p. 49)

"Today teachers know that there is no identical explanation for reading failures, and they seek a specific explanation for each individual case." (Karlin, 1964, p. 21)

"When six or more potential causes are present in a case history, it becomes practically impossible to determine how much or how little each of these may have contributed to the total problem. Sometimes an accumulation of minor handicaps may produce as much interference with learning as one major handicap, reminding us of the old saying about the last straw that breaks the camel's back." (Harris, 1960, p. 22)

"It is essential to recognize our own diagnostic limitations and when to call upon the other allied disciplines to fill in or correct the picture. We constantly need the advice of the pediatrician, the audiologist, the ophthalmologist, the counselor, school administrator, psychologist, psychiatrist, the professor, the social case worker, and the library science expert." (Wright, 1965, p. 16)

"The belief that the schools have a tremendous impact on ego-development or ego-starvation of pupils is gaining wider acceptance, and teachers are coming to realize that they are necessarily involved in the process of dealing with social and emotional maladjustments." (Heilman, 1961, p. 326)

REFERENCES

Bond, G. L. *The auditory and speech characteristics of poor readers.* Contributions to Education, No. 657. New York: Teachers College Press, 1935.

Bond, G. L., and Tinker, M. A. *Reading difficulties: Their diagnosis and correction.* New York: Appleton-Century-Crofts, 1957.

Brueckner, L. J., and Bond, G. L. *The diagnosis and treatment of learning difficulties.* New York: Appleton-Century-Crofts, 1955.

Challman, R. C. Personality maladjustments and remedial reading. *Journal of Exceptional Children,* 1939, **6**, 7–11.

Delacato, C. H. *The treatment and prevention of reading problems.* Springfield, Ill.: Charles C Thomas, 1959.

Durrell, D. (Ed.) Success in first grade reading. *Journal of Education,* 1958, **140**, 1–48.

Eames, T. H. Comparison of eye conditions among 1000 reading failures, 500 ophthalmic patients, and 150 unselected children. *American Journal of Ophthalmology,* 1948, **31**, 51–55.

Edson, W. H., Bond, G. L., and Cook, W. W. Relationships between visual characteristics and specific silent reading abilities. *Journal of Educational Research,* 1953, **46**, 451–457.

Eisenberg, L. The epidemiology of reading retardation and a program for preventive intervention. In J. Money (Ed.), *The disabled reader.* Baltimore: Johns Hopkins Press, 1966. Chapter I.

Fernald, G. M. *Remedial techniques in basic school subjects.* New York: McGraw-Hill, 1943.

Flom, M., and Neumaier, R. Prevalence of amblyopia. U.S. Public Health Service Reports, Department of Health, Education and Welfare, 1966, **81**, 310, 329.

Friedman, L. Z. Optometry and reading—An optometric problem? *The Oregon Optometrist*, McMinnville, Ore., May–June, 1967. P. 12

Frostig, M., and Horne, D. *The Frostig program for the development of visual perception*. Teacher's guide. Chicago: Follett Publishing, 1964.

Hage, D. S., and Stroud, J. B. Reading proficiency and intelligence test scores: Verbal and nonverbal. *Journal of Educational Research*, 1959, **52**, 258–262.

Harris, A. J. Corrective and remedial teaching. A Report of the 16th Annual Conference and Course on Reading, University of Pittsburgh, Pittsburgh, Pa., 1960.

Harris, A. J. *How to increase reading ability*. (4th ed.) New York: David McKay, 1961.

Harris, A. J. *How to increase reading ability*. (5th ed.) New York: David McKay, 1970.

Heilman, A. W. *Principles and practices of teaching reading*. Columbus, Ohio: Charles E. Merrill, 1961.

Karlin, R. *Teaching reading in high school*. Indianapolis: Bobbs-Merrill, 1964.

Karlin, R. *Teaching elementary reading*. New York: Harcourt, 1971.

Keeney, A. H., and Keeney, V. T. *Dyslexia-diagnosis and treatment of reading disorders*. St. Louis: C. V. Mosby, 1968.

Kephart, N. C. *The slow learner in the classroom*. Columbus, Ohio: Charles E. Merrill, 1960.

Kolson, C., and Kaluger, G. *Clinical aspects of remedial reading*. Springfield, Ill.: Charles C Thomas, 1963.

Ladd, E. T. Pills for classroom peace? *The Saturday Review*, November 21, 1970, 66–68, 81–83.

Money, J. (Ed.) *Reading disability*. Baltimore: Johns Hopkins Press, 1962.

Money, J. (Ed.) *The disabled reader*. Baltimore: Johns Hopkins Press, 1966.

Morrison, I. E., and Perry, I. F. Spelling and reading relationships with incidence of retardation and acceleration. *Journal of Educational Research*, 1959, **52**, 222–227.

Otto, W., and Smith, R. J. *Administering the school reading program*. Boston: Houghton Mifflin, 1970.

Pasamanick, B., and Knobloch, H. Brain damage and reproductive casualty. *American Journal of Orthopsychiatry*, 1960, **30**, 298–305.

Rabinovitch, R. D. Neuropyschiatric considerations in children's reading problems. In R. Strang (Ed.) , *Understanding and helping the retarded reader*. Tucson, Ariz.: University of Arizona Press, 1965.

Rabinovitch, R. D., and Ingram, W. Neuropsychiatric considerations in reading retardation. *The Reading Teacher,* 1962, **15**, 433–438.

Robbins, M. P. Test of the Doman-Delacto rationale with retarded readers. *Journal of the American Medical Association,* 1967, **202**, 389–393.

Roberts, J., and Dyan, K. U.S. Public Health Service: *Vital and health statistics, series 11, number 101.* Public Health Service Publication No. 1000, February, 1970.

Robinson, H. M. *Why pupils fail in reading.* Chicago: University of Chicago Press, 1946.

Robinson, H. M., and Huelsman, C. B., Jr. Visual efficiency and progress in learning to read. *Clinical studies in reading: II.* Supplementary Education Monograph No. 77. Chicago: University of Chicago Press, 1953.

Rosenbloom, A. A., Jr. Promoting visual readiness for reading. In A. J. Figarel (Ed.), *Changing concepts of reading instruction.* International Reading Association Conference Proceedings, Vol. 6. New York: Scholastic Magazines, 1961.

Schubert, D. G., and Torgerson, T. L. *Improving reading through individualized correction.* (2nd ed.) Dubuque, Iowa: William C. Brown, 1968.

Spache, G. D. *Reading in the elementary school.* Boston: Allyn and Bacon, 1964.

Strang, R. Relationships between certain aspects of intelligence and certain aspects of reading. *Educational and Psychological Measurement,* 1943, **3**, 355–359.

Taylor, S. E., Frackenpohl, H., and Pettee, J. L. Grade level norms for the components of the fundamental reading skill. *Research Information.* Bulletin No. 8. Huntington, N.Y.: Education Developmental Laboratories, 1960.

Thelander, H. E., Phelps, J. K., and Kirk, E. W. Learning disabilities associated with lesser brain damage. *Journal of Pediatrics,* 1958, **53**, 405–409.

Woolf, D. Dyschriesopia: A syndrome of visual disability. In R. Wold (Ed.), *Visual and perceptual aspects for the achieving and underachieving child.* Seattle, Wash.: Special Child Publications, 1969.

Wright, H. C. *Understanding and helping the retarded reader.* Tucson, Ariz.: University of Arizona Press, 1965.

Zangwill, O. L. Dyslexia in relation to cerebral dominance. In J. Money (Ed.), *Reading disability.* Baltimore: Johns Hopkins Press, 1962. Chapter VII.

Chapter 3

Approaches to Diagnosis and Remediation

Efficient instruction in the basic school subjects is always in tune with individuals' strengths and weaknesses in skill development and with their idiosyncrasies as learners. Corrective and remedial teaching, then, does not differ in intent from good classroom teaching. Nevertheless, Heilman (1969) has pointed out the chief cause for what may in fact amount to differences between remedial and regular teaching in the area of reading: ". . . in remedial reading we conscientiously adhere to the principles that we often only verbalize in the regular classroom instruction" (P. 457). Adherence to sound principles is made workable in part by modifications in the conditions under which teachers function, e.g., lower teacher: pupil ratios, availability of varied supplementary materials, more time allotted for skill development. Even more important, much stress is placed upon the fine focusing of instruction through careful diagnosis and consideration of the needs of individuals rather than upon the demands of curriculum guides. Good corrective and remedial teaching is good teaching at its best.

In this chapter the components of good corrective and remedial teaching are discussed. First, the relationship of corrective and remedial teaching to the overall instructional program of the school and the working relationships among school personnel are considered; next, fundamentals of diagnosis and of corrective and remedial teaching are presented; and finally, suggestions regarding the planning and organization of instruction are given.

CORRECTIVE AND REMEDIAL TEACHING IN CONTEXT

In the discussion that follows, corrective teaching and remedial teaching are placed within the context of an overall developmental program of instruction and a number of terms that are used throughout this book are defined.

The Overall Developmental Program

The term *developmental program* generally has a broad meaning, whereas the meaning of *developmental teaching* usually is somewhat more restricted. Typically, the goal of the developmental program is achievement in the basic school subjects that approaches the limit of each pupil's capacity. Thus, the developmental program subsumes the entire curriculum at all grade levels as well as specialized instructional programs designed for pupils with particular needs. Developmental teaching, on the other hand, usually is designed for the normal child who moves through the school experience without special problems. The result is that when we speak of a school's overall developmental program we typically are speaking not only of regular classroom instruction (developmental teaching) but of special instruction—corrective, remedial, adapted, accelerated—as well.

The overall developmental program as we conceive it is represented in the schema below (fig. 2). Developmental instruction is augmented by

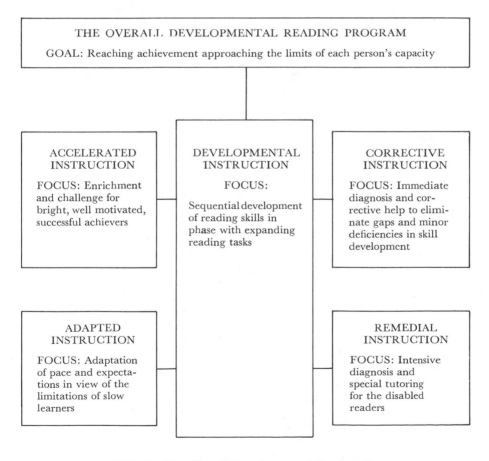

FIG. 2   The Overall Developmental Reading Program

special instruction with specific aims, and all instructional efforts are subsumed by the overall goal of near-capacity achievement for each pupil. A
more detailed discussion of the overall development program in reading is
given in Otto and Smith (1970, pp. 28–32).

Corrective Instruction

Corrective instruction can be differentiated from strictly remedial instruction in two ways. First, corrective instruction is given within the framework
of the regular classroom, whereas remedial instruction is offered apart
from the regular classroom instruction. Most corrective instruction is typically offered by the classroom teacher, but it is becoming increasingly common to make subject matter specialists who are skilled in diagnostic and
remedial techniques available to school staffs. Such persons often spend
part of their time providing traditional remedial instruction and part of
their time consulting with classroom teachers and actually offering some
corrective instruction by way of demonstration lessons, teaching particular
skills, etc. This appears to be an important step toward breaking down a
barrier in communication that sometimes exists between classroom teachers
and remedial specialists. Second, corrective instruction is given when it is
found that (1) an entire class is deficient in a particular skill or skills and/or
(2) a class or a group within the class is not achieving up to expectation in
a subject matter area. For example, if it were observed that all the members of a class appeared to be deficient in their mastery of the basic rules
of punctuation, the teacher might then begin a sequence of corrective instruction designed to improve the class level of mastery. Or, if it were found
that, say, five or ten children within a class were having more than normal
difficulty in understanding the process of long division, the decision might
be to offer corrective instruction in multiplication in order to prepare the
way for the more advanced understandings required by long division. Corrective instruction is provided when the nature and the degree of disability
is not such as to appear to demand intensive remedial instruction.

Remedial Instruction

Remedial instruction is appropriately reserved for the relatively few
pupils who have extreme achievement deficits in the basic school subjects
and whose deficits appear to stem from delimiting factors that demand
intensive, highly individualized attention. A child, for example, whose lack
of comprehension in reading is due primarily to his inattention to context
clues could probably benefit from corrective instruction, whereas a child
whose comprehension problems are accompanied by inadequate development of word attack skills, erratic study habits, and general inability to
sustain concentration would probably need prolonged, intensive remedial
instruction. As we conceive it, then, remedial instruction is offered to small

groups or individuals outside the regular classroom. Modification of the classroom setup is required to insure that adequate instructional time and materials and an optimum learning situation will be available for the intensive diagnosis and tutoring required to reach severely disabled learners.

We prefer to call children with severe learning problems *disabled* rather than *retarded* learners, and we prefer to avoid the use of the term *dyslexia* because it has been misused so often. *Retarded learner* often carries a connotation of mental retardation which is not intended. In our terminology, then, disabled learners are pupils who are capable, in terms of their general intelligence, of responding positively to remedial instruction when it is adequately focused.

Adapted Instruction

A fact too often ignored in considerations of corrective and remedial programs is that—given the normal, bell-shaped distribution of intelligence—about one-fourth of the children in a typical school have IQ's below 90. This suggests that a substantial number of children who fail to achieve at grade level are prevented from doing so mainly by their limited intellectual ability. These children do not need corrective or remedial help as much as they need instruction in which the pace and expectations are adapted to their slower rate of learning and lower capacity for achievement. In the public schools, they tend to have IQ's that fall roughly in the 70 to 90 range. We shall call them *slow learners* to differentiate them from *disabled learners.*

The methods and materials employed in adapted instruction will not differ much from those employed in remedial instruction. The critical difference is in terms of the expectation regarding the result of the instruction. We expect a disabled learner to overcome his disability and to function ultimately at or above his grade placement; we expect a slow learner to function at or near his capacity level, but this tends always to remain substantially below his chronological grade placement. When this difference in expectations is kept in mind, slow learners are not so likely to be casually referred for remedial instruction. When slow learners are indiscriminately mixed with disabled learners in remedial programs in the hope that all pupils will somehow "get up to grade level," both the remedial program and the slow learners are doomed to fail.

We feel that adapted instruction is best provided in the regular classroom or, where the classroom is not the basic instructional unit, in generally heterogeneous groups. Slow learners, as they are defined here, ought not to be segregated in homogeneous groups except for specific, short-term instruction, e.g., specific skill development activities. Nor should slow learners be arbitrarily excluded from remedial instruction. Slow learners, because they are apt to get off to a bad start in their school experience, are likely to fall substantially behind their capacity levels in achievement. Any child, regardless of his general ability, who is achieving substantially below his *ability level* ought to be considered for remedial instruction. If expectations are adapted in view of pupils' capacities, then there will be no problem.

The Pupil in the Program

A pupil's placement within the overall developmental program at any given time is determined mainly on the basis of information regarding his *(a)* general learning capacity, *(b)* actual achievement, and *(c)* estimated achievement potential. We shall consider first some points regarding estimates of capacity and achievement and then some rules of thumb for assigning pupils to programs.

Learning Capacity

A child's mental age is probably the most straightforward estimate of his learning capacity. Mental age is determined by the following formula:

$$\text{MA (Mental Age)} = \text{CA (Chronological Age)} \times \frac{\text{IQ}}{100}$$

Thus, on a straight $\text{MA} = \text{CAPACITY}$ basis, a ten-year-old with an IQ score of 90 would have a mental age of nine ($10 \times \frac{90}{100} = 9$), or the capacity of a nine-year-old. A ten-year-old with an IQ score of 120 would have a mental age of twelve ($10 \times \frac{120}{100} = 12$), or the capacity of a twelve-year-old.

While the $\text{MA} = \text{CAPACITY}$ conversion is uncomplicated, two points should be noted. First, IQ scores are not absolute numbers. They are only as good as the tests that are used to obtain them and evidence is accumulating that suggests they are subject to change. Second, the derivation of mental age ignores prior experience. Take the two ten-year-olds in the example above: the child with the IQ score of 90 might be expected to perform better than the average nine-year-old on the basis of more than a tenth of a lifetime's additional experience; and the child with the 120 IQ score might have difficulty in competing with average twelve-year-olds due to his relative lack of experiences.

Achievement

We have said that the ultimate goal of instruction is achievement that is at or near each child's capacity level. In the chapters that follow we shall discuss specific measures of actual achievement in the several basic school subjects. The essential fact here is that some children fail to achieve at their capacity levels.

Grade level is not a realistic achievement criterion, for some children have the ability to perform above their chronological grade-placement level and others are incapable of grade-level performance. The bright child who achieves only at grade level may need corrective help, whereas the child who achieves substantially below grade level may need adapted or remedial instruction, depending on his learning capacity. A child's learning capacity, not his grade placement, is the achievement criterion to which his actual achievement should be compared.

Estimated Achievement Potential

We have already noted that mental age, derived from IQ scores, is the most straightforward estimate of a child's learning capacity at a given point in time. To arrive at an estimate of achievement potential in terms of grade level, then, it is necessary only to subtract 5 from any given mental age:

$$\text{Achievement Potential (Grade Level)} = \text{MA} - 5$$

The typical ten-year-old, having entered first grade at age six, is in fifth grade. Thus, the ten-year-old with an IQ of 100 has an achievement potential of Grade 5, and the ten-year-old with an IQ of 120 has an achievement potential of Grade 7. For practical purposes, we feel that such estimates are adequate so long as there is awareness of their limitations. Harris (1970) and others have, however, pointed out that more precise procedures are desirable for certain purposes, such as establishing priorities among disability cases or conducting survey or experimental research studies.

Bond and Clymer (see Bond and Tinker, 1967, pp. 91–95) have suggested the following formula for estimating reading expectancy in terms of grade level:

$$\text{Reading Expectancy} = \text{Years in School} \times \frac{\text{IQ}}{100} + 1.0$$

In the Bond-Clymer formula the IQ factor is applied only to years in school, whereas in the straight MA conversion the IQ factor is applied to the entire chronological age. Della-Piana (1968) has pointed out the tendency of the Bond-Clymer formula to yield underestimates of actual achievement for high-IQ groups and of the MA conversion to yield underestimates of actual achievement for low-IQ groups and overestimates for high-IQ groups.

Harris (1970, p. 212) suggests the following formula for estimating a reading expectancy age:

$$\text{Reading Expectancy Age} = \frac{2\text{MA} + \text{CA}}{3}$$

The formula emphasizes the importance of intelligence but includes other age-related characteristics, thus taking note of one limitation of the straight MA conversion.

Our own preference is to stay with the straight IQ conversion $(\text{MA} = \text{CA} \times \frac{\text{IQ}}{100})$ in a corrective and remedial teaching context because it is extremely straightforward and its limitations are obvious. A more complicated formula is more likely to be accepted as a substitute for common sense. We believe that test scores must always be interpreted by teachers who are able and willing to bring to bear much additional information.

Assigning Pupils

The IQ conversion method for estimating learning capacity amounts essentially to a rule of thumb. Rules of thumb are useful so long as they are accepted for what they are and not transformed into rigid laws for governing behavior. In this spirit, then, some rules of thumb for providing pupils with appropriate instruction are suggested.

In general, regular developmental instruction is likely to be adequate to meet the needs of pupils in the average IQ-achievement range. "Average achievement" can be conceived roughly as grade placement plus or minus three months by the end of first grade to grade placement plus or minus about nine months by seventh grade and above. Corrective instruction is designed to help pupils overcome moderate deficiencies in learning that do not appear to require an intensive remedial approach. At the middle elementary level, corrective instruction should be considered when a pupil's achievement is one to two years below his capacity level. The rule-of-thumb gap should, of course, be increased for pupils at higher grade levels and decreased for pupils at lower grade levels.

Remedial instruction is reserved for pupils who are achieving substantially below capacity and who appear to require intensive diagnosis and tutoring outside the regular classroom. The following are commonly considered realistic criteria for judging the significance of achievement-capacity gaps:

Grade 2	six months or more
Grades 3–4	one year or more
Grades 5–8	two years or more
Grades 9–12	three years or more

Thus, say, a fifth grader whose actual achievement is two or more years below his capacity level would be considered, at least for screening purposes, a potential candidate for remedial teaching. (Ullman, 1969, has very legitimately pointed out the fact that when criteria such as the above are applied, a progressively larger percentage of children at each succeeding grade level will be defined as being in need of remedial help. This problem can be avoided by using such screening criteria as (1) achievement one standard deviation or more below mental test score on a common scale [Malmquist,

1960], (2) achievement two stanines or more below mental test score [Kelley, Madden, Gardner, and Rudman, 1964; Durost, 1962], or (3) an Expectancy Quotient below 90 derived from the following formula [adapted from Harris, 1970, p. 212]:

$$\text{Expectancy Quotient} = \frac{\text{Achievement Age} \times 100}{\text{Achievement Expectancy Age}}$$

Nevertheless, for practical purposes, we feel the rule-of-thumb criteria given above are adequate for screening purposes.) The fact, of course, is that in practice grade-placement level rather than learning capacity level may be the criterion to which actual achievement is compared. When this is so, bright children who achieve at grade level but below capacity tend not to get the attention they need.

Adapted instruction, in which the pace and expectations are modified in view of limited learning capacities, should be offered to children with IQ scores in the 70–90 range. Slow learners should not be excluded from remedial instruction when their achievement is substantially below their learning capacity level.

Some examples of appropriate assignments of pupils for instruction follow. In each case, the pupil is ten years old and in fifth grade.

1. Sam has an IQ score of 80, so his MA is 8.0 and his achievement potential is third-grade level. His actual achievement tends generally to be at third-grade level. He appears to be a *slow learner* who will profit most from *adapted instruction*.

2. Joe's IQ score is 110, his MA is 11.0 and his achievement potential is sixth-grade level. He reads at fourth-grade level. Depending on whether grade-placement or capacity level is the criterion for comparison, the achievement gap is one or two years. Our rule of thumb places him in the corrective category. The working hypothesis is that he can be adequately taught in the regular classroom with some special corrective help.

3. Sue's IQ score is 105, her MA is 10.5 and her achievement potential is at about mid-fifth-grade level. Her arithmetic achievement test shows performance at the 6.0 level. She appears to be responding well to regular developmental teaching.

4. Frank's IQ score is 100, his MA is 10.0 and his achievement potential is fifth-grade level. He reads at the second-grade level. He appears to be a candidate for remedial reading. But again, remedial reading as we define it should be reserved for pupils whose problems are so complex that they demand intensive attention outside the regular classroom. Whether corrective instruction would suffice or remedial instruction is needed can be determined through diagnosis and tentative teaching. Specifics are given in the chapters that follow.

Obviously, the assignment of pupils to categories will solve no problems unless the assignment of a pupil to a category leads to a sharper focus of instruction for him as an individual. In our experience the categories of instruction that we have suggested do help to demonstrate the range of instruction required in a balanced overall program. They also establish a framework for the screening that is a prelude to corrective and remedial teaching.

An Adjusted Curriculum

Although it may seem pessimistic in the context of a book on corrective and remedial teaching, we feel that it is realistic to acknowledge the occasional need for an *adjusted* curriculum. (See Otto and Smith, 1970, pp. 26–27, for an extended discussion.) Despite the best efforts of remedial teachers, the fact remains that some children with average or better intelligence appear to be incapable of responding to remedial teaching, particularly in reading. In such cases there is clearly a need for an adjusted curriculum that places minimum reliance on literacy. Too often children are endlessly referred from clinic to clinic and from summer program to summer program with no good results. Until the state of the art has advanced to where there are no failures, we are well advised in some cases to admit failure and to get on with the task of providing nontraditional but meaningful learning experiences.

WORKING RELATIONSHIPS

Many schools have remedial programs that, while they may have been originally intended to round out and firm up the total developmental program, have come to be quite apart from the day-to-day teaching program. When this is so, there is a tendency on the part of the school staff to look upon the remedial teacher as "somebody in special education," and there may be a tendency on the part of the remedial teacher to reciprocate by spending his working day within the confines of the remedial room. Furthermore, Lowe (1962) has pointed out the fact that there often is a lack of communication even between the services intended to prevent and/or remedy maladjustment, such as remedial education, school health, testing, counseling, speech therapy, etc. Lowe observes that

> . . . few pupil welfare workers confer with the youngster's teachers; few remedial specialists confer with the school counselor; and few psychologists confer with the school nurse. Typical school administrative arrangements almost penalize the specialist who would go 'over' or 'around' someone who feels he is in the line of authority for handling a pupil's case. All too frequently and unwittingly, lines of authority are designed to protect vested interests rather than to facilitate services to pupils. (Pp. 10–11)

In order to overcome the lack of communication among the various specialists, Lowe (1962, pp. 12–13) proposes greater efforts toward coordination of the special services provided by many school districts. In addition, it appears that some effort should be directed toward breaking down whatever barriers exist between the remedial specialist and the classroom teacher. Perhaps one of the most direct methods of breaking the barrier is to make the remedial specialist more available to the classroom teacher. This could be done by providing time for both teachers to confer regarding individual pupils and, equally important, providing time for remedial teachers to get into the classrooms to assist classroom teachers with diagnosis and corrective teaching. Where the latter has been tried (i.e., freeing the remedial teacher for a part of the day to work with classroom teachers) the results have been encouraging. Teachers are not reluctant to verbalize their belief that every child should be given every opportunity to progress to the ultimate of his capacity. Yet remedial specialists may guard their special knowledges and skills as "trade secrets" and classroom teachers may tend to see the remedial teacher as an outsider who is looking for evidence of poor teaching. The child who is a behavior problem may be referred for remedial help because he disrupts the class, not because he particularly needs remedial help. A teacher may refuse to give needed corrective instruction because he feels that "the students should have gotten that two years ago." Fortunately, such notions and practices are becoming more scarce as school staffs learn better to understand each other's roles and their interrelationships. Corrective and remedial instruction has an integral place in a school's overall developmental program. When this fact is fully recognized by both specialists and classroom teachers effective working relationships will follow.

DIAGNOSIS

Diagnostic instruments and procedures for specific skill areas are discussed in the chapters devoted to each of the several areas. The discussion here amounts to an introduction to diagnosis. The nature of diagnosis, levels of diagnosis, formal and informal approaches to diagnosis, and sources of diagnostic information are considered.

The Nature of Diagnosis

Diagnosis, we believe, ought to have a positive connotation. To diagnose in a positive way is not merely to seek and/or to classify the causes of malfunctions and breakdowns in the learning process; a sensitive teacher discovers strengths as well as weaknesses through diagnosis. Diagnosis, then, is by no means limited to corrective and remedial situations: it is basic to all efficient teaching. And, to be truly effective, diagnosis must be continuous. Harris (1970, p. 282) made a nice distinction when he said a "teach, test, reteach" sequence is desirable in developmental teaching but a shift to "test, teach, reteach" is best for remedial teaching; nevertheless, he was clearly calling for continuous diagnosis in both situations. The intent is to show that in developmental teaching we ought to check periodically to see how what was learned differs from what was taught and then fill in the gaps; whereas in remedial teaching it is most efficient to start with the gaps, to attempt to fill them with appropriate teaching, and then to see if we succeeded. The distinction is useful, and we shall preserve it in the discussion that follows.

The task of diagnosis with disabled learners is not an easy one. More often than not the problem is complicated by the presence of a number of interacting causal factors (see Chapter 2); seldom can a single factor be isolated as the key to the problem. Pressey, Robinson, and Horrocks (1959, p. 459) spoke to the point when they said that diagnosing a learning problem is quite different from attempting to isolate a germ that is causing an illness or to locate the defective part that is keeping an automobile from running. They concluded that diagnostic and remedial efforts must be guided by recognition of the complex nature of the individual and how he learns. Our purpose in emphasizing the complexities inherent in the diagnosis of learning problems is not to imply that attempts at diagnosis are necessarily destined to fail. On the contrary, the purpose is to point up the need for reasonable care and for proceeding with an open mind. Often teachers doing diagnostic work develop a "pet theory" that causes them to look for—and, consequently, to find—a common cause for most learning problems. Or, on the other hand, some teachers become convinced that all diagnosis is so complex that it is best left to the experts. Unfortunately, there are seldom enough experts to go around. Just as there are levels of disability, there are levels of diagnosis. The average classroom teacher is competent to do the diagnosis needed in day-to-day teaching and, usually, to do the diagnosis required for effective corrective instruction. For more severe disability cases requiring more intensive diagnosis, the teacher usually has a number of resource persons available to him. The truly competent teacher will know how far he can go in diagnosing the problems of his students and when he should make a referral to a specialist or an agency. The discussion that follows will help to clarify this point.

Levels of Diagnosis

All learning problems do not demand equally prolonged, intensive, or sophisticated diagnosis to permit successful treatment. Nor is it necessary or even desirable that all diagnostic work be done by highly trained specialists. The purpose of diagnosis is to discover the information that is required in order to devise a plan for efficient treatment. In some cases this may require examination of complex, underlying causal factors by specialists in a variety of fields, but in other cases a very straightforward assessment of individuals' skill development in the problem area by the classroom teacher may be adequate. The diagnostic process can be systematized if it is considered to involve several steps or levels.

Carter and McGinnis (1970, pp. 11–12) suggest four levels of diagnosis: (1) identification of the problem, (2) classification of the problem, (3) identification of instructional (skill development) needs, and (4) determination of causal factors. Brueckner and Bond (1955, pp. 63–65)—and Bond and Tinker (1967, pp. 154–158)—advocate three levels of study in educational diagnosis: (1) general, where areas of weakness are identified; (2) analytical, where specific strengths and weaknesses are examined; and (3) case study, where all information requisite to understanding the problem is gathered and considered. We feel that identification and classification of the problem actually amount to a single step in the diagnostic process, so we shall describe three levels: *survey, specific,* and *intensive.* The point is not the number of levels but the fact that a step-by-step approach to diagnosis can be efficient and effective.

Survey Level

Diagnosis at the survey level is generally carried out by the classroom teacher; in the main, it serves as the foundation upon which all subsequent diagnosis is based. At the survey level the teacher attempts to examine the level of performance of all his pupils in order to evaluate the success of the developmental teaching program, determine areas in which the whole class or certain groups need corrective instruction, and locate pupils who appear to be disabled learners and in need of more specific diagnosis. It is probably appropriate to think of the survey level as a classroom screening level.

The following are typical sources of information at the survey or classroom screening level of diagnosis:

1. *Achievement Tests* (in any or all of the basic skill and content areas) Comparison of class results with local or national norms helps the teacher to evaluate the performance of individuals and of the entire group.

2. *Group Tests of Mental Ability* It is useful to examine the results of achievement tests in the light of tests of ability because analysis of group mental test scores can give the teacher a rough estimate of the level of expectancy for the group in general and for individuals within the group.

3. *Cumulative Record Folders* When available and current, these can yield useful information about general health, home background, school history, etc. This kind of information can be useful in broadening the bases for better understanding both group and individual performance.

To sum up, as we conceive it, the survey level of diagnosis includes class-wide testing and evaluation. The main purposes of the survey diagnosis are to uncover strengths and weaknesses in general class achievement and to identify individuals who appear to have special instructional needs.

Specific Level

Specific diagnosis is essentially individual diagnosis for the purpose of isolating the weaknesses and gaps in skill mastery that are the immediate causes for poor performance. At the survey level the individual suspected of being a disabled learner is located; at the specific level, the tentative diagnosis of learning disability is thoroughly checked out and performance in the area or areas of difficulty is carefully examined for strengths and weaknesses.

Two kinds of tests are useful at the specific level:

1. An individual intelligence test, such as the *Stanford-Binet* or one of the Wechslers, may be given in order to check on group intelligence test results that may be available. Disabled learners tend to do poorly on group tests of capacity for a variety of reasons ranging from inability to read the items to adverse reaction to stress arising from the test situation. The best available measures of capacity should, therefore, be used in order that the disabled learner's level of expectancy may be estimated with some confidence. One point should be clearly in mind: strengths as well as weaknesses may be turned up by individual tests of capacity. There is a needlessly negative emphasis when tests are used primarily to point up a wide gap between potential and actual achievement for the purpose of clearly categorizing a child as a disabled learner. In a more positive vein, it is good to remember that an individual intelligence test often uncovers strengths that may be capitalized upon in overcoming learning difficulties.

2. Tests that are designed to give a detailed analysis of performance in the area or areas of difficulty may be given to assess achievement strengths and weaknesses of an individual pupil. These tests may be standardized or informal, oral or silent. At the level of specific diagnosis several tests of different types are often given to round out a complete sampling of skills. Analysis of the test results should provide the teacher with a clear, detailed picture of a pupil's skill-learning difficulties and, subsequently, enable him to outline the first steps to be taken in remedial teaching.

Because many of the tests for specific diagnosis are individual tests, they must necessarily be administered outside regular class periods. Some of the diagnostic tests discussed later may be given to small groups, but these, too, should be given under conditions that permit the tester to observe the test-situation behavior of each pupil being tested. In the final analysis, it is not so much the tests used as the purpose for which they are used that separates the survey from the specific level of diagnosis. One might use a particular test at either level: at the survey level to locate class weaknesses to be attacked through corrective teaching, and at the specific level to get a clearer picture of a disabled learner's performance in a particular area.

Survey diagnosis is most frequently handled by the classroom teacher. Specific diagnosis might be handled either by the classroom teacher or a remedial specialist, depending on such things as the time and facilities available, the complexity of the disability, and the classroom teacher's competence with diagnostic techniques.

Intensive Level

Intensive diagnosis is usually reserved for those learning disability cases that are unusually severe and appear to be complicated by factors that tend to impede learning even when well-planned remedial help is given. At the level of intensive diagnosis a complete case study in done to get an overall picture of a child and his needs. The purpose is to get at the basic defects or problems that are interfering with effective learning.

Chapter 4 deals specifically with case study procedures; sample forms and a rationale for the case study approach are presented there. Briefly, the case study provides a framework for (1) bringing together everything that is known about a pupil's academic performance, particularly in the areas of disability; (2) integrating information about the subject's home background, school history, health record, personality, and social adjustment; (3) translating all of the diagnostic information into recommendations for remedial treatment; and (4) describing and evaluating the results of the remedial treatment.

Case studies are usually undertaken by remedial specialists in either the school or a clinical setting. The remedial specialist is often well advised to seek the assistance of other specialists—eye specialists, pediatricians, psychologists, speech pathologists, social workers—in acquiring all of the information that may be pertinent to a case study. This is not to say, however, that a case study is taboo for a classroom teacher. If he can find time to do one occasionally, we feel that the discipline of a case study can be beneficial both for his understanding and teaching of the child directly involved and for his general understanding of the factors involved in good corrective and remedial teaching. In many school districts it is possible to find some classroom teachers with more training and competence in diagnostic techniques than some remedial specialists. It would appear to be pointless, therefore, to suggest that certain levels of diagnosis are the exclusive domain of any particular group. At any level of diagnosis, both remedial specialists and classroom teachers must be aware of their own competencies and limitations. They must recognize the point at which they should seek assistance from specialists and the point at which they should turn a case over to more highly trained persons.

As we conceive it, intensive diagnosis serves to round out the total picture of an individual disabled learner. At the survey level the disabled learner is first discovered; at the specific level, his strengths and weaknesses in academic achievement are thoroughly checked out; and at the intensive level the underlying causes of the learning disability are sought. Certainly the three levels are not discrete, one from another; rather, one level leads logically into the next as the need for further information becomes apparent.

The emphasis here should be upon "need for further information." While it is important to seek all the information that will be useful in most effectively tackling a case, it is also important to sense the time to stop. Diagnostic information is useful only when it dictates remedial treatment; beyond that, it becomes merely an academic gymnastic.

Approaches to Diagnosis

Diagnosis is much more than a labeling process, yet overdependence upon formal, standardized tests is likely to result more in labeling than in anything else. To decide—on the basis of either a group or individual intelligence test—that a child is a slow learner or to decide—on the basis of a test of perceptual-motor functioning—that he has a "visual-motor impairment" is but to take a step in what may turn out to be the right direction. Once a problem has been labeled the task of arriving at some sensible way of dealing with that particular problem still remains. That is, given a child with a visual-motor deficit the teacher is still confronted with the task of determining what deficiencies must be remedied before the child will be able to, say, produce legible handwriting. A combination of formal instruments and informal techniques can be useful in moving from labels to specifics.

Standardized Tests

As long as their limitations are clearly recognized, standardized tests have a role to play in the diagnosis of learning disabilities. Here we shall consider some guidelines for choosing and using them and some of their limitations. Specific tests are described in the discussions of diagnostic procedures in each of the several basic skill areas. The following points should be kept in mind as standardized tests are chosen.

1. *Define the purpose for testing.* Standardized tests may be given for any number of reasons—to compare class achievement with local or national norms, to determine the current achievement status of the class and/or individuals in order to learn whether corrective or remedial steps should be taken, to screen in order to determine the need for further testing, or to evaluate the developmental program. When the purpose for testing is clearly in mind, a decision can be made as to whether a *survey test* or an *analytical* test would be most appropriate. Generally, survey tests are group tests designed to provide an average score which will tell the teacher how well a class or a pupil compares with other pupils of the same age and grade. Survey tests are typically used at the survey level of diagnosis. Analytical tests may be either group or individual tests. They are designed to break down a total performance into specific strengths or weaknesses. Analytical tests may be given at either the survey or the specific level of diagnosis in order to examine the details of class or individual skill mastery

in a particular area. Group tests have the obvious advantage of testing more pupils in less time than individual tests, but the latter are likely to provide much more information regarding the idiosyncrasies of an individual's performance.

2. *Locate suitable tests.* From among the many tests currently available several will appear to be appropriate for the purpose identified. Probably the most useful single source of assistance in locating and sorting out suitable tests is *The Sixth Mental Measurements Yearbook,* edited by Oscar K. Buros. (Previous editions were published in 1938, 1940, 1949, 1953, and 1959.) Available tests in education and psychology are listed and described in the yearbook; a brief statement of such things as cost, coverage, source, and one or more critical reviews is included for each test.

Other sources of information about tests are journals in education and psychology and publishers' catalogs. The following journals commonly include reviews of and/or research relevant to tests and testing: *Journal of Educational Research, Perceptual and Motor Skills, Personnel and Guidance Journal, The Reading Teacher, Journal of Educational Measurement, School Review,* and *Elementary School Journal.* Publishers' catalogs naturally present the tests in their most favorable light.

3. *Evaluate before selecting.* Once the tests that appear to meet the requirements of a given situation have been identified, they should be carefully evaluated in terms of such things as reliability, validity, economy, ease of administration, adequacy of the manual, relevance of the norms provided, and appropriateness of the content for local pupils.

A test that is *reliable* yields consistent results. One common method of estimating reliability is to correlate the results of two administrations of the same test to the same groups. Another method is to correlate the results obtained with the odd- and even-numbered items on the test. A perfect correlation coefficient of 1.0 results if the test and retest or the odd- and even-item results are identical. In practice, a reliability (correlation) coefficient of .85 or above is usually acceptable. A reliable test, then, would yield similar results on Monday and Tuesday if no learning were interpolated. When there are two or more forms of a test, the inter-form reliability must also be high.

A test that is *valid* actually measures what it is supposed to measure. For example, it is conceivable that a test purporting to measure mental ability may, in fact, measure reading ability; such a test would not be valid, especially not for disabled readers. The validity of a test can be estimated by correlating individual scores on the test with performance on a previously selected task or test. Thus one might correlate scores on a group IQ test with scores on a highly regarded individual IQ test in order to estimate the validity of the group test. The individual test, then, is accepted as the criterion. Although one might question the validity of the criterion itself, this is actually a common practice. As in estimating reliability, the closer the relationship between the test score and the criterion the higher the validity. For most purposes, the validity (correlation) coefficient of a test should be .70 or better; but when a test is meant to measure a very complex performance or skill, a lower coefficient may be acceptable. The fact remains, of course, that many highly regarded, widely used tests have only *face validity*. That is, they *appear to* measure what they are *intended to* measure.

An adequate test manual includes the following kinds of information:

1. Clear and concise directions for administering the test. This is important because a major reason for using a standardized test is to secure data under stated conditions.

2. Adequate information regarding the reliability and validity of the test.

3. Norms based upon sound sampling procedures. That is, the sampling of scores upon which the norms are based should be large and distributed according to geographic location and socioeconomic areas. Both age and grade norms should be provided; and it is desirable to have means, percentiles, quartiles, and stanines provided to facilitate interpretation of scores. A good manual also includes instructions for creating local norms.

4. Aids for interpretation. Provision for profile analysis and illustrative interpretations can, for example, be useful.

Finally, a test must be readily and currently *available* if it is to be used in quantity. It should be *economical:* such things as initial cost of test booklets, reusability of the booklets, ease of scoring, and compatibility with machine scoring techniques must be considered. A test that is very reasonable in terms of initial cost could be prohibitively expensive in terms of time required for scoring or replacement costs. Availability of *alternate forms* is required if the test is to be used in test-retest comparisons.

The best way to become completely familiar with a test is to take it yourself and then administer it to a few children. There is no better way to discover problems in administration and scoring, inappropriate items, etc. Specimen sets of tests are readily available from publishers at a reasonable cost. For an extended discussion of things to consider in selecting tests consult *Standards for Educational and Psychological Tests and Manuals* (American Psychological Association, 1966).

Standardized tests share some rather severe limitations that ought to be kept in mind even after the "best available" are chosen. Some of the more salient limitations, particularly of achievement tests, are given here.

1. The very fact that they are "standardized" in terms of administration and scoring may make them inappropriate for use with certain groups. Norms may be unrealistic; items may be meaningless or placed at inappropriate levels; directions may be incomprehensible.

2. The test's quest for brevity, which unfortunately but pragmatically enhances the saleability of tests in some circles, may result in unrealistic time limits and a choice between depth and breadth in sampling. The scores achieved by children who work very slowly but accurately are likely to be meaningless; the sampling of behavior is likely to be superficial or constricted.

3. Group administration may work to the disadvantage of certain individuals. The group situation combined with the standardized conditions may, in fact, totally invalidate the test in some instances. For example, a child, who fails to understand one or two words in a set of directions may be completely precluded from responding to any of the items, which he may or may not have known.

4. The format of the test may restrict the type of items used. A machine scorable format, for example, virtually demands some form of multiple-choice items. Certain behaviors are not adequately sampled with multiple-choice items.

5. Tests at upper grade levels assume ability at lower levels. Thus, a pupil may be able to score at a certain base level simply by signing his name to the test booklet. Furthermore, the fact that standardized tests tend to yield overestimates of actual performance is generally acknowledged.

The main feature of the standardized test is that it is accompanied by norms that, presumably, are based upon the responses of large numbers of pupils at specified grade and age levels under specified conditions. Through the use of standardized tests the individual teacher is able to compare the performance of his pupils with the performance of many other pupils.

Informal Techniques

In the process of diagnosis a teacher will often find it necessary to seek information that is not available from standardized tests or to supplement information from standardized tests. When this is so, it is up to him to devise his own informal measuring device or to know where to find one that is appropriate. The following sequence can serve as a guide to the effective use of informal assessment: first, decide exactly what information is desired and what this means in terms of observable behavior; then devise new or adapt existing test items, materials, or situations to sample the behavior to be evaluated; keep a record of the behavior evoked in the test situation; analyze the information obtained; and, finally, judge how the information fits the total picture and how well it fills the gap for which it was intended.

Examples of some of the most useful and most used informal devices for gathering diagnostic information, particularly regarding strengths and weaknesses in specific skill development, follow:

1. *Informal Observation*   The most natural informal technique for gathering diagnostic information is informal observation of the pupil. This technique is often overlooked, but it is one that alert, skillful teachers can use effectively for a number of purposes—systematically observing a child's overall performance, learning about his interests and attitudes, finding out about his approaches to problem solving and to study situations, detecting physical problems and limitations, etc. Observing with a purpose can, for example, provide the teacher with real insight into the problems

a child may be encountering when he attempts to solve story problems in arithmetic, attack new words, or write legibly with his left hand.

2. *Anecdotal Records*   In its simplest form an anecdotal record can consist of a manila folder in which work samples and observations are kept in chronological order. The primary purpose for keeping such a record is to help the teacher keep in mind the developing characteristics of a child. Gradual but steady improvement may be seen as lack of improvement if there are no readily available check points. The record can be used to demonstrate gains resulting from remedial teaching. Obviously, the record loses its value if it is simply cluttered with an occasional drawing and general statements like "Clyde appears to be doing better." Entries must, of course, be dated.

3. *Informal Tests*   Many of the books, workbooks, and periodicals designed for school use include informal, nonstandardized tests that can be used for quick checks of pupils' comprehension, writing ability, grasp of arithmetic concepts, and the like. Similar informal tests can be constructed by the teacher to check on pupils' grasp of just-presented material or to get samplings of various kinds of behavior.

4. *Check Lists*   In this general category are included such things as interest and personality inventories; questionnaires of work habits, interests, activities, associates; and lists of specific skills that can be used to check a pupil's mastery of certain areas. The lists are a practical means for systematizing observations.

5. *Informal Reading Inventories*   In the area of reading, many teachers use an informal reading inventory to observe a pupil's oral and silent reading at several difficulty levels. The inventory consists of samples from the various grade levels of a basal reader series plus comprehension questions. Four levels of reading ability are typically identified through the use of the inventory: (1) independent level—the level at which the pupil can read independently with at least 99 percent accuracy in word recognition and 90 percent or better comprehension; (2) instructional level—the level at which the pupil can read with some help from the teacher; (3) frustration level—the level at which the pupil can no longer function effectively; and (4) hearing capacity level—the highest level at which the pupil can comprehend at least 75 percent of material that is read to him. With adaptations, the basic idea of the informal reading inventory can be very useful in other basic skill areas. In handwriting, for example, it would be useful to know both how well a pupil is able to write for special purposes (instructional level) and how well he writes for his own, outside-the-classroom purposes (independent level).

Each of the informal devices listed can be adapted in a number of ways to increase its applicability. Other informal sources of diagnostic information are interviews, autobiographies, sociometric procedures, projective and expressive techniques, and introspective-retrospective study. The latter merits special consideration.

Introspective-Retrospective Study

Strang (1969, Chapter V) has made the very legitimate point that teachers and students are partners in the diagnostic process, and she suggests introspective-retrospective study as a demonstration of the teacher's faith in the resources within each individual. Reduced to its essence, the approach is to encourage pupils to describe what goes on in their minds while they are engaged in an academic task. Such self-analysis can be encouraged through class discussion, the writing of reading autobiographies, questions immediately following an assigned exercise, and interviews. Strang's suggestion is eminently sensible. The teacher-pupil partnership deserves emphasis. How easy it is to become so engrossed in studying a pupil that we forget to ask him what he is thinking and experiencing!

A Final Word

The salient feature and key to the usefulness of informal evaluation is the flexibility such an approach affords the teacher. When used with discrimination, informal techniques can be used to obtain much information that is sound, current, and unique to the individual pupil being considered. The very informality and flexibility that most enhance the functional value of the informal technique, however, are also its most serious limitations. In the absence of standardized procedures and norms, the interpretation of data secured from informal evaluation must be based mainly upon personal judgments and feelings. Fortunately, there are many standardized tests available and, ideally, standardized and informal measures will be used to complement each other. In the process of diagnosis standardized tests can help provide the objectivity that is needed while informal techniques provide the flexibility and fill in the gaps.

While it is important to exercise care in choosing the best tests available for use in the diagnostic process, it should be clearly understood that this is not an end in itself. It is well to remember that the act of obtaining test data, as such, is not diagnosis; it is merely one of the steps preceding diagnosis, a seeking of data upon which a diagnosis can be based. Baron and Bernard (1958) have said it well: "Educational and psychological tests do not make analyses or suggest what should be done; they give indications which may serve to sharpen and clarify the judgments teachers make on the basis of experience, training, and understanding" (P. 3).

Sources of Diagnostic Information

The competent classroom or remedial teacher senses the point at which he needs to seek aid in his diagnostic work with individuals. In most communities certain resources are available; but, of course, they vary widely, depending upon such things as size of the community, wealth of the community, and the initiative of local leaders. Of the typical resources discussed here, some offer tutorial services as well as diagnostic assistance. The fact is, however, that they are likely to be useful mainly for diagnosis; the responsibility for remedial teaching almost invariably comes back to the remedial specialist in the school and, ultimately, to the classroom teacher.

Sources within the School

As school districts become larger through consolidation and as the districts move toward greater cooperation to provide special services, workers with a variety of specialties are becoming more commonly available for consultation and assistance. Some time ago, Lowe (1962) pointed out the desirability of having nine types of professional services available in order to work toward full development of student capabilities. Progress has been made, and many schools do have several or all of these services with the attending personnel available: pupil accounting service—pupil welfare worker; health service—school nurse; remedial education service—remedial specialist; speech/hearing correction service—speech/hearing therapist; home/school social service—school social worker; parent education service—school counselor or school social worker; counseling service—school counselor; assessment service—school psychologist; and research service—educational psychologist. The point here is that the resources and limitations of each service that is available ought to be known and all available services ought to be brought to bear when relevant. Both teachers and specialists can make referrals only when they know what is available to them.

College and University Clinics

In communities where teacher training institutions are located, clinics operated by the institutions may be available. Such clinics usually have a dual purpose: to offer diagnostic services and, in some instances, remedial treatment to disabled learners; and to provide a setting for practicum courses for students seeking advanced training in diagnostic and remedial techniques. Typically, the clinics accept a limited number of children for intensive diagnosis and limited treatment and send a report of diagnostic findings and suggested follow-up remedial treatment back to the school.

Community Services

Since the nature and number of community services available varies widely from community to community, it is not possible to generalize about the services likely to be found in any specific community. This makes it imperative for each teacher to be familiar with the services available in his particular community. One large metropolitan community offers a *Directory of Community Services* in which the health and welfare services available to individuals and groups are listed. Of the 150 services listed—ranging from Alcoholics Anonymous to the Crippled Children's Division of the University Medical School to the Salvation Army—several are potent resources for the teacher seeking aid in diagnosing learning problems. The Crippled Children's Division is a prime example: the staff of specialists offers diagnostic and treatment services to crippled children and to children with crippling conditions. Such an agency can offer invaluable aid, particularly in cases where brain damage or neurological damage is suspected. The Community Child Guidance Clinic, supported by United Givers, offers diagnosis and treatment for children with behavior disturbances. Working relationships between remedial teachers and staff members at such clinics are likely to be very productive: the clinic provides the intensive therapy and the school provides coordinated tutoring.

The remedial teacher is well advised to expend some effort to become aware of and to establish working relationships with the legitimate service agencies available in his community. Assistance may be forthcoming from a variety of sources. In smaller communities service clubs can often be called on to provide financial assistance for eye examinations and glasses or other services when there is a need. The range of possible sources for assistance is limited most by the limits of the remedial teacher's initiative.

REMEDIAL TEACHING

Just as children differ, so do their problems differ, and so too must approaches to remedial teaching differ. The purpose here is to show that remedial teaching must proceed from diagnosis, to suggest some guidelines for remedial teaching that can be adapted in view of specific needs, and to consider in detail certain aspects of effective remedial teaching. The specific strategies of a good remedial teacher are, of course, always worked out in response to the information and resources available in a given case.

The Diagnostic Base

Diagnosis is pointless unless the information gained is used to shape remedial teaching, and remedial efforts that are not directed by diagnosis are certain to be grossly inefficient. Yet in practice the gap between diagnostic and remedial efforts may be quite real for at least four reasons (from Strang, 1969, p. 12).

1. So much time can be spent on diagnosis that there is little time for instruction. (This, perhaps, is the most common but least excusable reason. An equally undesirable situation arises, though, when teachers claim they have no "time to test" because they must get on with their teaching. Unfocused, random teaching is as arbitrary and inefficient as indiscriminate testing and over-diagnosis.)

2. In some instances the main diagnostic work is carried out by one person and the remedial teaching by another with no adequate communication between them.

3. Some single cause of learning difficulty may be overemphasized. (The remedial teacher—whether dedicated zealot or impressionable faddist—who fixates upon a single cause is virtually certain to have a panacea for learning problems. Single causes and panaceas do not often square with the facts of diagnosis.)

4. Strictly quantitative diagnostic data are likely to be inadequate. (Quantitative data may tell very little about the nature and dynamics of a learning problem, and, as a result, be of little use in planning remedial teaching.)

The gap can be eliminated, or at least narrowed, if questions that are to be answered through diagnosis are kept in mind throughout a sequence of remedial teaching. The first question to be answered is whether an adapted or a corrective/remedial program of instruction is appropriate. The answer is important not because it dictates the nature of subsequent instruction but because, in effect, it sets the expectations and establishes a context for the instruction that follows. Having decided that a child is a disabled learner rather than a slow learner, the next question is whether corrective help is likely to be adequate or remedial help is required. The answer depends upon careful diagnosis to determine the degree and the nature of the disability. The very severely disabled learner may need intensive remedial help outside the regular classroom. The child's reactions to group situations must also be considered: while one child might benefit from the give-and-take in a group another might become hopelessly lost. The make-up of the child's class is relevant, too. If a number of children share similar strengths and weaknesses, corrective teaching may be feasible, whereas a child with a unique problem might best be taught individually. Most of these questions should be answered, at least tentatively, at the survey level of diagnosis.

Once the general approach has been determined, the answers to specific questions guide the teaching. The most basic information to be obtained through diagnosis must yield an estimate of the level at which instruction should begin. Related questions are: What is the exact status of the child's skill mastery in the area of difficulty? Are there special problems of motivation? Does the child have any strong interests? In what areas, if any, is the child experiencing success? What additional information is needed from other specialists (e.g., pediatrician, audiologist, speech therapist, optometrist). Answers to questions such as these direct both the remedial teaching and the quest for additional information.

As teaching progresses, evidence may accumulate to suggest that learning continues to be blocked by complex, deep-rooted problems. If this is so, then it will be necessary to move to the level of intensive diagnosis in order to seek the underlying causes for the problem. Information gained at this level may indicate a need to modify the remedial efforts in order to accommodate certain physical or psychological deficits, or the information may indicate that certain modifications in the child's environment are required before progress can be made.

If diagnosis is conceived primarily as a question-answering process, then diagnosis and teaching are likely to remain in balance and in phase. Seldom is a case so uncomplicated as to permit the teacher to gather all of the essential information before remedial teaching begins. In most cases the teaching process itself uncovers the need for additional information which, in turn, leads to further diagnosis and modifications in the teaching. To assist teachers in putting their observations and plans together in a systematic manner, a *Tentative Diagnosis, Prognosis, and Proposed Treatment* form is given in Chapter 4. The form provides guidelines for initial observation, a vehicle for estimating the rate and degree of progress expected on the basis of the known facts, and a repository for a description of the treatment proposed. The tentative diagnosis provides a rationale for the proposed treatment, which serves as a guide to the first steps in remedial teaching. The form can serve as an aid to both *planning,* as the remedial teacher works with a child, and *communication,* if and when the report is passed on to another teacher.

Adequate diagnosis reveals not only the degree of a learning problem but also the exact nature of the problem. The latter is, of course, much more critical to remedial teaching. Having found, for example, two sixth graders who read at the third-grade level, it would be absurd simply to start teaching both as if they were third graders. Chances are that in each case the disability is attributable to quite different factors. Getting at the different factors in each case is what diagnosis is all about, and reflecting those findings in a planned instructional program is what remedial teaching is all about.

Guidelines for Remedial Teaching

Again, the specifics of remedial teaching must be worked out in view of the information and resources available in each case. Nevertheless, we have found the following guidelines, which are based upon accepted learning principles, to be useful in the planning of remedial teaching efforts. Note that attainment of the goal inherent in the first guideline—*Secure the learner's cooperation*—is most effectively accomplished through application of the remaining guidelines.

1. *Secure the learner's cooperation.* An active participant is a more efficient learner than a passive spectator, and, ultimately, the success or failure of remedial efforts depends on the involvement of the learner. Each of the guidelines that follow is designed to secure the learner's involvement. Additional suggestions are given in the following sections on motivation, behavior modification, and selection of materials and in the final chapter.

2. *Offer instruction at the learner's level.* To do this, the teacher must have constantly in mind the pupil's present level of skill development and

his capacity level. The determination of a tentative diagnosis, prognosis, and proposed treatment as suggested in Chapter 4 will help to focus the instructional level. Access to and familiarity with a wide variety of instructional materials at various levels will permit the implementation of instruction.

3. *Take small steps.* The teacher will do well to borrow a basic tenet of programmed instruction: make each step so small that a correct response is virtually assured. For example, if the improvement of handwriting is the goal, it is realistic not to expect the pupil to move directly from his habitual illegible letter forms to the perfect models provided by commercial materials. Instead, the pupil should be led toward the goal through a series of minimal changes for which interim models are provided. Likewise, if the general goal is, say, improved language usage, the teacher should help the student to establish interim goals that emphasize the elimination of certain specific faulty forms.

In this connection the teacher should also help the pupil to set realistic goals for himself. Unless the pupil perceives a small step as one that is significant, he is not likely to be satisfied with the small step. Disabled learners often object, for example, to the "baby work" that necessarily underlies improvement in a skill area; they need to see that they must walk before they can run.

4. *Reinforce success.* In many instances a success experience is its own reinforcement. The assumption in most programmed learning is that small steps insure correct responses and that correct responses are rewarding to the learner. A related assumption is that the learner will have immediate *knowledge of results,* i.e., he will know whether or not his response was correct. The latter is particularly important if the learning experience is to be reasonably self-sustaining. One of the main advantages of one-to-one remedial teaching is that the teacher is constantly available to provide immediate knowledge of results.

Reinforcement can, of course, be either tangible (a jelly bean, a dime, a gold star) or intangible (a smile, a nod, confirmation of a correct response), depending upon the maturity, perceptions, and needs of the individuals involved. The effective teacher knows *when* a pupil perceives a success experience and *what* constitutes reinforcement for that particular pupil at that particular moment. Ultimately, the pupil must come to recognize his own mistakes and to derive satisfaction from his success, but as a disabled learner he will require considerable coaching along the way.

5. *Keep learning tasks and materials meaningful.* The results of countless research studies demonstrate the fact that meaningful tasks and materials are mastered more readily than materials that have limited meaning or tasks that are not clearly understood. While additional research regarding specific applications is needed (Mickelson, 1969), certain implications are clear. The problem in remedial teaching is not merely to be sure that tasks and materials presented have inherent meaning, for the use of nonsense materials is generally limited to experimental settings. The remedial teacher

must be constantly alert to see that materials are meaningful *for the particular pupils being taught* and that assigned tasks are understood. For example, the statement "Intelligence quotient equals MA divided by CA," has meaning for most teachers, but it is not meaningful to most pupils because they lack the basic concepts. Pupils must understand what is presented if they are to learn efficiently.

6. *Facilitate remembering.* Researchers usually get at memory by studying forgetting, and most psychologists agree that forgetting is due primarily to interference (Kausler, 1966). That is, old learnings tend to stand in the way of new learnings and new learnings tend to blur old learnings because similarities in what is known and what is freshly learned tend to merge, thus interfering with both efficient learning and remembering. The remedial teacher can combat interference by taking care to see that the unique features of each new learning are stressed and understood; the more clear the differentiation, the less likely that interference will cause forgetting. In spelling, for example, the *ie* in words like *field* and *yield* would be stressed; in letter perception, the difference between similar letters like *p* and *q* and *b* and *d*; in sight word recognition, the unique characteristics of *then* and *than.* But it should be remembered that while "merging together" causes interference and forgetting, a similar process also enables us to grasp useful relationships and to generalize. Thus, the suggestion here is not that teachers should refrain from pointing out similarities and relationships when appropriate.

With some tasks, the best means to facilitate remembering is to provide for overlearning. In the basic skill areas a number of tasks should be appropriately overlearned through repetitive practice (drill). Production of letter forms in handwriting, for example, should be overlearned to the point of being automatized (made without conscious thought of the muscular movements involved). Service words in reading (*this, that, then, and, but,* etc.) should be overlearned to the point where they are recognized instantly fairly early in the learning-to-read process. The multiplication tables and proper language forms, too, should be overlearned to the point of instant recall and automatic use.

7. *Encourage pupil discovery of relationships.* When pupils are able to discover important relationships and generalizations for themselves, transfer to new tasks and situations is better. For example, a phonics principle that is merely presented by the teacher and memorized by the pupil is not as likely to be applied in independent reading as a generalization that is discovered by the pupil. Likewise, relationships in arithmetic are more likely to be understood and applied when they are discovered by the pupil.

Of course we are not suggesting that the pupil be abandoned to proceed at random as he seeks to make his own discoveries. The point is that the learning sequence should be so structured that the pupil is led to the place where relationships and generalizations are clear and self-discovery is a logical next step. Many of the basal reader series do a good job of *leading* pupils to self-discovery of phonics principles. The teacher's role, then, is not to impose relationships but to provide the setting that permits them to emerge. The necessary next step is to provide opportunities for the pupil to apply the relationships he has learned.

8. *Guard against motivation that is too intense.* Too much of any good thing can be harmful. Motivation that is too intense is likely to be accompanied by distracting emotions and limited cue utilization, both of which interfere with efficient learning. Some workers have suggested that learning is facilitated until motivation reaches an intermediate level and that any further increase in motivation results in decreased learning efficiency (Weiner, 1969). Intense motivation appears to be particularly debilitating when the learning task is complex.

Movement along a continuum that goes from healthy achievement motivation to anxiety to fear will differ greatly from pupil to pupil, so it is difficult to generalize about optimum motivation for individuals. The remedial teacher can, however, be sensitive to symptoms of anxiety and fear and adapt his motivational techniques as needed.

9. *Provide spaced practice.* Perhaps little can be done to glamorize the overlearning recommended for certain basic tasks, e.g. sight recognition of frequently used words, automatized production of letter forms. Nevertheless, there is evidence that where there is high response similarity—e.g., where sight words are similar in configuration: *horse–house, then–them;* and where letter forms are similar in confirmation: *d–b, p–q, m–n*—spaced or distributed practice will produce better results than massed practice (Underwood, 1961; Keppel, 1964). There is evidence, too, that long-term retention is improved by spaced practice. Other research suggests that spaced practice may be preferable because it permits reactive inhibition to dissipate (Otto and Fredricks, 1963; Otto, 1965; Otto, 1966). Reactive inhibition according to Hull (1943) is a negative drive that results from sustained performance and its effect is decreased learning efficiency. For these and other reasons, the most obvious being simple relief from monotony, frequent rest periods and/or changes in activity during remedial work sessions is recommended.

10. *Build a backlog of success experiences.* Some years ago Hilgard (1956, p. 486) expressed his belief that tolerance for failure is based largely upon a backlog of success. On the basis of our observations, we agree. The child who has a history of success experiences in learning has that to sustain his efforts when he encounters difficulty. The child with learning problems, on the other hand, expects to fail in academic areas and has little reason to try again when he fails at a given task. An extremely important function of the remedial teacher, then, is to see that each pupil adds to his store of success experiences during each remedial session. A reserve of success experiences will help to sustain the effort required to adjust to the regular classroom program.

Attention to the ten guidelines in a remedial teaching sequence will help both to secure and sustain the learner's cooperation and to insure the success experiences that are so critical to long-term recovery from learning disability.

Motivation

Klausmeier and Goodwin (1966, p. 446) have pointed out a distinction between pupils that has considerable importance in the present context: some pupils come to school with a desire to learn everything the school and the teacher desire; others either do not want to learn what is offered or they do not want to learn it the way it is being presented. The distinction is important because it brings into focus the necessity of handling the techniques of motivation differently with different children. In remedial teaching the fact is that for a variety of fairly obvious reasons the disabled learner is likely to be in the latter category. This means that the remedial teacher is well advised to pay more explicit attention to sound principles of motivation than may be required in regular developmental teaching.

Principles for Motivating

Klausmeier and Goodwin (1966) have identified seven generalizations and accompanying principles for motivating pupils that amount to a worthwhile complement to the guidelines for remedial teaching given in the preceding section of this chapter.

GENERALIZATION	PRINCIPLE
1. When certain objectives are to be achieved, the students' attention must be directed toward those objectives.	1. Focus student attention on desired objectives.
2. Curiosity, interest and achievement are positive motives that may be manipulated readily to focus student behavior toward desired objectives.	2. Encourage the development of positive motives.
3. Meaningful learning sets and advance organizers enhance motivation for learning new material by relating previous abilities and knowledge to the present task.	3. Use learning sets and advance organizers.
4. Setting and attaining goals encourage consistent effort and permit knowledge of progress and feelings of success to operate effectively.	4. Help students to set and attain realistic goals.
5. A warm, businesslike environment promotes continued effort and favorable attitudes toward learning.	5. Create a warm, orderly atmosphere.
6. Rewards are effective with some children in initiating and directing behavior; punishment may suppress undesirable behavior.	6. Provide incentives and punish, if necessary.
7. Extended, intense motivation, accompanied by anxiety, disorganizes behavior and impairs learning efficiency.	7. Avoid high stress and disorganization. (P. 446)

In the same sense that diagnosis is the key to effective teaching, motivation is the key to effective learning. Motivating a child to learn amounts to involving him in the teaching/learning process. Some approaches to securing involvement through application of sound principles follow.

Demonstrate Success

Much has already been said about careful diagnosis and how it should enable the teacher to start remedial teaching at the child's level and shape the instruction that follows to meet the child's individual needs. This, of course, is the most basic step toward insuring success experiences. Instruction that can be understood and that results in measurable gains in skill helps to demonstrate to the child that he can succeed. Once a pattern of success has been established, the child has cause to re-evaluate his own worth as a learner.

Initial success needs to be followed by success at every stage in the remedial process. To insure continuing success, the teacher must carefully consider the pace at which to proceed and the times at which to move to successively higher levels of difficulty. The most practical way of realistically setting the pace of instruction is to take cues directly from the child: if a good relationship has been established, he will say when the pace is too fast or too slow. In addition, praise and encouragement should be freely used, but praise must be sincere and it must arise from a success that the child can recognize and understand. Most children are very sensitive to phony compliments and they are repelled by frozen smiles and solicitous behavior. The teacher should praise only when there is reason, but accept the child at all times. Thus, it is more important to gear instruction to insure real success than to attempt to contrive occasions for less than genuine praise.

One way of keeping praise genuine and evidence of success clearly in view is to make liberal use of progress records of various sorts. Such records can range from conventional bar or line graphs and thermometer charts to more whimsical progress records that are devised by the child and reflect a particular interest of his. An example of the latter would be a chart in the form of a football field, where progress is marked by moving a paper football down the field toward a touchdown. Whatever the form of the progress chart, it can serve the important function of showing real and measurable progress from day to day. Another value of such charts is inherent in the fact that they can start at the level at which the child starts and compare his performance only with his previous performance.

Keep the Problem in Perspective

Although disabled learners may often appear to have withdrawn from active participation in the learning experiences in the classroom, most of them respond with more enthusiasm in a small group or individual tutoring situation. The negative feedback the child may have come to expect in the larger classroom group is absent when he is the focus of a teacher's attention and has nobody to compete with but himself. Thus, typically, the tutoring situation itself is inherently motivating and the teacher can proceed directly to the business of remedial teaching.

Yet, there will be cases where the remedial teacher is best advised to take what might appear to be a less direct approach to the attack of the learning problem. For example, a child who has personal or emotional problems or an extremely negative outlook toward schoolwork in general is not likely to be highly motivated or to be capable of devoting much energy to school tasks. Compared to a child's real or imagined problems, the problem of learning to do long division or to write legibly may be small indeed. In such cases, the most direct attack on the learning problem is the indirect attack that begins with helping to clear up the negative feelings or the personal problems. We are not suggesting a "pussyfooting" approach to remedial teaching. The primary business of the remedial teacher is to provide remedial help. But zeal for getting on with the basic task should never cause a teacher to lose his sensitivity to the personal problems and needs of his pupils.

Seek Support from the Family

The importance of the home in most learning disability cases cannot be overemphasized. Parents frequently feel defensive about a child in need of remedial help. When this is so they are likely to exert pressures, ranging from the subtle to the physical, upon their child in attempts to get him to "work harder." They are also prone to want to "help" the child with his schoolwork—the very same schoolwork that he is resisting with a great deal of energy at school. Siblings, especially those who are doing well in school, also frequently get into the picture with their own special pressures, ridicule, and attempts to "help."

One of the jobs of the remedial teacher is to gain the cooperation of the family in attacking learning problems. Typically, this is more likely to involve getting the family to pay less attention rather than more, or at least getting them to shift the emphasis of their attention. In a desirable situation the family takes an interest, discusses problems quietly and objectively, helps the child in ways suggested by the remedial teacher, and—perhaps most important—offers sincere praise when the child makes progress. The remedial teacher can often accomplish much through a conference at school or in the home, in which he can relieve any guilt feelings of the parents. Often he can suggest certain ways in which the parents can work with the child for limited periods of time (e.g., listening to the child read or practice a short spelling list) in order to redirect parental efforts to "help." Frequent notes from the teacher to the parents pointing out gains and long-range progress can help to allay anxieties. All too often a child's apparent lack of motivation stems, at least partly, from his resentment or outright rebellion against pressures applied at home. Disabled learners have many problems. Every effort should be made to keep the home from being one of them.

Applications of Learning Principles

In discussing guidelines for remedial teaching, we advised that a basic tenet be borrowed from programmed instruction: take small steps in order to assure success. The fact is, of course, that programmed instruction represents but one systematic attempt to apply the principles of learning to the treatment of human behavior problems. Other applications that have attracted considerable attention in recent years are behavior therapy and behavior modification methods (Staats, 1968, Chapter 17). Up to the present time the efforts expended have yielded more promise than practice, but it seems quite clear that the emerging techniques of behavior modification in particular are quite relevant to the concerns of the remedial teacher.

Behavior Modification

Hewett (1968) has made the point that teaching machines are behavior modification devices in a pure form and that ". . . the programs presented on them adhere closely to basic learning theory principles: clearly defined stimuli and expectations, active responses required of the learner, immediate reinforcement through knowledge of results, use of prompts when necessary to guarantee success, and gradual increase in complexity of the material" (P. 32). Thus, while behavior modification depends on the application of operant conditioning principles and the operant conditioning philosophy (Staats, 1968, p. 349), the methods involved in behavior modification are not grossly different from the methods involved in good remedial (or developmental) teaching. In practice, though, the difference resides mainly in the precise planning required for a behavior modification sequence. Where a remedial teacher might ordinarily tend to "play it by ear," he would pay much more explicit attention to objectives, hierarchies of objectives, and reinforcement practices if he decided to use formal behavior modification techniques.

As already suggested, there is not yet any general agreement on a specific behavior modification "method." The results of studies of behavior modification techniques with disabled learners have been reported, and perhaps the best descriptions of these methods are to be found in the reports of specific applications, e.g., Birnbrauer, Bijou, Montrose, and Kidder (1965), Staats and Butterfield (1965), and Hewett (1964). In general, applications such as these have in common the reinforcement of correct responses and the nonreinforcement of incorrect responses. While this is hardly a bold new concept for the classroom, the fact is that in a behavior modification framework the emphasis is upon the *systematic* application of reinforcement. The learning situation is highly structured with regard to what is expected from the child, what is expected is clearly presented to the child, and the reinforcement is contingent upon his meeting the expectations. Reinforcement, or knowledge of results, is immediate, so the child knows how he is doing at all times and he knows the consequences of his actions (Hewett, 1968, p. 35).

Some corrective and remedial teachers may feel that a certain "humanization" of behavior modification techniques is desirable and that some loss of precision is not too high a price to pay. We tend to agree. Nevertheless, we feel that advances in behavior modification bear watching because teachers will continue to see techniques and ideas that they can adopt or adapt in their personal teaching. Two specific areas that have received impetus from the work in behavior modification merit special attention: reinforcement practices and the behavioral specification of objectives.

Reinforcement Practices

Reinforcers may have an informative and/or an incentive function. That is, reinforcement of a given behavior conveys information about the appropriateness of that behavior; and, once a correct behavior is established, anticipation of desired rewards for performing that behavior can maintain appropriate responding even though reinforcement is delayed. Both functions are important in corrective and remedial teaching: the first in establishing correct responses, and the second in sustaining correct responding after remedial teaching.

Bandura (1969) has identified three essential features in the successful application of reinforcement procedures.

> First one must select reinforcers that are sufficiently powerful and durable to maintain responsiveness over long periods while complex patterns of behavior are being established and strengthened. Second, the reinforcing events must be made contingent upon the desired behavior if they are to be optimally effective. And third, a reliable procedure for eliciting or inducing the desired response patterns is essential; otherwise, if they rarely or never occur there will be few opportunities to influence them through contingent reinforcement. (P. 225)

In practice this means that a good remedial teacher will consider carefully (1) *whether* initial reinforcement ought to be extrinsic (gumdrops, tokens) or intrinsic (praise or self-satisfaction) and *when* reinforcement can change from extrinsic to intrinsic; (2) *how* to insure that correct or desired responses are perceived as such by both teacher and pupil and *how* to insure that the reinforcement is in fact associated with the correct or desired response; and (3) *how* to elicit desired responses or to shape or modify incorrect responses until they become desired, reinforcable responses. The good remedial teacher can handle the first two items mainly on the basis of his knowledge of and rapport with an individual pupil; to handle the third, however, he must know the precise nature of the desired response. He should, therefore, give some thought to the behavioral specification of his objectives.

Behavioral Specification of Objectives

A meaningfully stated objective has at least two basic characteristics (Bandura, 1969; Mager, 1961): first, it identifies and describes behaviors considered appropriate to a desired outcome; second, it may specify the conditions under which the behavior can be expected to occur. Thus, once an objective has been sensibly stated in behavioral terms, reasonably straightforward decisions can be made regarding (1) experiences that are most likely to produce the desired behaviors, (2) situations in which the behaviors are appropriate, and (3) the success or failure of the approach designed to produce the behavior.

In a formal behavior modification sequence the behavioral specification of objectives is virtually imperative. The objectives, sequentially arranged, provide the framework for a treatment sequence, and the behavioral descriptions provide the specifics required to elicit and evaluate responses during each learning-reinforcing session. In a less formalized remedial teaching context behavioral objectives can serve a similar purpose. The main difference in the latter situation would more likely be found in the handling of reinforcement procedures than in the function of the objectives.

Of course curriculum workers have not been completely unrestrained in their support of behavioral objectives. Kliebard (1968) feels that more attention ought to be paid to the source of objectives, how they are stated, and the role they are to play in planning curriculums and guiding instruction. Eisner (1967) has said that even with urging teachers have not made much use of behavioral objectives and that there is little evidence that they make much difference in teaching, learning, or curriculum construction. Nevertheless, we feel that the behavioral specification of objectives can serve a useful purpose both in and out of the formal behavior modification framework for reasons we have already presented. The reader who wishes to examine an existing list of behavioral objectives designed for use by teachers is directed to a recent book by Otto and Smith (*Administering the School Reading Program*, 1970, Chapter 2).

Teaching Materials

If a child is to develop a feeling of success and accomplishment as a result of his positive experiences in a corrective or remedial situation, it is imperative that the instructional materials be appropriate both to his level of ability and to his specific but changing, instructional needs. Some considerations to be kept in mind in choosing and using teaching materials are discussed here.

Level of Difficulty

The task of selecting materials at the appropriate level of difficulty for disabled learners is complicated by the fact that formal test scores tend often to be spuriously high. Attempts to begin instruction at the tested level may, therefore, fail because the materials are too difficult. There are two main reasons for spurious test scores. First, the testing situation tends to evoke maximum effort from most children. Consequently, estimated ability is likely to be at the level the child can reach under optimum conditions, not at the level at which he can function for sustained periods. Second, when we convert raw test scores into grade-equivalent scores, we tend to lose sight of just what the raw score was to begin with. For example, consider a child who is ten years old, has an IQ of 120, and a mental age of twelve. If such a child has a tested grade equivalent of 3 in, say, arithmetic, he is supposedly performing as well as the average eight-year-old. But the fact is that our disabled learner brought to the test all of the background and general problem-solving ability of a child with a mental age of twelve. It is likely that his greater test sophistication and native ability tended to enhance the test score; it is also likely that his classroom performance in arithmetic is significantly different from that of the average third grader.

Much care must be taken, then, to select materials and exercises that are at the disabled learner's true level of achievement. Many times this level is better determined through the use of informal techiniques than through the use of standardized tests. We shall deal with the specifics of determining true level of ability in the chapters devoted to the several basic skill areas.

Teachers who work with disabled learners sometimes complain that there is a lack of material written at their pupils' interest level and, at the same time, at the proper level of difficulty. A sixteen-year-old, for example, is not likely to be enthralled with the idea of working with materials devised for eight- or ten-year-olds despite the fact that he is unable to work with more difficult material. Fortunately, much progress has been made in recent years toward making materials adapted for use by disabled learners widely available. This is especially true in the area of reading. Trade books that are written with interest levels to satisfy the older child but with lesser demands upon reading ability are now readily available (see Chapters 7 and 8).

Variety of Materials

Disabled readers need specific help to correct specific deficiencies: they are likely to need considerable work with exercises designed to develop specific skills, and they need opportunities for more general use and integration of multiple skills. If both of these needs are to be met, teachers must have access to and be willing to choose from a wide variety of materials and exercises.

Availability of Materials

Materials for remedial instruction are available from many sources. Of course, many of the materials designed for use in the regular classroom can be used in remedial teaching. Basal textbooks and their accompanying workbooks can, for example, continue to serve as a nucleus for instruction, for they provide systematic coverage of skills. There are also many materials that are designed specifically to be used with the disabled learner. The more useful aids are mentioned in the chapters dealing with specific skill areas.

ORGANIZING FOR INSTRUCTION

We have already discussed certain points that are relevant in organizing for corrective and remedial instruction: aspects of the overall developmental program, means for identifying children with learning problems of various degrees of severity, relationships among school personnel. In the pages that follow we shall consider the selection of cases for corrective and remedial help and the implementation of instruction.

Selection of Cases

When screening at the survey level of diagnosis locates a child with learning difficulties, a decision must be made about whether corrective, remedial, or adapted instruction is most appropriate under the given circumstances. We have suggested as a rule of thumb that remedial treatment might be reserved at the middle elementary level for cases where there is a gap of two or more years between capacity and achievement, or potential and actual performance; corrective teaching would be given when the gap is about one year; and instruction would be adapted in cases where limited capacity (IQ's in the low 80's and below) appears to be the main cause for low achievement. The rules of thumb are, of course, oversimplified and they can serve only as rough guides. Many factors in addition to a mental age/performance age comparison must be considered.

In some cases it will be virtually impossible to get an accurate estimate of capacity because of emotional problems, limited experiential background, bilingualism, etc. Rigid adherence to a rule-of-thumb definition or to a formula would be grossly inappropriate. Even when children appear clearly to be eligible for a certain kind of instruction, it is good to look beyond the strict definition of eligibility and exercise judgment in assigning them to instructional groups. Consider, for example, two children of the same chronological age: one a very bright child and the other a slow learner. The slow learner is performing not only below his grade level but also more than two years below his capacity level; he is, therefore, eligible for both adapted and remedial instruction. The bright child is performing above his grade level but more than two years below his capacity level; by our definition he is eligible for remedial instruction. By strict definition, both pupils could conceivably be placed in the same small group for remedial instruction; but it seems extremely doubtful that they could be taught effectively in the same group.

Where facilities and personnel are limited, remedial programs must be limited in scope. In such instances a choice between intensive help for relatively few severely disabled learners and corrective help for a larger number of less severe cases may be required. Such choices can be made only after careful consideration of local circumstances. Every attempt should always be made to provide the help each child needs at the earliest possible moment. A well-managed program of corrective instruction in the classroom can solve many small problems before they develop into full-blown, severe learning problems. Resources should be deployed with this fact in mind.

Implementation of Instruction

Implementation of a corrective-remedial program of instruction requires that consideration be given to grouping, work schedules, and record-keeping.

Grouping

Some severely disabled learners probably would benefit most from the careful diagnosis and intensive teaching that is most effectively handled on a strictly individual basis. Yet, owing to the high cost of teaching individuals, most instruction will probably have to be individualized instead of literally individual. Even in a remedial program two to five pupils may be scheduled for each session. Thus, it is up to the teacher to see that the instruction is truly individualized by carefully selecting group members, subgrouping for certain teaching, and working individually with each child during a portion of each session.

Corrective instruction may be provided by the classroom teacher or by a special teacher. When a special teacher is involved, he may simply replace the regular teacher for the duration of the corrective session, or he may teach special classes to which children with learning problems are assigned. Normally, less severe cases are scheduled for corrective sessions, while individual or small-group treatment is provided only for those pupils with severe learning disabilities.

Work Schedules

Whether a child is to be given remedial or corrective help, individually or in a group, there will be certain scheduling problems. Perhaps the most important thing to be considered, as far as the overall success of an individual's remedial program is concerned, is that the special help should not interfere with other necessary and enjoyable activities. A boy who must choose between the basketball team and a corrective reading class, for example, will probably find it impossible to make a "correct" choice. It is also important that the special help be offered at a regular, scheduled time. Casual scheduling can be disconcerting to both teacher and pupil and probably unproductive of any real gains.

Attempts should be made to schedule pupils with similar problems and ability levels at the same time. This, of course, increases the possibilities for total group instruction and increases the likelihood that individuals will identify with the group. Feeling that he is part of an academic group may be a child's first step toward returning to full participation in the learning experiences of the regular classroom.

The length of remedial sessions must vary, of course, according to the grade level and the idiosyncrasies of the individuals involved. Half-hour sessions, for example, are probably optimum for third or fourth graders; for eighth graders, sessions of about an hour's duration are probably realistic. Individual attention spans, too, should be considered; children who have difficulty concentrating or sitting still or who tire easily should be scheduled for shorter sessions than their peers. It is better to shorten the duration of the remedial session than to turn a full-length period into an arts and crafts session. A remedial session should not be a grim affair, but it should be devoted entirely to activities that are part of a planned sequence of instruction designed to overcome learning difficulties.

Record-Keeping

Records must be kept if long-range gains are to be recognized and if a remedial teaching sequence is to have direction. Some useful forms for recording case study materials, gathering information, writing tentative plans, and organizing reports are presented in Chapter 4. A record as detailed as a formal case study is probably needed only with the more complicated cases. Actually, the degree of severity of disability can dictate the complexity of the record-keeping. When a teacher is working with an entire class for corrective purposes, for example, the records and plans for the class as a whole might be stated in some detail; but the records for individuals might be confined to test results and occasional notations of such things as special problems, unusual behavior, and rapid gains. Perhaps the most realistic plan is to start with a manila folder for each child who receives corrective or remedial instruction. Test booklets, special reports, tentative plans, etc., can be inserted as they become available. The actual procedure can then be formalized as the teaching progresses. Different teachers will find different procedures helpful; some will need to "write everything down," others will not. The suggestions in Chapter 4 can be adapted to fit many different needs.

THOUGHTS FOR DISCUSSION

"Simple interpretations of the individual's behavior should have preference over the more complex. The individual's disability . . . should be explained in terms of the fewest possible causal factors. If one is sufficient, the others are superficial and of little consequence" (Carter and McGinnis, 1970, p. 157).

"In basing a remedial program upon a diagnosis, there is frequently the tendency to use one specific exercise to overcome a known deficiency. However, there are many ways to develop the various skills and abilities in the basic tool subjects. An effective program will employ a variety of techniques and instructional procedures. The teacher should keep an account of those that appear to be effective in specific types of learning disability problems" (Brueckner and Bond, 1955, pp. 79–80).

"If we sample a wide spectrum of verbal and perceptual behaviors, we have a 'wide-range' achievement test or a general aptitude test; an intelligence test" (Cohen, 1969, p. 33).

"A single total score gives a basis for comparison with students of the same chronological age or grade. But emphasis on norms runs counter to the point of view that every child should be helped to develop *his* potentialities, rather than be expected to reach a grade standard or national norm" (Strang, 1969, p. 135).

"When the classroom teacher fails to observe the signs of frustrated reading in a given child, one can be certain it will not escape the parents for long. The responsibility for the initial identification of the problem reader then often falls to the parents" (Wilson, 1967, p. 203).

"Experiencing success and anticipating further success result in higher achievement than do experiencing failure and anticipating further failure" (Klausmeier and Goodwin, 1966, p. 457).

". . . we do not need to 'motivate' children into learning, by wheedling, bribing, or bullying. We do not need to keep picking away at their minds to make sure they are learning. What we need to do, and all we need to do, is bring as much of the world as we can into the school and the classroom; give the children as much help and guidance as they need and ask for; listen respectfully when they feel like talking, and then get out of the way. We can trust them to do the rest" (Holt, 1967, p. 189).

"Whether teachers are better therapists or diagnosticians in the long run than psychiatrists and neurologists is of little consequence. But what is crucial is that a teacher can teach, and without a full commitment to that role the important contribution which only the school can make to the treatment of the emotionally disturbed child may be minimized" (Hewett, 1968, p. 43).

"The most basic prerequisite to individually prescribed instruction is the development of a list of skills. Ideally, pupils are expected to proceed at their own rates on development of skills in which they are deficient rather than to progress at a class-established rate" (Della-Piana, 1968, p. 18).

". . . even children with inappropriate behaviors can still learn normally if they are subjected to special learning procedures which involve an adequate reinforcement system. It may be suggested that through the use of such procedures it may be possible to prevent learning deficits from occurring in such children, to provide these children with adjustive repertoires which will replace the inappropriate behaviors, and thereby treat the inappropriate behaviors" (Staats, 1968, pp. 547–548).

"Because the need for communication and coordinated planning is acute, we feel that remedial teaching is, in general, better offered in each child's home school building than in a centrally located 'clinic' " (Otto and Smith, 1970, p. 37).

REFERENCES

American Psychological Association. *Standards for educational and psychological tests and manuals.* Washington, D.C.: Author, 1966.

Bandura, A. *Principles of behavior modification.* New York: Holt, 1969.

Baron, D., and Bernard, H. *Evaluation techniques for classroom teachers.* New York: McGraw-Hill, 1958.

Birnbrauer, J. S., Bijou, S. W., Montrose, M. W., and Kidder, J. D. Programmed instruction in the classroom. In L. P. Ullman and L. Krasner (Eds.), *Case studies in behavior modification.* New York: Holt, 1965. pp. 358–363.

Bond, G. L., and Tinker, M. A. *Reading difficulties: Their diagnosis and correction.* (2nd ed.) New York: Appleton-Century-Crofts, 1967.

Brueckner, L. J., and Bond, G. L. *The diagnosis and treatment of learning difficulties.* New York: Appleton-Century-Crofts, 1955.

Buros, O. K. (Ed.). *The sixth mental measurements yearbook.* Highland Park, N.J.: Gryphon Press, 1965.

Carter, H. L. J., and McGinnis, D. J. *Diagnosis and treatment of the disabled reader.* New York: Macmillan, 1970.

Cohen, S. A. *Teach them all to read.* New York: Random House, 1969.

Della-Piana, G. M. *Reading diagnosis and prescription.* New York: Holt, 1968.

Durost, W. N. *Manual for interpreting metropolitan achievement tests.* New York: Harcourt, 1962.

Eisner, E. W. Educational objectives—help or hindrance? *School Review,* 1967, **75**, 250–260.

Eisner, E. W. A response to my critics. *School Review*, 1967, **75**, 277–282.

Harris, A. J. *How to increase reading ability.* (5th ed.) New York: David McKay, 1970.

Heilman, A. W. *Principles and practices of teaching reading.* (2nd ed.) Columbus, Ohio: Charles E. Merrill, 1969.

Hewett, F. M. *The emotionally disturbed child in the classroom.* Boston: Allyn and Bacon, 1968.

Hewett, F. M. Teaching reading to an autistic boy through operant conditioning. *The Reading Teacher*, 1964, **17**, 613–618.

Hilgard, E. R. *Theories of learning.* (2nd ed.) New York: Appleton-Century-Crofts, 1956.

Holt, J. *How children learn.* New York: Pitman, 1967.

Hull, C. L. *Principles of behavior.* New York: Appleton-Century-Crofts, 1943.

Kausler, D. H. (Ed.) *Readings in verbal learning.* New York: Wiley, 1966. Chapters 10, 11.

Kelley, T. L., Madden, R., Gardner, E. F., and Rudman, H. C. *Stanford achievement test.* New York: Harcourt, 1964.

Keppel, G. Facilitation in short- and long-term retention of paired associates following distributed practice in learning. *Journal of Verbal Learning and Verbal Behavior*, 1964, **3**, 91–111.

Klausmeier, H. J., and Goodwin, W. *Learning and human abilities.* (2nd ed.) New York: Harper and Row, 1966.

Kliebard, H. M. Curricular objectives and evaluation: A reassessment. *High School Journal*, 1968, **51**, 241–247.

Lowe, R. N. *A rationale and models for organizing and administering programs of pupil personnel services.* Eugene, Ore.: Bureau of Educational Research, School of Education, University of Oregon, 1962.

Mager, R. F. *Preparing objectives for programmed instruction.* San Francisco: Feardon, 1961.

Malmquist, E. *Factors related to reading disabilities in the first grade of elementary school.* Stockholm, Sweden: Almquist and Wiksell, 1960.

Mickelson, N. I. Meaningfulness: A critical variable in children's verbal learning. *The Reading Teacher*, 1969–70, **23**, 11–14.

Otto, W. Inhibitory potential in good and poor achievers. *Journal of Educational Psychology*, 1965, **56**, 200–207.

Otto, W. Reactive inhibition as a contributor to school failure. *Journal of Special Education*, 1966, **1**, 9–15.

Otto, W., and Fredricks, R. C. Relationship of reactive inhibition to reading skill attainment. *Journal of Educational Psychology*, 1963, **54**, 227–230.

Otto, W., and Smith, R. J. *Administering the school reading program.* Boston: Houghton Mifflin, 1970.

Pressey, S. L., Robinson, F. P., and Horrocks, J. E. *Psychology in education.* New York: Harper and Row, 1959.

Staats, A. W. *Learning, language, and cognition.* New York: Holt, 1968.

Staats, A. W., and Butterfield, W. H. Treatment of nonreading in a culturally deprived juvenile delinquent: An application of reinforcement principles. *Child Development,* 1965, **36**, 925–942. (Also in W. Otto and K. Koenke (Eds.), *Remedial teaching.* Boston: Houghton Mifflin, 1969.)

Strang, R. *Diagnostic teaching of reading.* (2nd ed.) New York: McGraw-Hill, 1969.

Ullman, C. A. Prevalence of reading disability as a function of the measure used. *Journal of Learning Disabilities,* 1969, **2**, 6–8.

Underwood, B. J. Ten years of massed practice on distributed practice. *Psychological Review,* 1961, **68**, 229–247.

Weiner, B. Motivation. In R. L. Ebel and V. Noll (Eds.), *Encyclopedia of educational research.* (4th ed.) New York: Macmillan, 1969.

Wilson, R. M. *Diagnostic and remedial reading.* Columbus, Ohio: Charles E. Merrill, 1967.

Chapter 4

The Case Study

A sequence of diagnosis that proceeds from a survey to a specific, and finally, to an intensive level is described in Chapter 3. The suggestion is that diagnosis should proceed as long as the diagnostic findings continue to have clear implications for understanding and treating a given disability. Yet the fact remains that the depth and scope of a diagnostic investigation are determined not only by the complexity of the problem but also by the facilities and resources available. A staff of experts can do more than a remedial specialist, and a remedial specialist can do more than a classroom teacher. The availability of time for intensive diagnostic work can be as critical as access to tests, techniques, and expert opinions. A good deal of flexibility is required, for it is as indefensible to overcomplicate a case by adhering to rigid procedures as it is to stop short when further diagnosis is needed. This word of caution is interjected here because even the most productive case study techniques can become oppressive if they are not applied with discretion and judgment.

A case study is, essentially, a vehicle for gathering and systematizing information that is relevant to the understanding and treatment of a learning disability. A case study is virtually required at the intensive level of diagnosis where the focus is upon underlying causes for the learning disability, but much relevant information that has to do with the specifics of skill development and achievement is gathered at the specific level of diagnosis. While we shall present several forms that we have found useful in organizing information, it is the *function* not the *form* of a case study that is important. Each of the forms suggested ought to be adapted in view of the constraints and expectations in a given situation. See Harris (1970a) for other examples of case reporting.

The following topics, accompanied by model forms when appropriate, are discussed in this chapter: gathering background information from the home; gathering background information from the school; writing a case report; preparing a statement of tentative diagnosis, prognosis, and proposed treatment; focusing information for the classroom; compiling information for a thorough case analysis; and preparing a report to the school.

INFORMATION FROM THE HOME

Information from the home can be extremely useful in the diagnosis and treatment of learning problems mainly because (1) factors in the home may be contributing to the problem, and (2) resources in the home may be useful in overcoming the problem.

A Home Information Blank that we have used to gather preliminary information is given as a model. In practice it would be accompanied by an explanatory letter or presented in person. Spaces should be provided for answers to the queries. The information gained should be supplemented by a visit to the home after the remedial work has begun. While the example is designed specifically for use with a child disabled in reading, minor modifications can readily be made to cover other basic skill areas.

HOME INFORMATION BLANK

Date . . . .

Please supply the information requested below concerning . . . .
. . . . The information will be useful to us in planning the remedial help to be given your child.

1. Has your child any specific difficulties in seeing and hearing? If so, please describe, indicating how recently he has been tested, whether or not he wears glasses, etc.

2. Has your child a general health problem, or a history of health difficulties (other than vision or hearing), which has handicapped him in his work in school? If so, please describe.

3. Did your child have any difficulty in learning to talk? Has he had, or does he now have, any speech problem? If so, please describe.

4. How would you describe your child's general emotional adjustment? For example, is he inclined to be tense and to worry, or is he usually calm and carefree? How does he compare with other children in the family?

5. How would you describe your child's attitude toward reading and toward school? For example, does he like them, dislike them, or doesn't he care? Please describe any changes you have noted in his attitude.

6. Have you attempted to help your child improve his reading either at home or by tutoring? Please describe any specific steps you have taken, materials you have provided, suggestions received from the school, etc.

7. Do you have any suggestions on the probable causes of your child's reading difficulty? If so, please indicate.

8. Has the school ever suggested specific remedial help for your child (such as remedial reading, summer clinic, special tutoring, etc.)?

The home can provide concrete information regarding a child's preschool background and present outside-of-school behavior and attitudes. But information from between-the-lines can be equally important: the general tone of the responses may yield clues about the parents' attitude toward school, their perception of the child's learning problem, the pressure applied at home, and potential assistance and support from the home. Remember, though, that when you try to deal with information from between-the-lines you are not working with "hard data." Be sure to check out any hunches you may get from the information.

INFORMATION FROM THE SCHOOL

Just as information from the home is useful in getting an adequate picture of a child's background, so, too, is information from the school likely to be of significant value. The school information might, depending upon the circumstances, be gathered by a classroom or remedial teacher to be used within the school or to be forwarded to a clinic or other agency. In either instance, school records and school personnel can usually provide vital information from at least four areas. First, the history of a child's learning problem can be traced through careful scrutiny of cumulative folders and other records. Whether a learning disability was present from the very beginning of a child's school experience or appeared to emerge at a particular grade level can, for example, provide clues as to possible causes for the learning problem. Second, the results of past and current standardized tests can be summarized. Such records are, of course, a part of the child's school performance history and so are related to the previous point. In addition, a summary of existing tests can help to determine where further testing is or is not needed. If, for example, an individual intelligence test was given recently, knowledge of the results could preclude some duplication of effort. Third, the child's current behavior in an educational setting can be described. Behavior at home and at school may be quite different, for example; different teachers may perceive different values and attitudes on the part of the child, etc. Finally, the observations and feelings of various school people who have had contacts with the child may provide clues regarding possible causes for the learning problems.

We have found the following School Information Blank to be useful for gathering and organizing information related to school performance and behavior. Again, the blank is designed for use with reading disability cases; minor changes would be required to make it suitable for use in other areas. Some changes would also be indicated if the blank is to be used solely on an intraschool basis, by the classroom or remedial teacher, rather than as a résumé to be forwarded to a referral agency outside the school.

SCHOOL INFORMATION BLANK

Your cooperation will be greatly appreciated in supplying the information requested below regarding your student ....

1. What appears to be this child's specific reading difficulties? Please describe his current behavior in reading situations, both oral and silent.

2. Has this child a history of reading difficulties? If so, please describe the time and course of their development.

3. Please indicate the test data available for this child.

	Test	Date	Grade Score	Age Score
Silent reading	....	.....	....	....
Oral reading	....	.....	....	....
Other tests of achievement	....	.....	....	....

	Test	Date	CA	MA	IQ
Group test of intelligence*	....	......	......	......	......

* Give language and nonlanguage scores if available.

Binet	......	.....	.....	.....
Wechsler (total)	......	.....	.....	.....
(verbal)	......	.....	.....	.....
(nonverbal)	......	.....	.....	.....

Note: Please attach additional test data, if available.

4. To what extent is the child's performance in school in accord with the above test data? Please indicate particularly any respects in which the school's experience with the child is at variance with the test data.

5. Does the school have evidence of any particular factor or group of factors which may contribute to the child's reading difficulty? If so, please indicate below:
   a. health factors (especially vision, hearing, chronic illness)
   b. influence within the home or in the community (siblings, parental relationships, delinquency, etc.)
   c. the child's personal-social adjustment
   d. work-study habits, attitudes toward school, school success, etc.
   e. the basic plan of reading instruction (basal reader program out of phase with child's needs, child too dependent to cope with individualized instruction, hearing problem interferes with response to stress on phonics, etc.)
   f. other factors (as absenteeism, change of schools, etc.)

WRITING A CASE REPORT

Once information from the home, the school, and other pertinent sources has been gathered, the remedial teacher is confronted with the task of assembling the existing information into a meaningful case analysis. Sample forms to provide guidance in assembling salient points in diagnosis and treatment are presented in the pages that follow. But the forms merely suggest a framework; the major task of communication still falls to the remedial teacher who makes use of the forms.

The case analysis and subsequent reports should be conceived as vehicles for communication. Most fundamentally, the case study serves as a means for organizing background information for diagnostic purposes, which in effect facilitates the remedial teacher's communication with himself; it helps him to look systematically at what he knows and, as a result, gain in understanding. The teacher's increased understanding of the problem, in turn, makes for more effective communication between teacher and child. Communication with other teachers and specialists who might be working with a child on a follow-up basis can also be expedited by the case study and subsequent reports. The remedial teacher who makes a case study should always assume that what he has done will be followed up by somebody else and, therefore, write a report that will be meaningful and useful. All too often, a case study is seen as an end in itself or as the remedial teacher's personal document. Actually, a case study serves its optimum purpose only when it is passed on and used by all the people who can learn from it.

It is important, then, that the remedial teacher be familiar with a method for communicating information that accurately describes diagnosis and treatment. English and Lillywhite (1963) have outlined such a method, and the following discussion is based upon their semantic approach to clinical reporting. While we have retained the designation *clinical reporting* for this method, it will become clear that the term is not intended to be restrictive in any way. The method can be as appropriately used in a school as in a clinical setting. The four levels of communication—observation, description, evaluation, and emotion—described by English and Lillywhite can serve both as an aid to clear communication and as a guide to structuring diagnostic and remedial efforts.

Observation

The diagnostic process (the case analysis) begins with informal and formal observations of behavior. Observations may be made directly by the remedial teacher or they may be made through interviews or information blanks similar to those described. This is the level at which observations are made regarding a child's skills and deficiencies, his emotional status, his health, his motivation level, and his ability level. Some of the devices that might be used include: tests of skill mastery in the areas of disability; interviews with parents, teachers, the child; tests of mental ability; visual examination; and physical examination.

The raw material from which a case analysis is made is examined at the observation level; the remedial teacher merely observes but makes no attempt to evaluate or to categorize. Things are not good or bad, acceptable or unacceptable, passing or failing; they simply are. As English and Lillywhite sum it up, "The clinician 'senses,' merely this, and nothing more" (pp. 6–7). This is the nonverbal level, where the teacher simply gathers information and makes no attempt to record or describe.

Description

When he has a satisfactory sample of a child's academic performance and general behavior, the remedial teacher is ready to describe, in oral and written form, what he has observed. However, no attempt should be made to evaluate what has been observed; only "pure observations" should be recorded or reported. Language is important at this level: the reporter must consciously avoid influencing himself or others with his language structure. The reporter should say "The child did . . ." or "He performed thus . . ." or "The child's mother says . . ."; he should not say, "This child is obviously retarded" or "The child has never been taught phonics." In short, the reporter should merely describe what he has seen and guard against making evaluations. This is difficult, for most of what we see is colored by what we feel.

Much of what goes into a case study should be at the level of description. The bulk of the case analysis form that is presented in this chapter calls for statements at this level. Only after an adequate sample of observations has been described should evaluations be made.

Evaluation

At the evaluation level, an attempt is made to interpret what has been observed. As English and Lillywhite put it, the remedial teacher "attempts to make judgments, to formulate tentative hypotheses, develop certain inferences, and reach a number of 'guarded' conclusions as to causes, effects, etc. He takes particular care not to allow his evaluation to exceed his observations" (p. 648). With learning disability cases, the remedial teacher would make judgments about each child's capacity to learn and his degree of disability, venture hypotheses about the factors contributing to the learning problem, record a tentative prognosis for the case, and attempt to outline a tentative instructional program.

Again, language is important. When judgments have been made, the language should make this clear; judgments should not be stated nor accepted as facts. At the evaluation level the writing should contain many qualifying phrases such as these: "On the basis of tests and informal observations it appears . . . ."; "These observations tend to show . . . ." In the format of the case analysis, evaluations and judgments are typically stated in the portions which are concerned with summary, salient points, and evaluation of the teaching program.

Emotion

The fourth level is the emotional level. This is a "feeling" level, where the remedial teacher may verbalize about what he has seen, felt, or heard.

At best, the feelings of an experienced remedial teacher may point the way toward productive rechecking that can, in turn, lead to a clearer understanding of a case. That is, in working with a child, sensitive and experienced remedial teachers often develop hunches which cannot—at that point—be developed into conclusions and accepted as fact. Such hunches can be checked out through additional observation-description-evaluation or through the utilization of more appropriate techniques and resources. The language for reporting hunches should make use of such phrases as: "It is felt that . . ."; "This reporter is concerned about . . ."; etc. In the format of the case analysis, such statements would most appropriately be made in connection with recommendations for further teaching or checking of causal factors in the disability.

At worst, feelings may color and distort the whole case analysis. Feelings may cause the immature or inexperienced teacher to make snap judgments or to place children in categories which tend to shape future perceptions. A teacher who falls into this trap is likely to make such statements as: "John has a mental block which interferes with his learning." "The child cannot be taught because of his brain injury." "Jane comes from a normal, happy home that cannot be contributing to her emotional problems." Once such judgments are made and recorded they are likely not only to shape future judgments of the reporter but also to delimit the usefulness of the report to others who may see it.

To sum up, the four levels of communication include observation, description, evaluation, and emotion. The first three are highly interrelated, involving the gathering and reporting of the data pertinent to a particular case. The skilled remedial teacher moves freely from level to level as he works with a child; the important thing is to remember the level of operation at all times. If the level is kept clearly in mind, the likelihood of going beyond the data in reporting is minimized. When, or if, the remedial teacher moves to the fourth level, he must recognize that he is on the emotional level and guard against perceiving or reporting feelings as facts.

The novice writer of case reports will benefit from carefully analyzing case reports in terms of the four levels of communication. Some examples of acceptable case reporting are given in the pages that follow. In general, the level of communication is clear for each statement.

TENTATIVE DIAGNOSIS, PROGNOSIS, AND PROPOSED TREATMENT

The Tentative Diagnosis, Prognosis, and Proposed Treatment Blank that follows serves as a vehicle for organizing a statement that can provide guidelines for further diagnosis and teaching. Such a statement can usually be prepared after two or three weeks of working with a child. The completed statement might serve mainly as a prelude to an extended case analysis or it might serve as a summary statement to be passed on to another teacher, say, from the remedial specialist to the classroom teacher.

The statement serves three main purposes: (1) The tentative diagnosis pulls together the existing information and points up the need, if any, for additional diagnostic information; (2) The prognosis, which is an estimate of rate and degree of expected progress based upon the existing information, sets a level of expectation or an interim objective which, if it proves to be unrealistic, provides cause to re-examine the diagnostic base and/or the remedial teaching program; (3) The proposed treatment, based upon what is known about the child's problems and needs, serves as a guide to the first steps in remedial teaching.

The comments of a remedial teacher are given along with the outline of the blank in order to provide an example of acceptable case reporting. The comments were made by a remedial teacher who was working with a disabled learner, Roddy X., in a summer remedial program. While it is possible to identify statements at all three of the verbal levels of communication discussed above, it will be seen that a fairly substantial number of statements are at level four, the "feeling" level. This is as it should be, because the diagnosis and proposed treatment are still at a tentative stage; the remedial teacher is still seeking further information and attempting to define the teaching program. At this point, the feelings of a sensitive remedial teacher are invaluable—so long as they are based on facts and are recognized as feelings—because they can point the way toward the probing and rechecking that is needed as remedial work progresses.

TENTATIVE DIAGNOSIS, PROGNOSIS, AND PROPOSED TREATMENT FORM

Date . . . .

Pupil's name: Roddy X.   Age: 10–6   Last grade completed: 5

Estimated independent reading level: Oral 3^2 Silent 3^2

Estimated instructional reading level: Oral 4^2 Silent 4^2

Adequacy of Current Reading Habits (indicate whether mastery of each skill is below, at, or above grade level and describe performance):

1. *Sight vocabulary* (below-at-above): Roddy's sight vocabulary is relatively good. He sometimes mispronounces known sight words in context, however.

2. *Phonetic analysis skills* (below-at-above): He has a fairly good knowledge of the more consistent common vowel and consonant sounds but needs help with the less common and with application of phonic rules to his own reading.

3. *Structural analysis skills* (below-at-above): He is weak in syllabication (division of longer words into pronunciation units).

4. *Configuration clues* (below-at-above): He shows some awareness, but the clinician is not sure how much he uses these kinds of clues.

5. *Contextual clues* (below-at-above): These clues are used frequently, often at the expense of more careful analysis. He has a good experiential and informational background.

6. *Dictionary skills* (below-at-above): They are adequate in the few situations called for to date.

7. *Oral reading fluency* (below-at-above): Reading is quite fluent at his level, but he makes additions frequently and add his own "color."

8. *Comprehension skills* (below-at-above): Adequate if tested immediately but he forgets rapidly.

9. *Rate of comprehension* (below-at-above): Reading speed is low, due to frequent regressions.

10. *Other specific reading factors* (*name*): None observed.

Adequacy of Performance in the Other Basic Skill Areas (describe the level of performance in those areas which are presenting difficulty; point out specific deficiencies and strengths):

Roddy appears to be able to do grade-level arithmetic; but he is plagued by a certain amount of carelessness, which seems evident in other skill areas, too. His classroom teacher feels that his reading disability keeps his work in spelling, language, and social studies below grade level. The teacher states that "He just doesn't seem to be trying." His oral communication level seems slightly above other skill levels.

In writing experiences during remedial sessions, Roddy has demonstrated original ideas but he has difficulty organizing them effectively into sentences and paragraphs. He writes slowly and his handwriting, while usually legible, probably could be improved by greater care and consistency in producing the cursive letter forms.

Apparent Causes of the Learning Difficulty (specify and appraise significance):

1. *Intellectual factors:* Roddy has never had an individual intelligence test. Group tests place him in the low average range (i.e., *Lorge-Thorndike* IQ $= 94$, May, 1961). Present indications are that he has at least average ability. Further checking is needed.

2. *Physical factors:* There are no apparent physical disabilities which would cause the learning difficulty. Hearing and vision have been checked recently and are normal.

3. *Environmental factors:* (*a*) Home—Roddy is an only child and appears to lead a rather sheltered life. A brief meeting with his mother gave the clinician the impression that her life is centered around Roddy and that she might be a little overprotective. Roddy seldom mentions his father. (*b*) School—Roddy says he enjoys school and his social adjustment there is reported by his teacher to be "quite good." He wishes he could "read better" so he could read some of the "harder books." He says he liked "special reading" but his remedial teacher says "He loafed and did not make much progress." (*c*) Other—None.

4. *Personality (emotional) factors:* Roddy is very outgoing—he would visit during the entire remedial session if possible; but perhaps this is a passive defense to avoid the reading situation. He is eager to please and is quite skilled in using techniques designed to please—he always voices strong approval of everything we do; he wants to take three or four books home each day, etc. His "goodness" is his strongest attention-getting device, and it seems to work equally well both at home and in school.

5. *Educational and experiential factors:* It can only be hypothesized at this point, but it seems possible that Roddy has learned, first at home and then through reinforcing experiences at school, to play a passive, pleasant role. This may have influenced his functioning as a learner, creating what his teacher calls his "laziness" and the specific disability in reading.

Prognosis (rate and degree of expected progress):
Roddy's desire to please, alone, is likely to bring about a small amount of progress. If he can develop a simultaneous interest in actively "doing" he should be able to progress more rapidly. His current reading disability of approximately two years cannot be immediately erased, but an active, participating experience in the remaining remedial sessions could help him to develop more independence as a reader and more nearly approach the "harder books" in which he voices an interest. (See "Further investigations needed" below.)

Proposed Treatment:
1. *Major difficulties to be overcome:* (a) His "desire to please" energy needs to be channeled into a more active "desire to do." (b) He lacks systematic word attack skills, especially structural analysis (division of words into pronunciation and meaning units). (c) He has difficulty with comprehension of longer selections and with long-range retention.

2. *Further investigations needed:* A home visit would be of value both to get a feeling for the family atmosphere and to discover the parents' attitude toward Roddy's reading disability.

An individual intelligence test giving a Verbal/Performance breakdown and allowing a more careful study of the discrepancy between mental age and reading age might give a better idea of how much to expect from Roddy.

3. *Proposed line of treatment:* (a) Demonstrate (by the teacher) approval of reading accomplishment and provide more reading experiences and work responsibilities. (b) Provide exercises in syllabication as a method of analyzing words for pronunciation and meaning units. Choose pages from *Phonics We Use, Book C,* which illustrate principles that apply to his current reading (especially word endings). (c) Use *Reader's Digest Reading Skill Builder* (4^1 level) stories and follow-up discussion and comprehension exercises.

Have Roddy create his own booklet containing his own original stories and teacher-constructed exercises to illustrate appropriate principles growing from Roddy's reading needs.

(A listing of appropriate behavioral objectives could, of course, lend substance to the treatment proposed. See Chapter 3 for a general discussion and Chapter 7 for examples of specific objectives. Two main concerns should have prominence in offering such a list: (1) the objectives should proceed directly from the diagnostic information at hand, and (2) appropriate materials and/or procedures for attaining the objectives should be cited.)

A BRIEF CASE STUDY FORM

In many situations a brief, concise case report will be in line with the resources and expectations. The Case Study Form that follows is used by remedial reading teachers working in a public school setting. The completed form is passed on to the classroom teacher when the formal remedial work is terminated. Thus, the form serves as a vehicle for organizing information for the remedial teacher and as a tool for communication between the remedial teacher and the classroom teacher.

Again, a remedial teacher's comments are given along with the outline of the form. Note the use of phrases rather than complete sentences in deference to the brevity of the report. The tests listed by name on the form are tests that are used locally; changes would, of course, be required to adapt the form for other local situations.

Date . . . .

CASE STUDY FORM

Name   Robin W.

School   PS 53   Grade 5   Age 11–3   Teacher   Mr. Batman

1. *Mental Evaluation:*
   Individual tests
      a. Stanford-Binet   Year   Grade   IQ
      b. WISC   Year 1969 Verbal 95 Perf. 97 Total 95
   Group tests
      a. Kuhlmann-Anderson Year 1968 Grade 3   IQ 99
      b. Lorge-Thorndike   Year   Grade   IQ
      c. SCAT   Year 1969 Grade 4   P-Scores V. 35 Q. 38 T. 35
      d. SCAT   Year   Grade 7   P-Scores V.   A.   T.
   Comments: None

2. *Physical and Health Factors:*
   Vision   Normal

   Hearing   Normal

   Other

3. *Educational Factors:*

Schools attended		Days absent	Progress
Kgn	Dudley	7	immature
1st	"	9	", slow
2nd	"	7	" "
3rd	Quagmire	11	Below grade
4th	"		Slow
5th	"	5	Improving slowly
6th			
7th			
8th			

Grades repeated: Grade 3

Present School Status:
Interest in reading: Fair with easy material

Ability to maintain attention to tasks: Short attention span

Approximate reading level: Tests   V 3.2   C 2.5   Av 2.8   Book 3

Approximate arithmetic level: Grade 3 (Achievement test)

Comments: Tends to work slowly, somewhat carelessly. None of her work is up to grade level; claims to be uninterested in most school-related tasks, even when tasks are at her performance level.

4. *Social-Emotional Factors:*
Family pattern:
Lives with (circle) :
    M.   (F.)   St.M.   St.F.   Foster
    Other adults in home   None

    Siblings   Brothers
        Ages   16, 18, 21

Emotional adjustment (cooperation, self-control, fears, ability to tell the truth) :
Good in all grades according to information in cumulative folder.

Social adjustment (attitudes toward school, parents, siblings, adults, peers, self, play) :
Gr. K–3   Fair
Gr. 4–5   Good
Comments in cumulative folder show general improvement in adjustment over the last two years. Still lacks self-confidence.

Possible Causes of the Learning Problem (mental, physical, educational, emotional, environmental. Note duration.)
Characteristics reported in Grade 5 have been noted since kindergarten. According

to results on individual psychological examination, Robin may be expected to progress slowly. Her lack of confidence may be the result, partly, of overprotection and her place in the family—the youngest child and the only girl. Her "lack of interest" may be her way of protecting herself from failure.

Results of Reading Inventory
Estimate of sight word vocabulary   Dolch list OK, but miscalls occasionally. High 2nd level.

Estimate of word analysis skills   Unsure of more advanced skills. Single consonants and vowels OK. Blends known but less readily used.

Oral reading ability   2nd grade material, fine. Approaches frustration level with 3rd grade material.

Other   Reads slowly, hesitantly, no particular interest or enthusiasm; tends to confuse similar words; needs much support and encouragement. Embarrassed by reading errors and deficiencies.

Remedial Plan
Use variety of materials and techniques to stimulate interest and growth. Vary daily program. Use games, workbooks, recreational reading, plays: high 2nd easy 3rd level. Try SRA material *Cracking the Code*. Fill in skills as needed. Use tachistoscope to develop faster, more accurate recognition of words and phrases. Use reading accelerator when 4th level reached. Have Robin keep own notebook of work done, plus a simple graph of daily work and progress. Let Robin "read" through a hand puppet to shift attention from herself.

Remedial Teacher
Mr. Gordon

Use of a form such as the one given does not eliminate the need for verbal communication between the classroom and remedial teacher in situations where the remedial teaching is done by a specialist outside the regular classroom. The remedial teacher ought to obtain much information from the classroom teacher before the remedial sessions begin. Ordinarily, the classroom teacher has a good deal of general information about a child and this information can form a base for the remedial teacher's work, and the remedial teacher quickly acquires specific information that ought to be shared with the classroom teacher. A completed case study should not be a remedial teacher's monologue. A good case study—and a sensible working relationship—is based upon dialogue.

THE CASE ANALYSIS

The approach to the case study should, as we have already stated, be dictated by the nature of the learning problem involved. There is little need to do an exhaustive case study if it is apparent that the case is uncomplicated and the child is responding to a straightforward sequence of corrective teaching. Overcomplication of the problem is always indefensible. The following Case History Record for Analysis of Learning Difficulties is an example of a blank that might serve as a guide for an exhaustive case study. It is important to understand that many case studies do not require so extended an analysis, and that routine adherence to use of the form would be wasteful of both time and effort. We have, however, found the Case History Record to be extremely useful in working with severely disabled learners. Perceptive remedial teachers will be able to devise ways of adapting the form for optimum use with pupils having varying degrees of disability.

The Case History Record is organized to expedite examination of both formal and informal samples of performance in the basic skill areas. The emphasis is upon reading because in our experience disability in reading is the most common manifestation of a learning problem and often accompanies disability in other basic skill areas. The Record also provides for examination of physical and developmental data, environmental data, emotional and personality data, and educational data. Finally, there is provision for a statement of apparent causes of the learning problem, a summary and evaluation of the remedial approach, and recommendations for further treatment in the school and home. The final portion of the Record would normally be completed at the end of the remedial teaching sequence, and the summary statements would be the nucleus of any subsequent report.

The outline of the Record form is given, plus some concrete suggestions for observations (given in parentheses). The spacing would, of course, need to be adapted in actual use. Items I–VIII on the Record form call mainly for reporting of observations, test results, interview information, and information from outside sources; for the most part, this would involve straightforward reporting at the second, or descriptive, level of communication. Items IX, X, and XI call for summary statements, judgments, and feelings; these statements would tend to be at levels three and four, the evaluation and emotion levels. To illustrate a way of handling items IX, X, and XI, we have included sample completions for these items. The completions are from our files and demonstrate an acceptable style of writing and form of reporting.

CASE HISTORY RECORD FOR ANALYSIS OF LEARNING DIFFICULTIES

Date ....

I. *Referral Data*

Name: .... Birthdate: ....Sex: ......

Parent's name: .... Occupation: ....

Address: .... Tel. No.: ....

Age (as of current date) Years: .... Months: ....

School : .... City: ....

Principal: .... Last grade completed: ......

Teacher: .... Referred by: ....

Summary of the home's description of the learning problem:

Summary of the school's description of the learning problem:

II. *Capacity and Achievement Test Data* (list in order of date administered.)
   A. Tests of capacity:

			Verbal			Nonverbal		Total	
Test	Date	CA	MA	IQ	MA	IQ	MA	IQ
....	....	......	......		.....	......	.....	......	...
....	....	......	......		.....	......	.....	......	...

   B. General tests of achievement:

			Summarize part and total scores:
Test	Date	CA	age-grade equivalents, etc.
....	....	....	....
....	....	....	....

   C. Reading survey tests (silent):

Test	Date	CA	Summary of results
....	....	....	....
....	....	....	....

   D. Oral reading tests:

Test	Date	CA	Summary of results
....	....	....	....	....
....	....	....	....

   E. Diagnostic tests in the basic skill areas:

Test	Date	CA	Summary of results
....	....	....	....
....	....	....	....

   F. Appraisal of test results (discrepancies noted; pupil's behavior in test situation; correspondence of test performance with functional levels; further testing needed)

III. *Physical and Developmental Data*
   A. Developmental history:
      1. Age of first sitting: .... walking: ....
         use of first words: .... use of first
         sentences: ....
      2. Preschool language difficulties (evidence of delayed speech, stuttering, lisping, infantile speech habits)
      3. Adequacy of language development upon entrance to school (persistence of previous difficulties; onset of new difficulties; adequacy of vocabulary development)
      4. Experiential development upon entrance to school (breadth of experience; unusual opportunities and/or deprivations of experience; particular interests; extent to which school met or developed experiential needs)
   B. Health history (previous severe illnesses, operations, head or back injuries, and their effects; allergies, sinus difficulties, headaches, glandular deficiencies; extent to which health handicaps have interfered with schooling)
   C. Present health (current effects of adverse health history; general level of energy and activity; adequacy of sleep; diet problems; date of last physical examination; need for further physical examination)
   D. Vision:
      1. Glasses: .... when prescribed: ....
         why: .... worn regularly: ....

last visit to eye specialist: ....
recommendations: ....

2. Eyestrain: .... with or without glasses: ....
occurs only when studying: .... evidence of eyestrain
in reading (blurring, double vision, headaches, sleepiness, dizziness;
book held too close, too far): ....
....

3. Other data on visual efficiency: ....
....

E. Hearing:
1. Loss: L .... R .... how long: .... effect: ....
2. Discrimination: initial consonants ....
medial vowels and consonants ....
final consonants ....

F. Dominance:
1. Handedness: R .... L .... consistency ....
2. Eyedness: R .... L .... consistency ....
3. Attempts to change handedness (when; effect on pupil; on school
work): ....

IV. *Environmental Data* (social forces acting upon pupil)
A. Home (social, economic, and cultural level; special opportunities and/or
hindrances to self-expression; foreign language spoken in home)
B. Parents (living together, separated, divorced; evidence of parental rejec-
tion, overconcern, hostility; parents overly ambitious for children; evi-
dence of unfavorable comparisons with other siblings)
C. Siblings (names, ages, relationships with pupil)
D. Friends (age level preferred; things they like to do; close or casual; many
or few; ease with which pupil makes friends with those he likes)
E. Community activities (church, clubs, scouts, gangs; their effects)
F. Outside work (what, where, when; how much per week; satisfactions)
G. Other environmental effects (extent to which environment satisfies pupil's
needs)

V. *Emotional and Personality Adjustment Data* (pupil's reaction to self and
environment)
A. Attitude toward home (parents; siblings; extent to which security and
independence needs are satisfied in home)
B. Attitude toward school (rebellious, submissive, indifferent; attitudes
toward teachers; subjects strongly liked, disliked; reasons given)
C. Recreation (special abilities and interests; prefers group or individual
competition; avoids competition; reasons)
D. Emotional adjustment (degree of stability; evidence for this; results of
psychological inventories; learning difficulty a probable cause or result
of emotion; degree of tension normally present; reaction to frustration;
moods, fears)
E. Personality characteristics (degree of integration; effectiveness of general
adjustment socially and emotionally; outstanding traits)

VI. *Educational Data*
A. School progress:
1. Age entering: nursery ...... kindergarten ...... first grade ......

2. Schools attended: grades attended:

....

....

....

3. School grades: repeated .... skipped ....
4. Average school marks: low .... average .... high ....
5. Subjects: weak ....
   strong ....
6. Attendance (regular, irregular; note long absences; their cause and effect)

B. Study habits (regular routine established; effectiveness of concentration; distractions; use of study aids, as keeping record of assignments, note-taking, outlining, dictionary; general effectiveness of study techniques)

C. Adjustment of school to pupil's needs (has school met needs of pupil, which ones, which ones has it neglected, what adjustments can be made now)

D. Future educational and vocational plans (wants to go to high school, college, trade school; vocational interest; appropriateness of vocational choice in light of abilities)

VII. *Reading Data*

A. Reading readiness (evidence of pupil's readiness to read when introduced to oral and silent reading):
   1. Age when reading first introduced: .... years ....
      months; .... grade
   2. Mental readiness: ....
   3. Physical readiness: ....
   4. Social-emotional readiness: ....
   5. Experiential readiness: ....

B. History of reading difficulties (history of early difficulties, their nature, when encountered; pupil's explanation of difficulties; remedial training attempted; type of training—visual, auditory, kinesthetic; results)

C. Silent reading (see also test results):
   1. Observable habits (posture, distance from eye to book; moves head; moves lips; audible vocalization; points with finger; slow and inaccurate recognition habits; attention span long or short)
   2. Reported habits (reads much or little; extent of book, magazine, and newspaper reading; typical examples; use of library; tends to read slowly or fast, carefully or carelessly; depends more on aural ability than on reading ability in classroom work)
   3. Interpretation (significant characteristics; extent to which above data agree with test data)
   4. Instructional diagnosis (implications for remedial teaching)

D. Oral reading habits (see also test results):
   1. Defects and errors observed in informal oral reading (check):

...... stuttering	...... foreign accent	...... substitutions
...... lisping	...... hesitations	...... insertions
...... harelip	...... mispronunciations	...... repetitions
...... cleft palate	...... omissions	

2. Interpretation (seriousness of checked items; previous treatment attempted, when, by whom, results; extent to which above data agree with test data)

E. Current reading interests (books, magazines, etc.; maturity of interest for age, grade, sex)

F. Question: Does the student feel a real need for improving his reading? (Note here current attitude toward reading; degree of emotion involved in attitude; ways in which need can be aroused if lacking, capitalized upon if present.)

VIII. *Description of the Pupil's Performance in the Other Basic Skill Areas: Instructional Diagnosis of Typical Performance in Areas of Difficulty* (spelling, arithmetic, handwriting, and general language)

Examples of completions of points IX, X, and XI are given for two cases. The summary points draw together the information gathered through the use of the case study approach and describe the resultant remedial teaching and implications for follow-up. The first case, that of Vince, is an example of a disabled learner who, despite a substantial gap between capacity and achievement, is able to function at a fourth- or fifth-grade level in reading. The second case, that of Ben, is an example of a very severe reading disability; Ben is a seventh grader but virtually a nonreader. The two cases, then, provide examples of approaches taken with a pupil reading at the intermediate level and a pupil needing instruction at the primary level.

Summary of Vince's Case

IX. *Apparent Causes of the Learning Difficulty* (summary of salient points from the analysis of the pupil's developmental and present status):

The symptoms of Vince's reading disability are the typical ones for a context reader: carelessness; inattention to details; too rapid, inaccurate reading; plus lack of phrasing and inattention to marks of punctuation. This is combined with a tendency to guess at words rather than attack them by using techniques that are known to him. These, of course, are merely symptoms of more fundamental causes.

Personal and Emotional Factors:

Vince has an extremely short attention span and is always easily distracted. It is difficult for him to carry one task through to its completion before he is off to begin another. As a result, reading comprehension is low.

Vince works well as an individual. He is easily distracted, but alone he will cooperate and work willingly—as long as he is prodded occasionally. In a group, however, he wants to be the center of attraction. Typical behavior in a group will include criticizing the performance of others, making distracting noises, talking out of turn, and demanding the constant attention of the teacher.

The reason for this behavior may lie within the home.

Environmental Factors:

Vince's mother tends to be overprotective; and, although she apparently is aware of the fact, she remains so. His father says he wants Vince to "be a man"; however, in practice he fails to follow through and to set reasonable standards which he can expect Vince to meet. The mother tends to excuse everything on the basis of Vince's allergic condition. The inconsistency would be expected to be, and apparently is, confusing to the boy.

There is little acceptance of reading as a leisure activity in the home. Books and magazines are not in evidence and both parents frankly admit that they much prefer television to reading.

Physical Factors:

Vince was absent a great deal during the first three years of school, due to a severe allergic condition. At the present time, the allergic condition appears to be fairly well controlled through medication. Occasional headaches are still caused by congestion of the sinuses, however.

The mother has made and still makes a great deal of the poor health situation, which in reality no longer exists. Overindulgence and lack of disciplinary action appear to stem from this situation.

Vincent has worn glasses in the past. The mother reports that recent examinations indicate that correction is no longer necessary. Tests at the clinic, however, indicate that some visual impairment may exist.

X. *Summary and Evaluation of Treatment*

Treatment has been aimed primarily at encouraging more careful, accurate reading and at developing more systematic study habits.

In developing careful, accurate reading, emphasis has been placed upon: (1) Word recognition skills. The tachistoscope has been used to develop quick, accurate sight word and phrase recognition. This has worked out well—Vince can read simple phrases with fair accuracy at 1/100 of a second. Emphasis has been placed upon use of syllabication and recognition of known parts in attacking words. Vince is generally able to master a word with the skills at hand; but he must be encouraged to do so, since he will simply guess if left alone. (2) Reading for complete accuracy. Vince has been encouraged to slow down if necessary, but to read each word as it appears. The tendency to ignore final elements of longer words and substitute small words persists. Some work with reading thought groups within sentences has been done, but Vince continues to be misled by reasonable but inaccurate context clues. More reading of thought units is needed, plus emphasis on punctuation as a help in accurate, meaningful reading. (3) Reading to comprehend. Emphasis has been placed upon reading for comprehension of details which are commonly missed by a context reader. More work needs to be done to develop an awareness that accurate reading the first time leads to greater comprehension.

The need for good, steady study habits was also indicated. This was approached by outlining what needed to be done at the beginning of a study period. The importance of completing one assignment before beginning another was stressed and insisted upon. Vince responded well when firmly and clearly made to understand that an assignment needed to be completed. Vince needs, and will continue to need, a firm, if not heavy, hand to guide—and to prod—him. This is apparently not provided in the home. When Vince balked at some tasks, he was made to understand that he would not be given preferred treatment, that some things are expected of everybody. As Vince came to realize this, he showed improvement in length of attention span and in group behavior.

XI. *Recommendations for Further Treatment in School and Home*

The recommendations are directed to the school only, since past performance suggests that the kind of help needed could not be effectively provided by the home.

It is felt that establishing realistic goals and seeing that the goals are reached is the most important aspect of further treatment. In the past, Vince seems to have been overindulged, accused, and excused to such an extent that carrying a task methodically and diligently to completion is almost inconceivable to him. Vince needs to have realistic goals set; to have the means for attaining the goals outlined for him; to have consistent, steady pressure applied to insure constant effort; and, finally, to be helped to feel a sense of achievement upon reaching his goals.

Vince needs firm guidance, but he also needs to know that somebody is sincerely interested in seeing him do well and, more important, to realize that diligent effort can lead to real achievement and to personal satisfaction. The amount of material to be mastered and the reading level of material must be controlled to insure progress and ultimate achievement and to minimize the tendency to give up before anything has been attempted. Vince's present instructional level for reading is fifth grade; his independent level is fourth grade.

Vince should be examined by a competent eye specialist. Present findings are inconclusive but show some limitation of near-point vision.

Specific treatment of the reading problem, per se, should include the following: (1) Further development of syllabication as a method of word attack, as this seems to be the most natural method of attack in this case. (2) Drill in word-for-word accuracy in oral reading. This will contribute to more accurate reading and to comprehension. Each word missed should be individually pointed out and analyzed. The value of accurate reading in terms of comprehension should be stressed. Achievement here will be most difficult, and will most clearly reflect any progress made toward reading by thought groups. Drill in accurate reading should be combined with emphasis upon punctuation marks as useful sign posts in reading.

Summary of Ben's Case

IX. *Apparent Causes of the Learning Difficulty* (summary of salient points from the analysis of the pupil's developmental and present status):

Emotional Factors:

According to Dr. S., psychological consultant, "Ben is a frightened boy who feels he is the passive victim of a strong outside force." Dr. S. states that the emotional factors of this case cannot be overlooked. He recommends that "(1) Ben should become more self-assertive; (2) Ben be encouraged not to 'press' so much in his learning process; and (3) pressure should be released both at home and school." (Report dated 2/10/64.)

Dr. W., the school psychologist, indicated that "the reading situation appears to be highly emotionally charged." (Dated 2/12/64.)

Physical Factors:

Dr. M., the optometrist, reported that Ben has 20/200 vision in both eyes and that it has only recently been corrected to 20/20 for both near and far vision. Dr. M. states that one factor in his low achievement picture may be that he apparently needed glasses for some time before they were prescribed. This, combined with excessive absences in the first grade, points up the likelihood that there may be rather marked gaps in Ben's educational background. (Report dated 6/15/62.)

Social Factors:

Mrs. F., in particular, seems to feel that some of the difficulty might be related to earlier years in Ben's life when he was left very much on his own while both parents were working.

The County Child Guidance Clinic staff summarized their impressions as follows: "One must consider that this child has had very limited parental interest and time due to the work situation for both parents. One gets the feeling that the children may have been sacrificed, at least to a degree, in order to make a living which has required long hard hours for both parents." (Report dated 1/63 to 11/63, County Child Guidance Clinic.)

Instructional Factors:

It should be noted that Ben was instructed in reading for a period of time by his mother, who used a system of intensive phonics instruction. The method includes a series of flash cards with many groups of letters to be memorized. In evaluating the particular method, it appears likely that a certain amount of confusion would result if a disabled reader were required to memorize the many combinations. It would seem that increased tension and greater frustration would come from trying to learn the combinations and being unable to do so. Ben himself says, "When Mom tried to help me it seems my reading got worse."

The school has apparently shown concern for Ben's problem and special instruction has been given, but rather sporadically. At the present time all special instruction has been discontinued because a remedial teacher is not available.

(See also *Physical Factors* above.)

X. *Summary and Evaluation of Treatment*

During Ben's twenty, one-hour sessions at the clinic, considerable time was spent in administering formal and informal tests in order to determine specifically the nature of his reading disability and its degree of severity. Ben demonstrated a need for: (1) systematic instruction in the basic reading skills at the primer level; (2) better knowledge of the manuscript alphabet, upper and lower case; (3) multiple methods of word attack; (4) elimination of reversals such as *d* and *b*, *q* and *p*, *f* and *j*; (5) knowledge of consonant blends; (6) practice in reading stories at his level; and (7) many success experiences.

Systematic Teaching of Basic Reading Skills at the Primer Level:

Ben learned the short vowel sounds with the aid of pictures representing the sound (*apple, elephant, Indian, octopus,* and *umbrella*). He referred to these when he could not remember. Ben needs continued practice with the short vowel sounds. We also used Kirk's *Remedial Reading Drills, Part I.*

The short vowel sound was introduced and discussed. Then Ben was asked to read the words in the drill, which were rather simple (i.e., *sat, mat, cap, can, sad*). In all, there were forty words in Drill I. Ben read the words, without error and wrote the words when dictated, missing only one.

Knowledge of the Manuscript Alphabet, Upper and Lower Case:

Ben practiced printing the alphabet when a test revealed that he was confused about the order of the alphabet and the correct shapes of certain letters. He improved with practice.

Multiple Methods of Word Attack:

Ben has developed an overanalytical, letter-by-letter approach to attacking all words. To encourage sight recognition of frequently used words, the *Dolch Basic Word List* of preprimer and primer words was studied with the aid of a tachistoscope. By the end of the summer program, Ben was able to recall about 85 percent of the words as sight words. Configuration clues were also explained and Ben was encouraged to use them when appropriate.

Eliminating Reversals:

A need for accurate letter discrimination in order to correct certain reversals was apparent. A letter analysis was made and practice exercises found in the *Phonics We Use* (A) workbook were used. Ben still shows some confusion between *d* and *b*.

Knowledge of Consonant Blends:

In order to develop greater facility in this area Ben practiced with the *Dolch Consonant Blend Cards*. The cards were not too difficult for him and he enjoyed working with them.

Practice in Reading Stories at His Level:

During the clinic sessions Ben read three books: *Dan Frontier and the New House, Dan Frontier,* and *Jim Forest and Ranger Don*. As Ben reads he is visibly quite tense; therefore, reading periods were limited to ten or fifteen minutes at a time.

Success:

Ben experienced some degree of success in almost every reading exercise or story attempted this summer. His comprehension was above average and when relaxed he could recall familiar words much more readily than when he was tense.

Ben has a desire to learn how to read and he appears to possess the intellectual capacity for success in reading. After working with him it appears that now, in spite of emotional factors, he could achieve in reading if he were systematically instructed in basic reading skills in a situation free from pressure and tension.

XI.   *Recommendations for Further Treatment in School and Home*

School:

On the basis of compiled data and Ben's reading performance at the clinic, it is felt that he could profit from further instruction in the basic reading skills at this time. If possible Ben should be instructed by a remedial reading teacher or by someone familiar with primary reading skills. His intelligence test results, summer reading clinic performance, and interest seem to justify renewed effort. Ben needs practice in reading fluently and easily in a relaxed situation from materials at the primer level. Perhaps a teacher could be released to give Ben individual instruction in the basic reading skills for about thirty minutes a day.

Home:

Ben should be provided with some special help in reading by a qualified instructor if the school is unable to provide the special instruction needed.

In addition, he should read for short periods each day from books written on the appropriate grade level (primer, at the present time). The prevailing atmosphere during these sessions should be tension-free and relaxed, and supportive encouragement should be provided. Ben needs to read many easy books written on the appropriate grade level in order to gain facility in reading and a feeling of personal worth and self-confidence.

We made two points in introducing the case study form presented here: first, the form is designed for use with severely disabled learners; and second, the form should be adapted for use in specific settings. Both of these points should be explicitly clear. Because the coverage in the sample form is so exhaustive it should be relatively simple for individual remedial teachers to shorten and adapt the form to fit their mode of operation, their particular setting, and their unique students. In short, the form should not be adopted; it should be adapted. This is, of course, true not only for the case study form but also for all of the forms, methods, materials, techniques, and points of view we have suggested or shall suggest.

REPORT TO THE SCHOOL

A case study that is well done usually uncovers considerable information that can be useful to other teachers or specialists; therefore, a final report ought to be prepared in every instance. (We have arbitrarily chosen to call this report the Report to the School—despite the fact that it might be directed to a community agency, a private tutor, or an individual teacher—because it is likely that the school would be the final repository for the report and that the school would most often be responsible for any follow-up.) Some teachers are understandably reluctant to prepare final reports because they have seen such statements placed in cumulative folders and forgotten. Nevertheless, we prefer to err in the direction of writing a report that is not used rather than not writing a report that is needed.

Preparation of a final report can be a simple matter if care has been taken in preparing a case study. The Tentative Diagnosis, Prognosis, and Proposed Treatment statement could, for example, be used just as it is in reporting to the school. It is particularly appropriate for situations in which a disabled learner is referred mainly for diagnosis and then sent back to the classroom for extended corrective help. The treatment proposed must, of course, be sufficiently explicit to offer worthwhile guidelines to instruction. The brief case study form, too, can serve as a final report if it is carefully prepared. The form provides for a summary of diagnostic information and a statement regarding implications for further instruction, which together form the necessary elements of a meaningful report. If the more detailed Case History Record is used, we recommend that only selected parts be used in the report to the school: I. Referral Data; II. Capacity and Achievement Test Data; IX. Apparent Causes of the Learning Difficulty; X. Summary and Evaluation of Treatment; and XI. Recommendations for Further Treatment in School and Home. Taken directly from a carefully prepared Case History Record, the five parts together serve to identify the case, to summarize formal and informal diagnostic data, to recapitulate what has been done, and to suggest promising directions for the future. Needless to say, a brief but concise report stands a better chance of being read and used than one that is long and lacking in focus. The credibility of any suggestions for further treatment will, of course, be increased if classroom teachers and remedial specialists collaborate in working them out.

THOUGHTS FOR DISCUSSION

"The task of the person making a case study, after the separate data have been obtained, is to get an overall picture of the child and his needs. This task, never easy, is simplified somewhat if all the relevant information is briefly summarized in such a way that the interrelations can be seen." (Harris, 1970a, p. 312)

"Gathering all pertinent facts is, of course, a time consuming task and is not generally too popular with already overburdened teachers. The only answer, however, must be that teaching a child who is a remedial reading case is also a time consuming task and without the benefit of a case study, remedial work is not likely to be so effective as possible." (Barbe, 1959, p. 571)

"The case study synthesizes information on many abilities, attitudes, and conditions that may contribute to reading achievement. For example, both feeling and thinking affect reading development. . . . If enough were known about the child's developmental history, intelligence, language ability, personality factors, and environment, it would be easier to judge whether he was achieving as well as could be expected." (Strang, 1969, p. 229)

". . . effective teaching can be achieved without formal diagnostic examinations, but . . . for a reading disability case which has resisted normal growth in regular class instruction and in special individual instruction, diagnosis is needed. Expensive, time-consuming diagnostic procedures are recommended, particularly for those students not responding to regular classroom instruction or individualized classroom corrective treatment based on informal diagnosis." (Della-Piana, 1968, pp. 2–3)

". . . reports, written to accomplish a specific purpose, must place the welfare of the child first. His image and self-concept must remain unscathed, and no faulty characterization should be made by the professional workers charged with his diagnosis and treatment. In achieving this goal, it is suggested that reports be evaluated by at least two workers or staff members before being presented in final form." (Carter and McGinnis, 1970, pp. 283–284)

"It would be difficult to exaggerate the degree to which we are influenced by those we influence." (Hoffer, 1955, p. 115)

REFERENCES

Barbe, W. B. Preparation of case study reports. *Education,* 1959, **79**, 570–574.

Carter, H. L. J., and McGinnis, D. J. *Diagnosis and treatment of the disabled reader.* New York: Macmillan, 1970.

Della-Piana, G. *Reading diagnosis and prescription.* New York: Holt, 1968.

English, R. H., and Lillywhite, H. S. A semantic approach to clinical reporting in speech pathology. *Journal of the American Speech and Hearing Association,* 1963, **5**, 647–650. (Also in W. Otto, and K. Koenke (Eds.), *Remedial teaching.* Boston: Houghton Mifflin, 1969.)

Harris, A. J. *Casebook on reading disability.* New York: David McKay, 1970. (a)

Harris, A. J. *How to increase reading ability.* (5th ed.) New York: David McKay, 1970. (b)

Hoffer, E. *The passionate state of mind.* New York: Harper, and Row, 1955. Perennial Library edition, 1968.

Strang, R. *Diagnostic teaching of reading.* (2nd ed.) New York: McGraw-Hill, 1969.

Chapter 5

Diagnosis in Reading

Diagnosis is the foundation upon which effective corrective and remedial teaching is built. Fundamentals of diagnosis are discussed in Chapter 3 and the specifics of diagnosis in reading are examined in this chapter. The specifics of corrective and remedial teaching in reading are discussed in the chapters that follow. What is presented here, then, should be seen as the foundation for the further consideration of corrective and remedial teaching in reading.

No attempt is made in this chapter to present a comprehensive listing of the many formal and informal tools that are relevant to diagnosis in reading. The presentation is limited instead to representative standardized tests and informal tools for evaluation that we feel merit the attention of corrective and remedial teachers. More comprehensive lists with descriptions and, in some instances, evaluations can readily be obtained. Two prime sources are the works edited by Buros: the *Mental Measurements Yearbook*—the current yearbook is the *Sixth* (Buros, 1965), but updated versions are issued periodically—and *Tests in Print* (Buros, 1961). Another comprehensive list is *Guide to Tests and Measuring Instruments for Reading* (Farr and Summers, 1968), which is a publication of the ERIC/Clearinghouse on Reading (ERIC/CRIER). The document (accession number ED022973) can be obtained from the ERIC Document Reproduction Service (EDRS) in microfiche or hard copy. The Educational Testing Service (ETS) issues a quarterly *Test Collection Bulletin* in which new acquisitions are listed and briefly annotated. The bulletin is not, of course, limited to reading tests, but tests are cataloged as they become available. Composite issues of the bulletin can be obtained at no charge by directing an inquiry to Test Collection, ETS.

Other useful lists are given by Harris (1970), Bond and Tinker (1967), Della-Piana (1968), and Austin, Bush, and Huebner (1961). The latter source is now somewhat passé, but the discussion is still excellent.

SURVEY LEVEL OF DIAGNOSIS

At the survey level of diagnosis the teacher examines the performance of all his pupils in order to (*a*) examine the success of the developmental teaching program, (*b*) determine areas in which the whole class or certain groups appear to need corrective instruction, and (*c*) locate individuals whose problems need more specific diagnosis. The major sources of information considered are survey tests of reading ability, group tests of scholastic aptitude, and cumulative record folders.

Survey Tests of Reading Ability

When used with discretion, a standardized survey test of reading ability yields a fairly accurate basis for estimating the difficulty level at which a child can read. If the test is part of a battery of tests designed to measure achievement in several skill areas, comparisons can be made to identify pupils who are doing less well in reading than in other areas. Most survey tests in reading yield a vocabulary score, a general comprehension score, and a total reading score; some yield a reading rate score and/or specialized comprehension scores—e.g., literal and inferential—as well. More highly focused tests are required for a detailed analysis of specific reading strengths and weaknesses. Survey tests are sometimes called *power tests* because they are designed to show the difficulty level of the material a child can read. Some examples of widely used standardized survey tests follow.

The *Metropolitan Achievement Tests, Revised* (Harcourt, 1958–1962) are an example of survey tests that are available at several levels and in several equivalent forms as a part of an achievement test battery. The *Primary I Battery,* for use at the end of grade 1, includes measures of word knowledge, word discrimination, reading (general), and arithmetic concepts and skills. The *Primary II Battery,* for use at the end of grade 2 or beginning of grade 3, includes measures of word knowledge, word discrimination, reading, spelling, and arithmetic. The *Elementary Reading* (grades 3, 4), *Intermediate Reading* (grades 5, 6), and *Advanced Reading* (grades 7, 8) tests include measures of paragraph comprehension and vocabulary and yield part and total scores. Other widely used survey tests available at several levels and in several forms are: the *Diagnostic Reading Tests, Survey Section* (Committee on Diagnostic Reading Tests); the *Durrell Reading-Listening Series* (Harcourt), which replaces the *Durrell-Sullivan Reading Capacity and Achievement Tests;* the *Stanford Reading Tests, 1964 Revision* (Harcourt); the *Sequential Tests of Educational Progress—STEP* (Educational Testing Service); the *Gates-McGinitie Reading Tests* (Teachers College Press), which replace both the *Gates Primary Tests* and the *Gates Reading Survey;* the *California Reading Tests, WXYZ Series, 1963 Norms,* also part of the *California Achievement Test Battery* (California Test Bureau); and the *Developmental Reading Tests* (Lyons and Carnahan).

When the reading survey is a part of a battery of tests covering several basic skill areas, it can often be purchased separately if this is desired. A test that is available at several levels and in several forms can lend continuity to a sequential testing program designed to measure growth over a period of years. Often there is marked disparity between the format, type of questions, norms, etc., of tests from different publishers; thus, test results from a single series may be more clearly comparable. However, care must still be exercised in test selection because there may be little relationship between the several levels of tests in a single series.

Some survey tests are designed for use only at given levels, particularly the junior and senior high school levels. Some examples are: the *Cooperative English Tests: Reading Comprehension* (Educational Testing Service), with multiple forms available for grades 9–12 and grades 12–14; the *Davis Reading Test* (Psychological Corporation), with multiple forms for grades 8–11 and grades 11–13; the *Kelley-Greene Reading Comprehension Tests* (Harcourt), for grades 9–13; the *Nelson-Denny Reading Test, Revised Edition* (Houghton Mifflin), for grades 9–12; the *Nelson Silent Reading Test, Revised* (Houghton Mifflin), for grades 3–9; the *Schrammel-Gray High School and College Reading Test* (Bobbs-Merrill), for grades 7–12 and college; the *Traxler Silent Reading Test* (Bobbs-Merrill), for grades 7–10; and the *Traxler High School Reading Test, Revised 1967* (Bobbs-Merrill), for grades 10–12.

The *Wide Range Achievement Test, Revised Edition* (Psychological Corporation, 1965), which has performance norms for age five through college in word recognition, spelling, and arithmetic, is rather widely used for screening reading performance at the survey level of diagnosis. Because of its wide range, the test does have considerable appeal as a quick screening device and it can serve a useful purpose. But teachers who use it should recognize that it is a test of *word recognition,* not a test of *general reading ability.* We agree fully with Harris' (1970) observation: "It is . . . not a satisfactory measure of general reading ability, despite the fact that it has been used for that purpose in a number of research studies" (p. 189).

Perhaps some final words of caution are in order. Survey tests of reading ability tend generally to overestimate individuals' reading achievement levels. That is, a survey test score will tend to place a pupil's reading achievement level somewhat above his actual ability level in reading. Furthermore, a pupil's scores on several different tests may differ substantially. Kottmeyer (1959, p. 85) feels that this may be due, at least in part, to the tendency of older tests to yield lower scores than more recently published tests; but unfortunately he offers no data to support his observation. Regardless of the reasons for the variability among individuals' test scores, two points regarding survey tests should be kept in mind. First, test scores are not absolute values; they can be as fallible as subjective judgments. A sensible procedure is to seek corroboration of test scores by informal observation and vice versa. Second, tests should be chosen with care. If the remedial teacher will experiment with a number of tests to assess their strengths, weaknesses, and limitations he will be in a position to interpret the results obtained with the one he finally chooses. Chall (1970) said it extremely well: "There is more to interpreting the results of standardized tests than drawing profiles of grade scores or percentile ranks arrived at miraculously by modern scoring machines. As in medical diagnosis, the final decision about what the scores mean rests with human interpretation. The data secured from our more elaborate tests must ultimately gain their meaning and wise use from the teacher, the psychologist, and the administrator" (p. 59). Finally, if a survey test is to be used in program evaluation, parallel forms must be available for pre- and post-testing; and it must have sufficient range to assure that few pupils will score at the test ceiling.

Group Tests of Scholastic Aptitude

Specialists in testing and test construction have repeatedly made the point that so-called *intelligence* or *IQ* tests do not truly measure "intelligence" at all. They suggest that such tests be called something like "scholastic aptitude tests" because they merely attempt to predict how well a child will do in school—*if he chooses to work up to capacity* (Pine, 1969). We agree. It would, however, be naive to think that changing the name changes the product. The fact remains that the tests in question have severe limitations, some of which are discussed in this chapter. We feel, however, that when they are used with discretion, tests of scholastic aptitude have something to contribute to corrective and remedial teaching.

Estimates of scholastic aptitude are useful at the survey level of diagnosis because they help to establish a level of expectation both for individual pupils and for classes. Before a child is selected for remedial help, for example, there should be evidence that he has the capacity to improve. Similarly, if an entire class has limited ability it may be better to think in terms of adapted rather than corrective instruction. Individual "intelligence" test scores for each pupil would be valuable because the scores tend to be both more valid and more reliable than group test scores. It has become almost a cliché to point out the fact that a poor reader's performance on a typical group intelligence test may be limited by his inability to cope adequately with the written portions of the test. Unfortunately, individual tests are very costly to administer and to interpret; therefore, they are normally given at the specific level of diagnosis, after screening with group tests has been completed.

Most *scholastic aptitude*—intelligence—tests designed for use in the primary grades are reasonably satisfactory for use with disabled readers because they use pictures and no reading matter. One such test that is widely used is the *Otis Quick-Scoring Mental Ability Test, New Edition, Alpha Short Form* (Harcourt), which is for group use in grades 1 through 4 and requires no reading. Others are the *Kuhlman-Anderson Measure of Academic Potential, 6th and 7th Editions* (Psychological Corporation), through the fourth-grade level; the *Detroit Beginning First-Grade Intelligence Test, Revised* (Harcourt); the *Pintner-Cunningham Primary Test* (1965), for kindergarten through grade 2 (Harcourt); and the *Cognitive Abilities Test,* for kindergarten through grade 3 (Houghton Mifflin).

Many of the group tests of scholastic aptitude that are intended for use with pupils in the fourth grade and higher demand reading ability because the items are in printed form. Poor readers' scores on such tests may be low because of their lack of reading *ability,* not because of their lack of reading *potential.* Typical of the group tests with high reading demands are the following: the *Henmon-Nelson Tests of Mental Ability, Revised* (Houghton Mifflin); the *Otis Quick-Scoring Mental Ability Tests: New Edition, Beta Test* and *Gamma Test* (Harcourt), the more recent *Otis-Lennon Mental Ability Test, Elementary II, Intermediate* and *Advanced* (Harcourt); and the *Pintner Intermediate Test* (Harcourt).

Some of the group tests yield both a verbal and a nonverbal score, with the verbal score based upon items that demand reading ability and the nonverbal score based upon nonreading (pictorial, numerical, etc.) items. When both scores are available from a single test, the remedial teacher may get some additional clues for diagnosis. If, for example, a child's verbal score is substantially below his nonverbal score, there is good reason to suspect that his total performance is delimited by his lack of reading ability. On the other hand, if a child does equally poorly on both parts, there is reason to suspect that he is a slow learner rather than a disabled reader. Among the most widely used tests of this type is the *California Test of Mental Maturity, 1963 Revision* (California Test Bureau). Available at six levels ranging from kindergarten through college, the test yields language (reading dependent), nonlanguage (no reading required), and total scores. Other tests that yield both verbal and nonverbal scores are the *Pintner-Durost Elementary Test, Scale 1* (picture content) and *Scale 2* (reading content), for grades 2–4 (Harcourt); the *Lorge-Thorndike Intelligence Tests, Multi-Level Edition,* for grades 3–13 (Houghton Mifflin); the *Detroit Alpha Intelligence Test,* for grades 4–8 (Bobbs-Merrill); and the *School and College Ability Tests* (SCAT), for grades 4–16 (Educational Testing Service).

There are a few group intelligence tests available that require no reading. One example is the *Davis-Eels Test of General Intelligence or Problem Solving Ability* (Harcourt), *Primary Test* for grades 1 and 2, and *Elementary Test* for grades 3 through 6. The test is said to be "culture-free" because it measures the aspects of intelligence (problem-solving ability) that are relatively uninfluenced by a limited or severely deprived experiential background. Unfortunately, this very attribute limits its value as a means for estimating reading potential. Reading ability is very highly related to the verbal skills that children acquire through education and cultural backgrounds; a test that eliminates cultural and educational influences is unlikely to be a good tool for estimating potential in reading. The *Chicago Non-Verbal Examination* (Psychological Corporation), for age seven through adult, is another nonverbal group intelligence test that requires no reading. It is designed for children who are handicapped in the use of the English language, and directions for the test can be given verbally or in pantomime. Like the *Davis-Eels Test* it does not predict school achievement as well as do verbal tests. However, both tests may be useful with disabled readers if they are conceived as supplementary sources of information about general ability to be used with other sources. Three other nonverbal tests are: the *Cattell Culture Fair Intelligence Tests* (Institute for Personality and Aptitude Testing), with three scales for age four through adult; the *Raven Progressive Matrices* (Psychological Corporation), for age eight through adult; and the *Goodenough-Harris Drawing Test* (Harcourt), for ages three through twelve. The latter yields a score based upon pupils' ability to draw a human figure.

At the opposite extreme from the nonverbal intelligence tests are the picture vocabulary tests. One example of such a test is the *Peabody Picture Vocabulary Test* (American Guidance Service), for ages two through eighteen, which is designed to estimate a child's verbal intelligence by measuring his hearing vocabulary. In the testing procedure the examiner enunciates a word and the subject chooses a picture that matches the meaning of the word. (Actually, visual perception is as important as hearing vocabulary, for the pupil must interpret the picture as well as understand the word enunciated to make a correct response.) The test requires no reading, so nonreaders and poor readers are not directly penalized by their reading disability. Of course, it is difficult to determine just how adversely a child's vocabulary development may have been affected by limited reading experiences. Similar tests are the *Full Range Picture Vocabulary Test* and the *Quick Test* (Psychological Test Specialists), both appropriate for the preschool through adult range, and the *VanAlstyne Picture Vocabulary Test* (Harcourt), appropriate for mental ages two through seven. Actually, all four tests are individual tests and would, therefore, normally be used at the specific level of diagnosis. They are mentioned here because they can be administered very quickly (three to fifteen minutes, depending on the test and the subject) and scored in a straightforward manner. These two attributes make them potentially useful for screening purposes. The substantial relationship between verbal understanding and reading potential appears to imply that a picture vocabulary test, which tests understanding of spoken words, is likely to have diagnostic and prognostic value with disabled readers.

Again, some final words of caution appear to be in order, but at the same time some reassurance may be needed. Lyman (1970) has made some eminently sensible observations regarding IQ and the tests from which IQ's are derived:

> We need first to recognize that the IQ is only a way for expressing the performance of an individual on an intelligence test. (Note: '*intelligence* test,' NOT 'IQ test.') The IQ is *only* a type of test score.
>
> Intelligence tests and their resulting IQ's have been criticized in recent years because:
>
> 1. *IQ's are not constant.* Of course they're not! What is? Just as with any other type of test score, a person's IQ may change if: (1) he is given a different test;

(2) he is tested at a different point in time; (3) he is facilitated (or handicapped) by the particular circumstances (physical environment, etc.) of the test administration; (4) he is helped (or hindered) by his interaction with the examiner; and, (5) his motivation is enhanced or depressed, for whatever reason.

2. *Intelligence tests are unfair to minority groups.* Absolutely true, but not to the extent that some believe. And IQ's are helpful because they do relate positively to academic achievement, many job criteria, etc. But the cultural fairness of tests still needs much study.

3. *Intelligence tests are not culture-free.* Very true—neither is anything else! (This criticism, of course, is similar to the one above.) [Parenthetically, it is amusing to note another man's response to this criticism. Adrian Dove, a sociologist, devised the *Dove Counter-Balance Intelligence Test,* dubbed the CHITLIN TEST, because he feels that the standard tests are geared to middle-class white society. With tongue only partially in-cheek, he suggested that items such as the following would best reflect the culture and knowledge of the Negro slum:

Cheap Chitlings (not the kind you purchase at the frozen food counter) will taste rubbery unless they are cooked long enough. How soon can you quit cooking them to eat and enjoy them?—(A) 45 minutes, (B) 2 hours, (C) 24 hours, (D) 1 week on a low flame, (E) 1 hour.

'Bo-Diddley' is a—(A) game for children, (B) down home cheap wine, (C) down home singer, (D) new dance, (E) Moejee call.]

4. *IQ's tell us nothing about creativity.* True. Neither do IQ's tell us anything about the individual's personality, vocational interests, or color of hair! Creativity is a different entity [or set of entities] that is best measured with separate tests.

The point here is that *scholastic aptitude, intelligence,* or *IQ* tests—whatever they may be called—have useful functions as well as limitations. Used with discretion, they can help us to make reasonable estimates of reading potential (or, in other terms, reading *expectancy* or *capacity*). In a later section of this chapter some other types of tests that are also intended for this purpose are discussed. But the fact remains that whatever test or method is employed, estimating reading potential is no easy task. Things have not changed significantly since Spache (1958) came to the conclusion that follows:

> Practically all the methods of estimating reading capacity have sought a one-to-one relationship between some predictor and capacity. But the problem of predicting future performances in reading cannot be simplified in this fashion. Reading is not a simplified intellectual function reflecting only the intelligence of the learner, or his age, or his years in school. A multitude of samples has shown that success in reading is determined by multiple factors. Learning to read is an expression of the internal needs of the child as well as an answer to the external pressures. Because all these factors enter into reading capacity, it is very doubtful that we shall ever find a single test that will accurately predict reading capacity. We should continue to look for such tests, however, to add them to the measure of intelligence, auditory comprehension, and learning rate that we now find helpful.

Examples of Test Scores and Interpretations

Taken together, reading survey tests and group tests of scholastic aptitude yield data that can be useful in examining the performance of an entire class and in locating individuals who appear to be in need of further diagnosis. Perhaps the most satisfactory way of establishing a procedure for making use of test results at the survey level is to inspect test scores from an entire classroom and to examine certain inferences and conclusions derived from the data.

Test scores from an actual seventh-grade classroom are presented in Table 1. Scores are given for thirty-six pupils, who were tested at the beginning of their seventh-grade year. The scores were compiled before final class assignments were made; shifting in class assignments finally made it possible to reduce the number of pupils in each of four seventh-grade classrooms to about thirty-two. Thus, one function of the present data was to aid the teacher to make recommendations for reassignment of four pupils.

(An interjection is in order here. The seventh-grade analysis is given by way of a concrete example. It should be clear that if a similar analysis is done for a lower grade the differences between the various scores are not likely to be as great. A one-year gap between capacity and achievement would, for example, be as great for a third grader as would a two-year gap for a sixth grader. As we pointed out in Chapter 3, a one- or two-year criterion can be useful for screening purposes when children in need of corrective and remedial help are being located; but adaptations must be made. In practice the teacher will want to adapt the gap to the specific grade level; to screen remedial cases, for example, one year in third grade, two years in sixth grade, and three years in ninth grade would be realistic criteria. Of course, even when screening criteria are adapted the final decision on whether a disability calls for corrective or remedial help must be made individually on the basis of further diagnosis.)

The columns of Table 1 present: (1) *Chronological Age* (CA), which is the actual age in years and months of each child; (2) *Mental Age* (MA), or expectancy age based upon each child's IQ; (3) *Reading Age* (RA), or level of actual achievement in reading for each child; (4) *Arithmetic Age* (AA), each child's level of actual achievement in arithmetic; (5) a comparison between each child's mental age and arithmetic age; and (6) a comparison between each child's mental age and reading age. The scores are from tests that are typically used at seventh-grade level for screening purposes. (Since the emphasis here is upon the technique for utilizing test scores in screening and not upon a discussion of specific tests, the actual tests used are not named.) The mental ages are based upon scores from a group intelligence test that yields only a verbal (language) score. Reading ages are based upon total scores from a reading survey test that measures ability in vocabulary and paragraph comprehension. Arithmetic ages are based upon total scores from a standardized arithmetic computation test.

TABLE 1

Comparisons of Chronological, Mental, Reading, and Arithmetic Ages of
Seventh-Grade Pupils

Pupil	Chrono-logical Age (CA)*	Mental Age (MA)*	Reading Age (RA)*	Arithmetic Age (AA)*	Difference Between MA and AA	Difference Between MA and RA
1	12.0	14.3	15.0	13.2	− 1.1	+ 0.9
2	11.11	15.0	15.0	13.2	− 1.10	—
3	12.5	16.1	15.0	14.8	− 1.5	− 1.1
4	12.2	14.9	15.0	13.9	− 1.0	+ 0.3
5	12.4	15.2	15.0	14.1	− 1.1	+ 0.2
6	12.0	17.1	15.0	14.2	− 2.11	− 2.1
7	12.0	14.8	15.0	14.5	− 0.3	+ 0.4
8	11.2	14.3	14.6	14.0	− 0.3	+ 0.3
9	12.1	14.8	14.6	13.7	− 1.1	− 0.2
10	11.9	16.7	14.6	14.5	− 2.2	− 2.1
11	11.6	14.0	13.9	13.9	− 0.3	− 0.3
12	12.3	13.7	13.4	14.2	+ 0.7	− 0.3
13	11.7	13.7	13.3	12.2	− 1.5	− 0.4
14	12.5	13.1	14.2	14.4	+ 1.3	+ 1.1
15	12.1	12.11	13.2	12.3	− 0.8	+ 0.3
16	11.7	12.3	12.6	13.0	+ 0.9	+ 0.3
17	11.11	12.0	12.6	14.4	+ 2.4	+ 0.6
18	12.1	11.4	12.4	12.1	+ 0.9	+ 1.0
19	12.3	11.8	12.3	12.5	+ 0.9	+ 0.7
20	12.9	12.0	11.6	11.4	− 0.8	− 0.6
21	11.7	11.7	11.3	12.3	+ 0.8	− 0.4
22	12.6	12.0	10.9	11.9	− 0.3	− 1.3
23	12.4	12.3	10.7	11.9	− 0.6	− 1.8
24	12.1	12.9	10.7	12.5	− 0.4	− 2.2
25	11.11	11.0	10.6	13.8	+ 2.8	− 0.6
26	12.6	10.8	10.4	11.1	+ 0.5	− 0.4
27	12.4	10.9	10.2	12.0	+ 1.3	− 0.7
28	12.2	10.8	10.1	10.7	− 0.1	− 0.7
29	12.0	10.6	9.9	10.6	—	− 0.9
30	13.3	10.5	9.9	11.2	+ 0.9	− 0.8
31	12.7	10.4	9.8	11.7	+ 1.3	− 0.8
32	13.2	10.6	9.5	12.8	+ 2.2	− 1.1
33	13.3	10.3	9.3	12.1	+ 1.10	− 1.0
34	12.1	9.7	9.2	11.0	+ 1.5	− 0.5
35	11.8	12.0	9.1	11.2	− 0.10	− 2.11
36	13.0	10.4	9.0	10.7	+ 0.3	− 1.4
Range	13.3–11.2	17.1–9.7	15.0–9.0	14.8–10.6		
Mean	12.2	12.9	12.8	12.8		

*All ages are in years and months.

There is a reason for including arithmetic test results in a chapter on
diagnosis of reading problems. Arithmetic computation does not require
reading ability; consequently, a measure of performance in arithmetic computation yields information regarding achievement in a basic skill area

not dependent upon reading. Such a measure can be especially useful when only a verbal intelligence score is available.

We can first examine the test results for the entire group. The mean (average) scores for the group are shown in the last row of each column on Table 1. The mean chronological age is 12.2, which is fairly typical; if each child had entered school on his sixth birthday, the mean chronological age would have been exactly 12.0 years at the beginning of seventh grade. The mean mental age is 12.9, which is not significantly greater than chronological age; the mean age would appear to indicate that this is an average group in ability. The mean performance ages in arithmetic and reading are identical at 12. (Performance age is equal to achievement grade equivalent plus five; thus, achievement at exactly the seventh-grade level would equal a performance age of 12.0.) Thus, the mean scores indicate that this is a class with mental age, achievement age in reading arithmetic, and chronological age all in virtual agreement. The implication appears to be that the group is surprisingly homogeneous and average in ability and achievement. But mean scores can be rather deceptive, as a closer examination of the group test results will reveal.

The second-to-last row of each column in Table 1 shows the range of age scores in the several columns. The chronological ages range from 13.3 to 11.2. A two-year gap in ages at grade 7 is very common; in fact, a greater gap would very often be found. The mental ages range from 17.1 to 9.7, which means that the IQ's of the pupils range from over 150 to less than 70. The reading ages range from 15.0 to 9.0. The upper limit is depressed by the fact that the particular test used has a ceiling at the tenth-grade level; that is, the norms for seventh graders do not go above grade 10. Thus, the seventh graders in the group are reading from the fourth-grade level to above the tenth-grade level. Arithmetic ages range from 14.8 to 10.6, almost as widely as the reading ages.

Table 2 (p. 108) serves to demonstrate the wide ranges in the several age scores. The picture one gets from Table 2 is rather different from the one implied by the comparison of mean ages. It seems clear that the bright pupils in the class are not achieving at their capacity level and that reading achievement tends generally to lag below the expectancy level. Comparisons of mental age with reading and with arithmetic age show that a substantial number of pupils are reading below their capacity levels. Thus, in spite of mean scores that appear to indicate that all is well, closer examination indicates that some pupils may be in need of further diagnosis. Inspection of individual scores on Table 1 is the next step.

The far right column on Table 1, which presents a comparison between mental age and reading age, contains a useful summary of information for screening purposes. An example will serve to clarify: Pupil 3 shows up in the right-hand column with a − 1.1, which appears to indicate that he is reading 1 year and 1 month below his capacity level. This is cause to examine his scores more closely. Further examination shows that the reading

TABLE 2

Frequency Distribution of Chronological, Mental, Reading, and
Arithmetic Ages of Seventh-Grade Pupils

Age in Years and Months (midpoint)	Chronological Age	Mental Age	Reading Age	Arithmetic Age
17.0		2	—	—
16.0		1	—	—
15.0		5	7	1
14.0		5	4	12
13.0	6	3	4	4
12.0	28	8	4	11
11.0	2	5	5	7
10.0		7	7	1
9.0		—	5	—

age is 15.0 which is the top of the scale for the particular reading test used; thus, it seems likely that the reading lag is due to the limitation of the test rather than to any need for corrective help in reading. The procedure, then, is to look for discrepancies in the right-hand column and to seek implications from the remaining columns. The following observations demonstrate the procedure in operation. (The procedure here is to make direct comparisons of mental age and achievement age. See Chapter 3 for alternative procedures.)

Pupil 6. The − 2.1 lag in RA would at first appear to suggest that this child is in need of remedial help. However, the reading test score is at the top limit for the test, so there is no way of telling how well Pupil 6 might have done. The − 2.11 lag in AA may indicate that this bright child (IQ above 140) is generally achieving below his potential level, although he is achieving substantially above grade level. This would not be a high priority case; but some further testing in reading would be desirable because of the limitations of the present data.

Pupil 10. This appears to be a very bright child with an IQ above 150. Both RA and AA lag more than two years below MA. The child is a disabled reader by our screening criterion (RA two or more years below MA). His achievement is good for his grade level, but he probably needs some help in refining the higher level reading skills if he is to approach his potential level of achievement.

Pupil 14. Both RA and AA are about one year above MA. It would be good to get a recheck on mental ability because the existing test score does not appear to be valid. Of course, there are those who would say that Pupil 14 is simply an overachiever and that we should rejoice at his good fortune. Such a possibility is sufficiently remote to give little cause for not getting a recheck. In practice, the teacher's judgment should be exercised in making a decision about whether another mental ability test should be given. The existing scores simply indicate that perhaps a closer look should be taken.

Pupil 22. The − 1.3 lag in RA with almost no lag in AA appears to indicate that this child would benefit from corrective instruction in reading. It will be recalled that by our criterion corrective instruction may be indicated if RA lags a year or more below MA. In this case, the child is achieving more than a year below grade level as well as mental age expectancy.

Pupil 23. The − 1.8 lag in RA appears clearly to identify this child as a corrective case in reading. Actually, he is close to being a disabled reader. Both further diagnosis and corrective or remedial teaching are needed.

Pupil 24. The − 2.2 lag in RA appears to indicate that this is a disabled reader. Achievement in arithmetic is good, so further evaluation may indicate an even greater MA-RA gap.

Pupil 32. The − 1.1 lag in RA appears to indicate a need for corrective teaching; but achievement in arithmetic is + 2.2 above the expectancy level. Thus, there is reason to suspect that the mental ability test score may have been depressed by limited reading skill. Further evaluation is needed; the child may actually need remedial help.

Pupil 33. The test data are very similar to those of Pupil 32 and similar comments are appropriate.

Pupil 35. There is a − 2.11 lag in RA and virtually no lag in AA. The pupil appears clearly to be a reading disability case.

Pupil 36. The − 1.4 lag in reading appears to indicate a need for corrective teaching; but MA is substantially below CA and AA is in virtual agreement with MA. The child's IQ, then, appears to be about 69 and the indication is that he would probably benefit most from adapted instruction in reading.

Pupils 17 and 25. Both of these pupils have AA's that are more than two years above MA. The substantial gap strongly suggests that the mental ability score may be in error. While both pupils appear to be reading at about their expectancy level, reading achievement is substantially below arithmetic achievement. Further checking is needed.

Pupils 30, 31, and 34. We have pointed out that Pupil 36 probably needs adapted instruction if he is to achieve even at his limited ability level. According to the present data, Pupils 30, 31, and 34 also appear to be in need of adapted instruction, because a comparison of their respective MA's and CA's indicate that the IQ's are between 75 and 83. In each case, however, AA is substantially higher than MA but RA is not markedly below MA. It is possible, then, that the mental ability score is in error or that the needs of these children are being adequately met in the regular classroom. Additional checking should be done before any decision is made about assigning any or all of these pupils to an adapted instructional group.

The screening procedure yields data that are useful in several ways. A few applications can be shown. First, it will be recalled that four of the thirty-six pupils in our example were to be transferred to other classrooms.

On the basis of the screening, probably Pupils 3, 6, 10, and 36 should be transferred to another classroom if conditions permit. Pupils 3, 6, and 10 have MA's substantially above those of the other pupils. If an accelerated or enriched program is available, these pupils probably should be in it. On the other hand, Pupil 36 would probably benefit most from an adapted program if there is one. Removal of these four pupils from the classroom would also reduce the extreme IQ range noted in Table 1. Second, several remedial or probable remedial cases were located. Pupils 24 and 35, and possibly 23, 32, and 33, appear to be disabled readers. Specific diagnosis is the next step for them. Finally, in a number of instances there is reason to question the present IQ's. Retesting should be done before decisions are made on the basis of invalid test results.

To some extent, the nature of the analysis of survey level data will depend upon the information sought. We have illustrated one kind of analysis for screening purposes. As the teacher looks at test data from his classes he should remember that he also has bases for making personal judgments and evaluations. Whenever possible, it is desirable to temper objective test scores with considered judgments based upon informal observations.

SPECIFIC LEVEL OF DIAGNOSIS

As we said in Chapter 3, it is not so much the particular tests used as the purpose for which they are used that separates the specific from the survey level of diagnosis. Certain tests may be given at the *survey level* for class analysis and for screening purposes and/or at the *specific level* to obtain specific information about the capacity and the performance of individuals. In the pages that follow, individual intelligence tests, formal and informal tests of performance in reading, and selected specialized tests of reading and reading-related performance are discussed. But first some observations regarding the diagnostic process are in order.

Lowery (1950), a psychiatrist, once observed that ". . . there is a danger of jumping headlong into therapy, and in recent years I have been puzzled by what seems to be a tendency to treat first, and then inquire afterwards what was the matter." The same tendency can all too frequently be observed in the area of remedial reading. Some teachers, for example, routinely begin a remedial reading sequence with the intensive teaching of word attack skills despite the fact that as often as not the real problem turns out to be lack of comprehension skills and/or study skills or, even more basic, poor motivation to read. The procedure should be to find out what *is* the matter and then to provide instruction that is relevant, not to use a favored approach first and inquire later what *was* the matter. The problem seems to be that teachers are sensitive about taking time for testing when they feel that they ought to be getting on with the business of teaching reading. The business of teaching reading can best be got on with *after* sufficient information has been gathered to permit the focusing of instruction. The purpose of specific diagnosis is to permit the focusing of instruction.

Teachers often want to know just *how specific* and *how intensive* their diagnostic work must be. Of course there is no stock answer. While it is wasteful to overcomplicate simple problems, it is unrealistic to oversimplify deep-rooted problems by proceeding as if we thought that all disabled readers respond to the same remedial procedures. The nature of the diagnosis in a given case must be dictated by the nature and degree of the disability. Early diagnosis leads to a tentative teaching program and the emerging results help to determine what additional information is needed.

Individual Intelligence Tests

At the specific level of diagnosis it is useful to have an estimate of a pupil's mental ability that is reasonably valid and reliable. Such an estimate helps the remedial teacher judge the severity of the reading disability with some confidence and, consequently, to arrive at a realistic prognosis. As we have pointed out, individual tests are generally to be preferred to group tests because scores on the latter are more likely to be adversely influenced by a child's disability in reading. It should be kept clearly in mind, however, that it is extremely difficult to separate verbal ability from general mental ability even when individual tests are used. The very factors which tend to disable a child in reading tend also to interfere with performance on most tests of general ability.

Among the most highly regarded and widely used individual intelligence tests are the *Stanford-Binet Intelligence Scale, Third Edition* (Houghton Mifflin, 1960) for ages two through adult, and the Wechsler tests (Psychological Corporation), which are available in three separate scales for preschool through adult. Each of the tests requires considerable study and practice if it is to be efficiently and effectively administered and interpreted; and examiners are typically required to have formal training and supervised practice before they use the tests. Thus, in some localities these tests have taken on an aura of mystery because they are jealously guarded as the exclusive property of certain vested interest groups, who claim that only they can be trusted to do an adequate job of administering and interpreting them. This is unfortunate, because many people become so mystified or so alienated that they do not make use of the test results. Of course we agree that people who are to make appropriate use of the tests need some special training and experience; but we see no need to bar classroom and remedial teachers who have completed the training from making direct use of the tests. Nor do we feel that teachers who have not completed the specific training are too ignorant to be given the test results when they are accompanied by a reasonable explanation.

The *Wechsler Intelligence Scale for Children* (WISC) is suitable for most children from ages five to fifteen. The test measures both verbal and non-verbal aspects of intelligence and yields Verbal, Performance, and Full Scale scores. The Verbal Scale includes subtests on Information, Comprehension, Arithmetic, Similarities, Vocabulary, and Digit Span. The subtests included in the Performance Scale are Picture Completion, Picture Arrangement, Block Design, Object Assembly, Coding, and Mazes. The *Wechsler Adult Intelligence Scale* (WAIS) is similar to the WISC and is useful with older pupils and adults. The *Wechsler Preschool and Primary Scale of Intelligence* (dubbed the WOOPSI) is also similar in format and it is intended for use with younger children, ages four to six years and five months.

Some clinicians feels that the verbal and intellectual abilities which are closely related to reading potential are more adequately sampled by the *Stanford-Binet* than by the Wechsler tests and so prefer the former in working with reading disability cases. Others feel that the *Stanford-Binet* places too much emphasis upon the language factor, thereby penalizing the poor reader. This feeling, along with the fact that the Wechslers tend to be easier to administer and to score, has led many clinicians to use the Wechslers almost exclusively. Under ideal conditions it would probably be most desirable to use both tests, supplementing a *Stanford-Binet* score with a Wechsler Performance Scale score; but it is seldom economically feasible to administer both.

The picture vocabulary tests described above on p. 103—the *Peabody Picture Vocabulary Test*, the *Full Range Picture Vocabulary Test*, the *Quick Test*, and the *VanAlstyne Picture Vocabulary Test*—are all individual tests of verbal capacity that can be useful at the specific level of diagnosis. Otto and McMenemy (1965) have reported favorably on the use of the *Quick Test* with disabled readers. They concluded that "in situations where group tests are questionable (as with poor readers), testing time is at a premium, and outside psychometric services are limited, the QT can provide some additional objectivity where objectivity might otherwise be lacking" (p. 197).

Still another picture-type test, the *Pictorial Test of Intelligence* (Houghton Mifflin), should be mentioned here. The format is similar to that of the picture vocabulary tests, in that the pupil responds to the oral questions of the examiner by attempting to select the appropriate picture from a stimulus card. The test is more than a picture vocabulary test, however, for it includes six subtests: picture, vocabulary, information and comprehension, form discrimination, similarities, size and number, and immediate recall. The range includes children between the ages of three and eight, so teachers may find the test useful with beginning readers. It has all the advantages of the picture vocabulary tests without the limitation of getting at just one facet of mental functioning. There are no time limits, but the entire battery can be administered in about forty-five minutes. An attractive feature is that the testing can be stopped at the end of any subtest and resumed at a later session as time permits. Norms are provided in the form of deviation IQ's, MA's, and percentile ranks.

Finally, another test that can be given quickly and interpreted in a reasonably straightforward manner is the *Slossen Intelligence Test* (SIT) (Slossen Educational Publications). Items included in the SIT are adapted from the Stanford-Binet and the Gesell Developmental Schedules, so they are somewhat more diverse than the items on the picture-vocabulary tests. The SIT items, which range in difficulty from infant through adult levels, deal with motor coordination, arithmetical operations, serial memory, and vocabulary. Each item is read to the pupil, who then responds verbally; thus reliance on reading is minimal. The SIT takes approximately twenty-five minutes to administer and score. After comparing pupils' performance on the *SIT*, the *Quick Test,* and the *Wechsler Intelligence Scale for Children,* Houston and Otto (1968) concluded: "Both the *SIT* and the *QT* are appropriate for preliminary screening of students with reading disabilities, and both provide a rough measure of intelligence which requires little testing time. The small savings in time of the *QT* over the *SIT,* however, would seem to be outweighed, on the basis of the present sample, by the superior reliability and concurrent (with WISC) validity of the *SIT.*"

Informal Tests of Reading Ability

Much insight into the nature of a reading problem can be gained through the use of informal tests. Such tests can be patterned after formal, standardized tests but tailored to a given program of instruction and to given instructional materials used in day-to-day teaching. Of course, informal tests have no norms; but they can aid the teacher by permitting him to focus on the reading behavior that he feels is relevant at any given time. Informal tests can be broad in scope—designed to determine overall reading achievement levels—or very specific—focused upon a single, specific skill. The term *informal* should not imply that such tests can casually be thrown together. Quite the opposite. If it is to be useful an informal test must be *interesting,* pitched to the *appropriate difficulty level,* and aimed at a *specific objective.*

A general discussion of informal testing and data gathering is given in Chapter 3. Some approaches to informal testing in reading—word lists, informal inventories, and assessment of specific skills and abilities—are discussed here.

Word Lists

Word lists are useful in informal diagnosis for three closely related reasons:

1. A pupil's ability to respond quickly to the words in a given list can reflect his sight vocabulary, which is essential to fluent reading.

2. A graded list can be used to arrive at a quick estimate of the level at which a pupil has little difficulty with word attack and can, therefore, read with comfort and fluency.

3. A pupil's basic attempts to analyze words not known as sight words can reveal basic weaknesses in word attack techniques.

A number of prepared word lists—such as the list included in the *Wide Range Achievement Test* and the lists by Dolch (1942), Durrell (1956), and Stone (1950)—are readily available and widely used. (See also Chapter 6 for other lists and suggestions for their use.) Lists of words used at the various grade levels are also found at the end of most primary-level and many intermediate-level basal readers. Teachers can easily devise their own word lists by taking systematic samples from books at various grade levels. The procedure would be to include on the list, say, the first word on the third line of every fifth page.

The latter lists are particularly useful in making quick checks to see if pupils are able to handle the vocabulary of particular books. Likewise, the teacher can estimate a pupil's word recognition ability by observing his performance with words from different grade-placement levels of difficulty and, thus, begin to determine whether the pupil can read, for example, third-, fourth-, or fifth-grade materials. Such a procedure is often the first step in administering an informal reading inventory.

Informal Reading Inventories

The general idea of the informal inventory is discussed in Chapter 3. The construction and use of informal reading inventories (IRI's) was first discussed in detail by Betts (1957, Chapter 11). Such inventories offer a number of advantages:

1. Materials commonly used in the classroom are employed, so they are readily available and inexpensive.

2. Estimates of ability levels are likely to be valid because actual teaching materials are used and the overestimates commonly obtained with standardized tests are avoided.

3. There is great flexibility because the teacher can sample the variety of skills and the difficulty levels he chooses.

Check lists of skills to be observed can be used in conjunction with the IRI to systematize the record keeping. The discussion that follows is based on views expressed by Otto and Smith (1970, pp. 129–131).

IRI's *should—must*, if they are to serve their optimum purpose—be constructed from materials actually in use in the classroom. The generally accepted and probably most straightforward procedure in preparing an IRI is to select passages from the ascending difficulty levels of a basal reader series. A sound practice is to choose selections from well within the books rather than from the beginning pages. From the preprimer through first-grade books the passages should be 100 words in length, followed by five comprehension questions; from the 2^1 to 3^2 level books the passages should be 150 words long, followed by six questions; and from books at the 4^1 level and above the passages should be 150 words long followed by eight questions. The total number of words in each passage is, of course, an approximation, for complete sentences must be given. The comprehension questions devised by the teacher should deal with (1) the literal meaning of the entire passage or parts of it, (2) meanings that are not explicitly stated but can be inferred from what is given, and (3) the meaning of individual words (vocabulary), when appropriate. In our experience the questions devised too often deal only with specific, literally stated facts. The questions should be revised on the basis of some initial try-outs.

Otto and Smith (1970) go on to state:

> The inventory is administered by having the child begin at the level where he can comfortably handle both the word-attack and comprehension tasks and continue to read through more difficult levels until he can no longer do so. He may be asked to read passages of comparable difficulty silently and orally. With the oral reading, which should be unrehearsed, the focus is upon his word attack skills; with the silent reading the focus is upon his comprehension. In oral reading, the following are noted as "errors":
>
> *Omissions.* Technically, all words left out are "omissions," but a word inadvertently skipped probably does not reflect the same sort of problem as a word refused. We are inclined to encourage teachers to use their judgment and to record an error only when they feel a child has omitted a word because he doesn't know how to tackle it.
>
> *Substitutions.* Again we are inclined to be less concerned about substitutions that make sense in context than about *confabulations,* or obvious guessing.
>
> *Mispronunciations.* These are "miscalls" and evidence of inability to attack new words.
>
> *Insertions.* These are words that are interjected as the passage is read.
>
> *Repetitions.* There is little agreement as to *whether* or *when* repetitions should be counted as errors. A child may repeat a word or phrase simply to stall for time to analyze a troublesome word. On the other hand, persistent, habitual repetitions may be evidence of a serious problem. Again, teacher judgment is probably a better guide than any arbitrary criterion regarding when to count an error.
>
> Some writers feel that there should be a third passage at each level of difficulty to be read to the pupil in order to establish the highest level at which he can respond to questions unhampered by his own ability to cope with the reading task.
>
> The following levels can be established through use of the inventory:
>
> *Independent Reading Level.* The pupil reads with about 99 percent accuracy in word attack and about 90 percent comprehension. This is the level at which he could reasonably be expected to read with virtually no help from anyone else.
>
> *Instructional Reading Level.* The pupil reads with about 95 percent accuracy and a minimum comprehension of about 70 percent. At this level he can read and comprehend with some teacher supervision and assistance.
>
> *Frustration Level.* The pupil reads with less than 90 percent word attack accuracy and less than 50 percent comprehension. At this level he can no longer function adequately. Johnson and Kress (1964) have, however, made a worthwhile

point regarding the frustration level: "If the child is ready for instruction at one level and completely frustrated at the next, there is clear-cut evidence that he has many problems to be overcome through instruction at the appropriate level. . . . If there is considerable spread between the instructional and frustration levels, there is a better chance for fairly rapid progress. There is evidence that he can continue to use his reading abilities with fair effectiveness when he meets more difficult material than that truly appropriate for instruction."

Hearing Capacity Level. This is the highest level at which the pupil can comprehend at least 70 percent of material read to him. Theoretically, it is the level at which he *could* read if he had no problems with the mechanics of reading. In fact, as often as not, the task simply reflects the pupil's effectiveness as a listener, so the hearing capacity level may turn out to be *below* his instructional level in reading. Caution should, therefore, be used in interpreting the meaning of an individual's hearing capacity level.

Informal reading inventories need not, of course, be constructed only within the context of a basal reader series. Although the gradation of the basals provides a useful format for identifying more than one level of ability, more often than not a teacher's main interest will be in finding out whether a particular person can read a specific book. In such cases the informal inventory procedure can be adapted to a single book in the following way: Select a passage of 100–150 words, formulate appropriate comprehension questions, then administer by having the pupil read the passage orally and respond to the questions; an estimate of whether the book is at his independent, instructional, or frustration level can readily be made. Such an approach, combined with judgments based upon other knowledge of individuals—i.e., interests, background, prior instruction—can help to insure not only proper matching of books and readers but also adequate comprehension of essential content.

A self-administering informal inventory can also be useful, especially at the upper elementary and secondary levels. Passages of 150 words can be marked off in any text or library book and comprehension questions provided—either inserted in the book or kept in a file. Students who know the criteria for establishing independent, instructional, and frustration levels can then determine for themselves the suitability of any book for their particular ability and purpose. If this approach to book selection can be established, there is likely to be much less frustrated plodding through too difficult or too easy materials and much more rewarding, self-motivating reading.

Assessment of Specific Skills and Abilities

Informal tests may be more useful than standardized tests when teachers seek answers to certain questions regarding a child's reading skills and abilities. A few examples of informal testing are given here.

If a remedial teacher wants to know whether a pupil can use context clues, some information can be obtained by watching to see whether the pupil makes use of context while reading orally. More direct information can be obtained by determining whether the pupil can complete from context such items as these:

The big dog was ——— loudly, but he was wagging his ———.
A big, red fire ——— came down the ———.

To differentiate between a pupil's skills in word discrimination and word analysis is important. For example, a child who has difficulty in identifying a word presented for word analysis (or simple sight recognition) may recognize the word when he is asked to select it from a group of words. To make the distinction, the teacher might select, say, four words and tell the pupil, "One of these is *dog;* point to *dog.*" In that way the teacher can determine whether the pupil is able to discriminate words better than he is able to recognize them. Formal tests often get at word discrimination skills better than word recognition skills, so an informal test can be very useful in this regard.

Teachers can also give informal sound-blending tests to assess ability to *apply* knowledge of letter sounds. They can compare a pupil's speed of oral and silent reading to see whether development of fluency in silent reading is resulting in increased speed. They can note flexibility (or the lack of it) in reading speed by comparing a pupil's reading speed at various reading levels. They can, in short, shed more light on many problems with informal techniques than with more formalized testing.

An excellent collection of suggestions for informal assessment in reading is given in *Locating and Correcting Reading Difficulties* (Ekwall, 1970). The author has identified a number of common faults—e.g., word-by-word reading, incorrect phrasing—and given suggestions for assessing the difficulty and for correcting the problem. The approach taken by Ekwall can also serve as a model for supplementary efforts by teachers.

If behavioral objectives relative to specific reading skills are stated, the objectives can serve as the basis for constructing informal, criterion-referenced tests. (See also Chapters 3 and 15 regarding behavioral objectives.) Once such objectives are stated the specific skills involved can be examined by focusing upon the behaviors called for in the statements. This is, of course, one of the main advantages offered by behavioral objectives. Additional discussion of behavioral objectives and a number of examples are given by Otto and Smith (1970, Chapter 2).

Standardized Reading Tests (Group)

Several standardized reading tests—*analytical* tests—that are useful at the specific level of diagnosis can be administered to groups and tend to be relatively easy to administer and score. In general, group analytical tests differ from survey tests in that they yield a profile of a pupil's strong and weak points in silent reading ability. The profile is typically based upon the results of subtests that sample from a variety of skill areas. Unfortunately an attempt is made in some tests to sample from so many areas in a limited time that the several subtests are too short to yield accurate information. The remedial teacher must, therefore, choose tests for specific diagnosis with caution.

A few examples of group reading tests for specific diagnosis are discussed here. No attempt is made to present a complete list.

The *Silent Reading Diagnostic Tests* (Lyons and Carnahan), devised by Bond, Clymer, and Hoyt, yield a profile of eleven subtest scores. The subtests are presented in a single test booklet and provision is made for plotting a graphic profile based upon the test data. The following subtests are included:

I. Word Recognition. Each of the fifty-four items consists of a picture and five words, one of which tells about the picture. Initial, middle, and final letter as well as reversal errors can be spotted with this test.

II. Recognition of Words in Context. There are twenty-eight "fill in the blank" type items. The correct word is chosen from five that are given.

III. Recognition of Reversible Words in Context. The test consists of a short story in which twenty-three words can be reversed.

IV. Word-Recognition Techniques: Visual Analysis—Locating Usable Elements. The thirty-six items consist of pictures and "long" words; the pupil identifies the "little" word, illustrated by the picture, within each "long" word.

V. Word-Recognition Techniques: Visual Analysis—Syllabication. The pupil divides the twenty-four polysyllabic words into syllables.

VI. Word-Recognition Techniques: Visual Analysis—Locating Root Words. There are thirty long words which contain shorter root words; the pupil circles the root.

VII. Phonetic Knowledge—General Word Elements. The examiner pronounces a word element and the pupil chooses, from five possibilities, the corresponding letter combination. There are thirty items.

VIII. Recognition of Beginning Sounds. The examiner pronounces a word and the pupil chooses a printed word that begins with the same sound. Thirty items.

IX. Rhyming Words. The pupil chooses a printed word that rhymes with a word pronounced by the examiner. Thirty items.

X. Letter Sounds. The examiner enunciates a letter sound and the pupil chooses, from a group of four, the letter that stands for the sound. Thirty items.

XI. Word Synthesis. The test measures ability to blend parts of a word into a whole. Short paragraphs are so printed that certain words are divided after the initial consonant or syllable. The pupil must blend the parts correctly in order to be able to answer comprehension questions based upon the paragraphs.

The *Silent Reading Diagnostic Tests* can be used by the classroom teacher without extensive clinical training. Administration is uncomplicated and the scoring procedure is straightforward. Two types of diagnostic scores can be derived from the subtests: scores in word recognition (sight recognition); and scores in word-analysis (word-attack) techniques. The tests are intended for use in grades 3 through 6, but they are useful with disabled readers through senior high school. The general limitations of the tests are typical for group analytical tests: they are not designed for use with extreme disability cases and there is no provision for oral reading. Specific limitations of the tests are: they are rather laborious to administer; scoring tends to be time consuming; and if the profile is to be completed according to the manual, achievement tests by Bond, Clymer, and Hoyt must be administered.

Another group test that is widely used for specific diagnosis is the *Stanford Diagnostic Reading Test, Level I* for grades 2.5 to 4.5, and *Level II,* for grades 4.5 to 8.5 (Harcourt). The test yields scores for comprehension, vocabulary, and rate as well as for syllabication, auditory skills, and phonic analysis. While these scores can be useful, additional checking is usually required to complete the tentative picture that this battery of subtests yields.

The *Doren Diagnostic Reading Test* (American Guidance Service) measures mastery of word recognition skills. It can be administered to groups; it requires no special training for administration and scoring; and it yields specific information regarding pupils' word recognition skills. Subtests sample skills in the following areas: letter recognition (manuscript and cursive), beginning sounds, whole-word recognition, words within words, speech consonants, ending sounds, blending, rhyming, vowels, sight words, and discriminate guessing (use of context clues). The test can be used at any grade level when a thorough analysis of word recognition difficulties is desired. No attempt is made to examine comprehension difficulties. The lack of norms has been criticized, but the manual explains that the test is designed to assess *mastery* of certain skills and that, therefore, there is no need for norms.

The *McCullough Word Analysis Tests* (Ginn), for grades 4-8, include subtests of the following skills: initial consonant clusters, comparing vowel sounds, matching symbols with vowel sounds, identifying phonetic spellings, using a pronunciation key, syllabication, and finding root words. Harris (1970) says, "These are practical, useful tests of reasonable length" (p. 162).

The *Diagnostic Reading Tests* (Committee on Diagnostic Reading Tests) include, in addition to *Survey Sections* at several levels, separate tests of a number of reading skills. In the diagnostic battery for grades 7-13, for example, there are eight tests available: vocabulary, silent reading comprehension, auditory comprehension (listening), general rate, rate in social studies materials, rate in science materials, oral word attack, and silent word attack. There are two forms, A and B, for each part. The tests for grades 7-13 are the *Higher Level* tests; there are also tests for grades 4-6, *Lower Level,* and for kindergarten through grade 4.

When Tests A and B are used together, the *Iowa Every-Pupil Test of Basic Skills* (Houghton Mifflin) can be useful for specific diagnosis in reading. The tests are available for grades 3-5, *Elementary,* and grades 5-9, *Advanced.* Test A, *Silent Reading Comprehension,* measures vocabulary and paragraph comprehension. Test B, *Work-Study Skills,* covers such skills as map reading and use of indexes, references, and the dictionary. In addition to the reading tests, two other tests are included in the battery: Test C, *Basic Language*

Skills; and Test D, *Basic Arithmetic Skills.* Four forms—L, M, N, and O—are available for each test. Taken as a battery, the tests can be useful when an assessment of performance in the several basic skill areas is needed.

The *Comprehensive Tests of Basic Skills* (California Test Bureau) are available at four levels: *Level 1,* for grades 2.5-4; *Level 2,* for grades 4-6; *Level 3,* for grades 6-8; and *Level 4,* for grades 8-12. Subtests of vocabulary, comprehension, and certain study skills are included.

Some other widely used tests that yield part scores that can be useful for specific diagnosis are: the *Iowa Silent Reading Tests, New Edition* (Harcourt), *Elementary* for grades 4-8, and *Advanced* for high school and college, which include tests of rate, comprehension, vocabulary, sentence and paragraph meaning, and locating information; the *Iowa Tests of Basic Skills* (Houghton Mifflin) for grades 3-8, which include five major areas—vocabulary, reading comprehension, language skills, work-study skills, and arithmetic skills; and the *New Developmental Reading Tests* (Lyons and Carnahan), *Primary,* for grades 1-3, and *Intermediate,* for grades 4-6, which include tests of vocabulary, reading for information, reading to discover relationships, and reading appreciation.

Standardized Reading Tests (Individual)

While certain diagnostic information can be obtained quite efficiently through the use of group tests, severe disability cases usually demand extensive and detailed analyses that are best pursued on an individual basis. And, of course, oral reading performance must be examined individually. Selected oral tests and comprehensive tests of reading skill development are discussed here.

Oral Reading Tests

Certain inadequacies in reading, such as word recognition and phrasing difficulties, are revealed most clearly in oral reading. The typical oral reading test consists of a series of short paragraphs of increasing difficulty. As a pupil reads the increasingly difficult material, the examiner has an opportunity to observe methods of word attack, fluency, and phrasing. The examiner, then, can note the kinds of errors made on a record form. Analysis of oral reading performance can yield much diagnostic information about a pupil's method of word attack: whether he has an adequate sight vocabulary; whether he has a method of attacking unknown words; whether he tends to overanalyze unknown words; whether he uses context clues; etc. The examiner also has an opportunity to note faulty reading habits such as word substitutions, omissions of letters and words, lack of phrasing, disregard for punctuation, and repetition of words and phrases.

The *Gilmore Oral Reading Test, New Edition* (Harcourt) is a good example of a standardized test of oral reading. The test consists of ten paragraphs of increasing difficulty, which are designed to provide a means for analyzing the oral reading performance of pupils in grades 1 through 8; but the test can be profitably used with disabled readers in higher grades. The paragraphs are printed on heavy cardboard and are spiral bound, a paragraph to a page, into a booklet that presents a continuing story as the pupil progresses from one difficulty level to the next. Separate record booklets are available and they provide a convenient form on which the examiner can record errors, reading time, and answers to comprehension questions. The manual explains a method of noting several types of errors: substitutions, mispronunciations, words pronounced by the examiner, disregard of punctuation, insertions, hesitations, repetitions, and omissions. There are norms for accuracy, comprehension, and rate of oral reading. The test is very useful and it can serve as a model for teachers who want to devise informal oral tests of their own. Forms A and B from the original edition are still available and new Forms C and D were added in 1968. A limitation to be considered is the fact that comprehension is tested after *oral* reading. This, we feel, is generally not a defensible procedure.

Other standardized oral tests tend to be rather similar in form to the *Gilmore Oral*. The *Gray Standardized Oral Reading Paragraphs Test* has been very popular since it was first published in 1926. The test consists of twelve paragraphs of increasing difficulty for use with children in grades 1 through 8. A revision of the test was published in 1963 under the title *Gray Oral Reading Test* (Bobbs-Merrill). The revision includes thirteen paragraphs which, according to the manual, provide an objective measure of growth in oral reading from early first grade through college. The revision is a significant one that has made a very widely used and respected test even more useful. The revised test is available in four forms, all similar in length, organization, and difficulty. Grade-equivalent scores are based upon both reading time and number of errors. The *Gray Standardized Oral Reading Check Tests* (Bobbs-Merrill), too, continue to be popular and useful. They are available at four levels—Set I, for grades 1 and 2; Set II, for grades 2-4; Set III, for grades 4-6; and Set IV for grades 6-8—in five equivalent forms at each level. The tests are well suited for the longitudinal follow-up or oral reading skill development. The *Durrell Analysis of Reading Difficulty*, the *Gates-McKillop Reading Diagnostic Tests*, and the Spache *Diagnostic Reading Scales*—each of which is described in the discussion section that follows—include oral reading tests as part of the overall batteries.

Comprehensive Tests of Skill Development

In instances of severe reading disability, comprehensive testing of a variety of skills may be required before a tentative remedial sequence can be planned. Several tests are available for broad sampling of reading behavior.

The *Durrell Analysis of Reading Difficulty* (Harcourt) is designed for use with pupils at the nonreading through sixth grade reading ability levels; it can be profitably used with severely disabled readers at the junior high school level and above. The test is rather complex, so the teacher who uses it should be thoroughly familiar with the procedure for administration and experienced in interpreting the results. Typically, it takes an hour or more to administer the test to one child. An Individual Record Blank, to be used with each pupil who takes the test, provides space for recording such things as background information, tentative remedial plans, and a profile of test performance, as well as check lists of difficulties observed during the testing. It should be clearly understood that the check lists of errors are in many ways more important than the norms for the test. Despite the fact that Durrell points this out in the *Manual of Directions,* many teachers seem to get so bogged down in converting raw scores to grade equivalents and the like that they lose sight of the really valuable information that is recorded on the check lists.

The following subtests are included in the *Durrell Analysis:*

1. *Oral Reading.*   Eight paragraphs of increasing difficulty are included. A check list for recording errors and behavioral symptoms while reading is provided, but grade norms are based upon time required to read the several paragraphs. Probably it would be more meaningful to base the norms upon accuracy rather than upon rate. Comprehension questions are provided for each paragraph.

2. *Silent Reading.*   Eight paragraphs, parallel to the oral, are included in the silent reading test. As the pupil completes each paragraph he is asked to tell everything he can remember from the story. Grade norms are based upon reading time and memory scores. Because the silent and oral test paragraphs are parallel, a pupil's difficulties with silent reading can be compared directly to his difficulties with oral reading.

3. *Listening Comprehension.*   Eight paragraphs of the same difficulty levels as the paragraphs comprising the two preceding tests are used. The purpose of the test is to determine reading capacity, the highest level at which a child can comprehend material that is read to him. Such a test is extremely useful for prognostic purposes because it helps to define the level at which a child could operate if his reading disability were removed.

4. *Word Recognition and Word Analysis.*   Lists of words printed on cardboard strips are used with a cardboard tachistoscopic device that permits flash presentation. Word recognition is tested by one-second exposure of the words; when the pupil misses a word he is given an opportunity to analyze it. Difficulties in word recognition and word analysis can be recorded on a check list that is provided.

5. *Naming Letters—Identifying Letters Named—Matching Letters—Writing Letters* (optional).   These tests are provided for the nonreader or for any pupil who is suspected of having difficulty with letters.

6. *Visual Memory of Words—Primary/Intermediate.*   In the primary test the pupil is shown a letter or word for 2 to 3 seconds; when the stimulus is covered, he is asked to mark it from memory in the record book. In the intermediate test the pupil is asked to write the word from memory.

7. *Auditory Analysis.* Several types of tests are included here: *Hearing Sounds in Words-Primary; Learning to Hear Sounds in Words* (to determine the severity of difficulty exhibited in the preceding test); and *Sounds of Letters* (to discover which letter sounds and blends are not known). The tests are reserved for pupils whose reading level is below grade 3.

8. *Learning Rate.* The test is designed to determine the degree of difficulty a pupil has in remembering words that have been taught. The test is given to nonreaders or preprimer readers. The procedure is to teach the pupil a list of words and then to check recall after 20 minutes or more of interpolated activity.

9. Additional tests: *Phonic Spelling of Words; Spelling Test; Handwriting.* These tests are designed mainly to provide samples of performance in the above areas.

The subtests of the *Durrell Analysis* sample from a number of skill areas that are essential for adequate progress in reading. As a whole, the test is generally adequate for the specific diagnosis of all but the most severe reading difficulties. The complete test kit contains spiral-bound testing material, a very useful examiner's manual, individual record sheets, and a tachistoscopic device.

The *Gates-McKillop Reading Diagnostic Tests* (Teachers College Press), which comprise a battery that is generally similar to the *Durrell Analysis,* include the following subtests.

1. *Oral Reading.* The test consists of seven paragraphs of increasing difficulty, ranging roughly from second- to eighth-grade level. Errors are recorded for each paragraph and suggestions and norms are provided to assist in the diagnostic interpretation of a child's performance. Elimination of norms for assessing speed of reading from the present revision is an improvement; the test does not appear to be an appropriate basis for estimating reading speed, as was suggested on the older form.

2. *Words: Flash Presentation.* Two columns of twenty words each are used in this test; in each column the progression is from short, easy words to longer, more difficult words (i.e., from "so" to "superstition"). The examiner uses a hand tachistoscope (a card with a rectangular opening) to expose each word for about one-half second. Incorrect responses are recorded in order that they may be examined later for significant and consistent errors.

3. *Words: Untimed Presentation.* The test is similar to the flash presentation test except that the child is encouraged to take all the time he needs to figure out each word. A total of eighty words is provided to give the examiner ample opportunity to observe the methods a child employs in working out the recognition and pronunciation of words.

4. *Phrases: Flash Presentation.* The test is similar to the *Words: Flash Presentation* test except that more than one word is presented. Twenty-six phrases—ranging in difficulty from "a boy" to "park your car here"—are used.

5. *Knowledge of Word Parts: Word Attack.* Four subtests are employed to assess knowledge of word parts.

(a) Recognizing and Blending Common Word Parts: Nonsense words (e.g.,

"drite," "frable," "brome") are used to test a child's ability to blend commonly occurring word parts into wholes. Twenty-three nonsense words are presented. If a child fails to pronounce the "word," it is broken into its component syllables and he is then asked to blend them together (e.g., slidge: sl—idge—: slidge).

(b) Giving Letter Sounds: Lower-case letters are presented to the child and he is asked to "tell what the letter says."

(c) Naming Capital Letters: Naming Lower-Case Letters: These last two tests simply measure a child's ability to name individual letters; only the most severely disabled readers need to be tested.

6. *Recognizing the Visual Form of Sounds.* Four subtests are employed to assess ability to associate sounds with their visual (word or letter) equivalents.

(a) Nonsense Words: In this test the examiner enunciates a nonsense word (e.g., "tabe") and the child is asked to circle its visual equivalent in a row of four (e.g., "tode," "tabe," "kib," "bate") nonsense words.

(b) Initial Letters: The examiner enunciates a word (e.g., "luscious") and the child is asked to pick its initial letter from a list of five letters.

(c) Final Letters: The child is asked to pick the final letter of a word enunciated by the examiner from a list of five letters.

(d) Vowels: The examiner enunciates a short nonsense word with a vowel sound in the middle (i.e., "keb," "kine") and the child is asked to identify the vowel that "makes the sound."

7. *Auditory Blending.* The examiner enunciates fifteen words part by part. The child is asked to listen to the parts of each word and then to "tell what the word is" (e.g., f—ire—crac—ker: firecracker).

8. *Supplementary Tests.* Four supplementary tests are included with the battery. They may be used if certain information is lacking or when evidence has been turned up by previous subtests that some further checking is needed.

(a) Spelling: The child is asked to spell orally the forty words from the flash presentation list. The examiner records the child's method of attacking the spelling. For instance, the child may spell letter by letter or he may use phonetic elements (e.g., c—a—n or c—an).

(b) Oral Vocabulary: The manual suggests that this test be used in the absence of the *Stanford-Binet* oral vocabulary test. It is also pointed out that the test is not very reliable for children of average or lower ability in the lower three grades.

(c) Syllabication: The child is asked to divide a number of nonsense words into commonly occurring syllable units. The test measures ability to recognize syllables when they occur in combinations that do not make up meaningful words.

(d) Auditory Discrimination: The examiner enunciates a pair of words ("do"—"to") and the child is asked whether they are the same or different.

No norms are given; analysis of the child's errors indicates those sounds between which the child fails to distinguish.

The *Gates-McKillop* is, in our opinion, the most complete battery for specific diagnosis that is readily available. The complete testing kit, which includes two equivalent forms, contains spiral-bound testing material, pupil record blanks, an examiner's manual, and tachistoscopic cards. The examiner's manual includes helpful references to remedial techniques that can be used to attack difficulties identified through the use of the tests.

Teachers who expect to use the *Gates-McKillop* should be thoroughly familiar with the sequence and procedures for administration and scoring. The test is not designed for casual use even by experienced remedial teachers; it is sufficiently complicated and involved to demand a fairly high degree of sophistication from the examiner if it is to be used optimally. The *Gates-McKillop* probably should be reserved for pupils who are very severely disabled in reading and other tests should be used with less severe cases; judiciously used it is an excellent test, but there is little point in overtesting when the need is not apparent.

A third comprehensive test of reading skill development that has proved to be extremely useful is the Spache *Diagnostic Reading Scales* (California Test Bureau). The battery, which is similar in format to both the Gates-McKillop tests and the Durrell analysis, includes three word recognition lists, twenty-two reading passages of graduated difficulty, and six supplementary phonics tests. The examiner's manual states that the *Scales* have three main purposes: to estimate the pupil's instructional reading level; to reveal the pupil's method of attack and analysis; and to evaluate the pupil's sight vocabulary. We feel that each of these purposes is reasonably fulfilled. Harris (1970) has, however, made a pertinent observation: "Spache considers 85 per cent comprehension desirable for the instructional level, but 60 per cent is his minimum for independent reading level. Most reading authorities use quite different standards for comparison; a minimum of 70 per cent for instructional level and 85 to 90 per cent for independent level" (P. 186).

Remedial teachers will find it useful to be familiar with all three tests, whether they expect to use them routinely or not, because, taken together, they cover a wide variety of specific skills. In practice, selected subtests from any or all of the batteries will probably be used more frequently than an entire battery. The subtests relevant in a particular case can be given as needed. The subtests can also serve as models for teachers who wish to construct informal skill tests of their own.

Two other tests that may be useful at the specific level are the *Standardized Reading Inventory* (Pioneer Printing) and the *Botel Reading Inventory* (Follett). The former is, essentially, a formalized informal reading inventory that can be used to establish frustration, instructional, and independent reading levels. The latter includes phonics mastery, word opposites (essentially a vocabulary test), and word recognition tests that are intended to determine instructional levels of pupils. The Botel inventory can, with the exception of the word recognition subtest, be administered to groups, which enhances its appeal for the busy teacher. Neither test yields the specific information that is required in order to plan intensive remedial instruction.

Specialized Tests

Several tests of reading and reading-related abilities that have gained some degree of acceptance do not clearly fall under any of the categories discussed up to this point. They are grouped here for discussion purposes, not because they share any common focus or function but simply because they are used and we feel they merit some comment.

The *Wisconsin Tests of Reading Skill Development: Word Attack* (National Computer Systems), developed at the Wisconsin Research and Development Center for Cognitive Learning. The University of Wisconsin, Madison, comprise a battery of tests, each of which focuses on a specific word-attack skill. The tests are available at four levels of difficulty (A, B, C, and D) to assess thirty-eight word-attack skills commonly taught at the kindergarten through third-grade levels. The individual tests are short, usually fifteen items, but they have demonstrated reliability at acceptable levels, generally in the .80's. Each test is available bound in a booklet by level in a machine-scorable form or singly in hand-scorable form. The tests can help teachers to focus on the specific skill development strengths and weaknesses of individuals. The tests are criterion—rather than norm—referenced, the expectation being demonstration of mastery by correct responses to at least 80 percent of the items on any given test.

The *Learning Methods Test* (Mills) is designed to aid teachers in determining individual student's ability to learn new words under four different procedures: (1) the *visual* method, where word recognition is taught by stressing the visual appearance of words; (2) the *phonic* or *auditory* method, where stress is placed upon sound qualities; (3) the *kinesthetic* or *tracing* method, where the Fernald method (see Chapter 7) is employed; and (4) the *combined* method, where equal stress is placed upon the visual, auditory, and kinesthetic approaches. The aim is to identify the method by which an individual learns new words most efficiently. The procedure is very simple: ten words are taught to the subject by each of the four methods, one set of words on each of four consecutive days. A delayed recall test is given the day after each training session and a mean "delayed recall" score is computed by summing all correct responses and dividing by four. Any score for a particular method that deviates substantially from the mean in a positive direction is assumed to be the best method for the individual. In practice, many individuals will attain score patterns that do not differentiate among methods; then the assumption is that there is very little difference in learning efficiency under the different procedures. The test has high "face" or "content" validity—the test directly samples the behavior of interest—and the reliability is reported to be high (Mills, 1964). We feel that although the predictive validity of the test needs to be demonstrated it serves as a source for tentative hypotheses regarding approaches to teaching.

The *Marianne Frostig Developmental Test of Visual Perception* (Follett) has found favor with some reading teachers. The test was constructed to assess childrens' ability in each of five areas of visual perception which are believed by Frostig to be most relevant to school performance. The five subtests assess pupils' ability in *eye-hand coordination, figure-ground discrimination, form constancy, position in space,* and *spatial relationships.* Subsequent research has shown that certain of the subtest scores are related to reading performance, but not more substantially than readiness test scores or scores from other visual-motor tests. There is a related *Frostig Program for the Development of Visual Perception* (Follett) that is designed to provide practice in the five perceptual areas. After reviewing the research evaluations of the Frostig Program, Myers and Hammill (1969), reached this charitable conclusion: "In summary, assessments of the Frostig-Horne training program differ, rendering additional research necessary in order to conclusively establish its efficacy. At present, the reactions of educators and researchers who have used the program vary widely regarding the effect of such training on the development of basic academic skills" (P. 250). Others—notably Cohen (1969)—have not been so charitable. Rosen (1966), on the basis of a careful, large-scale study, reported that the Frostig training had some effect on the behaviors measured by her tests but no effect on reading performance.

The *Bender Visual-Motor Gestalt Test* (Psychological Corporation), which is an ostensible measure of childrens' visual motor development, is used by some psychologists to gain insight into mental development and language ability. The test comprises nine designs that are copied by the subject. The drawings are then judged for distortion, rotation, perseveration, and other factors. In our opinion the results obtained are not sufficiently definitive to recommend the test very highly to reading teachers.

The *Harris Tests of Lateral Dominance, Third Edition* (Psychological Corporation) are a set of tests of hand, eye, and foot dominance. Harris (1970, pp. 236–246) feels that lateral dominance—or, more properly, lack of it—is sufficiently related to success in reading to merit examination, particularly in cases of disability in reading. He feels that directional confusion, as revealed by the Harris tests, is most closely associated with reading problems. A number of studies have shown no such relationship, but the fact is that the studies tend to be based on too few observations or to have other serious limitations. Harris presents the case convincingly enough to justify spending the small amount of time required to check for directional confusion.

The *Illinois Test of Psycholinguistic Abilities* (ITPA) (University of Illinois Press), now available in a 1968 *Revised Edition,* is used in some circles for language evaluation. The ITPA comprises ten subtests and two supplementary subtests: Auditory Reception, Visual Reception, Auditory Association, Visual Association, Verbal Expression, Manual Expression, Grammatic Closure, Visual Closure, Auditory Sequential Memory, Visual Sequential Memory, Auditory Closure, and Sound Blending. The norms permit an examiner to derive both psycholinguistic age equivalents and scaled scores, which serve as referents in judging a child's performance in any of the twelve abilities tested. The test permits broad examination of intra-individual differences in the psycholinguistic functions tapped by the several subtests. At the present time, however, there is only limited definitive evidence to show that training a child in the abilities assessed by ITPA will result in improved performance in reading. The approach is reasonably promising, however, and additional work ought to, and undoubtedly will, be done.

Finally, deHirsch, Jansky, and Langford (1966) have reported on their work in developing a battery of tests for use in predicting reading failure. While the approach is promising and clearly appealing to people who are concerned about reading failure, the authors themselves have termed their work as "preliminary in nature." The deHirsch battery clearly needs more work before it will take a place among the tests that are unequivocally useful to the remedial teacher.

INTENSIVE DIAGNOSIS IN READING

Intensive diagnosis typically is reserved for children whose severe reading disabilities appear to be complicated by physical and/or psychological problems that stand in the way of successful remedial teaching. Thus, in most cases the remedial teacher will move to the intensive level of diagnosis only after a number of carefully planned remedial sessions have failed to yield results. For this reason, the practice of putting down a tentative diagnosis, prognosis, and proposed treatment (see Chapter 4) is a sound one because it provides a framework of expectation. That is, the teacher makes judgments about the rate and degree of progress expected when specific instruction is provided; then, if the progress is not forthcoming, there is good reason to go on to seek underlying causes for the disability at the intensive level.

A general orientation to intensive diagnosis is given in Chapter 3; and a vehicle for implementing intensive diagnosis, the case analysis, is described in Chapter 4. As we have described it, diagnostic testing—of ability, general achievement, and specific abilities and disabilities—is done at the specific level of diagnosis. Usually the specific information gathered provides the teacher with all the data he needs to devise a successful sequence of remedial teaching. But when such specific efforts fail to produce results, then there is need for a closer look, for consultation with other specialists, for careful analysis of experiential and developmental background. In short, the teacher turns from the relatively straightforward procedure of dealing with specific gaps in skill development to a more intensive attempt to uncover causes for the gaps.

THOUGHTS FOR DISCUSSION

"I sometimes think the most important service we could achieve is somehow to get every test-user or interpreter to take a good hard look at the test whose score he is proposing to use or interpret. A good hard look means a look inside the test book at the tasks and items, not just at the title on the cover. A diagnostic test of poetry reading looks less exciting when scrutiny shows it to be a highly analytic test of the meaning of words and phrases in a single poem. A good hard look means a look at the manual and the test norms. A difference of half a grade in the grade norms for a test somehow shrinks back to proportion when it is seen as just two more items answered correctly and when the standard error of measurement is seen to be three raw score points." (Thorndike, 1969)

"Obviously, even the best tests and the best testing methods will not guarantee that all children will do well on tests, and therefore, the primary source of public resentment against testing will remain. Perhaps the only real answer to the whole argument over testing is to improve education for all children. 'You won't eliminate educational problems by doing away with the tests or even by changing them,' Thorndike replies to the critics. 'If nothing else, testing makes us face our educational problems. It keeps us from thinking that maybe if we don't look at them, they'll just go away.' " (Pine, 1969, p. 4)

"Too many teachers think that they must depend upon test results. It is better to select a few reliable instruments that the teacher can interpret and apply than to administer many tests whose results are poorly interpreted and used unwisely. Many teachers underestimate the diagnostic possibilities of their day-by-day contacts with students. Many do not realize that they themselves are the most important influence on students' reading achievement." (Strang, 1969, p. 43)

"The diagnosis and evaluation of student reading abilities should be continuous and contiguous with classroom instruction. This means that classroom teachers need to develop techniques they can apply as part of their daily reading instruction." (Farr, 1970, p. 167)

"Diagnostic teaching is the technique of teaching each child the specific skills he has not mastered but must know before he can progress in the sequence to more difficult learning." (Zintz, 1970, p. 523)

". . . on the basis of present data, I would play the visual perceptual game if I were in the visual perception or the IQ business. But in the reading field, the surest way to get urban ghetto kids to read is to teach them letters and words and to do it thoroughly." (Cohen, 1969, p. 503)

"If learning disordered children formed a homogeneous group, all reflecting the same types of problems in learning, both diagnosis and remediation would be immeasurably simpler. Unfortunately, children with specific learning disabilities exhibit all of the variation found in unaffected children as well as a variety of problems in learning, some of which are related to the vocal symbol system, some to the graphic system, and others to the subtle and pervasive elements of learning subsumed under such categories as attention and memory." (Myers and Hammill, 1969, p. 67)

"Unless we select students for the special reading program carefully, we may dissipate our time and energy and neglect those who can most profit from instruction." (Schell and Burns, 1968, p. 113)

REFERENCES

Austin, M. C., Bush, L., and Huebner, H. *Reading evaluation, appraisal techniques for school and classroom.* New York: Ronald Press, 1961.

Betts, E. A. *Foundations of reading instruction.* New York: American Book, 1957.

Bond, G. L., and Tinker, M. A. *Reading difficulties: Their diagnosis and correction.* New York: Appleton-Century-Crofts, 1967.

Buros, O. K. (Ed.) *The sixth mental measurements yearbook.* Highland Park, N.J.: Gryphon Press, 1965.

Buros, O. K. (Ed.) *Tests in print.* Highland Park, N.J.: Gryphon Press, 1961.

Chall, J. S. Interpretation of the results of standardized reading tests. In R. Farr (Ed.), *Measurement and Evaluation of Reading.* New York: Harcourt, 1970.

Cohen, A. S. Studies in visual perception and reading in disadvantaged children. *Journal of Learning Disabilities,* 1969, **2,** 498–503.

deHirsch, K., Jansky, J.J., and Langford, W. S. *Predicting reading failure: A preliminary study.* New York: Harper and Row, 1966.

Della-Piana, Gabriel M. *Reading diagnosis and prescription: An introduction.* New York: Holt, 1968.

Dolch, E. W. *The basic sight word test.* Champaign, Ill.: Garrard, 1942.

Durrell, D. *Improving reading instruction.* Yonkers, N.Y.: World Book, 1956.

Ekwall, Eldon E. *Locating and correcting reading difficulties.* Columbus, Ohio: Charles E. Merrill, 1970.

Farr, R. (Ed.) *Measurement and evaluation of reading.* New York: Harcourt, 1970.

Farr, R., and Summers, E. G. *Guide to tests and measuring instruments for reading.* Bloomington, Ind.: ERIC/Clearinghouse on Reading, 1968.

Harris, A. J. *How to increase reading ability.* (5th ed.) New York: David McKay, 1970.

Houston, C., and Otto, W. Poor readers' functioning on the WISC, Slossen Intelligence Test and Quick Test. *Journal of Educational Research,* 1968, **62**, 157–159.

Johnson, M. S., and Kress, R. A. Individual reading inventories. In *Sociological and Psychological Factors in Reading,* Twenty-first Annual Reading Institute, Temple University, 1964, pp. 48–60.

Kottmeyer, W. *Teacher's guide for remedial reading.* St. Louis: Webster, 1959.

Lowery, L. G. Training in the field of orthopsychiatry. *American Journal of Orthopsychiatry,* 1950, **20**, 667.

Lyman, H. B. Talking test scores. *Measurement News* (Official Newsletter of the National Council on Measurement in Education), 1970, **13** (3). (pages not numbered)

Mills, Robert E. *The teaching of word recognition.* (Rev. ed.) Fort Lauderdale: The Mills Center, 1964.

Myers, P. I., and Hammill, D. D. *Methods for learning disorders.* New York: Wiley, 1969.

Otto, W., and McMenemy, R. A. An appraisal of the Ammons Quick Test in a remedial reading program. *Journal of Educational Measurement,* 1965, **2**, 193–198. (Also in W. Otto, and K. Koenke (Eds.), *Remedial teaching: Research and comment.* Boston: Houghton Mifflin, 1969, pp. 112–116.)

Otto, W., and Smith, R. J. *Administering the school reading program.* Boston: Houghton Mifflin, 1970.

Pine, P. What's the IQ of the IQ test? *American Education,* 1969, **1** (9), 2–4.

Rosen, C. L. An experimental study of visual perceptual training and reading achievement in first grade. *Perceptual and Motor Skills,* 1966, **22**, 979–986.

Schell, L. M., and Burns, P. C. (Eds.) *Remedial reading: An anthology of sources.* Boston: Allyn and Bacon, 1968.

Spache, G. D. Estimating reading capacity. In H. M. Robinson (Ed.), *The evaluation of reading.* Supplementary Educational Monographs, No. 88. Chicago: University of Chicago Press, 1958.

Stone, G. R. *Progress in primary reading.* St. Louis: Webster, 1950.

Strang, R. *Diagnostic teaching of reading.* New York: McGraw-Hill, 1969.

Thorndike, R. L. Helping teachers use tests. *Measurement in Education* (A series of special reports of the National Council on Measurement in Education), 1969, **1** (1). (pages not numbered)

Zintz, M. V. *The reading process.* Dubuque, Iowa: William C. Brown, 1970.

Chapter 6

Remedial Reading: An Overview

The purpose of Chapter 6 is to give an overview of the nature of reading and to offer some broad suggestions for providing corrective and remedial reading instruction that teaches attitudes and concepts as well as skills. There are various philosophies regarding remedial reading instruction and various approaches to improving reading ability. Our ideas and suggestions are only one point of view. However, the philosophy and the teaching practices that are recommended in the present chapter are derived not only from our personal teaching experiences but also from the experiences of other teachers whose ideas we have incorporated into our discussion. In the present chapter we have emphasized and discussed explicitly aspects of remedial reading that are less prominent and more implicit in similar discussions.

We are most concerned in Chapter 6 with establishing a conceptual framework within which corrective and remedial reading teachers may plan and implement the variety of instructional approaches that are required to meet the many different needs of disabled readers. Although Chapter 6 does offer some definite suggestions for teaching disabled readers, the suggestions are offered primarily to illustrate practical applications of theoretical or philosophical positions.

READING AND READING INSTRUCTION

Moffett (1968b) has expressed succinctly and well the reason for learning to read: "Symbol systems are not primarily about themselves; they are about other subjects. When a student 'learns' one of these systems he 'learns how' to operate it. The main point is to think and talk about other things by means of this system" (p. 6). Obviously, reading instruction which falls short of enabling pupils to use reading "to think and talk about other things" is a failure. The objective of corrective and remedial reading instruction is the improvement of pupils' reading ability to a level that enables them to use reading for functional and recreational purposes. This does not mean that unless disabled readers can become highly sophisticated readers, they should not be given special instruction. Reading ability is like most other human abilities in that some people outperform others. In itself reading has little value, but as a source of information and pleasure it has few if any equals. The reading teacher should strive to make his pupils "readers" in the fullest sense of the word. To lose sight of this ultimate objective is to run the risk of teaching a symbol system as a goal in itself and to evaluate success in terms of completed exercises rather than in terms of personally enriching experiences.

Pupils' attitudes toward reading are a major concern in any remedial teaching that has life betterment through reading as its objective. Pupils who can but will not read are no better served by print than those who cannot. Students for whom skill development is difficult will tend to develop negative attitudes toward the object of their distress. Therefore, skill development and attitude development must be taught simultaneously and with equal devotion. Consequently, the teacher of corrective and remedial reading must be a superior teacher of attitudes as well as a superior teacher of skills. Moffett (1968a) says:

> Conventionally . . . poor readers whose problems go beyond decoding . . . are made to undergo the sort of dull, mechanical course that actually requires the 'most' motivation, confidence and maturity to get through. They submit to 'practice readers,' 'word study' workbooks, 'skill builders,' 'spellers,' and so on. Remediation that consists of relentless drills and comprehension questions is based on a false assumption that the underlying problems are reading problems, whereas the problems are ones that 'manifest' themselves in reading as elsewhere. For these children reading should be more, not less, fun than for others. (P. 112)

The teacher's concept of reading will strongly influence the nature of the reading instruction he offers, and this in turn will determine the concept of reading developed by the student. Gans (1967) comments, "When I go into a group, I realize first of all that I carry something in. I reflect what I think reading means" (p. 65). Unless both teacher and pupil understand that their goal is the utilization of reading for personal enrichment of one kind or another, it is unlikely that this goal will be reached. Too often remedial reading instruction deteriorates to an artificial kind of operation that reinforces the pupil's notion of reading as a series of meaningless encounters with words rather than reading as a flow of ideas and feelings.

The following excerpts from a remedial reading teacher's progress report for one of her pupils illustrates how instruction and learning can become poorly focused because of the teacher's, and hence the pupil's, lack of a clear conception of the objective of remedial reading instruction.

Student: William
Grade: 6.4
Classroom teacher: Mrs. Johnson
I. Q. (WISC): Performance 108, Verbal 88, Full Scale 100
Gilmore Oral Paragraphs (Accuracy): Grade 3.2
Stanford Diagnostic Test, Level II, grade equivalent for Reading Comprehension
   Total: 3.0

Brief description of classroom work

From the middle of second grade, William's teachers reported a lack of interest in reading and an inability to master phonics. He has always had difficulty with medial vowels, blending and syllabication. Except for a short time in the first grade, William was consistently placed with the low reading group although he was considerably brighter than most of the students in that group and appeared to be bored with the progress of the group. In the basal series used, William was always working about two years below grade level with difficulty. He has had some success with supplementary reading materials, especially the *Science Research Associates Reading Laboratory* where he averaged about 80 percent comprehension with easy selections.

Brief description of the home situation

Both of William's parents have worked since he entered school. He is often in the care of an older sister who reportedly is herself a poor reader. She and William spend a great deal of time watching television together and the primary topic of conversation in the home is favorite family television programs. Both of William's parents are concerned with their children's poor reading and are pleased that William is receiving special help, a service not available to their daughter. William's father is an assembly line worker at a local factory, and William's mother is a tailor's helper in a local department store. There appears to be no financial difficulty. The home has a set of encyclopedias and a newspaper is received every day. The *Reader's Digest* is also purchased regularly.

Interpretation of diagnostic findings

The Gilmore Oral Paragraphs revealed a preponderance of mispronunciations, hesitations and substitutions. This suggests an inability to attack words phonetically, a finding that is in accord with the observations of his classroom teachers. Obviously, William needs to learn how to relate letters to sounds and blend these sounds to produce words. His performance on the Stanford Diagnostic Comprehension Sub-test indicates that at the same time he needs to improve his comprehension skills by answering questions about selections at his reading ability level. He also needs much motivation to learn to read, which means that he needs many success experiences with reading.

Brief description and evaluation of remedial program

William has been receiving remedial reading instruction three times a week for approximately four months. During this time the focus of the remedial teaching has been upon helping him to attack words in a systematic way. Various word games have been employed to motivate William to use both phonic and contextual analysis skills to attack unfamiliar words. Special attention has been given to medial vowels and word endings. Exercises from several different workbooks have been used regularly for instructional and evaluative purposes. Easy selections from an *SRA Reading Laboratory* have also been used regularly to improve William's comprehension and to give him success experiences with reading comprehension exercises. He was also given help in finding a library book about horses (his stated interest), and he is being encouraged to discuss the book in his remedial reading class and at home.

There is some evidence that William is making slow but steady progress. He is doing much better on the workbook exercises and occasionally gets 100 percent on an SRA exercise. He is only on page 48 in his library book but insists that he is enjoying it and doesn't want to change it. It is understandable that he is only on page 48 as he still has difficulty in applying word-attack skills when he reads from a book. His teacher reports that his attitude is somewhat improved and that he answers questions about stories and completes his seatwork much better and faster than he did before remedial instruction was started. It is still difficult for William to read, but a retest with the Gilmore Oral Paragraphs indicates he is improving (grade 3.8). William still watches too much television at home, but his parents have agreed to send him to bed earlier so that he will be more alert at school the next day. William's success with the work he is doing seems to be improving his self-concept and increasing his motivation to improve his reading.

William's self-concept may be improving, but it is doubtful that his concept of reading is improving. Obviously, some change in William's behavior has occurred. However, the change does not appear to be in the direction of using reading for truly self-satisfying purposes, but rather for the extrinsic rewards that accompany the completion of developmental exercises. William and his teacher have yet to begin their major task—the discovery of reading to satisfy personal needs. Unfortunately, both seem so satisfied with their path they may fail to realize that it doesn't lead where they want to go. Eventually the enthusiasm of William and his teacher may wane in the realization that William's "progress" is for all practical purposes of little value to him. If this happens, each may feel betrayed by the other. And just as the battle was lost for want of a nail, so William's chance to be a reader will have been lost for want of a proper concept of reading and reading instruction. Remedial instruction must never become so occupied with the various components of reading that the actual nature of reading is obscured.

READING AS A COGNITIVE AND AFFECTIVE EXPERIENCE

Often the two purposes of information getting and enjoyment are both served during the reading act. However, depending upon the specific reading activity, one may be more directly sought and obtained than the other. For example, a pupil who studies a history book to find the causes of the American Revolutionary War is searching first of all for information which he will use to satisfy some cognitive need. However, in the process of getting this knowledge he will in all likelihood experience certain attitudinal changes, value adjustments, and other affective responses. At another time this same pupil may be reading a historical novel of the American Revolutionary War purely for recreational purposes. However, he will undoubtedly respond cognitively as well as affectively to the ideas he encounters. He will comprehend them, analyze them, apply them, and perhaps evaluate them, all in the pursuit of his primary purpose of reading for pleasure. The interdependence of the cognitive and affective domains requires that reading evoke behaviors in both. Combs and Snygg (1959) say, ". . . no behavior can ever be purely intellectual or emotional. . . . We cannot separate intellectual from feeling functions" (p. 235).

Krathwol, Bloom, and Masia (1964) have discussed the interaction between the cognitive and affective domains for instructional purposes as follows:

> Some of the more interesting relationships between the cognitive and affective domains (and some of the clearer indications of the interrelatedness of the two domains) are those in which the attainment of a goal or objective of one domain is viewed as the means to the attainment of a goal or objective in the other. In some instances we use changes in the cognitive domain as a means to make changes in the affective; e.g., we give the student information intended to change his attitude. In other instances we use an affective goal as a means to achieve a cognitive one; e.g., we develop an interest in material so the student will learn to use it. (P. 54)

Of particular interest to corrective and remedial reading teachers is the following observation by Krathwohl, et al. (1964) regarding curricula which seek to develop attitudes and cognitive skills simultaneously:

> In some instances the joint seeking of affective and cognitive goals results in curricula which use one domain as the means to the other on a closely-knit alternating basis. Thus a cognitive skill is built and then used in rewarding situations so that affective interest in the tasks is built up to permit the next cognitive task to be achieved, and so on. (P. 60)

The job of the remedial teacher is to teach reading to children for whom reading is a difficult and sometimes threatening task more to be avoided than sought. Consequently, special attention must be given to the child's affective development as well as his cognitive development. Too often remedial reading instruction focuses so intently on word attack or other cognitive skills in need of development that the child never experiences reading as a means to an end but rather as an end in itself. Word attack and word-calling are not reading. Unless remedial reading instruction produces pupils who do successfully use reading to satisfy cognitive and affective needs, which might be otherwise expressed as using reading for information and pleasure, the instructional process is certainly wasteful and perhaps harmful. Johnson and Kress (1969) have pointedly observed that, "A reader is one who reads." The difference between knowing how to read and being a reader is substantial. The remedial reading teacher must always be keenly aware of the difference.

THE ROLE OF THE READER

Background Experiences

Jennings (1965) has commented that, "What we are and what we are living through at a particular time reworks what we read and makes it a unique experience fraught with new meanings that we never suspected" (p. 139). Anyone who has observed people discussing something they have read in common must be impressed with the different interpretations each reader takes from the same selection. What a reader "takes" from a selection depends in large measure upon what he "brings" to the selection. This is so because reading is an activity which involves the reader as a unique personality with an author's message. Reading, then, is a cognitive and affective process that cannot be considered apart from the existing cognitive and affective development of the person doing the reading. Macdonald (1965) talks about "the person in the curriculum," and Otto and Smith (1970, p. 5) talk about "the person in the reading program." We are talking here about what might be called "the person in the reading selection."

Teachers are aware of the effect of background experience on pupils' reading and usually attempt to provide their students with the experiential background that is needed for a correct and satisfying interpretation of a particular reading selection. Most teachers are also aware of the need to permit pupils some individual interpretations with material that is not completely factual. With some selections, the most satisfying personal experiences are the result of creative thinking relative to an idea or ideas. Russell (1961) tells of a fourth grader who once remarked, "I like stories that mean more than they mean" (p. 454). Reading, then, is an active interaction between an author and a reader. For a productive interaction to occur, it is essential for the reader to have a background of experience that allows him to know what the author is saying and in some instances to go beyond what the author has said. The message of a particular piece of writing lies not only in the writing itself but also in the behavior of the reader. Jennings (1965) says, "The same piece of writing may be read at many different levels, regardless of the author's obvious intent" (p. 138).

A book that has been a favorite of students for many years is *The Yearling* by Marjorie Kinnan Rawlings (1938). Early in the novel the main character is described as follows: "He moved a stone that was matching its corners against his sharp ribs and burrowed a little, hollowing himself a nest for his hips and shoulders. He stretched out one arm and laid his head on it. A shaft of sunlight, warm and thin like a light patchwork quilt, lay across his body." During a class discussion of the chapter in which this quotation is found, a pupil of ours said, "You know, I did that once; and when I read about it I could remember how it felt." For that child, this short passage triggered a very private series of associations and reflections. For other pupils, reading that passage was obviously a much less profound personal experience. Johnson (1956) says, "Reading is something we do, not so much with our eyes, as such, as with our knowledge and interests and enthusiasms, our hatreds and fondnesses and fears, our evaluations in all their forms and aspects" (p. 123).

If the effects of reading are dependent upon the reader's condition at the time of reading, then the teaching of reading must include readying the student to interpret and respond to ideas we want him to experience. From this point of view a reading readiness program cannot be pressed into several workbooks, some experience charts, and a book of "stories children love to hear." Rather, reading readiness must be concerned with the child's total development as a person in addition to selected instructional readiness activities. And readiness should not be thought of only as instruction which precedes initial formal reading instruction. Developing readiness for reading is necessary at every academic level and is a factor in the effect any given reading selection will have on an individual regardless of how much previous reading instruction he has received. In this sense, the individualization of reading instruction is a matter of bringing pupils to reading selections for which they are presently "ready" and, therefore, from which they can derive worthwhile cognitive and affective experiences. Unfortunately, remedial reading instruction too often ignores the readiness of a child as a total personality. When this happens, the instruction amounts to little more than laboriously getting pupils through practice exercises. And although the students may become more proficient with the exercises they are assigned, there is no assurance that they are in fact becoming readers or, for that matter, are developing a proper concept of reading.

Concept of Reading

We have referred throughout the present chapter to the importance of providing disabled readers with a proper concept of reading. We have also placed considerable importance on the teacher's concept of reading because so much of a child's concept is learned from his teacher. The home is another potent force in the development of a child's concept of reading. Regarding the importance of school and home "models" in the formation of a child's reading concept Johnson and Kress (1969) have commented as follows:

> It certainly is a strong desire of most teachers and parents that children read widely. However, these same adults seem to work actively as well as passively, *against* the actualization of this goal. . . . Much in the way of recognition of the importance of reading could be gained by the child's seeing his teachers and parents absorbed in reading which had nothing to do with school work, father's business, or the running of the house. Having to wait occasionally for the next lesson to begin because the teacher was stealing a few minutes to read (not that lesson) might be a fine experience for many children. (P. 594)

Johnson (1956) says, ". . . a fondness for reading is something that a child acquires in much the same way as he catches a cold—by being effectively exposed to someone who already has it" (p. 123).

The models presented by his classmates are also important to the development of a child's concept of reading. The child who is receiving remedial reading instruction is likely to have experienced his classroom instruction as a member of the poorest reading group. Consequently, in his exposure to other student readers he has probably been more impressed with the laborious nature of reading than with reading as a flow of meaningful ideas and feelings. Therefore, he needs most of all to be oriented to reading as an idea-getting and pleasure-getting enterprise rather than an adventure in attacking words.

Downing (1969) studied the research on young children's thinking and drew up a list of conclusions which seem especially pertinent to reading instruction that is concerned with concept development as well as skill development. The following four conclusions from Downing's list of five may be especially helpful to the remedial reading teacher who must work with children who have a distorted notion of the nature of reading as well as skill deficiencies:

1. Children's thoughts about reading, their notions or conceptions of its purpose and nature, present the most fundamental and significant problems for the teacher of reading.

. . . .

3. The very different logic of young children causes two serious difficulties in teaching them to read and write.

    a. They have difficulty in understanding the *purpose* of the written form of their language.

    b. They cannot readily handle the *abstract* technical terms used by teachers in talking about written or spoken language.

4. Teaching formal rules (e.g. of phonics or grammar) for their thinking (a) is unnecessary and (b) may cause long term reading difficulties.

5. It is vitally important to provide rich and individually relevant language experiences and activities which (a) *orientate* children correctly to *the real purposes* of reading and writing, and (b) enable children's natural thinking processes to *generate understanding of the technical concepts of language.* (P. 217)

THE READING PROCESS

For instructional purposes reading may be conceptualized as a hierarchy of three complex behaviors: (1) translation-comprehension, (2) organization-internalization, and (3) utilization. We feel that these three behaviors, although hierarchical, should be a part of nearly every reading experience a child has from his initial reading instruction. We are aware that certain instructional reading approaches separate these different stages with no apparent detriment to most pupils. On the other hand, we have observed that many children with reading problems lack a proper understanding of reading as an enjoyable meaning-getting process. Therefore, we feel it is especially important for remedial teaching to emphasize that reading is for getting ideas and enjoyment. In too many cases the poor reader is seldom, if ever, lifted above word-attack exercises and, consequently, he never grasps the real reasons for reading. Needless to say, it is important that the teacher also have a proper perspective of reading. Although translation-comprehension is the first step in the reading act, organization-internalization and utilization must also be considered basic components if reading is being conceptualized as a thinking process.

Translation—Comprehension

Although translation and comprehension could be discussed as separate processes, we have chosen to combine them. Our rationale for this combination is that we believe the first stage in reading is the establishment of "meaningful" relationships between the written language and the spoken language. To discuss the process of making letter-sound relationships apart from getting meaning from those relationships would in our judgment unwisely depart from the position that reading is not a symbol system, but rather the operation of that system to get meaning. The understanding of this position and its implications for instructional materials and practices is critical to the kind of reading instruction we advocate. Reading instruction that does not keep the making of letter-sound relationships in close relation to the comprehension of ideas is, we feel, dangerous to the successful reading growth of some children. Individual words that are sounded out or analyzed in some other way should be taken from *meaningful* sentences and after they are analyzed discussed in their contexts. The emphasis should always be upon getting and reacting to ideas in print, not analyzing individual words. Lefevre (1964) contends that misapprehending the relationship between the spoken and the written language is the most decisive element in reading failure. Whether the misapprehension Lefevre refers to is or is not the "most" decisive element in reading failure is debatable and depends upon one's interpretation of Lefevre's contention. There is little doubt, however, that misapprehension of the relationship between the spoken and written language is a factor in some reading disability cases. And remedial reading instruction for these cases that does not closely integrate translation and comprehension may cause the reading disorders to persist and even worsen. A major task of the remedial teacher is the construction of sentences and paragraphs that are meaningful, interesting, and useful for teaching word analysis skills so that students can have thoughtful reading experiences and interesting reading-related activities at the same time they learn word analysis skills.

As was pointed out earlier, some instructional approaches stress the separation of translation and comprehension during the initial stages of formal reading instruction; and these approaches have been used successfully to teach many children to read. Although we do not favor these approaches, we do not strongly oppose their use with pupils who do not have learning disabilities. Nor do we object to teaching translation of letters to sound without major concern for comprehension as initial remedial instruction for children who have certain severe reading disabilities. We do feel strongly that for most pupils who are in need of remedial instruction, translation and comprehension should be closely integrated at all times.

Most teachers have encountered "word-callers" who decode print by making accurate letter-sound associations, but who fail to obtain meaning from their efforts. The problem is often the pupils' lack of insight regarding the entire relationship between writing and speaking. For these students "reading" often remains at the word-attack stage. They in fact do not know the potential reading has for getting ideas and pleasure. Niensted (1969) comments on her observations of children who have mastered the translation stage of reading but who have not progressed beyond it as follows:

> Too many students have cracked the symbol-sound code and yet remained reading cripples. Although they read so someone else could understand the message, they themselves fail to understand what they read either orally or silently. For instance, after pronouncing, 'The cat sat on a mat,' a first grader drew a picture of the cat and the mat widely separated. Certainly the words had meaning for him or he could not have pictured the cat or the mat; but the sentence had no meaning. A fifth grader read a paragraph correctly and answered the question, 'What did you read?' with 'I don't know.' A seventh grader answered the question, 'How fast did the boat go?' with 'It didn't say,' although it plainly did. Obviously, cracking the code had not allowed these children to attach meaning to what they read aloud. (P. 112)

It is not difficult to find children who give proof of their ability to translate letters to sounds by good oral reading performances but learn little and enjoy nothing from their silent reading. To comprehend a written message the reader must do more than react to the individual words that constitute the message. The concept of the whole as being equal to the sum of its parts is not true for reading as it is for mathematics. In reading, the whole is greater than the sum of its parts.

To comprehend a reading selection the reader must organize his reading in a way that places the ideas in the selection in their proper relationship to each other. Thorndike (1917) says, "In correct reading (1) each word produces a correct meaning, (2) each such element of meaning is given a correct weight in comparison with the other, and (3) the resulting ideas are examined and validated to make sure that they satisfy the mental set or adjustment or purpose for whose sake the reading was done" (p. 326). Two elements, then, must be interfused for comprehension: the particular structure or organization of the material being read and the cognitive structure provided by the reader.

Establishing letter-sound relationships is the base which makes reading for meaning and pleasure possible. However, in itself making letter-sound relationships is not reading and, therefore, must be kept in perspective by both teacher and student. The teacher must understand certain linguistic principles so that instruction can proceed according to the nature of the English language and the psychological processes necessary to translate it to its equivalent in sound. The following five principles are basic to a proper concept of reading as a thinking process.

1. The English language is basically a systematic arrangement of meaningful sounds.

2. English writing exists for the purpose of recording and preserving those sounds.

3. English spelling is a system for recording sounds as they combine to form words. Words may carry meaning individually but usually carry meaning only as they combine in sentences. The sentence, therefore, is the basic unit of meaning in the English language.

4. English grammar is a system for combining words in meaningful sentence patterns.

5. To extract meaning from writing, the reader must decode the recorded sentences in terms of an oral language background common to him and the writer. The ability to extract meaning from print, then, depends not only upon the ability to decode the spelling system but also upon previous oral language experience with the grammar employed by the writer.

Translation-comprehension is the basic reading process whereby the encoded message of an author is communicated to a reader by means of associating meaningful symbols arranged in meaningful patterns with meaningful oral language experience. The object of the process is to extract sentences, not words, from print because ideas are embedded in sentences, not words.

Many disabled readers have not experienced reading as an idea-getting process. Vernon (1958) notes:

> . . . almost the only fact which appears clearly at the first sight is the heterogeneity of cases of reading disability—heterogeneous both in the origin and in the nature of their disability. But there does seem to be one fairly universal characteristic of the disability, namely, the child's general state of doubt and confusion as to the relationship between the printed shapes of words, their sounds and their meanings. This confusion resembles that of a young child who is just beginning to read (P. 186).

Remedial reading teachers must strive to overcome this confusion by helping disabled readers to discover reading first of all as the translation of a printed message to an idea that would mean the same if it were spoken to them.

Organization—Internalization

When a printed message has been translated to meaningful sound in the mind of a reader, the idea of the message must be incorporated into the reader's existing cognitive structure. Regarding this process, Ausubel (1964) says, "Subject matter can at best have logical or potential meaning. Potential meaning becomes converted into actual meaning when a 'particular' individual, employing a meaningful learning set, incorporates a potentially meaningful proposition or unit of information within his cognitive structure" (p. 223). The integration of new ideas within an existing cognitive structure gives new dimensions to the reader's previous cognitive structure and in fact a new structure emerges.

In keeping with the discussion earlier in this chapter regarding the interrelationship between the cognitive and affective domains, we have borrowed the term *internalization* as delineated by Krathwohl, et. al. (1964) to describe the affective behavior that accompanies the cognitive process of organizing an idea:

> The process of internalization . . . begins when the attention of the student is captured by some phenomenon, characteristic, or value. As he pays attention to the phenomenon, characteristic, or value, he differentiates it from the others present in the perceptual field. With differentiation comes a seeking out of the phenomenon as he gradually attaches emotional significance to it and comes to value it. As the process unfolds he relates this phenomenon to other phenomena to which he responds that also have value. This responding is sufficiently frequent so that he comes to react regularly, almost automatically to it and to other things like it. Finally the values are interrelated in a structure or view of the world, which he brings as a "set" to new problems. (P. 33)

Organization

According to our delineation of the reading process, organization is essentially a matter of establishing ideational relationships. Using the *Taxonomy of Educational Objectives* (Bloom, Engelhart, Furst, Hill, and Krathwohl, 1956) as a reference point, we would place organization at all levels above the first level of "Comprehension." According to Bloom et al., the first level of comprehension is the lowest level of understanding. "It refers to a type of understanding or apprehension such that the individual knows what is being communicated and can make use of the material or idea being communicated without necessarily relating it to other material or seeing its fullest implications" (P. 204). Since we combined this first level of comprehension with the translation of letters to sounds and presented "translation-comprehension" as the first stage in the reading process, we shall discuss "organization" as the higher-level thinking behaviors that follow the translation-comprehension stage. These higher-level behaviors include analyzing the extracted ideas, applying them in different situations or circumstances, evaluating them, or creating new ideas relative to them.

It is the organization of ideas encountered in print that develops the reader's cognitive structure and enlarges the understanding he has of his world with its myriad interrelationships. Teaching pupils who have difficulty mastering the translation-comprehension stage to organize their reading requires skillful teaching. The primary requirements for the teacher are a knowledge of the reader's experiential background, a knowledge of the material being read, and good questioning techniques that bring the two together. The time required for pupils receiving remedial instruction to organize their reading is often substantial. However, if remedial reading instruction is to improve pupils' reading ability to a level that enables them to use reading to enrich their personal lives, the process of organization must figure prominently in the instruction.

Internalization

The affective counterpart of cognitive organzation is internalization which, as we pointed out earlier, is a term we have borrowed from Krath-wohl, et. al. Essentially, internalization is a process of incorporating an individual's affective response to a newly perceived phenomenon into his existing value system. In regard to remedial reading instruction the objectives are (1) to help pupils perceive reading as having potential for shaping their values and (2) to help them perceive reading as a potentially aesthetic experience. Arnstine (1964) defines an aesthetic experience as follows:

> Aesthetic experience, or experience considered in its aesthetic dimension, will . . . be taken to mean any experience had by an individual which fulfills, minimally, the following two conditions. First, the experience is taken to be valuable on its own account. Whether or not the experience is instrumental to the attainment of other experiences, it is felt to be satisfying, fulfilling in itself. . . . Second, the experience is marked by the arousal of affect (or emotion) as a result of the individual's having perceived some formal articulation and integration of the elements of which the cue for that experience is composed. Combining these conditions, we may say that when an individual is undergoing a terminal (in-trinsically valuable) experience marked by the appearance of affect cued by his perception of a formal pattern within the occasion for that experience, then his experience may be described as aesthetic. (P. 243)

The concept of reading as an aesthetic experience that is internalized and thereby shapes the reader's total value system is an important one for the remedial teacher. Instructional objectives, materials, and practices will all depend heavily on the importance the teacher attaches to internalization as a product of reading experiences. We have observed many teachers doing corrective and remedial work who rely solely on extrinsic motivation to keep pupils reading. The typical motivation is some kind of reward given for the number of questions answered correctly following a reading experi-ence. The reward given for correct answers may be an approving remark, recognition on a chart or bulletin board, a letter or number grade, candy, toys, and even money. Unfortunately, in too many instances the only rewards a child gets for reading are of this "extrinsic" nature. Rarely or never does he come to value a reading experience because of an "intrinsic" satisfaction. For poor readers, reading too often becomes a game of "please the teacher" or "answer the questions and win a prize." And when the prizes stop so does the reading. The desired products of reading instruction are pupils

who use reading to enrich their lives. Obviously, students will read volun-
tarily and without extrinsic rewards only if they learn to value reading as
an enriching activity that is intrinsically rewarding. This is not to say that
extrinsic rewards have no place in remedial instruction. It would be naive
to dispense with all extrinsic rewards for motivating problem readers. Before a horse can quench his thirst he must be led to water. The point here
is that students must enjoy reading as an aesthetic experience before the job
of the remedial teacher is finished. Internalization is as important to the
objectives of reading instruction as translation-comprehension and organization. We believe that master teachers will conduct their instructional sessions so that even children for whom reading is difficult will learn that
reading can change personal values and can be intrinsically satisfying.

Utilization

The difference between knowing how to read and reading is decisive in
terms of the potential reading has for personal growth. It is unfortunate,
but true, that many pupils who have well-developed reading skills are seldom
if ever inspired by the literature they read in school. For these pupils the
teaching of literature has been a failure either because of the students' lack
of readiness or the nature of the teaching. The same is true of remedial
reading instruction. A pupil who completes his assigned exercises, answers
the correct number of questions about reading selections at specified difficulty levels, and is stamped as "sufficiently improved to resume developmental instruction" is not necessarily a reader. As a matter of fact, we have
known children who concluded their special reading instruction and were
less inclined to read than they were before they received special help. Obviously, their special help was more harmful than helpful to the attainment
of the desired objectives.

Pupils who are not learning to read according to their intellectual poten-
tials are identified and given special instruction so that they can make
better use of reading in their daily lives. Yet, in the business of remediation
it is not unusual for teacher and pupil to lose sight of reading for functional and recreational purposes because of the intense concentration needed
to develop specific skills. To maintain a proper perspective of instructional
objectives, remedial teachers and their pupils must be ever mindful of
the many utilitarian purposes which can be satisfied through reading. The
following lists of functional and recreational reading purposes are by no
means exhaustive. They are representative of the many utilitarian purposes
for improving reading ability.

FUNCTIONAL READING PURPOSES (in school)

to understand what is asked for in a math problem
to follow the sequence of a science experiment
to see the cause-effect relationships of historical happenings

to understand a question on a teacher's test
to understand a question on a standardized test
to detect subtlety in a poem
to gain a general impression from an essay
to interpret the constitution of a club
to learn the new cheer that has been printed up and distributed before the big game
to learn the school song that is printed and given to all new students
to follow directions for registering to use the tennis courts
to read the pamphlets distributed by the guidance office
to read a report to the class of a project done independently
to report on current events in the newspaper
to participate in choral reading for the Christmas program
to read training rules for school athletes
to draw a picture about a story as one part of a group reading project
to find the dates of the Civil War
to find the names of some famous black scientists
to find out what siestas are and why they are popular with Latin Americans

FUNCTIONAL READING PURPOSES (out of school)

to read a menu in a restaurant
to follow directions for assembling or operating a Christmas present
to read the note left by some member of the family
to follow a recipe
to interpret signs for automobile drivers and pedestrians
to read the advertisement that came in the mail
to interpret the questions in the driver's test
to find who is advertising to give puppies a good home
to follow the map to a new friend's house
to read the instructions for operating the automatic washer and dryer
to learn the regulations for use of the YMCA swimming pool
to read a blueprint
to follow instructions for using a popular car wax
to learn the fishing regulations for inland lakes
to find a number in the phone book
to order from a catalogue
to learn the new regulations for newspaper carriers
to read the instructions left by a neighbor for a Saturday cleaning job
to learn the material of an article of clothing on a shopping trip
to read the "caution" message on a dangerous product

RECREATIONAL READING PURPOSES

to pass the time on a bus, train, or plane trip
to improve morale with some "words of wisdom" after a difficult day
to enjoy the Sunday comics
to follow the careers of favorite sports figures
to play games with road signs on a family auto trip
to empathize with people who write letters to Ann Landers
to compare the different features of the new model automobiles

to take "shopping trips" through the catalogue
to learn the scenes and characterizations from the program at a play
to learn the background of a musical rendition from the concert program
to escape from the world in a novel
to find relief from a particular burden as someone else did
to enjoy descriptions of characters or places that are familiar
to read a part for the school play auditions
to enjoy a crossword puzzle
to learn the name of an actor from the list of credits after a TV show
to read the subtitles in a foreign film
to enjoy the cleverness of some billboard advertisements
to appreciate the messages on greeting cards
to ease the strain of a wait in the dentist's office

The line separating functional from recreational reading purposes is not entirely clear-cut. However, the ultimate objective of all reading purposes is the same: the improvement of a person's well-being through reading. It is crucial to the success or failure of remedial instruction that this ultimate objective does not become lost in the more immediate objectives of sounding out words, proper phrasing, and answering comprehension questions after each selection.

In a questionnaire survey Weingarten (1954) found that nearly two-thirds of 1,256 college students thought that reading had changed their attitudes, stimulated them to imitate the characters portrayed, and helped them to find their ideal self and develop some of the personal qualities they had read about. And nearly everyone can cite numerous acquaintances who use reading to make their livings, pursue their vocations, and guide them in the various responsibilities of citizenship in a democratic society. Reading, then, is an activity that extends deeply into human development. It is the responsibility of remedial teachers to effect that extension as part of their instructional programs.

REMEDIAL READING INSTRUCTION

The Teacher

Herrick (Macdonald, Anderson, and May), wrote: "The most important educational experience happening to a student is his teacher" (p. 68). And Harris (1970) says, "The most important characteristic of a good remedial teacher is a real liking for children" (p. 284). We concur with these observations. A pupil with learning problems needs above all a teacher who understands his needs and is responsive to them. We have known teachers who were extremely knowledgeable about curriculum theory, diagnostic tests and procedures, instructional materials, and other components of remedial instruction, but who were unsuccessful in their attempts to improve the reading ability of disabled readers. While their academic qualifications were excellent, they were personally not well suited for teaching disabled readers.

There is little doubt that at least a portion of poor readers' improvement in remedial situations is attributable to the special attention they receive from accepting, sympathetic, and optimistic adults. Learning, especially for those who have experienced failure, requires emotional support as well as intellectual exercises. The personality projected by the teacher sometimes causes students to attempt tasks they were previously unwilling to try, and to be successful with them. A teacher who sincerely believes in the value of reading projects this belief to students and thereby motivates them to learn. In addition, a child's self-concept is extremely important to his academic improvement, and his self-concept can be built through the personal relationships that occur between himself and his teacher. All in all, the contribution of the teacher as a person to the improvement of disabled readers cannot be overemphasized.

Although the teacher's personality is a major factor in the success of remedial reading instruction, remedial teaching is much more than a personality game. Remedial teaching includes careful diagnosis, assignment of appropriate instructional materials, skillful questioning techniques, frequent assessments of skill development, and numerous other specialized instructional practices. Remedial teachers should be cautious about relying too heavily on their personalities for stimulating student achievement. It is easy for some teachers who are highly personable in their work with pupils to let remedial reading sessions become "gab fests" or pseudo-psychotherapy sessions. Teachers and students often receive considerable ego-gratification from these meetings and perceive them to be truly helpful. Unfortunately, when this happens, the true objectives of remedial reading training are forgotten and both teacher and pupil become progressively more reluctant to get to the business of reading improvement.

Instructional Materials

It is unfortunate that some teachers permit instructional materials to pre-empt them from center stage in their instructional programs. In fact, some teachers have relegated themselves to being little more than record-keepers who move mechanically through various self-correcting exercises. The instructional materials trap is easily fallen into. Pupils are initially attracted to the nicely packaged competitive games, exercises, and devices. And while the novelty and appeal of one product is diminishing, others are being marketed. In addition, the ostensibly self-motivating and self-correcting features of certain materials give the impression that the teacher who employs them is able to teach many more pupils than the teacher who does not. And finally, students do often improve their performance with these materials, as improvement is measured by the accompanying tests and exercises. Unfortunately, the improvement does not always transfer to the pupils' performance with functional and recreational materials. Consequently, the remedial program that depends too much upon developmental instructional materials must often be judged a failure in terms of the program's objectives regardless of how successful the program appears in terms of students' improved performance with certain materials.

Despite the limitations of developmental instructional materials, they are helpful to the remedial reading teacher. They can be used to motivate reluctant pupils to try reading, to help the teacher teach specific skills, and to provide helpful practice exercises. However, to be maximally effective with remedial readers the materials must be accompanied by large amounts of pupil-teacher interaction. Pupil-teacher interaction can set the purpose for using the materials, evaluate the effectiveness of specific materials, and transfer the skills that were practiced with the materials to relevant and interesting functional and recreational materials. We have found that a little pupil-teacher interaction with study-type or recreational reading matter is more helpful to the attainment of the ultimate objective of remedial instruction than many completed practice exercises in materials designed expressly to teach reading skills. Pauk (1968) says:

> With the prodigious outpouring of techniques and methods, gadgets and gimmicks of reading, it is small wonder that having become so engrossed with the nuts and bolts of our profession we seldom lift our eyes to the horizon to see where we are going. . . . It is true that we need the nuts and bolts to carry on, but perhaps we teachers of reading have placed too much faith in the powers of our own techniques which we think will automatically open wide the doors of learning. The fallacy may be that we view the best techniques as ends rather than means for learning. (P. 507)

The increased production of instructional materials to be used with poor readers in no way decreases the need for skillful teaching. Remedial reading instruction that does not go beyond the "nuts and bolts" is not good instruction.

Going beyond the nuts and bolts means getting students reading about things that are meaningful to them. Johnson and Kress (1969) point out that one learns to read by reading. They say, ". . . reexamination of reading instructional programs per se is certainly indicated. For how much actual reading do they provide? Only by reading extensively will the child become a facile reader. Learning about reading or learning how to read may not be either learning to read or the path to becoming a reader" (p. 706). Obviously, seriously disabled readers cannot read "extensively" until their level of improvement permits. But functional and recreational reading experiences should be a major part of every student's remedial program as soon as his ability permits. Teachers need to have faith in the act of reading itself to develop vocabulary, comprehension, and rate skills. This approach demands, of course, truly interesting material that the student is able to read with a minimum of teacher help.

Prereading Preparation

The preparation a student receives prior to reading an assigned selection is as important to his reading growth as the help he receives after reading. As a matter of fact, most poor readers need considerable help before they read if they are to have productive reading experiences.

Disabled readers should not be asked to read a selection "cold." They usually need some background information for what they will read, some preparation for certain vocabulary words, and some help with setting reading purposes. For prereading preparation to be maximally effective the teacher must have read carefully the selection he is assigning. The prereading structure provided by the teacher must be skillfully planned to help students get the author's message and to emphasize the development of specific reading skills at the same time.

Postreading Discussion

Having read an interesting selection students should have an opportunity to communicate orally with another person about the ideas and feelings they have experienced as a result of the reading. The remedial teacher is probably in the best position to help the student discuss his reading experience and in so doing help him learn much about reading. We feel that postreading discussions with students about selections they have read is a major function of the remedial teacher. A list of questions with several options from which to select the best answer will not suffice. The child needs to talk and the teacher needs to respond. Perhaps the best test of a remedial teacher is his ability to structure good postreading discussions. A good remedial teacher is skillful at eliciting responses from the student and in reacting to the student's comments. These dialogues are useful for diagnostic, teaching, and evaluation purposes. As is true of prereading instruction, for postreading instruction to be maximally effective the teacher must have read what he and the student are discussing. We do not endorse hurried conferences between a student and a teacher who is poorly prepared to discuss a particular selection. Nor do we in most cases endorse assignments that require disabled readers to write more than two or three sentences about a selection they have read. Poor readers are usually poorer writers, and the prospect of a writing assignment to be completed after reading a selection is enough to defeat most poor readers before they begin.

A Sample Program

Earlier in the present chapter we presented excerpts from a remedial reading teacher's progress report for one of her students. We think the following excerpts from a different teacher's report for one of his students provides an illustration of a remedial reading program consistent with the philosophy we advocate.

Student: Davy
Grade: 5.3
Classroom teacher: Mr. Kenton
I. Q. (WISC): Performance 104, Verbal 86, Full Scale 93
Gilmore Oral Paragraphs (Accuracy): Grade 4.0
Stanford Diagnostic Test, Level II, grade equivalent for Reading Comprehension
    Total: 3.0

Brief description of classroom work

Davy's oral reading performance is characterized by repetitions, omissions, and substitutions. His silent reading comprehension is so poor that he is rarely able to discuss orally or in writing anything he has read. However, he participates eagerly in class discussions and in projects that do not require him to read and often makes a significant contribution. When he is given a reading assignment in any subject matter area or a library book to read he fidgets, daydreams, or engages in generally disruptive behavior that annoys his classmates and his teacher. Regardless of how much time he is given to read a selection his comments about the selection are confused and irrelevant. If he is required to return to a selection to locate his errors, he can usually find and correct them. However, locating and correcting errors in his responses to a reading selection is upsetting for him and doesn't seem to improve his performance with subsequent assignments. On one occasion he read an entire story about a dog that was "nearly as big as a horse" and reported on the story as a funny story about a horse. This lack of accuracy is not reflected in his art work or in science experiments which he does with relish. His work with tasks that do not require reading is usually precise although his attention span is shorter than the attention spans of most of the other children in his class. These characteristics are reported by all of his past teachers except his first-grade teacher. She reported that Davy was sometimes restless but that he made good progress in the top reading group which used programmed reading as the basic instructional approach.

Brief description of the home situation

Davy's home is definitely not lacking in comforts or in recreational diversions including books, magazines, and newspapers. Davy has his own room with a well-stocked shelf of books which Davy claims he read but has forgotten what they are about. He has a rock collection, a chemistry set, a telescope, and various games such as Monopoly, Clue, and Careers. He also has a radio and a television set in his room.

Davy's father owns a very successful real estate business. Both of Davy's parents are college graduates and extremely concerned about Davy's reading. They have obviously tried to provide him with a variety of interesting and educational experiences. They report that they try to get Davy to listen to stories they read to him and to encourage him to read for himself; however, he is a restless and inattentive listener and often falls asleep when left alone to read by himself. Davy has a dog, but no brothers or sisters. He belongs to a neighborhood "gang" and participates in the gang's activities with vigor and good acceptance by his peers. He also participates eagerly in his parents' country club activities for children.

Interpretation of diagnostic findings

Davy's performance on diagnostic reading tests is characterized by carelessness and inability to attend to the presented task. His oral reading has many repetitions, omissions, and substitutions. His answers to comprehension questions are generally inaccurate. He appears to guess, rather than read, his way through a selection. Although he knows the sounds of letters individually, his ability to blend the sounds is poor. Words that he frequently uses in informal conversation he misses in his reading. In conversation his intonation patterns are appropriate and expressive, but his oral reading is rapid and jerky with few hesitations. He claims that (1) he likes reading, (2) reading makes him sleepy, and (3) he is a good reader when he wants to be.

Apparently, Davy has had few, if any, meaningful experiences with reading. At any rate he does not seem to recognize reading as essentially a meaning-getting process. Davy's many possessions may have been more distracting than helpful to his concentration and may have kept him "too busy" to involve himself with ideas in print. He would rather "do" things than think about someone else's ideas.

Perhaps the programmed approach used for Davy's initial reading instruction taught him to regard reading as a series of challenges rather than the process of extracting ideas from print. His first-grade teacher may have rewarded him for decoding the language without requiring him to deal with the ideas he decoded. If, indeed, this was the case, it is understandable that he could have developed a faulty concept of reading.

All of the diagnostic evidence that has been collected indicates that Davy's faulty concept of reading is preventing him from developing good reading concentration, good word-attack skills, and good comprehension. His intellectual potential, oral language development and environmental advantages, if properly tapped, should be sufficient to help him understand that reading is an excellent way to get information and pleasure. Until Davy can be taught to understand what reading is and how beneficial reading can be for him, specific word attack and comprehension skill training is likely to reinforce his existing poor concept, attitudes, and habits and do very little to correct his skill deficiencies.

Brief description and evaluation of remedial instruction being provided

For three months Davy has been receiving remedial reading instruction with two other boys from his class forty minutes a day, three days a week. The boys have been using a language experience approach to create radio plays which are tape recorded and played to their classmates. The boys dictate original lines for a script which is typed and which they then read and record. The boys "try-out" for several different parts so that it is very difficult for them to memorize their parts and thereby avoid reading. When the boys run short of ideas, their remedial teacher reads to them from various sources while they listen to get ideas for their play. Sometimes they are asked to search for ideas or facts for a particular play in newspapers, magazines, and reference books. The meaning of all dialogue is discussed before it is typed for inclusion in the play. The use of a particular word to communicate a particular idea is often discussed. When the teacher is reading aloud, she frequently stops and asks the boys to predict what will happen next. Davy has been given paragraphs with titles to read silently after he has made some predictions about the content of each paragraph from the clues supplied by the title. Phonics skills are being taught to Davy only as he needs them to attack unknown words he wants to use in a play.

Although he has been receiving special instruction for only a short time, Davy's attitude toward reading and his concept of reading appear to be improving. His reading is more accurate as is evidenced by his reading-related writing and speaking activities. His ability to use phonics to attack unknown words is improving although he still has a strong tendency to look at the first part of a word and guess the rest.

However, if his attention is focused on an isolated word and he is given some help with blending, he can usually sound it out and repeat it correctly when the word is returned to context. The main improvement is that he is beginning to see many reasons for reading.

THOUGHTS FOR DISCUSSION

"The structure of the subject must be meshed with the structure of the student. A major failure of education has been to consider the logic of the one almost to the exclusion of the psychologic of the other." (Moffett, 1968b, p. 13)

"Obviously motivation is critical to learning and thus is one of the major ways in which the affective domain is used as a means to the cognitive." (Krathwohl, et al., 1964, p. 57)

". . . the humane teacher cannot stop when his students 'recognize' words and 'comprehend' stories. He must acquaint children with the greatness inherent in their civilization." (Stoops, 1967, p. 41)

"A good teacher is not merely a person with a deep knowledge and love of a subject, but one who has an excellent understanding of basic principles, a love of people and children in particular, an ability to awaken and maintain interests, to direct those interests towards successful experiences and above all to foster wonder, curiosity, patience and an appetite for understanding. Brilliance in teaching is an acquired skill and it is not necessarily spectacular. It grows readily when the teacher has access to good materials." (Jennings, 1965, p. 61)

"In general, lower class children are more dependent upon the school in learning to read, write and do arithmetic than are middle class children. Middle class children are 'smarter' only in the sense that they are better prepared to read at the outset of their education and so sustained in that preparation by their home environments and by their teachers' expectations that the current poor or mediocre methods are sufficient." (Cohen, 1969, p. 8)

REFERENCES

Arnstine, D. Shaping the emotions: The sources of standards for aesthetic education. *School Review,* 1964, **72,** 242-271.

Ausubel, D. P. Some psychological aspects of the structure of knowledge. In S. Elam (Ed.), *Education and the structure of knowledge.* Chicago: Rand McNally, 1964, 221–249.

Bloom, B. S., Engelhart, M. D., Furst, E. J., Hill, W. H., and Krathwohl, D. R. *Taxonomy of educational objectives.* New York: David McKay, 1956.

Cohen, S. A. *Teach them all to read.* New York: Random House, 1969.

Combs, A. W., and Snygg, D. *Individual behavior.* New York: Harper and Row, 1959.

Downing, J. How children think about reading. *The Reading Teacher,* 1969, **23**, 217–230.

Gans, R. Meeting the challenge of the middle grades. *What is reading doing to the child?* Danville, Ill.: The Interstate Printers and Publishers, 1967, 65–72.

Harris, A. J. *How to increase reading ability.* (5th ed.) New York: David McKay, 1970.

Jennings, F. *This is reading.* New York: Bureau of Publications, Teachers College, Columbia University, 1965.

Johnson, M. S., and Kress, R. Readers and reading. *The Reading Teacher,* 1969, **22**, 594.

Johnson, W. *Your most enchanted listener.* New York: Harper and Row, 1956.

Krathwohl, D. B., Bloom, B. S., and Masia, B. B., *Taxonomy of educational objectives, handbook II: Affective domain.* New York: David McKay, 1964.

Lefevre, C. A. *Linguistics and the teaching of reading.* New York: McGraw-Hill, 1964.

Macdonald, J. B. The person in the curriculum. Unpublished speech delivered at the 1965 Teachers College Curriculum Conference, Columbia University, November, 1965.

Macdonald, J. B., Anderson, D. W., and May, F. B. *Strategies of curriculum development.* (Selected writings of the late Virgil E. Herrick.) Columbus, Ohio: Charles E. Merrill, 1965.

Moffett, J. *A student-centered language arts curriculum, grades k–6: A handbook for teachers.* Boston: Houghton Mifflin, 1968. (a)

Moffett, J. *Teaching the universe of discourse.* Boston: Houghton Mifflin, 1968. (b)

Niensted, S. Meaninglessness for beginning readers. *The Reading Teacher,* 1969, **23**, 112–115.

Otto, W., and Smith, R. J. *Administering the school reading program.* Boston: Houghton Mifflin, 1970.

Pauk, W. Beyond nuts and bolts. *Journal of Reading,* 1968, **11**, 507–508.

Rawlings, M. K. *The Yearling.* New York: Grosset and Dunlap, 1938.

Russell, D. *Children learn to read.* New York: Ginn, 1961.

Stoops, J. A. Reading and the crisis of values. *What is reading doing to the child?* Danville, Ill.: The Interstate Printers and Publishers, 1967, 31–43.

Thorndike, E. L. Reading as reasoning: A study of mistakes in paragraph meaning. *Journal of Educational Psychology,* 1917, **8**, 323–332.

Vernon, M. D. *Backwardness in reading.* London: Cambridge University Press, 1958.

Weingarten, S. The developmental values of voluntary reading. *School Review,* 1954, **62**, 222–230.

Chapter 7

Word-Attack Skills in Reading

The most common deficiency of children who are poor readers is a lack of word-attack skills. Developing this most basic of reading skills often becomes the major objective of corrective and remedial teaching. The decision on how this task is to be accomplished often determines the success or the failure of the instruction. Three factors loom large in this decision: (1) In remedial teaching there is no one approach that is universally effective. A method that works well with Dick may have little value with Jane. The merit, or lack of merit, can only be judged in relation to its success or failure when used by a particular teacher with a particular pupil under particular conditions. In the selection of the method, it should be clear that techniques become useful only when they are applied in response to a need that has been identified through careful diagnosis. (2) Teachers need more than the conventional basal reader to correct word-attack deficiencies. A wide variety of supplementary material is needed in order that a high degree of individualization can be practiced. It should go without saying that if more of the same methods with which the pupil has already failed are applied, the likelihood of success is small. By providing the teacher with a wide range of materials, the options of materials and strategies for teaching greatly increase the chances for success. (3) One of the few constants in remedial teaching is the necessity for a patient, positive, enthusiastic approach that characterizes successful teachers whether they operate as remedial specialists or as regular classroom teachers. In the following discussion of the remedial teaching of word-attack skills it should be clear that all three factors are assumed.

Both careful studies and experience have shown that reading disability is more often caused by a series of interacting deficiencies than by a single deficiency. For this reason, each of the problem areas discussed will be of interest to the teacher doing remedial teaching. The areas discussed in this chapter include basic sight vocabulary, reversals, substitution and confabulation, repetitions and regressions, word-by-word reading, and general word analysis, which includes both phonic and structural analysis. Chapter 8 deals with vocabulary, comprehension, rate of reading, and study skills.

CORRECTION OF WORD-ATTACK DEFICIENCIES

Skill in word attack—whether it be through sounding and blending letters, through sight vocabulary, or through any of the other known processes by which children recognize words—is basic to the development of skill in reading. Word attack is the foundation upon which the superstructure of comprehension, fluency, and appreciation is built. Thus, with many disabled readers the teacher must begin not—as the cliché has it—where the child is, but at the very beginning stages of reading instruction. In the opinion of many highly successful remedial teachers the development of a basic sight vocabulary is a desirable first step in the remedial teaching of word-attack skills.

Sight Vocabulary

In selecting the basic sight words to be taught, the remedial teacher has several options. The following are but a few of the possibilities open to him. With the exception of the classic Dolch list, only the more recent lists are mentioned.

"A Basic Sight Vocabulary" by E. W. Dolch, in the *Elementary School Journal,* 36: 456–460, February, 1936.

This is perhaps the most widely used basic sight word list. According to Dolch, 220 words comprise about 65 percent of the service words used in the reading material in the first three grades.

The list also has significance beyond the third-grade level, for the percentage of the frequency of use drops only to about 60 percent through the intermediate grades. It can be readily seen that the list has considerable utility because once the words have been mastered, a pupil can apply his mastery in most of his attempts at connected reading and gain fluency at an early stage of the instructional sequence. All of this, of course, can lead to the much-needed success experience which disabled readers invariably need.

(Parenthetically, we must point out a recent piece of work by Johnson, 1971, pp. 449–457. His point is that because the Dolch list is derived from work done in 1920, it has become somewhat passé. The point is well taken, and we agree. The reader should examine the Johnson article and the updated word list suggested. We feel that the Johnson list can and will supersede the Dolch list in the near future. Until the transition has been made, however, the Dolch list will remain important simply because the teaching materials based on it exist and will continue to be used. The suggestions we have made regarding the Dolch list can, of course, be applied to the Johnson list.)

Because of the abstractness of many of the Dolch words—such as *with, where, there, their*—disabled readers may have difficulty in remembering them. This fact suggests that wherever possible the words should be used and taught in context in order to strengthen understanding and subsequent retention. A method of teaching service words by use of context is to use them in simple sentences. In the examples below the word *house* is the only word not from the Dolch list.

1. We went to their house to play.
2. Will you come to my house?
3. I have not seen him today.
4. This is the way we will do it.

Several other methods have proved successful in teaching a sight vocabulary. We feel that in some cases relatively isolated drill can be beneficial. Using the words in sentences or experience stories, tracing, and work with flash cards have also been found effective in some cases. Here again, the method to be used in an individual case is the one by which the pupil seems to learn most efficiently. This is, in fact, a basic tenet in all remedial teaching.

In working with a group of youngsters in need of sight word training, pleasurable practice can be provided by using the Dolch Basic Sight Vocabulary Cards or Sight Phrase Cards (Garrard Press) in a "game" situation. One method is to mark numerical values of one, two, or three on the face of each card and then place the cards face downward on the table. The words of preprimer and primer difficulty level would have a value of 1; the words of first- and second-grade difficulty would have a value of 2; and the third-grade level words would have a value of 3. Then each player takes a turn in selecting a card and reading it. If the card is read correctly he may keep it, but if he cannot read the card he must return it to the bottom of the pack. In either event, the next pupil takes his turn. After all the cards have been read, the pupils determine their scores by adding up the numbers on the cards they have read correctly. The pupil with the most points is the winner. A teacher-made set of cards with other words or phrases can, of course, be used in the same way. Russell and Karp (1956) have collected some three hundred activities similar to the above that may be found useful, with adaptation, in corrective and remedial teaching.

Other useful sight word lists are:

"Bucks County 1185 Common Words," by Morton Botel, in *How to Teach Reading* (Chicago: Follett, 1963), pp. 103–113. The list is subdivided as follows: 41 words at preprimer level; 67 at primer level; 124 at first-grade level; 152 at beginning second-grade level; 207 at high second-grade level; 283 at beginning third-grade level; and 311 at high third-grade level.

"Durrell Intermediate Grade Word List" by Donald Durrell, in *Improving Reading Instruction* (New York: World Book, 1956) pp. 367–392. A list of words at fourth, fifth, and sixth grade level of difficulty derived from fifty-six reading, social studies, and natural science texts at the indicated grade level.

A Revised Core Vocabulary: A Basic Vocabulary for Grades 1–8—An Advanced Vocabulary for Grades 9–13, (Huntington, N.Y.: Educational Developmental Laboratories, 1969). A highly useful list which, at primary level, is taken from the basal texts of nine major publishers. At middle grades the Rinsland (1945) and Thorndike (1944) lists were added to the nine basic series used at the primary level. Other resources were used at upper grade levels. Grade level word counts at the various grade levels were: primary 68, first 311, second 527, third 850, fourth 992, fifth 1201, sixth 1378, seventh 802, and eighth 862, for a total of 6,991 words. Word counts in grades 9–13 varied from 420 to 542 for a total of 2,411. The careful research and recency (1969) make this an especially valuable list.

In addition, the teacher may wish to teach as sight vocabulary the most common words from the basic material he intends to use with a pupil. We feel, however, that it is wise to use a researched list as well in order to insure that words of more universal usage will be taught.

In general the lists suggested above would be appropriate for children in the elementary grades; lists of words more suitable for older pupils are suggested in the following chapter.

Games For Use in Teaching Sight Vocabulary

A wide variety of games, flash cards, and instructional devices is available for use in correcting sight word deficiencies. A note of caution needs to be sounded, however, regarding indiscriminate use of games in any form of remedial teaching. While each game or device has some merit, the teacher must be careful that the fun of the game does not overshadow its instructional purpose. Games and instructional devices such as those listed below need careful supervision on the part of the teacher if full benefit is to be obtained.

Basic Sight Vocabulary Cards (Garrard Press). The 220 Dolch Basic Words on flash cards. These may be used by individual children and pupil teams or in a group game as described earlier.

Basic Sight Word Phrases (Garrard Press). These are the 220 Dolch words described above, used in phrases. They can be used as flash cards as mentioned above. Additional possibilities will occur to the teacher.

Group Word Teaching Game (Garrard Press). A word "Bingo" game aimed at teaching the Dolch list. Can be used by pupil teams or larger groups.

Linguistic Block Series (Scott, Foresman). *The First Rolling Reader* consists of a set of ten blocks on which fifty primer level words are printed. *The Second Rolling Reader* contains fifty-four verbs, nouns, and adjectives at first-grade level. *The Third Rolling Reader* contains blocks with fifty-four auxiliary verbs and negative constructions. Can be used by an individual child, pupil teams, or small groups of children.

Educational Password Game (Milton Bradley). This game is based on the television show "Password." It teaches basic sight and picture words found in beginning basal series. For use with pupil teams or with groups.

There is no consensus among remedial experts regarding the efficacy of teaching large sight word vocabularies. Some very telling criticisms have been made of basal reading programs that depend too much on memorization of sight words. The critics claim it is much more profitable to limit sight words to a minimum and spend the time thus saved in teaching phonic skills or the word patterns more recently advocated by the linguists. The determining factor regarding how long to dwell on sight words is tied to the success rate of the learner. Experience has shown that children with good visual memories do best with sight words; if this condition does not exist, it would appear wise to limit the number of sight words to be taught. In any event, one would want to move rather quickly to some word-attack skills based on sound, tracing, word families, or whatever seems to be effective.

Reversals

In the beginning stages of reading it is fairly common for youngsters to reverse words—*saw* becomes *was*, *mad* becomes *dam*, *dig* becomes *big*, etc. Or, they may reverse individual letters; e.g., *p* for *q*, *u* for *n*, *b* for *d*. These kinds of errors often cause much greater concern than is justified. Parents, for example, are sometimes unduly alarmed when reversals are said to be symptomatic of "mirror vision." An indication of the rarity of true mirror vision is evidenced by the fact that when one of the writers polled a large staff of remedial reading teachers who collectively had over four hundred years of experience in teaching disabled readers he found only one true case of mirror vision. Maturation will, in the great majority of cases, erase or dispel reversal tendencies in young children. Nevertheless, if reversal tendencies persist beyond the primary grades remedial instruction may be needed.

While reversals may be attributed to many factors, they are most often related to left-right discrimination ability, incomplete or confused dominance, fusion and eye-coordination problems, or immaturity. As in the case of most reading disabilities, the remedial measures to be taken will be dictated by the diagnosis.

Fernald (1943), Gillingham and Stillman (1956), and many other authorities advocate a kinesthetic method for eliminating persistent reversal errors. By this method, the pupil traces frequently reversed words—which have been printed or written on cards in large letters—while he says the word in syllables; he then writes the word from memory without reference to the card. Actually, many techniques of instruction that direct the attention of the pupil to the proper left-to-right sequence, whether of words or letters, have been found to be effective. Strang, McCullough, and Traxler (1961) have made the pertinent observation that whatever the error involved in such cases, the remedial teacher should direct the pupil's attention to the specific point of difficulty rather than to the vague, general area of reversals. They also caution against isolated drill, but here again the present writers can find no fault with limited amounts of isolated drill if it is not overdone. If teachers have an antipathy toward the word *drill,* they have the writers' permission to call it *focused practice.*

Substitutions and Confabulation

The term *substitutions* usually refers to the practice of substituting a contextually correct word in place of the literally correct word. This may be
done through honest error in not correctly identifying the proper word.
Such errors as reading *pan* for *pot, home* for *house,* etc., usually indicate
that the pupil is fully aware of thought content but has hurriedly miscalled
a word because the substitution seems to fit the context. *Confabulation,* on
the other hand, usually refers to an attempt—using whatever context picture,
or other clues that can be utilized—to offer a substitute that the pupil hopes
will conceal the fact that he cannot read a particular word; the word read
may or may not have any relation or resemblance to the correct one. Substitutions are generally no great cause for concern; frequently, even good
readers may make this kind of error if they have done wide reading with
little or no supervision. In cases of confabulation, however, the reader is
most likely attempting to read material too difficult for his ability. Either
type of error can be readily detected by listening to a student read.

Some substitutions, such as *horse* for *house,* may be due to the fact that
the pupil is looking only at the initial letters or general configurations of
words. This fault is sometimes used to support the argument against learning by the sight method alone. An accepted remedial procedure is to make
a practice card or sheet that contains many words that begin in the same
way and have the pupil practice reading them. An example of such a card
is shown in figure 3. As the pupil progresses in his ability to distinguish
the words when he sees them in pairs, the list may be scrambled to give
him additional practice. As a final step, the teacher would do well to give

FIG. 3   Exercise to Overcome Substitutions

horse	track	space
house	trick	spade
slim	will	tin
slam	well	tan
plant	flop	clan
plans	flip	clam

the pupil further practice in recognizing the words in the context of simple sentences. Another suggested technique for drill is to use multiple-choice items which offer choices of words with like beginnings. Two examples follow:

1. The boy rode to the $\frac{\text{house}}{\text{horse}}$.

2. We will eat the $\frac{\text{food}}{\text{fool}}$.

Many workbooks contain material of this type that will be found useful.

If the errors made in substitutions are in the middle or end of words, a different remedial technique is indicated. Miscalling middle sounds is most frequently due to vowel confusions or unfamiliarity with the consonant-final *e* rule. An acceptable remedy is first to give the pupil practice on words that differ only in the middle vowel, such as *pat, pet, pit, pot, put.* Practice then should be given with words in which the other letters are different and only the middle vowel is the same, such as *rat, bar, saw, can, pad.* Research by Burrows and Lourie (1963), Clymer (1963), and others questions the use of the "when two vowels go walking the first does all the talking" rule when teaching middle sounds, inasmuch as it applies less than 50 percent of the time.

In the case of final errors the difficulty may be failure to note or discriminate between endings such as *-s, -es, -er,* etc. This type of error is usually comparatively simple to correct, requiring only a little practice in being careful to note endings. A good instructional procedure is to point out how endings can change the meaning of a word.

With most substitution errors, any practice that encourages the pupil to make an orderly inspection of words is usually effective. It is well to remember that if the pupil makes logical or reasonable substitutions, such as reading *ocean* for *sea* or *house* for *home*—substitutions that do not destroy the meaning and do not occur too frequently—it should not be a cause of great concern. Undue attention to trivialities sometimes creates more problems than it corrects. In the case of frequent confabulation, however, it may be that retraining in the basic word-recognition skills is in order.

Repetitions and Regressions

Many disabled readers persistently repeat words or phrases and sometimes whole sentences. This type of error may or may not be significant. Even the best of readers will, if confronted with unfamilar vocabulary or concepts, occasionally regress in order to understand a particularly difficult passage. Such labored reading is of no concern to the remedial teacher. It is another matter, however, when the difficulty level of the reading material is well within the reader's range of ability. A teacher needs to consider carefully whether or not the problem should be of concern. Of course, repetitions and regressions occur in silent reading as well as in oral reading, and the former can best be ascertained by eye-movement photographs. However, Harris (1970) has described a useful informal technique for easy, spontaneous observation of regressive movements. This is called the "mirror method." The pupil is seated at a table to read and the teacher holds a small rectangular mirror at such an angle as to reflect the pupil's eye movements. In the case of a pupil who is old enough to have some insight into his reading problem, it is not uncommon for him to realize he does regress and often he will tell the remedial teacher he has this habit. In any event, perhaps the best and simplest remedial procedure is to encourage the pupil to practice with very easy reading material and to use a 3×5 card as a screen coming down the page to cover the material already read, thus discouraging regression. A useful mechanical device to correct regressions, the Controlled Reader, is discussed in Chapter 8. It should be clear that in oral reading repetition errors may be created by nervousness over the audience situation and may not be a problem when the pupil is reading silently. Many adults who read very adequately silently are prone to make repetitions in an oral reading situation; it is likely that this is even more prevalent among youngsters.

Word-by-Word Reading

A great deal of planning is done by authors of basic readers at the pre-primer, primer, and primary levels to foster the habit of reading in thought units or phrases and most pupils have little difficulty in this respect. Yet, most teachers are probably familiar with the youngster who painfully reads word for word with no expression and little natural flow of thought units; even prepositional phrases, where one might most expect flow, are read word for word. This fault may be associated with one of several causes: (1) a habit of word-by-word reading formed over the years, (2) excessive use of phonics, (3) short fixation unit, (4) low intelligence, or (5) slowness with only certain difficult words due to their unfamiliarity. In the latter case, the pupil may have basic word-recognition difficulties which would necessitate slow, plodding reading. A perceptive teacher can readily determine the cause by administering an informal reading inventory or, perhaps, by merely listening to the pupil read orally. If the problem is due to the difficulty of material the solution is obvious. If the problem is caused by inadequate sight vocabulary, tendency to overanalyze, inattention to thought units, etc., the following remedial techniques and materials designed to develop quick recognition of words and phrases may be useful.

Dolch has developed useful Sight Phrase Cards (Garrard Press) made from the basic sight vocabulary list discussed earlier; and his ninety-five commonest nouns list (Garrard Press) has also proved beneficial in flash card drill. Some teachers prefer to use them simply as flash cards with individuals or with pairs of students having the same deficiency, but they may be used in a variety of ways. The phrases may, for example, be used as a game by having a group of pupils see who can make the greatest number of meaningful sentences from them.

A teacher-made tachistoscope, similar to that shown in figure 4, may

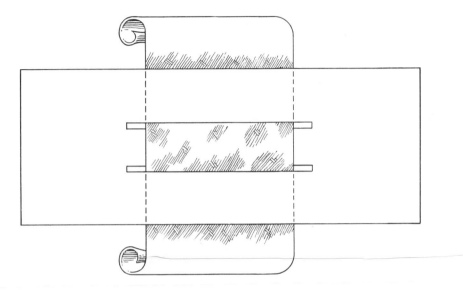

FIG. 4   A Teacher-made Tachistoscopic Device

also be used to provide practice in quick recognition of words and phrases. The slot through which the pupil sees the words simply needs to be made wide enough to accommodate phrases. Words and phrases should be typed with double or triple spacing between the lines in order that only one word or phrase at a time appears in the window. The phrases may be taken from a story the pupil is reading or from the Dolch Sight Phrase Cards described earlier. Care should be taken that only phrases containing words well within the pupil's reading ability are used. Additional suggestions for improving phrase perception will also be found in Chapter 8.

A commercial tachistoscopic device, the Flash-X Tachistoscope (Educational Developmental Laboratories), that exposes words at a fixed controlled rate of $\frac{1}{25}$ of a second is also available. Word wheels containing basic sight words, spelling words, etc., are available for use with the Flash-X. This device offers advantages over the teacher-made variety in that the time of exposure is known and fixed and therefore does not allow the student to vary from the set exposure. A possible disadvantage is that one must use the printed material available and teacher-made phrases or words cannot readily be used. Two other commercial tachistoscopic devices, which are excellent for working with groups of children, are the Keystone Overhead

Projector and Flashmeter (Keystone View Company) and the Tach-X (Educational Developmental Laboratories). The former is a device that projects $3\frac{1}{4}'' \times 4''$ glass slides on a screen; the length of exposure may range from 1 second to $\frac{1}{100}$ of a second. There is a wide range of material, from Dolch basic sight words to long, difficult phrases, available for use with the Keystone tachistoscope. The Tach-X operates on a different principle in that it uses film strips rather than slides. There is also a wealth of commercial material available for use with this instrument. All three devices have been found helpful in speeding up word recognition and getting pupils to read in phrases.

Word Wheels and Phonic Devices

The literature describes many variations of word wheels and phonic devices, both commercial and teacher-made, to provide training in word attack and add interest to what might be a monotonous chore. A resourceful teacher should have little difficulty in finding or making the kind of wheel or device that will best suit a particular problem. Examples, with a brief explanation of each, are given below.

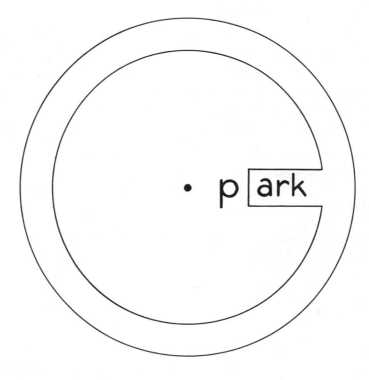

FIG. 5   Circle-type Word Wheel

Circle Type Two circles, one larger than the other, are fastened together by a brass paper staple or other means that allows each circle to be rotated freely without moving the other. Initial consonants, consonant blends, etc., can be printed on the inner circle and word endings, suffixes, etc., can be put on the outer circle. Many variations can be devised or are available commercially. A circle-type word wheel is illustrated in figure 5.

Strip Tachistoscopic Device This type of tachistoscope is made by cutting a 4″ × 6″ window in a piece of oak tag board or similar material; the window card is then attached by stapling or gluing to another card of like size to form a backing. Individual words or phrases can then be typed or lettered on a strip of paper the width of the window and the pupil can draw the card past the window at any desired speed. A strip-type tachistoscope is shown in figure 6.

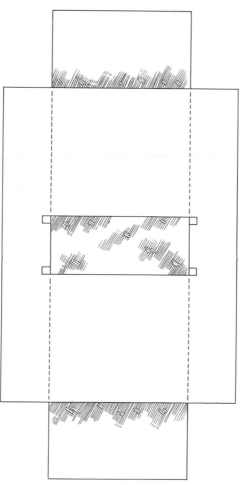

FIG. 6 A Strip Tachistoscope

Commercial Materials Commercial word wheels and devices have an advantage over teacher-made devices when the series comprises a carefully thought-out program. Two widely used sets of materials can be mentioned here. The Webster Word Wheels (Webster Publishing) include a series of sixty-three beginning blend, prefix, and suffix wheels and fourteen common beginning blend wheels (*sh, ch, th, wh, cl, dr, br, st, fr, tr, pl, sp,* and *fl*) ranging from easy to more difficult words. The Phono-Word Wheels (Steck) have five sets of blending, prefix, and suffix wheels. Set A, initial consonants, has 120 words with 15 beginning consonants; Set B consists of 110 words using initial consonant blends, digraphs, and word endings.

A word of caution is in order regarding wheels, devices, and games and their proper role in remedial teaching. Such devices are useful when used for short, concentrated drill and practice, or as motivators in reinforcing some newly learned skill. They do not take the place of direct teaching.

MECHANICAL DEVICES

Several mechanical devices, e.g., Controlled Readers, tachistoscopes, reading accelerators, etc., have been developed to teach almost all aspects of corrective and remedial reading. Opinion is mixed regarding their effectiveness with severely disabled readers but is somewhat more favorable in the case of corrective reading. Most reading specialists feel that for remedial teaching nothing can take the place of the warm, supportive teacher who provides highly individualized instruction on a one-to-one basis or in very small groups. Teachers of corrective reading are more enthusiastic about mechanical devices, often finding them effective for increasing the perceptual skills of reading, the rate of reading, and the motivation of some pupils to read.

The writers neither oppose nor advocate the use of mechanical devices; it does need to be pointed out, however, that research on their effectiveness, other than that performed by the manufacturers of the machines, is sparse and inconclusive. Several companies now engaged in performance contracting are using the mechanical devices, and it may be that out of these experiments new evidence on their effectiveness will emerge.

APPROACHES TO WORD ATTACK

The term *word attack* is the generic term applied to all methods of attacking and pronouncing words. It is a more comprehensive designation than the term *phonics* alone because it includes not only phonetic analysis and structural analysis but also the more recent terminology, *word patterns,* used by the linguists. Regardless of the approach used, all reading authorities recognize the need for independence in word attack before a pupil can advance from the sight word stage of reading. A brief discussion of a phonic approach to word analysis is presented below, followed by a discussion of structural analysis and a description of one linguistic approach.

Phonic Approaches

Phonic analysis may be described as a systematic study of words by sound units. In order to become proficient at analyzing words phonically, the pupil needs to learn the sounds of letters or combinations of letters. The complexity of such a task becomes evident when one considers the fact that in English there are more sounds than letters, which means that there must necessarily be inconsistencies and confusion. A number of "systems" for teaching phonics have been proposed, but basically they are typified by two approaches: (1) word-family phonics, and (2) single-letter phonics.

Word-family phonics consists mainly of sounding the initial consonant, or consonant blend, and then sounding the remainder of a word as a phonogram (e.g., *m-an, p-an, r-an*, etc.). Thus, the system avoids the need for blending individual letter sounds by making use of "families," such as *an, at, ell, in*, etc. In the beginning, the pupil usually learns the consonants in isolation; later consonants are coupled with the phonograms to make actual words. In most systems, drill is used to give the pupil practice. The method has a great many critics who point out that it fosters word-calling and tends to be isolated from meaningful reading.

Single-letter phonics consists of blending individual consonant and vowel sounds from the very beginning. Typically, the phonically regular monosyllables with short vowel sounds are taught first. Care must be exercised to insure that the pupil does not distort the consonant so that an *uh* sound is added and, e.g., *b* becomes *buh* or *d* becomes *duh*. In advocating single-letter phonics, Kottmeyer (1959) claims several advantages over family phonics: it leads to less confusion later on when structural generalizations are taught, for the pupil will not look for family units that are likely to be crossed by syllabic divisions; it strengthens spelling ability because it is directly applicable; and because it is relatively simple it can be taught faster and applied earlier than the more complicated family system.

Whichever phonic approach is attempted, the teacher will usually find the basic disability to be in the area of blending of sounds. Many pupils know virtually all they need to know about letter sounds, phonic rules, etc., but cannot utilize what they know because they are unable to blend the sounds into words. Basically, there are four general rules to remember in the teaching of this very important skill.

1. *Provide a great deal of practice in auditory perception.* Before any pupil can master phonics, he must be able to recognize similarities and differences in beginning, middle, and ending sounds. McKee (1948) and Durrell (1964) are but two of the many authorities who point up the importance of phonic readiness and how vital adequate auditory perception is.

2. *Sounds should be smooth and continuous.* Inaccurate and careless pronunciation, as well as the tendency to add extraneous sounds to consonants, are frequent stumbling blocks to phonic skill and successful blending of sounds. Confusion on the part of the pupil is understandable when, for instance, an *uh* sound is added to consonants; pupils are all too frequently told that *k* says *kuh* and *p* says *puh,* etc. It is also well to remember that the time interval between letters needs to be kept almost imperceptible when blending.

3. *Proceed from the whole word to its parts.* Less confusion arises if the entire word is presented and pronounced than if the letter sounds are studied first.

4. *Keep phonic and blending instruction brief.* The best reinforcement is that which provides ample but pleasant practice. High-interest low-difficulty level books, well within the range of the pupil's capability, are the best way to accomplish this.

Phonic Systems and Workbooks

There are many widely used commercially prepared systems and workbooks for teaching phonics that would be of interest to the experienced or the prospective teacher. The question of the proper place of workbooks in a developmental reading program continues to go unresolved. There is little dispute, however, over the use of such material in a remedial or corrective program. Virtually all teachers who work with children who have learning problems have found workbooks indispensable for reinforcing and practicing the skills taught. Some cautionary words regarding the use of workbooks are in order, however, and the chart below probably covers the most important points regarding their use. An annotated list of phonic systems and workbooks that have been found useful for teaching or reinforcing beginning instruction follows the chart.

ADVANTAGES OF WORKBOOKS

Workbooks—

provide needed additional practice
meet a specific need, teach a specific skill
provide work to do independently
are a "time-saver" for teacher
help provide for individual differences:
    slow children can take all the time they need
    fast children can go on to other things, i.e., creative writing, additional
        reading, story illustrating, any other enrichment
are really liked by children if properly used
have some diagnostic value for the teacher (provide a "check" on where a
    child is in the instructional sequence)

PITFALLS OF WORKBOOKS

Workbooks—

can engender criticism from administrators if indiscriminately used
evoke the legitimate charge of "busy work" if not properly supervised
create friction with parents if they are not carefully checked
promote copying if teacher doesn't create a favorable climate
destroy individualization of instruction if same workbook used for all
  children

SOME DO'S AND DON'TS ON USING WORKBOOKS

Don't—	Do—
say, "Work pages 24 and 25 in your workbooks"	make sure children get clear and sufficient instruction for what is to be done
allow children to read several days and then *catch up* in workbook assignments	work out a system for checking workbooks; if students correct each other's work, teacher must be sure to check up on them frequently
allow children to merely *correct* their workbooks but have no understanding of the errors made	try to see that the student knows his errors and *why* they are errors; group discussion is good for this

Reading With Phonics, by Julie Hay and Charles E. Wingo (Lippincott). This material, commonly referred to as the Hay-Wingo System, consists of a hard-cover book and three workbooks for the pupil, plus a teacher's manual. Practice exercises place emphasis upon isolated words. The main approach is through initial consonant-vowel combinations. The hard-cover book is printed with red and black ink, more clearly to show the phonic units.

Building Reading Skills, by Rowena Hargrave and Leila Armstrong (McCormick-Mathers). This material consists of six text-practice workbooks, a teacher's guidebook, and practice cards. The six books are sequential in difficulty. Phonic skill-builder cards are bound into the center of each of the first three workbooks. The "Teacher's Phonic Skill Builders" are a set of 104 large key cards for teaching the phonetic elements. This is really a combination system in that phonic methods are used in connection with sight vocabulary, structural and comparative analysis, and other methods of word attack.

Remedial Reading Drills, by Thorleif G. Hegge and Samuel A. and Winifred D. Kirk (George Wahr). This is a single book originally intended for use with mentally retarded pupils but now in general use, particularly with children who have extreme learning problems. This is a single-letter phonics system that makes use of kinesthetic reinforcement in teaching the extensive word lists that constitute the book. It is not intended primarily as a supplemental system but rather as a complete method in itself; however, the authors know of many instances where it has been used supplementally with a great deal of success. One of the strengths of this system is that it is constructed in such a way that the child has but one response for each symbol. This eliminates confusion until the pupil can better cope with more sounds.

Functional Phonetic Books, by A. D. Cordts (Benefic Press). This is a series of three workbooks that advocates the whole word approach, used contextually. It is said to be compatible with a sight method of teaching.

Phonics, by Selma Herr (Educational Research Associates). This set of three workbooks has one of the most complete and thorough presentations of phonics available. A wealth of practice drills and activities are illustrated with drawings. A most complete work that is recommended for neophytes in the area of phonics.

Phonetic Keys to Reading, by T. L. Harris, Mildred Creekmore, and Margaret Greenman (The Economy Company). A highly structured traditional phonic approach. Almost all the materials are expendable. Latest copyright date is 1964.

The Structural Reading Series, by Catherine Stern, T. S. Gould, Margaret Stern, and K. Teague (Random House, 1972). An updating of the 1963 series that has proved to be effective with the disadvantaged, the perceptually handicapped, and children learning English as a second language. Eight colorful workbooks, readers, and ancillary components, plus an excellent teacher's manual.

Open Court Remedial Program, by Ann Hughes (Open Court). This program consists of a kit of classroom materials including teacher guides, wall cards, flash cards, phonograph records, and progress charts. Pupil materials consist of a basic student text, student reader, student response cards, plus twenty loose-leaf stories for supplementary reading. This is a highly structured teaching program designed to be covered in seventy-five to ninety instructional hours. One hour per day minimum teaching time is required but two to two and one-half hours is recommended. The program is for the whole class and for use by grade 4 children and above who have not learned to read fluently. The company offers a performance contract plan for those who wish it.

Individualized Phonics, by Richard E. Wylie and Marie Jonke (Teachers Publishing Corporation, Collier-Macmillan School and Library Services). A program aimed at supplementing a basal reader program in grades 1 through 6. Materials consist of liquid duplicator masters, primary wall charts, flash cards, and teachers' guides.

Structural Analysis

Structural analysis is a method of word study which enables a child to recognize variations that are based upon inflectional, derivational, or compound forms by identifying the pronunciation and meaning of the base or root word. When a child has a basic sight vocabulary, he can learn to attack unknown words through structural as well as phonic analysis. Instruction in structural analysis is usually divided into four areas: inflected forms of known words; derived forms of known words; syllabication; and compound words.

In the primary grades' or in remedial instruction, the structural analysis skills need to be taught with something of a light touch. The list below incorporates those elements of structural analysis, together with examples, that most authorities agree are necessary to teach in the primary grades.

1. compound words (always begin with known words): cowboy, afternoon, doorway
2. plurals formed with -s, -es, and -ies: ball–balls, potato–potatoes, fly–flies
3. doubling consonants before adding endings beginning with a vowel: can–canned, stop–stopped
4. base words with variant endings: wanted = when -ed says ed, tricked = when -ed says t, loved = when -ed says d
5. contractions: I am = I'm, I will = I'll, he is = he's
6. possessive forms: boy's hat, boys' hats
7. base words with prefixes: unkind, refill, export
8. base words with suffixes: fearless, thankful, eagerly
9. base words with both prefixes and suffixes: unkindly, unhappiness, unthankful

The knowledgeable teacher will realize that as the pupil passes from the decoding stage of reading to mastery of the higher skills of reading, a greater knowledge of structural analysis skills is both possible and profitable. Structural analysis is a method of word study used continuously until the pupil reaches the most advanced levels of reading. It is an approach that can and should be used in conjunction with phonic analysis. Virtually all of the conventional developmental series of basal readers make careful provision for growth in structural analysis. If a serious deficiency in this area is found in disabled readers, one effective way to increase a pupil's skill is to stress the same techniques that are suggested in the basic series teachers' manuals. While it is true the pupil may already have been exposed to these methods, it may also be true that he was not ready to learn at that time and such a presentation may now be effective. It is the authors' opinion that a great many of the skills of structural analysis are learned inductively by many pupils after a general foundation of awareness of words and word patterns is laid.

Linguistic Systems

Reading systems based on an approach long advocated by linguists seem to be gaining recognition and acceptance at a rather rapid rate. While no two linguistic systems are identical, any more than no two phonic systems are precisely alike, the techniques of the sequencing of word patterns and minimal use of sight vocabulary are virtually the same in all. The sample word patterns from Science Research Associates Basic Reading Series shown in figure 7 are representative of several systems. Teachers who are not familiar

FIG. 7   Sample Word Patterns from Science Research Associates Basic Reading Series

Level	Description of patterns and examples	Approximate Grade Level
A	**A B C* (a b c)** can cap dip big Dan lap hip dig fan rap lip pig man nap rip rig ran tap tip wig	Alphabet Book Preprimer
B	get bed cot hop bun wax let fed dot mop gun fix met led hot pop fun mix net red lot top run box set Ted not sun fox	Primer
C	bell kick end dust skid span black fell lick bend gust skim sped crack sell pick lend just skin spin smack tell sick mend must skip spot stack well tick send rust skit spun track	1^1
D	king banging hush thin bath chin catch quit ring hanging mush thing Beth chip latch quiz sink ringing rush think with chimp match quick Bing singing flush thick fifth chick patch quill sting swinging brush sixth chill snatch quilt	1^2
E	hunted seven travel bee beat moon fail bay die fine tested linen gravel see meat noon nail day lie line filled kitten camel wee seat soon pail pay pie mine robbed mitten level free treat hoop rail say tie vine picked bitten panel tree wheat boot sail way nine	2^1
F	fair care more bird burn bar dear all blue book date age cough knee hair dare sore dirt hurt car fear ball glue took late cage rough knew pair fare tore girl turn far hear call true cook mate wage tough knife chair hare wore shirt curl jar near tall cruel foot fate huge laugh knock stair share store third curve mar year small value hate large enough know	2^2

with the linguistic approach should understand that this list of word patterns constitutes only a portion of the program through the decoding process. There are no phonic rules to learn, and there are a minimum number of sight words to master. The approach is inductive, rather than deductive. For practical purposes, the pupil is an independent reader when he masters these patterns.

For corrective and remedial teaching, the following linguistic programs offer a promising and different approach that has been used effectively with severely disabled readers.

Cracking the Code, by Donald Rasmussen and Lynn Goldberg (Science Research Associates, 1968). This material consists of a student workbook, a 215-page reader entitled *Cracking the Code,* and a very complete and very necessary teachers' guide.

Merrill *Linguistic Refresher Program,* by Charles C. Fries, Rosemary G. Wilson, and Mildred K. Rudolph (Charles E. Merrill, 1966). This is a hard-bound special edition made up from the six books that comprise the Merrill Basic Program. It consists of four books: Book A (made up of Books 1, 2, and 3 of the basic program); Book B–Reader 4; Book C–Reader 5; Book D–Reader 6. In addition to older disabled readers, the program is also successful with the emotionally disturbed, the brain-damaged, the mentally retarded, and with adult illiterates.

Briefly stated, the following points can be made for both of these programs:

1. Both are intended specifically for the middle- and upper-grade pupil who has so many gaps in his knowledge of reading skills that the best corrective or remedial strategy is to start again from the beginning.

2. The format of the systems is quite acceptable to older pupils. No tell-tale pictures are used in the Merrill program and there are only a few pictures in the SRA program.

3. The pupil has had no prior knowledge of the material; he has had no past failing experiences with it.

4. The programs are straightforward and simple to teach; pupils experience success and progress almost immediately.

5. Sight words are held to the very minimum, and there are no phonic rules to be learned.

6. Pupil progress is simple to check, thus the teacher need not wonder how the youngster is doing.

A SUGGESTED SEQUENCE OF READING SKILLS

Presented below is a sequential list of basic reading skills that will furnish some practical guidelines for the remedial or corrective teacher. The list is in some respects unique in that it embodies the best features of a traditional approach as well as a great many of the word patterns (word families) that have proved so helpful in the approach advocated by the linguists. The list begins with some *minimum essentials of readiness,* which are included because it has been observed that many remedial teachers often assume that the basic readiness tasks have been mastered by the older disabled reader only to learn after some unsuccessful teaching attempts that such an assumption was erroneous. It is suggested that very little time would be lost in checking the pupil on these essentials; a great deal might be gained by uncovering some very basic inadequacies that have been interfering with learning.

The readiness objectives are stated in behavioral terms. The list is divided into levels A, B, and C. These levels only approximate grades 1, 2, and 3. A remedial teacher would be well advised to ignore the grade equivalencies and concentrate on the sequential aspects of the list, realizing that if the major portion of the skills on the list is successfully taught, the pupil will have completed the decoding process and will be well on the way to becoming an independent reader.

THE BASIC READING SKILLS
Minimum Essentials of Readiness

The pupil will:

demonstrate ability to trace over a dotted line and draw both vertical and horizontal lines between designated points

perform the finer motor skills such as holding and manipulating chalk and pencil correctly

identify likenesses and differences in shapes, letters, numbers, and words

demonstrate ability to hear rhyming elements in simple verse, in phrases, and in isolated pairs of words

recognize and name letters of the alphabet, both in and out of sequence, and in upper and lower case

demonstrate ability to hear the differences between the long and the short sound of the vowels

Level A Skills

The pupil will be able to recognize the following basic sight words in isolation as well as in context. The words are listed in order of difficulty and frequency, so that they should be taught in approximately the order given.

SIGHT WORDS

Preprimer difficulty

1. a	9. down	17. I	25. my	33. stop
2. and	10. find	18. in	26. no	34. the
3. at	11. for	19. jump	27. not	35. to
4. away	12. funny	20. little	28. on	36. up
5. big	13. go	21. look	29. play	37. we
6. can	14. good	22. make	30. run	38. yes
7. car	15. help	23. may	31. said	39. you
8. come	16. here	24. me	32. see	40. who

Primer Difficulty

1. all	9. do	17. now	25. say	33. too
2. am	10. eat	18. on	26. she	34. under
3. are	11. get	19. our	27. so	35. want
4. ate	12. have	20. out	28. soon	36. was
5. be	13. he	21. please	29. that	37. well
6. but	14. like	22. ran	30. there	38. went
7. came	15. must	23. ride	31. they	39. what
8. did	16. news	24. saw	32. this	40. will

First-Grade Difficulty

1. after	9. every	17. him	25. may	33. some
2. again	10. fly	18. his	26. of	34. stop
3. an	11. from	19. how	27. old	35. take
4. any	12. give	20. into	28. once	36. thank
5. as	13. going	21. just	29. open	37. them
6. ask	14. had	22. know	30. over	38. then
7. by	15. has	23. let	31. put	39. were
8. could	16. her	24. live	32. round	40. when

PHONICS

The pupil will be able to make the sounds of the consonants in the initial position. First *M, T, B, H, P, N;* then *D, W, G, C, J;* then *F, L, R, S;* finally *V, X, Y, Z, K,* and *Q.* (Order as suggested by Dechant, 1964.)

The pupil will:

know consonants in ending position of words

know consonants in middle position of words

know short vowel sounds: a, o, i, u, e

know beginning consonant blends: *sh, st, tr, cr, dr, fr, pl, sp, bl, br, cl, ch, dr, fl, gl, gr, sk, sm, sp, sw, sn*

STRUCTURAL ANALYSIS

Compound words are introduced: upon, cannot, into, etc.

The pupil will:

know common word patterns and apply consonant substitution

an	od	it	un	en
at	og	in	ug	ed
am	ot	im	ut	et
ap	ob	id	um	
ag	op	ig		

know common word endings, *-s* and *-ing*: sing–singing, ball–balls

know various sounds of *-ed,* i.e., *ed* in looked (sound of *t*)

                                     ed in wanted (sound of *ed*)

                                     ed in played (sound of *d*)

know about most frequently used contractions: it's, I'm, can't, that's, don't, etc.

COMPREHENSION

The pupil will:

recall what has been read silently

recall what has been read orally

draw conclusions from given facts

follow simple printed directions

place events in sequence

SILENT READING

The pupil will:

read without lip movement, vocalization, or whispering

read without head movement

recall what has been silently read

follow directions gained from silent reading

ORAL READING

The pupil will:

use proper phrasing

draw conclusions from stated facts

demonstrate knowledge of periods, commas, interrogation and exclamation marks through voice inflection in oral reading

demonstrate understanding of what he is reading through voice intonation

Level B Skills

The pupil will be able to demonstrate mastery of all skills at "A" level.

The pupil should be able to recognize the following sight words in isolation as well as in context.

SIGHT WORDS

1. always	13. cold	25. off	37. us
2. around	14. city	26. or	38. use
3. ahead	15. does	27. pull	39. walk
4. because	16. don't	28. read	40. wash
5. been	17. fast	29. right	41. which
6. begin	18. first	30. sing	42. why
7. before	19. found	31. sit	43. wish
8. belong	20. gave	32. sleep	44. work
9. best	21. goes	33. tell	45. would
10. both	22. its	34. their	46. write
11. buy	23. made	35. these	47. yet
12. call	24. many	36. those	48. your

PHONICS

The pupil will:

learn additional word patterns with consonant substitution:

ell	ust	ump	ank
ick	ack	ast	ent
end	est	ake	ant
ate	and	ill	ing

learn, also, other helpful patterns:

oi as in oil	er as in her
oy as in boy	ur as in fur
ou as in out	ir as in bird
ow as in cow	oo as in book
ow as in show	oo as in balloon

know two sounds of *c*: hard as in *cook* and soft as in *ceiling*

know two sounds of *g*: hard as in *goose* and soft as in *gentle*

recognize and sound three-letter blends:

str	spl	spr
sch	thr	squ
shr	chr	scr

know the short vowel generalization (when a vowel is in the middle of a one-syllable word, vowel sound is short)

know the final *e* in short word rule (when there are two vowels, one of which is final *e*, the first vowel is long and the *e* is silent)

STRUCTURAL ANALYSIS

The pupil: recognizes root words

acquires confidence with possessives

extends knowledge of contractions; differentiates between contractions and possessives

COMPREHENSION

The pupil can: draw conclusions and predict outcomes

gain meaning from words, sentences, selections

use punctuation meaningfully

SILENT READING SKILLS

The pupil can: read without lip or head movement, pointing, or whispering

recall and follow directions gained from silent reading

ORAL READING SKILLS

The pupil can: read with fluency and expression

convey meaning to listeners

demonstrate eye-voice span of three words

Level C Skills

The pupil should be able to demonstrate mastery of the skills of levels "A" and "B." The pupil should be able to recognize the following sight words in isolation as well as in context.

SIGHT WORDS

1. able	11. eight	21. keep	31. parent
2. about	12. fall	22. kind	32. pick
3. better	13. far	23. laugh	33. rescue
4. bring	14. full	24. light	34. shall
5. carry	15. got	25. long	35. show
6. clean	16. grow	26. much	36. start
7. cut	17. hold	27. myself	37. today
8. done	18. hurt	28. never	38. together
9. draw	19. if	29. only	39. try
10. drink	20. island	30. own	40. warm

PHONICS

The pupil should:

learn additional word patterns and apply consonant substitution:

ail	one	are	ear
ine	air	ore	all

learn most commonly used prefixes and suffixes:

un-	dis-	sub-	-ful	-ment
ex-	in-	re-	-less	-ty
be-	th-	anti-	-ness	-ion

STRUCTURAL ANALYSIS

The pupil should:

reinforce skills previously taught

learn most basic syllabication rules:

> the number of vowel sounds in a word determines the number of syllables in a word
>
> when there is a double consonant in a word, the syllable break is between two consonants
>
> prefixes are separate syllables

COMPREHENSION

The pupil should:

practice identifying author's purpose

practice identifying main characters' traits

become proficient in finding the main idea of a selection

learn to use dictionary and reference works

learn rudiments of note-taking from reading

SILENT READING

The pupil should:

reinforce skills previously taught

increase rate of silent reading

ORAL READING

The pupil should:

consolidate skills previously taught

If the pupil masters the basic requirements above, he should then be exposed to a great deal of high-interest low-difficulty reading material which will give him many success experiences and enable him to practice his newly acquired skill. The more advanced aspects of reading development are dealt with in the following chapter on vocabulary, comprehension, study skills, and reading rate.

ANCILLARY SERVICES IN A READING PROGRAM

Teachers and administrators, particulary in large school systems, are constantly seeking ways to provide the large numbers of children with reading problems some means of getting badly needed individualized and personalized instruction. It seems obvious strained school budgets will never provide sufficient remedial teachers to meet the ever present need. The following is a description of a plan that may be helpful in making use of community resources. The description is the text of a presentation made by one of the authors at a conference at Western Washington College of Education, Bellingham, Washington, that dealt with approaches to solving reading problems.

VIP's IN YOUR READING PROGRAM

One of the very few issues in education that everyone can agree upon is the need for improvement in reading instruction. Most school systems promote a reading program that seeks to meet the needs of *all* youngsters.

In the Portland, Oregon, school system, a valuable program was instituted to assist in meeting the needs of poor readers. The plan grew out of the ashes of a levy defeat which necessitated several remedial teachers being assigned to the classroom as regular teachers, resulting in a considerable number of youngsters being dropped from the remedial program. Thus began the parent-tutoring program. It was a serendipitous event for two reasons. First, more tutoring help could be provided. Second, it was a program that would get the patrons involved with the school by allowing them to see firsthand some of the problems facing most school districts.

Once the idea of enlisting parent volunteers was formulated, things moved very rapidly. Acknowledgment must go to the principals who enlisted the aid of their PTA boards. Radio and newspapers gave good coverage and television stations were happy to cover the first tutor-training sessions.

The following ground rules were formulated:

1. Volunteers were asked to contribute two hours per week, preferably in three forty-minute periods on different days of the week.

2. All tutoring would be on a one-to-one basis.

3. The necessity of training was emphasized. This consisted of two two-hour sessions plus one monthly meeting after the tutoring was under way.

4. Any and all adults were welcome: parents, grandparents, nonparents.

5. If a volunteer had a youngster with a reading problem, he would not tutor his own child.

6. Volunteers were furnished with all supplies and materials and, when possible, worked with the age/grade youngster they preferred within the limits of the 3–8 grade span.

In the training sessions, the tutor was given the philosophy of a remedial program, some basic and very simple phonic lessons, the rationale of a basic sight vocabulary, and finally a presentation of the materials they would be using. In each of the sessions a pattern evolved that generally followed this outline.

1. A general discussion was held which sought briefly to answer the questions: "Just what is a remedial case? " "How did he get that way? " "Are there different kinds of remedial cases? " "Can they be helped? "

2. By way of providing them with a philosophy upon which to base their teaching, each tutor was given a copy of Edward Dolch's 1953 article in *Elementary English* entitled "Success in Remedial Reading." Briefly stated, it points out that every remedial case is a case of failure, thus the first step is to remove fear, frustration, and insecurity. The next step involves discovering the pupil's "area of confidence." The third step consists of advancing from the area of confidence by a continual series of success steps.

3. Using the *Barbe List of Basic Reading Skills,* some basic phonic indoctrination was presented. Rules were not emphasized but the importance of helping youngsters to develop good auditory perception was stressed.

4. The Dolch Basic Sight Vocabulary was explained with greater emphasis on the previously mentioned word-attack skills and the need for some sight recognition of utility words pointed out.

5. Finally, the materials were presented and each group was given a chance to examine and hear a presentation of the following:

a. Dolch Sight Vocabulary

b. *Go Fish* initial consonant game

c. *Go Fish* initial blends game

d. *Conquests in Reading,* W. Kottmeyer, both pupil book and teacher's manual

e. some district-made diagnostic and prescriptive reading exercises

f. many of the better known high-interest/low-ability books, such as:

Morgan Bay Mystery	*Sailor Jack*
Deep Sea Adventure	*Checkered Flag*
Jim Forest	*Dolch Basic Vocabulary*
Dan Frontier	

These were supplemented by a great many of the Dr. Seuss books, the Bennett Cerf riddle books, books of plays such as *The Straw Ox,* and many other old standbys effective with disabled readers.

This, then, was the major portion of the "training" given the tutors. The sessions concluded with a two-page *Tips for Tutors* which reviewed many of the items that had been previously stressed. In addition to the summing up done in this two-page handout, there were tips for the first session and suggestions for varying the pace in all sessions, closing with the inspiring quote from President John F. Kennedy, "One man can make a difference and every man should try."

What were the results? Objectively we cannot say, no initial or final testing was done. Subjectively, there is considerable proof of progress. Teachers reported improved reading by the tutees and a better attitude toward school. Tutors began to see changes taking place in children. As an example, at the start of the tutoring sessions a boy somewhat skeptically said to his tutor, "How much are you getting paid for this?" The tutor explained she was unpaid and was there merely to help him. The boy plainly showed by his look that he was doubtful of such altruism. After a few weeks of triweekly sessions, the tutor told her pupil that they wouldn't meet at their appointed time the next day because she needed to keep a doctor's appointment. The youngster then asked in a somewhat grieved tone, "Couldn't you have made your appointment for a day we didn't have a lesson? "

In the year-end meeting with the tutors, most expressed a new awareness and understanding of the problems facing the classroom teacher.

A frequent comment was, "I wish I'd had this training and experience when my own youngster had trouble with reading. I just didn't understand it then." These remarks serve to illustrate the point that not only did children profit from the program but patrons gained an appreciation of the task done by the school. Some teachers, it might be added, grew a little also. Many commented, with some surprise, that "these parents really do make a difference, and they had the perseverence to stay with their job, too! "

Parents and other adult tutors can make a genuine contribution to the reading program. They won't solve all the problems; they can, however, provide a valuable ancillary service in the day-to-day struggle to keep ahead of the reading problems.

THOUGHTS FOR DISCUSSION

"If a child has remedial reading on an irregular schedule, such as every other day, the classroom teacher must continue with the same program as the one prescribed by the remedial teacher." (Byrne, 1968, p. 22)

"Remarkable success has been achieved by our educational system, but so long as there is one boy or girl who leaves school unable to read to the full extent of his capability, we cannot escape the charge of failure in carrying out the responsibility entrusted to us." (Allen, 1969, p. 5)

"Developmental instructional material should be designed to unfold gradually and systematically a logical sequence of skills or concepts to be mastered. It must be of optimum difficulty for the learner. A child should not be introduced to more difficult material until he has thoroughly mastered all that is foundational or prerequisite to it." (Schubert and Torgerson, 1968, p. 66)

". . . the research from 1912 to 1965 indicates that a code-emphasis method— i.e., one that views beginning reading as essentially different from mature reading and emphasizes learning of the printed code for the spoken language—produces better results, at least up to the point where sufficient evidence seems to be available, the end of the third grade." (Chall, 1967, p. 307)

"The problems of beginning reading instruction have been greatly overdramatized. There are many communities in all parts of the country in which reading failure is seldom encountered in the first grade. All that we need is efficient instruction which is adjusted to individual subskill needs and which conforms to the nature of the learning task. The nonreader is a child who has been inadequately served in the classroom."(Durrell, 1964, p. 71)

"A long list of mental activities that any psychologist would consider general properties of thinking that occur in many different areas of human experience have somehow or other all been tucked under the skirts of reading. 'Recalling,' 'comprehending,' 'relating facts,' 'making inferences,' 'drawing conclusions,' 'interpreting' and 'predicting outcomes' are all mental operations that go on in the head of a non-literate aborigine navigating his outrigger according to cues from weather, sea life, currents, and the positions of heavenly bodies. Not only do these kinds of thinking have no necessary connection with reading, but they have no necessary connection with language whatever." (Moffett, 1968, p. 16)

REFERENCES

Allen, J. E., Jr. The right to read—Target for the 70's. Paper read at the 1969 Annual Convention of the National Association of State Boards of Education.

Burrows, A. T., and Lourie, Z. When "two vowels go walking." *The Reading Teacher*, 1963, **17**, 79–82.

Byrne, R. L. *Remedial reading.* Washington, D.C.: Education, Inc., 1968.

Chall, J. *Learning to read.* New York: McGraw-Hill, 1967.

Clymer, T. The utility of phonic generalizations in the primary grades. *The Reading Teacher*, 1963, **16**, 252–258.

Dechant, E. V., *Improving the teaching of reading.* Englewood Cliffs, N. J.: Prentice-Hall, 1964.

Durrell, D. D. Learning factors in beginning reading. *Teaching Young Children to Read*, Bulletin No. 19. Washington, D. C.: U.S. Government Printing Office, 1964, 71–72.

Fernald, G. M. *Remedial techniques in basic school subjects.* New York: McGraw-Hill, 1943.

Gillingham, A., and Stillman, B. W. *Remedial training for children with specific disabilities in reading, spelling and penmanship.* Benton Harbor, Mich.: Educational Service, Inc., 1956.

Harris, A. J. *How to increase reading ability.* (5th ed.) New York: David McKay, 1970.

Johnson, D. D. The Dolch list reexamined. *The Reading Teacher*, 1971, **24**, 449–457.

Kottmeyer, W. *Teacher's guide for remedial reading.* St. Louis: Webster, 1959.

McKee, P. G. *The teaching of reading in the elementary school.* Boston: Houghton Mifflin, 1948.

Moffett, J. *A student-centered language arts curriculum, grades k-13: A handbook for teachers.* Boston: Houghton Mifflin, 1968.

Rinsland, H. D. *A basic vocabulary of elementary school children.* Oklahoma City: University of Oklahoma, 1945.

Russell, D. H., and Karp, E. E. *Reading aids through the grades.* New York: Bureau of Publications, Teachers College, Columbia University, 1956.

Schubert, D. G., and Torgerson, T. L. *Improving reading through individualized correction.* (2nd ed.) Dubuque, Iowa: William C. Brown, 1968.

Strang, R., McCullough, C. M., and Traxler, A. E. *The improvement of reading.* (4th ed.) New York: McGraw-Hill, 1961.

Thorndike, E. L., and Lorge, I. *The teacher's word book of 30,000 words.* New York: Bureau of Publications, Teachers College, Columbia University, 1944.

Chapter 8

Vocabulary, Comprehension, Study Skills, and Reading Rate

While the remedial or corrective pupil is mastering the decoding process of reading he needs also to be developing his vocabulary, comprehension, study skills, and rate of reading. The vocabulary and comprehension skills needed in the early grades are relatively simple because some control is generally used in presenting both vocabulary and concepts. Beginning in the fourth grade, however, the teacher is often faced with a task different from initial reading instruction. Both vocabulary and concepts are more difficult in the reading material assigned in middle and upper grades, and instruction must take this into account. Study skills and an increased rate of reading are additional skills that are needed to complete the task of producing an able reader at this academic level.

The following discussion assumes the disabled reader has mastered a basic sight vocabulary; that he has learned a definite system of word attack involving phonics, structural analysis, or a combination of both; and that his greatest need in order to become an adequate grade-level reader is adjusted but specific developmental teaching. While these components of reading skill are discussed separately, it will be evident to the teacher that they are not separable. Beginning about fourth grade, the greatly increased demand made upon the pupil by more difficult concepts, increased vocabulary load, the greater self-discipline required in terms of study skills, and the necessity for increased rate of reading becomes apparent for even the able student and is greatly compounded for the reader who is trying desperately to "catch up." If the teacher accepts the accuracy and truth of the above premise, he must also accept the implications for adequate diagnosis and purposeful, palatable teaching. The methods presented have been found effective by many remedial teachers.

VOCABULARY

Consensus regarding the need for systematic and extensive vocabulary development is unanimous among authorities in reading instruction; and the need is recognized, too, by teachers who work with disabled readers. Kottmeyer (1959) has accurately pointed out that disabled readers are usually aurally familiar with a much larger vocabulary than they can recognize in print. As a consequence, word meaning is not likely to be a problem in the beginning stages of word recognition skill development; but the need to be concerned with the development of word meanings becomes more vital as the disabled reader progresses beyond a minimal sight vocabulary. Botel (1963) not only stresses the need for teaching vocabulary as part of the reading lesson but also makes a point for relatively isolated vocabulary work. He feels that vocabulary training needs to be both *horizontal* and *vertical* (learning more about words already known is horizontal improvement, and learning new and unfamiliar words is vertical improvement). While this concept was intended for developmental reading instruction, it is also well suited for work with disabled readers. It is in agreement with this point of view that the following suggestions and techniques are offered. The problem of diagnosis is discussed first.

Diagnosis of Vocabulary Inadequacies

The initial problem in diagnosing or determining where to begin vocabulary instruction with the disabled reader is usually not complicated. It can be done either formally or informally. The formal method typically involves the use of a standardized test which contains a separate vocabulary section. Most of the survey-type reading tests discussed in Chapter 5 include a vocabulary subtest. The inadequacy of this method is fairly obvious in that formal vocabulary tests usually yield only a grade-level score, a standard score, or some equally nebulous figure that has little meaning for the teacher insofar as telling him where to begin instruction. A more practical approach, in the view of the writers, may be for the teacher to try to examine the pupil's understanding and functional ability by one of the following methods.

1. *An informal inventory*—using a text judged to be at or near the pupil's instructional level of reading. By informally quizzing the pupil on the meanings he derived from context it is often fairly easy to determine not only the quantity but the quality of vocabulary work needed.

2. *An accepted frequency list*—such as Durrell's (1956), which contains words for fourth through sixth grades, or the Dolch Sight Vocabulary (see Chapter 7), or the McMenemy Functional Literacy List presented later in this chapter. Such lists enable a teacher to make a quick but accurate check on a pupil's mastery of words at various difficulty and/or frequency levels, and provide a valuable list of words pupils need to know if they are to attain a level of functional literacy.

3. *Word lists*—obtained from a book the pupil is going to be called upon to use. This is, of course, similar to the first method mentioned; but it offers the advantage of dealing with the specific words the pupil can expect to encounter in his assigned reading.

Remedial Guidelines

Once the scope and sequence of vocabulary instruction have been determined, many ways have been evolved to make vocabulary work pleasurable and productive. Before enumerating some of the techniques and methods that have proved to be effective for many remedial teachers, the following basic guidelines should be reviewed, for they are appropriate regardless of the specific method chosen.

1. Each pupil should be allowed to work on his own instructional level and at his own pace.

2. Wherever possible, words should be used and taught in a contextual setting. The words should have utility for the pupil. Motivation must be maintained and a variety of approaches used to keep the sessions alive and interesting.

3. When a word is chosen for study, multiple—but not obscure—meanings should be taught. Synonyms or different words which mean approximately the same thing should be taught.

4. A progress chart or record of new words learned should be maintained. This is for the pupil's benefit and inspiration. Consequently it should be simple and imaginative lest it degenerate into the drudgery and boredom of merely maintaining a card file or notebook that is too cumbersome and detailed. It is the authors' view that unless such records are handled with a light touch they often stifle interest.

Methods and Techniques

Following are some suggested methods and materials for teaching word meanings that many remedial teachers have found to be effective.

Preview Method   A very common method is as follows: The teacher previews a selection to be read and selects the most difficult words for discussion or explanation. This method needs to be handled with a certain degree of finesse, however, lest interest in the story be destroyed by too much discussion of isolated words. In using this technique the teacher has an excellent opportunity for expanding definitions and pointing out, perhaps, other ways to say the same thing, or, as the case may be, other meanings and uses for the same word.

Directed Word Study   Directed word study can be accomplished in several interesting ways.

1. Pupils can contribute specialized lists of words that apply to subject matter areas, such as social studies, mathematics, etc.

2. Pupil-made or commercially made crossword puzzles can interject an element of fun if they are not too difficult.

3. Practice in recognizing meanings of the common prefixes, suffixes, and roots can be useful with more mature pupils.

4. Practice in being specific in shades of meaning and in discovering unfamiliar uses of words.

5. Practice in recognizing synonyms, antonyms, and homonyms.

6. Learning about sources of words; the derivations of many words involve interesting stories.

7. Arranging lists of words in some special interesting ways. A pupil (or groups of pupils) can contribute a list of words appropriate to his hobby or favorite sport, such as the following lists for baseball and art:

diamond	perspective
home-run	canvas
Texas-leaguer	pallette
pitcher's mound	charcoal
batter's box	shading
hickory stick	infinity
glove	primary colors
mitt	secondary colors
mask	pastels
bag	easel
foul	texture
curve	portrait
box score	sketch
batting average	highlight

Wide Reading Method Wide reading and the consequent enrichment of vocabulary it brings is the most natural and, perhaps, the most effective way to develop vocabulary. The only difficulty with this method is that the pupil with whom we are concerned here is not (and may never become) an avid reader. Because of this fact it behooves the teacher doing the remedial work to take steps to insure that in whatever reading the pupil does, he is able to get meaning from context. Teachers cannot assume that the poor reader will be able to learn this incidentally. An effective approach for helping students develop facility in the skill of deriving meaning from context is described below.

1. Explain to the student, in terms he understands, that more often than not he can derive the meaning of a word from context. Start with simple sentences to prove your point, e.g., "He went to the *stationery* department to get paper for school." Explain that most authors try to supply their readers with clues to the meanings of unfamiliar words.

2. Show, by example, the type of clue sometimes designated as inferred or built-in meaning, e.g., "There is a city *ordinance* which prohibits speeding."

3. Go on to the contrast-type of clue wherein an author first uses a word in such a way that its meaning might not be clear and then quickly does an about-face in the next sentence to show in simple terms what the unknown word means, e.g., "He had *misgivings* about the outcome of the election. I told him he shouldn't have any doubts about our candidate's ability to win."

4. Illustrate the common-sense type of clue wherein the meaning is quite apparent if the pupil takes time to think. An example of this type would be,

"The pitcher was *downcast* over his defeat so his teammates tried to cheer him up."

Dictionary Method The use of the dictionary to improve vocabulary is often found to be the least productive method to use with poor readers. It has been the authors' experience that usually dictionary exercises are either too complicated or too dull to produce good results. While it may not be invariably true, it seems clear that if a pupil could and would make proper use of a dictionary, he probably wouldn't be a poor reader.

Each of the publishers of school dictionaries publishes teaching suggestions for use with the dictionary. The teacher may find it profitable to use such materials but again care must be exercised to avoid unproductive "busy work" that may stifle interest in words generally. Each case must be considered individually.

Books and Workbooks for Vocabulary Development Reading workbooks, written to accompany a basic series, as well as many of the supplemental skill-type workbooks, contain good suggestions for vocabulary building. The annotated list at the end of the section on comprehension skills in this chapter may prove helpful in locating materials for teaching vocabulary skills.

Functional Literacy Vocabularies Because of the recent interest and need for a functional literacy vocabulary list for use where a functional level of reading is the only realistic goal, attempts have been made to produce such a list. One of the most practical efforts has been made by M. Adele Mitzel (1966), who has compiled a pragmatic list of five thousand words gleaned from many sources, e.g., government publications and forms, employment forms, nonacademic magazines, menus, signs, union literature, political campaign literature, labels, religious tracts, and many similar sources. The list appears to have considerable utility in that it could serve as a basic reading, thinking, and speaking vocabulary for use with adult Americans in need of functional reading instruction. One of the writers has used the list as a basis for developing a very utilitarian functional literacy list of two thousand words, carefully graded by difficulty levels, which should be helpful in working with severely disabled readers of junior and senior high school age. In the list below, the first section consists of approximately five hundred of the most basic words; the second section consists of the next fifteen hundred words most frequently encountered:

THE McMENEMY FUNCTIONAL LITERACY LIST

Part I

Primary

a	can	down	good	home
and	car			house
at	come	for	have	
away			he	I
	did	get	help	in
big	do	go	here	is

it	be	ice	room	apartment
	before	if		arm
like	best	into	saw	
	better		school	because
make	boat	just	she	been
may	box		shoe	begin
me	bus	know	show	belong
my	but		snow	beside
	buy	last	so	between
not	by	live	some	bill
now		long	stay	block
	call		store	board
on	children	made	street	bread
	coat	man		break
red	cold	many	take	breakfast
	color	men	than	building
said	could	milk	that	butter
see		Miss	their	
stop	day	money	them	care
	don't	more	there	city
the	door	Mr.	these	clean
this	dress	Mrs.	they	clothes
to		much	those	corner
two	egg	must	time	cream
	every		too	cross
up		name	train	dinner
	feet	near	truck	dollar
want	fine	new		done
we	fire	next	under	drive
what	first	night		driver
will	fish	no	walk	
with	found		was	easy
work	from	of	water	edge
		off	way	evening
yes		old	were	ever
you	game	one	when	eye
	give	or	where	
		other	who	fat
1st Grade	had	our	window	finish
about	hand	out	word	floor
after	has	over		food
all	head		year	foot
an	hear	paint	yellow	front
any	her	park	your	full
are	high	picture		
as	him	please	*2nd Grade*	glass
ask	his		able	goes
	hot	right	ahead	
back	how	road	air	hair

join	shall	coffee	plan	area
	shop	company	police	avenue
keep	should	continue	price	
kind	shut	cost		business
kitchen	side		reason	
	sign	danger	record	check
large	slow	dime	repair	condition
leave	small	doctor		
left	stand	dry	safety	date
life	start	during	sale	delivery
line	station		save	department
low	stone	earn	serve	distance
	such	east	signal	duty
machine	suit	enter	since	
mail		escape	single	electric
mean	telephone		size	experience
minute	television	free	smoke	express
most	ticket	Friday	sold	
move	turn		son	furniture
		gas	south	information
need	use	group	special	
number		guard	speed	married
	wait		stamp	material
office	wash	half	state	modern
only	watch	heart	strike	
open	week	heat	Sunday	national
own	which	hospital		nurse
	wife	hour	Thursday	
	write	husband	tire	opposite
paper			trade	
part	*3rd Grade*	law	traffic	period
pass	add		travel	person
pay	address	mark		private
pick	age	meat	United States	property
place	also	metal	upon	
point	American	mile		quarter
present	army	Monday	vegetable	
	automobile	month		rent
quiet		motor	weight	
	bar		west	self
radio	beauty	narrow	women	service
real	birth	nickel		steel
rest	body	north	yet	supply
return				
roof	case	oil	*4th Grade*	type
	cause	order	accept	
safe	charge		admit	*5th Grade*
Saturday	church	page	altogether	account
say	class	paid	amount	aid

benefit	loss	vehicle	occupation	residential
credit	male	*6th Grade*	rate	sex
	member	available	register	
daily	military			
district		cigarette	satisfaction	unite
	p.m.			
emergency	prompt	employ	tavern	welfare
equipment	provide	employment		
establish	public	estate		
		estimate	*7th Grade*	*8th Grade*
female		etc.	complete	application
furnish	quality		dealer	finance
		former	dependent	
gasoline	restaurant			installment
		income	exceed	
height	social	individual	exit	lease
	society			
include	stock	local	insurance	maximum
	system		liquor	mortgage
license		manager		
limit	tax	mechanical	payment	
loan	term	medical	prohibit	security

Part II

Primary

ball	*1st Grade*	cake	garden	light
		came	gave	lost
fast	again	can't	girl	lunch
father	alone	cat	glad	
fun	along	catch	gone	met
	am	cry	got	morning
	animal		grass	
green	another	dark	ground	never
	around	does	grow	nothing
little		dog	guess	
	baby			oh
	basket	each	happy	once
mother	bear	eat	hard	
	bed		hat	painter
play	began	far	heard	party
	behind	farm	hill	peanut
ride	being	find	hold	people
run	birthday	fit	honey	pet
	black	five	hurry	pocket
	book	flower		pretty
something	boy	fly	laugh	prize
	bring	four	let	pull
toy	brown	friend	letter	put

rain	ago	country	heavy	outside
ran	almost	cover	held	oven
read	always	cut	himself	
ready	anger		hit	pair
	answer	dance	hole	past
sat	anyone	dear	hope	pie
sing	anything	deep	horn	piece
sit		didn't	hungry	pile
sleep	bad	different	hunt	pipe
soon	bake	dish		plant
spring	beautiful	drink	idea	poor
step	beginning	drop	I'll	print
story	believe		I'm	push
sun	bell		important	
surprise	bone	ear	inside	question
	both	early	isn't	quick
tail	bottle	eight	its	
talk	bought	else		race
tell	branch	end		railroad
then	bridge	engine	kept	reach
thing	bright	enough	key	really
think	broken	even	kill	remember
three	brother	everything	knew	ring
told	brought	everywhere		river
took	build			rock
town	burn	face	ladder	roll
tree	busy	fair	lady	rope
try		fall	lake	round
	camp	family	land	
us	candy	farther	late	sad
	cannot	feel	lay	same
very	cap	felt	leg	seat
	card	fence	library	second
went	careful	few	left	secret
wet	carry	field	listen	seed
white	caught	fight	lock	seem
why	cent	fill	lot	seen
wish	chair	fix	loud	sell
within	change	flag	love	send
woman	chicken	flash		sent
would	Christmas	follow	maybe	set
	climb	fourth	middle	seven
yard	clock	fruit	might	short
	close		mouth	silver
2nd Grade	coal	gate		sister
above	cook	gold		six
across	corn	great	nail	sky
afraid	couldn't		neck	smile
afternoon	count	happen	neighbor	soft
		haven't	nine	

someone	well	belt	disappear	given
sorry	wheel	bend	discover	grain
sound	while	beyond	divide	guide
soup	wide	blind	doesn't	gun
stick	win	blood	drag	
still	wind	bold	draw	hall
stood	winter	born	dream	handle
storm	wonder	brick		hang
straight	wonderful	brush	earth	harm
strange	won't	built	easily	highway
strong	wood		eighty	holiday
summer	world	cabin	either	hose
sure	wrong	calendar	eleven	hundred
swim		camera	enjoy	
swing	young	center	event	ill
	you'll	certain	everybody	impossible
table	yourself	chain	example	inch
tag		chance	except	indeed
taken	*3rd Grade*	cheer	exercise	instead
tall	act	cheese	expect	intend
teach	against	chief	explain	interest
teacher	aim	child	extra	interesting
ten	airport	choose		invite
tent	alarm	circle	fail	iron
third	alike	clear	famous	
thought	alive	clip	fan	job
through	already	cloth	fault	judge
throw	America	clothing	February	juice
tie	among	cloud	fifth	July
today	announce	club	fifty	June
together	appear	comfortable	finger	
tomorrow	April	common	flat	kiss
tonight	arrange	cool	flow	knife
top	arrive	copy	fold	known
track	August	correct	force	
tractor	average	course	forest	lead
trip	awful	crowd	forgot	lean
trouble		cup	forgotten	learn
	bargain		form	led
until	base	darkness	forty	less
useful	baseball	daughter	forward	lesson
	bath	dead	fourteen	lie
visit	beach	decide	fresh	list
voice	beat	depend	fur	load
	became	deserve		lumber
warm	become	diamond	garage	
wave	bedroom	die	gentle	main
wear	begun	difference	giant	map
weigh	below	direction	gift	March

market	pound	simple	unless	bound
marry	pour	sixteen	usual	brain
master	power	sixty	usually	bury
match	practice	skin		
matter	prepare	slip	wall	cast
mayor	president	smart	war	character
meal	press	smooth	warn	china
meet	promise	soap	waste	citizen
message	prove	sort	weather	claim
mind		space	welcome	coin
mine	queen	speak	whip	collect
mirror	quite	spirit	whole	collection
mix		spoke	whose	comfort
model	raise	spot	willing	committee
moment	rather	spray	wipe	contain
mount	rear	spread	wire	control
	receive	stage	worth	convenient
	refuse	star	wouldn't	couple
nation	remain	steal	wreck	court
net	respect	steam	written	creature
nobody	reward	stretch		cruel
none	rich	strip		current
note	rose	sudden	you're	curve
notice	route	sweet	you've	custom
November	rubber			customer
	rule	tank	*4th Grade*	
ocean		taste	accident	
offer	salt	team	according	damage
often	sand	teeth	action	dangerous
ought	satisfy	test	adjust	deal
	scene	themselves	afford	death
pack	season	thick	agree	December
package	seize	thin	although	declare
pale	sense	though	ancient	deed
parent	serious	thousand	anybody	deliver
passenger	several	till	appearance	demand
path	shade	tip	approach	design
pen	shadow	touch	arrest	destroy
perhaps	shake	toward	article	develop
pillow	shape	tower	attention	difficult
plain	share	trail	avoid	direct
plate	sharp	trust		disease
pleasant	sheet	tube	balance	dock
plenty	shell	tune	battery	doubt
pool	shine	tunnel	battle	dozen
porch	ship	twenty	bay	
possible	shore		beef	eastern
post	shot	understand	bet	effect
potato	sick	understood	bid	eighteen
			blame	encourage

entire	instrument	perform	success	attach
envelope		persuade	suffer	attempt
equal	janitor	phone	sugar	attend
especially	January	popular	suggest	award
examination		position	support	
exchange	knowledge	possession	surface	bind
expert		powder	surround	bomb
	lamp	problem		border
fact	lawn	program	tailor	bore
factory	league	proof	tape	brake
familiar	least	protect	tea	brand
favor	leather	protection	tear	broad
favorite	level	pump	temperature	burden
figure	locate		tile	
final	luck	quarrel	ton	cab
flavor			trailer	cabinet
flood	manner	range	transfer	cafe
fought	measure	rat	treat	cafeteria
freedom	medicine	refrigerator	trim	capital
freight	mention	regular	tub	casual
frozen	midnight	relief	Tuesday	cell
furnace	million	remind	typewriter	century
further	motion	remove		cereal
future	music	report	uniform	certificate
		result		cheap
general	natural	rough	view	choice
God	nature	rug		college
golden	navy		Wednesday	column
government	necessary	salad	whether	community
grade	neighborhood	scale	whom	compare
gradually	news	score	wine	concrete
grand	nineteen	scout		confidence
greet	noon	screen	yesterday	Congress
grind	nor	seal		connect
grocery	northern	September	zone	consider
		sew		construction
handsome	obey	shoulder	*5th Grade*	convention
health	object	sight	accompany	county
hesitate	October	silk	addition	craft
hire	officer	sink	admission	crime
hotel	opinion	speech	adopt	curb
however	owe	spend	advance	
human		spent	advantage	decision
	pain	sport	advice	delay
immediately	pants	square	affect	dentist
improve	patient	stable	agent	deny
improvement	pattern	statement	alcohol	describe
insist	peace	stove	appeal	desire
instant	perfect	strength	athletic	detail

determine	mat	select	adult	disturbance
device		separate	affair	drug
dial	native	series	alert	
division	neglect	shock	allowance	employee
double	Negro	sickness	alteration	employer
due		sincerely	alternate	engage
dues	observe	situation	antique	erect
dump	obtain	soda	apply	exit
dye	occasion	soil	appointment	expense
	operate	stationery	approve	expose
ease	opportunity	steak	arouse	extreme
education	original	study	artificial	
effort		style	assistance	false
elect	peculiar	subject	assistant	feature
election	permit	successful	association	federal
electronic	physical	suggestion	assume	
enclose	pier		attitude	grief
entrance	pill	taxi	authority	guilty
equip	pleasure	territory		
evidence	poverty	theatre	barber	handicap
extend	practical	title	bond	handy
	presence	tobacco	breast	headquarters
fashion	pressure	total		household
file	prevent	tour	campaign	
foreign	principle	tow	capacity	importance
fuel	produce	transportation	cash	impression
funeral	product	trial	caution	independent
	profit		cease	industry
gain	progress	university	combine	inform
generally	proper		commercial	injury
governor	purchase	vacuum	commission	inspection
grant	pure	valuable	consist	install
gum		value	constitution	issue
	rail	various	contact	
ham	reasonable	vision	contract	judgment
hamburger	recently	vote	contrary	jury
	relative		coupon	
idle	remark	weapon	create	label
increase	rust	wedding	criminal	laundry
				legal
justice	salary	youth	decline	location
	sample		decoration	luggage
labor	science	*6th Grade*	defense	
lawyer	scrap	accomplish	democracy	maintain
liberty	secretary	acid	democratic	major
liquid	section	acquire	deposit	manual
	secure	active	detour	marine
machinery	seek	activity	diet	marriage
manufacture	seldom	adjustment	display	mechanic

mental	qualify	yacht	murder	economy
method	quantity	yield		eligible
monument			obligation	exclusive
movement	radiator	*7th Grade*	organization	
	receipt	actual		financial
necessity	recent	administration	policy	
notify	recommend	amusement	provision	intersection
	recover		publicity	investment
	recreation	bail	pursue	
occupy	reduce	boulevard		justify
occur	reference		reliable	
operation	relation	chauffeur	render	
opposition	relieve	civic	rental	liberal
overtake	religion	culture	Republican	lounge
	religious		resident	
panel	replace	Democrat	riot	maintenance
pave	representative	depart		merge
pavement	request	development	sanitary	minimum
per	require	diaper	suburb	
percent	research	director		nominate
performance	resort	directory	veteran	nomination
permanent		discount	vital	
personal	schedule	domestic	vitamin	ordinary
pest	senate	drapery		
photograph	senator		*8th Grade*	pedestrian
physician	session	efficient	ample	pharmacy
plastic	source	enforce	apparel	prescription
plumber	standard	executive	appliance	
plus	storage		applicant	
political	submarine	fee	authorize	registration
portable	sufficient	florist		reproduction
portion	suspend		beverage	requirement
possess		guarantee	budget	retail
powerful	tackle			
prefer	throughout	institution	clergy	surgeon
previous	toll	insure		surplus
prime	tone		defect	
privilege	treatment	latter	delicatessen	transit
process		lubricate	dental	trend
production	union		discharge	
professional		merchandise	divorce	
proportion	x-ray	mobile	duplicate	vacancy

In summary, we repeat that development of vocabulary is a continuous process. An extended, enriched, accurate, and meaningful vocabulary is a necessity, not only for adequate comprehension of what is read but for complete enjoyment of what is read. Whatever the means used by the teacher—directed word study, puzzles, workbooks, dictionary work, contextual means, etc.—the poor reader has a great need for growth in vocabulary. Any method that accomplishes this or even moves the pupil a little way down the road to better reading is well worth the time and effort expended.

COMPREHENSION

An acceptable goal for all disabled readers is the development and refinement of adequate comprehension skills. In this section we shall suggest formal and informal methods of diagnosing comprehension difficulties and remedial and corrective techniques aimed at helping the disabled learner in this most important area.

Diagnosis

Essentially, the same factors that were mentioned in connection with diagnosis of vocabulary deficiencies also apply to diagnosis of comprehension inadequacies. The comprehension score obtained from a typical standardized reading survey test may not be too helpful except as an indication of the need for further testing. At the specific level of diagnosis, there are several good diagnostic tests available (described in Chapter 5) for determining inadequacies in the several skill areas. Yet, there is a dearth of formal instruments designed to get at specific comprehension difficulties discretely. Part of the reason for this shortcoming in diagnostic tests is undoubtedly that there is (a) lack of agreement as to what all the components of comprehension are, and (b) a great degree of overlap in word recognition, understanding, interpretation, study skills, and other types of reading.

It is the view of the authors that much of the diagnostic work in the area of comprehension needs to be informal and highly individualized. The broad areas which seem to cover the basic aspects of comprehension are:
  1. understanding sentences
  2. understanding the paragraph
  3. understanding the whole selection
  4. understanding nonliteral language
  5. critical reading
  6. use of study skills
A separate treatment of critical reading and the use of study skills appears later in this chapter; remedial methods for the remaining components of comprehension are briefly discussed below.

Comprehension of Sentences

In the expression of thoughts and ideas, the smallest and basic unit is the sentence. If disabled readers can learn to apply to written sentences the things they have learned about sentences in oral expression, the task of correcting comprehension difficulties is well on the way to being accomplished. When the pupil uses oral language he almost always knows the proper way to put meaning into a sentence. Even though he may not know the technical terminology, he knows the subject generally comes first with the verbs following and he knows the placement of modifiers, articles, and conjunctions. Thus, if the disabled reader can be helped to understand that what he already knows may enable him to find key words that are useful in deciphering what printed sentences are about, his improvement may be nothing short of spectacular. There is no value to comprehension in conducting a formal study of English grammar.

The most accepted teaching procedure for helping a disabled reader improve his ability in comprehending sentences is to begin with extremely simple sentences and proceed with a series of success steps to those of more complex construction. The purpose here is to give the pupil a great deal of practice in answering the key questions of who, what, where, when, why, how, etc. Following is an example:

1. Tom swims well.
   Q. Who swims?
   How does he swim?

2. Tom swam and played in the pool.
   Q. What did Tom do?
   Where did he do it?

3. Tom swims in the pool every day.
   Q. What does Tom do?
   Where does he do it?
   When does he do it?

4. Tom, an expert swimmer, is so fond of swimming that he visits the pool in the park almost every day.
   Q. Who swims?
   Where does he swim?
   Why does he swim?
   How does he swim?
   When does he swim?

Another procedure that may help a pupil to see key words and to develop sentence sense is to present him with some scrambled sentences and give him practice in unscrambling them. He might be asked also to judge whether the sentence is fact or fiction. For example:

1. Columbus was thought the round world
   (Columbus thought the world was round.)

2. Seaport large New York a is City
   (New York City is a large seaport.)

Very often the pupil's inability to read in phrases or thought units is partly responsible for poor sentence comprehension. If this is found to be the case, he should be given practice with phrase material well within his independent reading level. A good place to start might be with the Dolch Sight Phrase Cards (Garrard Press). For a more naturalistic presentation of thought units, the teacher may type sentences that are artificially divided into meaningful phrases. For example:

The black horse/has run away/down the street.

Her mother/is coming/to the school/at three.

The teacher will want to move quickly from the easy examples given to materials from a book or a workbook. Pupils can be asked to supply the slashes that mark off thought units after they have had some practice in reading the premarked material.

Another device sometimes used by remedial teachers is the teacher-made tachistoscope described in the preceding chapter. The phrases are merely typed on a long sheet and pulled past the opening. Here again, the setting is not as natural as it is in actual reading material.

In a few cases the pupil may need some instruction and practice in the use and function of the more elementary punctuation marks. This is especially true of the period, the comma or pairs of commas, and perhaps the colon and semicolon.

Comprehension of Paragraphs

The paragraph is not only a longer unit of written expression but it is a more complicated unit as well. After the disabled reader can handle the skill of "solving" the sentence, he should then be given practice with the paragraph. The three factors that usually need the greatest amount of emphasis in helping a pupil better to comprehend a paragraph are the concept of main idea, the use of pronouns, and careful attention to words that show relationships (i.e., words that introduce phrases and clauses, and words that connect ideas).

It is imperative that the teacher start main idea instruction with ideal paragraphs (i.e., those paragraphs that begin with a topic sentence) rather than with the more complicated paragraphs in which the topic sentence is buried somewhere within the body of the paragraph. The most complicated type of all, those in which the topic sentence is only implied, are often beyond the disabled reader. This is something the teacher must decide on an individual basis.

A good technique for remedial work with paragraphs is first to have the pupil develop some paragraphs of his own. Another technique practiced by some remedial teachers is to ask the student to number the sentences, in paragraphs of three or four sentences at the start, in order of their importance to the main idea of the paragraph. With this procedure, the teacher should then point out how the subordinate sentences emphasize detail, lend importance to the topic sentence, explain or develop the substance of the paragraph.

Newspaper articles, screened by the teacher, are often excellent examples of expository writing at its best and usually are concise, interesting, and timely. The nature of news stories provides excellent practice in finding the answer to "who, what, when, why," etc. questions. An effective variation of newspaper reading is to have the pupil write a news story.

Remedial teachers frequently find that a contributory factor to poor paragraph comprehension is lack of knowledge on the part of the pupil about how pronouns are used. Comprehension frequently is dependent upon recognition of the antecedent, but the antecedent may not be the noun immediately before the pronoun. Bond and Tinker (1957) suggest having pupils practice designating to whom or to what the pronouns in practice sentences refer. For example:

We wanted to play with Tom and Mary, but *they* were not home.
The work was difficult but *it* was fun.
Showing me his new pencil, Bob asked, "Have you seen *this*?"

"Why," "how," "when," and "where" questions help students develop the habit of paying close attention to words that show relationships.

Comprehension of the Whole Selection

The ultimate goal of most reading instruction is to enable the pupil to understand a whole selection of printed material. He must not only comprehend words, sentences, and paragraphs but also grasp the author's purpose, his organizational plan in developing the selection, and the way in which the subordinate ideas are presented in order to support the main idea. He needs also to be able to draw conclusions and to generalize from what he has read.

In the case of poor readers it may occur to the teacher that these refinements of reading are too much to expect from a pupil who may only recently have had difficulty with much more basic skills in reading. Yet, if instruction begins with smaller units and if the development of the comprehension skills that follow is thorough and sequential, corrective cases can and do profit from instruction in this area.

Some suggestions for remedial work aimed at helping pupils develop skill in this important area are given below. Inasmuch as the ability to understand a whole body of material is an important study skill, the reader should also refer to the section of this chapter devoted to study skills.

1. Point out to a student that well-written material usually follows a pattern of introduction, body, and conclusion. This is often a good beginning toward helping him see the writer's overall plan. Examples should be given, beginning with short, well-written articles that conform to the pattern. Only after some understanding and insight is gained can the teacher advance the pupil to writing that deviates from this routine.

2. Have the pupil make a very general outline of the whole selection. A short, general outline is suggested since the purpose is not to teach outlining but to help the pupil gain insight in seeing the overall plan of the author.

3. Use a method similar to the scrambled sentence previously suggested for helping the pupil with sentence comprehension. The scrambled paragraphs may be pasted on cards, one to a card, and the pupil merely needs to arrange them in proper sequence. Explaining the reason for his choice of order often helps the pupil clarify his own thinking and gives the teacher opportunity for discussion and guidance.

Comprehension of Nonliteral Language

In the context of this discussion, nonliteral language includes similes, metaphors, euphemisms, colloquialisms, poetic expression, etc.; in short, it includes all figurative or imaginative speech.

Poor readers frequently find figures of speech very puzzling. When this is so, both comprehension and enjoyment are likely to suffer. Yet, the existing literature on recommended remedial methods in this area is both scant and vague. The suggestions and points made below may aid the teacher in this somewhat difficult and nebulous area.

Most important, the teacher should avoid technical terms. In the opinion of the writers it would be better, for corrective cases, to categorize all items under "figures of speech" rather than to confuse the pupil with terminology that may be both ambiguous and difficult for him. For these pupils, it is better practice to illustrate with several examples than to depend too much on vague definition.

If a pupil can be helped to see that similes, metaphors, and personification have comparison as their base, it gives him an insight that may help him to "solve" these sometimes puzzling usages. It can be pointed out to the pupil that the power of the sentence rests upon the comparison. For example, in the simile "John ran like a deer" nothing more than speed is implied, but in the metaphor "The wind clutched at the shutters with frantic fingers" a much stronger, more imaginative comparison is made.

It has been found helpful and pleasurable for most pupils to try their skill at deciphering figures of speech. A few suggestions are:

1. "His eyes are as big as saucers" does not really mean he has big eyes. It means. . . . .
2. "He shed crocodile tears" does not really mean he shed anything but human tears. It means . . . .

3. "It was raining cats and dogs" does not really mean it was raining anything but rain. It means..

4. "He was chicken-hearted" does not really mean he had the heart of a chicken. It means..

5. "Her eyes were bigger than her stomach" does not really mean she had huge eyes. It means ....

Some teachers have found that pupils like to write as well as "decipher" these. Paraphrasing is another helpful exercise for students who have trouble with figurative language.

A final cautionary word regarding the teaching of comprehension skills needs to be emphasized. It has been the experience and observation of the writers that too often the remedial teaching of comprehension, vocabulary, and other subskills of reading deteriorates into the manipulation of bits and pieces, i.e., skills and materials. Often, the teacher *and* the pupil lose sight of the total act of reading. Ideas and an organizational plan to assist teachers in putting the bits and pieces of remedial teaching together, and applications in the content areas, are presented in Chapter 6; a combining of the suggestions contained in Chapter 6 with those presented above would insure a worthy and effective remedial approach.

WORKBOOKS

Virtually all teachers who work with children who have learning problems have found workbooks indispensable for reinforcing and practicing the skills taught. The following annotated list is far from a complete one; it merely includes a representative sample of those books found helpful for development of the basic reading skills. In most cases, these workbooks contain valuable practice material in both vocabulary and comprehension. A teacher would want to examine them individually before selecting one or more for use with his pupils. It would also be well to review the discussion of workbooks in Chapter 7.

Anderson, Murray et al., *Merrill Reading Skilltext*. Columbus, Ohio: Charles E. Merrill, 1970. Skills developed in this program are the five major skill areas constantly stressed by reading experts: *understanding words, knowing the facts* (direct recall), *extending ideas* (judgment and interpretation), *organizing ideas,* and *studying word structure.* Two diagnostic tests are provided; one to be given before the *Skilltext* is started and one to be administered upon completion. Wholesome stories, designed to interest the today's pupil.

Bammon, Henry A. et al., *Kaleidoscope Readers*. San Francisco: Field Educational Publications, 1969. This series of paperback books is designed to increase the reading ability of junior and senior high school pupils. The range of difficulty is from second to ninth grade. The subject matter is of interest to teen-agers because of its relevance; topics include selections about careers, dating, authority, drugs, hot rods, social relations, sports, space,. and other subjects equally interesting to this age group. Virtually all skills are covered. Format is colorful and attractive.

Gates, A. I., and Peardon, C. C., *Reading Exercises.* New York: Bureau of Publications, Teachers College, Columbia University, 1963. This series of reading exercises is designed to give pupils specific and concentrated practice in reading for different purposes, e.g., Reading to Comprehend the Main Idea of a Selection, Reading to Understand Precise Directions, Reading to Note and Recall Details. Two preparatory level booklets, Levels A and B, are appropriate for better second-grade readers, average third, and less able fourth and fifth graders. Elementary and intermediate levels are also available at progressively harder levels. Use of *Gates Basic Reading Tests* is suggested to determine specific needs if in doubt.

Gray, W. S., Monroe, M., and Artley, A. S., *Basic Reading Skills for Junior High School Use.* Chicago: Scott, Foresman, 1970. This well-planned workbook for mildly disabled readers or corrective cases covers vocabulary, comprehension, and word analysis skills. A teacher's edition is available.

McCall, W. A., and Crabbs, L. M., *Standard Test Lessons in Reading,* revised. New York: Bureau of Publications, Teachers College, Columbia University, 1961. This series of workbooks that has been a standby with remedial teachers for almost forty years has been recently revised. Books A, B, C, D, and E range from about third to seventh grade in difficulty. Designed mainly to increase rate of comprehension, each book consists of a series of short articles with many comprehension questions. Pupils can score and keep track of progress. Scores are by grade level. Pupils find material interesting and grade-level scoring is a motivating factor.

Parker, D. H., *SRA Reading Laboratory,* elementary edition. Chicago: Science Research Associates, 1969. This multilevel developmental reading improvement program consists of material at ten difficulty levels, each consisting of approximately fifteen individual reading lessons. Comprehension, vocabulary, word-attack skills, and other aspects of reading are covered in each lesson. Also included are an equal number of Rate Builders, three-minute rate exercises at various levels of difficulty. Although the lab is a developmental reading program supplement, it is also valuable in a corrective-type program. Spelling, social studies, and study skills labs are also available, as are reading labs at specific grade levels.

Rambeau, John R., and Rambeau, Nancy, *A Guidebook to Better Reading.* Oklahoma City: Educational Guidelines, 1968. This paperback book assumes the student has acquired at least a first-grade reading vocabulary. Upon completion of the book, he should be reading on a fourth-grade reading level or higher. After completing the fifteenth daily lesson the student will be ready to begin reading the first of six high-interest low-vocabulary paperbacks. The material has been tailored for the older underachiever.

Lessons are colorfully illustrated and contain fictional and factual material. Teacher's guide is available and should be used. The titles of the six readers are *Jinx Boat, Explore, Venture, Quest, Peaville Adventure,* and *Polecat Adventure.*

Reading Attainment System. New York: Grolier, 1967 and 1970. This material consists of two kits; one at third- and fourth-grade level difficulty, the other at fifth- and sixth-level difficulty. Designed to fill the needs of corrective or remedial type classes, it includes 120 individual color coded reading selections, 120 skill cards, self-scoring answer cards, student record books, an instructor's manual, and a wall chart. Highly motivational subject matter.

Stern, Catherine, Gould, T. S., Stern, Margaret, and Teague, K. *New Structural Reading Series.* New York: Random House, 1972. An updating of the 1963 series that has proved to be effective with the disadvantaged, the perceptually handicapped, and children with English as a second language. Eight colorful workbooks, readers, and ancillary components plus excellent teacher editions.

Stone, C. R., and Grover, C. C., *Practice Readers,* Books I, II, III and IV. St. Louis: Webster, 1961. The old *Practice Readers* have been revised. The format is bright and the material updated. Practice in vocabulary, comprehension, main ideas, etc. is provided.

Wagner, G. L. et al., *Reader's Digest Reading Skill Builders.* New York: Reader's Digest Educational Service, 1958. This complete series, consisting of books at the first- through eighth-grade levels, is similar in format to the adult *Reader's Digest.* It contains highly readable stories and articles and is well illustrated. At the end of each article are comprehension, vocabulary, and discussion questions. The number of words in each article is given to permit reading for rate improvement. The format and material do not appear juvenile, thus this series can be used for all ages. A teacher's edition is also available.

Wagner, R. F., and Wagner, Marney H., *Stories about Idioms.* Portland, Maine: J. Weston Walch, 1961. An excellent source of idioms and phrases that remedial and classroom teachers have found helpful for enlivening the study of figures of speech.

STUDY SKILLS

An important and somewhat neglected area of corrective and remedial teaching, in the authors' view, is that of study skills. Smith (1963, p. 307) suggests that the term *study skills* may be such a recent addition to the nomenclature of reading that there is considerable misunderstanding or confusion over its exact meaning. She feels that in some people's minds, the term simply means habits and attitudes conducive to study. Her own definition more specifically applies to reading: ". . . skills used when there is *intention to do something with* the content read." The writers, while not quarreling with this definition, wish to suggest a more inclusive one broadened to include areas other than reading and *all* aspects of study. The point here is that in the case of disabled learners, entirely too much attention has been paid to the *methods* of study and too little to the elements involved in a *self-direction* (personality-oriented) approach to "how to study." Such an approach would help to solve some of the problems the teacher is not able to solve when the presentation is limited to methods alone. The discussion that follows will clarify the importance of self-direction conception of study skill development.

An interesting and pertinent attempt at factor analysis of study skills was made by Entwhistle (1960), who found the components to be: (1) morale and self-confidence; (2) scholarly drive and values; (3) study mechanics; and (4) planning to get work done. Three of the four factors have to do with aspects of self-direction instead of skills per se. Schneyer (1961) reports that to concentrate on the assignment is the most pressing reading-study problem reported by 39 percent of the pupils he studied. Admittedly his finding is based upon observations of college-age subjects and may not be applicable to younger students, but it is unlikely that the problem was recently acquired by the pupils studied. Another college-level study that may have implications for teachers of younger children was done by Gladstein (1960); he found that even gifted students need individual methods of study suited to their personalities, rather than the conventional, stereotyped techniques usually taught.

Studies like the three cited as examples seem to suggest a need for self-direction in study skill development. Of course there is need for additional research, especially at elementary and secondary levels. But lack of research notwithstanding, all teachers with experience know that a child's personality plays an important part in his ability to learn. All too frequently personality inadequacies or maladjustments appear to interfere with motivation and self-direction. Specifically, the following are commonly apparent in children with severe learning problems: generally damaged self-image, inability to concentrate, frustration and blocking, general feeling of discouragement, lack of interest, inability to establish or achieve goals, and overt or covert aggression.

Thus, it is frequently observed that a child with an extreme learning problem is one who has lost confidence in himself due to years of failure. He cannot concentrate and often displays evidence of frustration and blocking. He has little or no interest in academic learning, often professing to see no point in learning to read. He cannot see that learning has a direct bearing on achivement of future goals. Finally, he is frequently the pupil who learned early in his school career that there are satisfactions and rewards to be derived from *not* learning. As psychologists have often pointed out, many children find "not learning" an effective weapon for striking back at parents, teachers, or the world.

If one concedes the accuracy of the above he will concede the need for a definition and conception of study skills that encompass both the mechanical and the self-directional aspects of study. Then, the task of the remedial teacher is to help the disabled learner to increase his skill in the mechanics of study and to guide him toward self-direction. It is upon this dual concept that the following suggestions for diagnosis and remedial teaching are based. The factors involved in self-direction are termed *nonspecific* study skills and the mechanical aspects are termed *specific* study skills.

Diagnosis of Nonspecific Factors

The area of nonspecific study skills is often the area of greatest weakness in a diagnostic work-up. All too frequently a teacher will explore all the important causal factors—environmental, physical, and mental—and administer tests of *specific* aspects of study but neglect to assess the pupil's "will to learn," his capacity for *self-direction*. Lack of knowledge regarding this factor often leads to teacher frustration and discouragement, whereas knowledge relating to this important area enables the teacher to view his teaching task more realistically and to plan and implement a program aimed at strengthening the pupil's capacity for self-direction. In defense of the teacher, however, it should be pointed out that there are few, if any, instruments or tests available that adequately measure the nonspecific aspects of study. Interest inventories, sociograms, conferences with parents and the pupil, cumulative folders, etc., all contribute to a teacher's appraisal and help him to evaluate the pupil's strengths and shortcomings relative to self-direction. But in reality it is possible to arrive at a true estimate only by subjective judgment based upon knowledge gained from getting to know the pupil well and by working with him for some time. A classroom teacher has an advantage over a remedial teacher in this respect because the former usually has had more opportunity to evaluate the pupil's personality and to observe his performance in many areas and in many different situations.

Relative to the diagnosis of nonspecific study factors, the point needs to be re-emphasized that the scope of *any* diagnosis is not limited to formal tests and that reliance must sometimes be placed upon other forms of appraisal, such as informal observation and sound professional judgment based upon experience and training. In the areas of assessing a pupil's desire to learn, his capacity for self-direction, and similar nonspecific factors, there is nothing that can surpass the judgment and appraisal of the insightful teacher.

Remedial Help with Nonspecific Study Skills

Just as it was not possible to recommend specific tests to diagnose nonspecific aspects of study, neither is it possible to recommend a specific remedial method to be used with pupils who need help in this area. Some general recommendations follow.

1. Demonstrate a genuine acceptance of the pupil regardless of his deficiency or shortcomings.

2. Provide a pleasant, nonthreatening atmosphere that promotes learning.

3. Begin instruction at the pupil's true level of ability—not where he should be. (*It is much better to start too low than too high.*)

4. Make learning its own reward. Praise only for genuine accomplishment.

5. Do not proceed too rapidly. Make sure the pupil has opportunity for ample reinforcement before proceeding to new skills or concepts.

In summary, diagnostic and remedial techniques for helping disabled learners reach the goal of self-direction are perhaps more dependent upon a philosophy of teaching than on a method. A fuller discussion pertinent to this problem, with suggestions for application, is given in Chapter 15.

Diagnosis of Specific Factors

To develop independence and skill in the techniques of study is an educational goal for all children; it assumes special importance for disabled learners. Teachers sometimes assume that if a pupil knows how to read he will also know how to make use of reference and illustrative material. Experience has taught us that such an assumption is erroneous and that most, if not all, disabled learners need the following kinds of help:

1. practice in the use of reference material
2. practice in the reading of maps, graphs, tables, etc.
3. development of outlining, note taking, and summarizing skills
4. development of efficient study patterns

The discussion which follows will suggest some diagnostic and remedial techniques for each of these areas.

In disabled learners, the absence of or weakness in study habits and skills is usually so obvious that it makes survey diagnosis superfluous. At the specific level, the teacher can use (1) formal tests which are typically designed mainly to measure locational skills and ability to use maps, charts, graphs, and other illustrative material; and (2) informal procedures which consist of observation and evaluation of classroom performance. Most remedial teachers like to use both informal and formal measures.

To locate suitable tests for measuring the specific aspects of study skills, a very useful and authoritative source of information is the most recent edition of the *Sixth Mental Measurements Yearbook,* edited by Oscar K. Buros (1970). The *Yearbook* is more fully described in Chapter 5.

Remedial Help with Specific Study Skills

Practice in the Use of Reference Material

The ability to use reference materials is perhaps the most basic of the specific skills. Use of a dictionary or an index is usually the first area of concern in teaching the reference skills. Teachers have found that a thorough grounding in this particular skill goes a long way toward making study less difficult and time consuming.

One of the most effective tools for teaching beginning reference skills is a local telephone directory. The directory more than meets the criterion that remedial materials should be fresh, interesting, and utilitarian. It has several advantages over a conventional text, the most salient of which is the fact that it provides a range of practice from the simple but interesting task of having a pupil locate his own or his friends' names to the more complicated task of finding answers to specific questions. Some examples of questions and activities follow:

1. How many pediatricians are there in our town?
2. Find and list the places one might go to buy skis.
3. If a man were unemployed, how could the classified section of the directory help him?
4. List the pages of the classified section in which the following are listed: department stores, lumber yards, physicians, creameries, etc.

Other more directly applicable and meaningful questions and exercises will occur to the teacher. (Some remedial and classroom teachers have been successful in securing several directories from their local telephone companies.)

Another interesting and readily accessible device for use in teaching locational skills and the use of tables, graphs, and charts is the daily newspaper. Here again, pupils who may find a text dry and somewhat uninviting can see more practicality in the use of this medium. The teacher can improvise many activities to make use of the information found in newspapers.

Practice in the Use of Maps, Graphs, Tables, etc.

A disabled learner usually needs all the supportive aid to understanding and comprehension that he can get. Maps, graphs, tables, charts, and other illustrative devices can often be extremely useful to poor readers, who need more than a written account to fully understand a selection. Remedial teaching in this area does not ordinarily present a great problem if the approach is a functional one. The pupil needs to see that what he is studying has practical value, and the practical value of maps, tables, graphs, charts, etc., can readily be demonstrated.

Highway maps obtainable at local service stations are excellent sources of practice work in map reading. They have the advantage of allowing the teacher to introduce an area with which the pupil is familiar and about which many things are already known. The progression of skills from easy to difficult is then possible because few maps would present serious problems to a pupil who had already mastered the map of his own state.

A readily available and utilitarian table that has been used in remedial teaching is that given on federal income tax forms. Pupils find it interesting to determine the tax rate for various income brackets and varying numbers of dependents. Schedules of rates charged by local utilities companies also provide excellent practice in interpreting tables and scales of charges. Motivation is sometimes increased if it can be pointed out to the pupil that in some cases he is acquiring knowledge that many persons do not possess.

Social studies and arithmetic texts are, of course, also sources of remedial practice material. We have not attempted to imply that all instruction in the specific study skills needs to, or should, avoid the academic materials. The principal point to be made here is that the disabled learner is often more highly motivated with the kinds of materials mentioned above; sooner or later he will need to transfer his skill to text and reference books. A common-sense progression from the simple to the complex—or from the familiar to the unfamiliar—should be followed in teaching the specific study skills; the imaginative teacher should have little difficulty in finding materials.

Outlining, Note Taking, and Summarizing Skills

Outlining, note taking, and summarizing are study skills that sometimes present a problem for even the best of students; in the case of underachievers, the problem is compounded. A great deal of guidance as well as direct instruction is usually required by pupils who are weak in these important areas. Basically, the three skills are the same; the outline is merely a more formal and structured series of notes. Note taking and summarizing are, by and large, merely a condensation in narrative form of something spoken or read. If pupils can be made to see the similarity between the three skills the remedial task is often simplified, because summary skill has usually been practiced to some degree from primary grades on.

Some remedial teachers have found that each of these areas can be taught through the use of the same technique outlined previously for promoting paragraph comprehension. Others prefer the procedures often found in reading workbooks whereby practice is given in following the author's plan for outlining a paragraph, etc. Language arts texts are also a good source of practice and remedial material; the skills, after all, are basic to that area.

Developing Efficient Study Patterns

A comparatively recent and important development in teaching study skills is the evolution of several study formulas which, put into practice, encourage structured, efficient study. The method known as *SQ3R* (Survey-Question-Read-Recite-Review) is perhaps the most widely used. The method, as outlined below, can be useful in providing the poor reader with a systematic approach to study.

THE SQ3R METHOD OF STUDY-READING

Survey   1. Glance over the headings in the chapter to see the big points which will be developed. Read the summary.

Question 2. Turn the first heading into a question. It demands a conscious effort on the part of the reader to make this a question for which he must read to find the answer.
Ask: Who, what, when, why, where, or how?

Read   3. Read to find the answer to your question.

Recite   4. Look away from your book and briefly recite the answer to your question. Jot down cue phrases in outline form. *REPEAT STEPS 2, 3, AND 4 ON EACH SUCCEEDING HEADED SECTION.* Complete the entire lesson in this way — question, read, recite over each section.

Review   5. Look over your notes to get a bird's-eye view of the points and their relationships and check your memory of the content by reciting major subpoints under each heading.

In connection with the above formula, Parker (1969) has pointed out that the latter two *R*'s of the formula are usually legitimately omitted for youngsters below the seventh grade. Policy in this regard should be dictated by the ability of the group being taught.

The strength and value of the *SQ3R* approach stem from the fact that the pupil is forced to read thoroughly and aggressively. He is not only asked to survey, or preview what he reads, he is also asked to raise questions about it and then read the selection. The final "recite and review" steps provide confirmation of what he has read.

In the opinion of the writers, it is most important to emphasize the role of study skills in improving the pupil's comprehension ability. The following account of a study made at Harvard University by Perry (1959) illustrates this point.

In exploring the reading skills of fifteen hundred Harvard and Radcliffe freshmen, Perry assigned a thirty-page chapter of a history book. No specific instructions were given the students other than, "Study the chapter; you will have a test later which will require you to write a short essay and identify important details." After twenty-two minutes the pupils were stopped and asked how they had approached their task. Over 90 percent reported that they had simply started at the beginning and read straight through the chapter. A multiple-choice test on the chapter yielded results that Perry termed "impressive." Perry then found that only 150 or 10 percent (!) of the students had taken a look ahead in their twenty-two minute struggle with the chapter; this in spite of the fact that the chapter contained excellent marginal glosses, and at the end of the chapter "like a bold flag" was a section headed *Recapitulation* in which the entire purpose and structure of the chapter was set forth. Perry's report then relates the revealing and crucial point:

> We asked anyone who could do so to write a short statement about what the chapter was all about. The number who were able to tell us . . . was just one

in a hundred—or a total of fifteen! As a demonstration of obedient purposeless-ness in the reading of 99 percent of freshmen we found this impressive . . . after twelve years of reading homework assignments in school they had all settled into the habit of leaving the point of it all to someone else. . . . (P. 3)

The lack of study skills and purposefulness in the reading of these other-wise excellent students amply illustrates the appallingly inadequate teaching of study skills. *Setting a purpose for reading* is perhaps the most basic of all study skills; *real comprehension* is "getting the point of it all." Clearly, this was a skill that 99 percent of these superior students had never been taught. Also, it is important to note that all were "impressive" when given a multiple-choice test. This would seem to corroborate our long-standing opinion that such tests often do not measure what they claim to measure.

RATE OF READING

If one thinks of rate of reading as having to do with speed alone, he might well wonder why such a topic is discussed in a text dealing with corrective and remedial problems. In reality, rate involves a much broader concept than mere words read per minute. A more realistic view of rate was suggested by Brueckner and Bond (1955): "A true measure of rate of reading is how rapidly a child can read material of a given difficulty with good understanding, taking into account the purpose for which he is read-ing" (p. 181). This definition has implications for all pupils, disabled readers or not; knowledge of the purpose for reading and adjustment of rate to that purpose is a great deal more important than absolute number of words read per minute. Very often poor readers need help in developing flexibility in their approach to reading because they have developed the habit of approaching all reading tasks as if they were the same. They need instruction and practice in recognizing and adapting to the following broad categories of reading.

1. *Study-Type Reading.* The rate here should permit thoughtful read-ing; it should allow time for the reader to reflect upon what he has read. Evaluation and the drawing of conclusions are required by study-type read-ing; the rate is necessarily low.

2. *Recreational Reading.* The rate and type of reading here is normally reserved for newspapers, magazines of a nontechnical nature, and most fiction. Typically, there is no need for a high level of comprehension or recall of specific facts, so the rate can be quite high.

3. *Accelerated Reading.* A very rapid rate can be attained through skimming and scanning when only main ideas are sought. Such reading is sometimes referred to as selective reading. The reader proceeds rapidly, selecting only the material that fits his immediate purpose for more careful scrutiny.

Some general suggestions for teaching and providing practice in the areas of skimming and scanning and thoughtful, or study-type, reading are given below.

Accelerated Reading

A good technique for teaching accelerated reading is to provide the pupil with short paragraphs, well within his reading ability, and check the time it takes him to find the main idea. If paragraphs are chosen carefully a pupil can scan several a minute and he will soon learn the advantage of the technique in finding topic sentences. At first the teacher will want to select only paragraphs that begin with topic sentences. As skill increases the topic sentences may become less obvious.

Another valuable type of practice is that of underlining the key words in a paragraph to give the pupil practice in reading rapidly only the underlined words. As his skill increases, he can underline his own words and finally progress to where he can find key words without the underline.

A motivational device for accelerated reading is to have the pupil keep a chart indicating the number of words read per minute. It should, however, be explicitly called a skimming and scanning chart and the pupil should understand that this is just one of the reading skills he needs to master.

Study-Type Reading

Careful study-type reading can also be taught with well-constructed paragraphs. As pointed out earlier in discussing the development of comprehension skills, the pupil should read for answers to "who," "what," "when," "where," and "why" questions.

Another study-type technique that has been found helpful is to have the pupil turn the headings and subheadings of the paragraphs in a textbook into questions. He then reads to find the answers to the questions. A social studies text typically lends itself to this technique.

Newspapers can provide valuable practice. The editorial page is excellent for practice in study-type skills. One technique is to have the pupil underline the main idea in red pencil and contributory ideas in blue pencil.

To summarize, teachers should make sure the pupil knows the purpose of his practice—whether it be practice in accelerated reading or thoughtful reading. The need for flexibility must be stressed and practice sessions should be brief. A good rule is to limit the practice session to ten or fifteen minutes for any single type of reading matter.

Factors Affecting Rate

Two inadequacies which are common to underachievers and which impede rate of reading are:

1. *Word-by-Word-Reading.* This is painfully slow reading where the pupil often loses the train of thought before a sentence or paragraph is finished. The most frequent cause of word-by-word reading is inadequate word-recognition ability. To overcome the fault the teacher can work to improve the pupil's sight vocabulary and word-attack skills and provide

practice in phrase reading. Specific techniques to accomplish this task are discussed in Chapter 7.

2. *Vocalization.* This is the habit of forming words either visibly with the lips or invisibly in the throat (subvocally). The trait is thought to be the result of too great an emphasis upon oral reading during the beginning stages of learning to read. The chief objection to vocalizing is that the pupil who vocalizes is unable to develop a rapid rate of reading because he can read only as fast as he can speak. The most common remedial technique is simply to have the pupil hold a finger to his lips as a reminder not to vocalize. Another technique that has been found helpful is to use some means to force the pupil to accelerate his reading. With older pupils it is possible to use a commercially made mechanical device, but some teachers have found "pusher" cards effective. A "pusher" card is nothing more than a 3 × 5 card which the pupil pushes down the page to force himself to read at a more rapid rate.

THOUGHTS FOR DISCUSSION

"For a remedial reading program to be successful, adequate materials must be available for use by the teacher and by the pupils. A well qualified teacher, with originality and adaptability, can do reasonably well with a minimum of materials and instructional aids. But, with proper materials, the same teacher may be able to develop a superior program." (Gilliland, 1965, p. 7)

"The only safe generalization regarding approaches to corrective and remedial teaching seems to be that there are few safe generalizations. The appeal, the use, and the ultimate success of an approach is likely to be determined as much by the point of view of the remedial teacher as by the specifics of the approach. The appropriateness of a principle may be dependent upon the interaction of disabled learner, teacher, and approach." (Otto and Koenke, 1969, p. 123)

"Let your child alone! or Don't worry, we'll handle it, are quite often the only suggestions that teachers have to offer parents who are seeking ways to help their child with reading difficulties. Today such advice is inappropriate and will likely fall upon deaf ears, for parents want to help their child, can help their child, and will help their child!" (Wilson, 1967, p. 201)

"The most important use of reading tests is as an aid to teaching. If a test does not help a teacher, directly or indirectly, teach better, there is not much point in administering it. Much effort and money are wasted by giving tests that are not needed and by failing to use the results of tests that are given." (Strang, 1964, p. 143)

"In reviewing the vast amount of research studies and articles about reading, I failed to find any program expressly geared for the vocationally interested students. The existing reading and study programs offer very little, if anything, to the student who is vocationally inclined. Often such programs are weighted heavily with exercises in classical literature which, at this stage of the student's development, is not appealing to him since such programs do not meet his immediate needs." (Pauk, 1970, p. 48)

"One of the reasons for failure to develop a life-long interest in reading in so many children may stem from the discrepancy between the type of material used to teach reading and the reading skills that children are expected to learn. Almost universally the material used for teaching reading is of a narrative type. Most of these narratives are fictional. The skills emphasized in reading instruction are much more suitable to expository material. Therefore the present practice of using narrative fiction to learn these skills is probably partially responsible for the low level of interest in reading in the majority of the adult population." (Johnson, 1970, p. 209)

REFERENCES

Bond, G. L., and Tinker, M. A. *Reading difficulties: Their diagnosis and correction.* New York: Appleton-Century-Crofts, 1957.

Botel, M. *How to teaching reading.* Chicago: Follett, 1963.

Brueckner, L. J., and Bond, G. L. *The diagnosis and treatment of learning difficulties.* New York: Appleton-Century-Crofts, 1955.

Buros, O. K. (Ed.) *The sixth mental measurements yearbook.* New Brunswick, N. J.: Rutgers University Press, 1970.

Durrell, D. D. *Improving reading instruction.* Yonkers, N. Y.: World Book, 1956.

Entwhistle, D. R. Evaluations of study skill courses: A review. *Journal of Educational Research,* 1960, **53**, 243–251.

Gilliland, H. *Materials for remedial reading.* Billings, Mont.: The Reading Clinic, Eastern Montana College, 1965.

Gladstein, G. A. Study behavior of gifted stereotype and non-stereotype college students. *Personnel and Guidance Journal,* 1960, **38**, 470–474.

Johnston, T. D. Must it always be the three little pigs? *The Reading Teacher,* 1970, **24** (3), 209.

Kottmeyer, W. *Teacher's guide for remedial reading.* St. Louis: Webster, 1959.

Mitzel, M. A. A literacy vocabulary for adults. *Adult Education,* Winter, 1966, **68**.

Otto, W., and Koenke, K. (Eds.) *Remedial teaching.* Boston: Houghton Mifflin, 1969.

Parker, D. H. *Teacher's handbook: Reading laboratory IIb.* Chicago: Science Research Associates, 1969.

Pauk, W. Reading needs of vocationally inclined students. *Reading Improvement,* Fall, 1970, **7** (2), 48.

Perry, W. G., Jr. Students' use and misuse of reading skills: A report to the faculty. *Harvard Educational Review,* Summer, 1959, **29** (3), 193–200.

Schneyer, J. W. Problems of concentration among college students. *The Reading Teacher,* 1961, **15**, 34.

Smith, N. B. *Reading instruction for today's children.* Englewood Cliffs, N.J.: Prentice-Hall, 1963.

Strang, R. *Diagnostic teaching of reading.* New York: McGraw-Hill, 1964.

Wilson, R. M. *Diagnostic and remedial reading.* Columbus, Ohio: Charles E. Merrill, 1967.

Chapter 9

Reading: Specific Remedial Approaches

Most remedial reading teachers employ an eclectic approach when they teach remedial reading. That is, they use a variety of instructional materials and practices designed to strengthen specific diagnosed weaknesses in a pupil's skill development. They may, for example, use a workbook from a particular publishing company for practice exercises in phonic analysis, a kit with multilevel reading selections from another publishing company for comprehension development, and some play reading to improve phrasing ability and oral reading expression, all in some logical sequence that is based upon the instructional objectives they have established for each pupil. And this eclectic approach is probably the best approach for most pupils whose disabilities are mild to severe. However, for certain severely disabled children an eclectic approach may exacerbate the problem rather than eliminate it.

There are several reasons for suggesting that an eclectic approach to remedial teaching may for some pupils be more harmful than helpful. First, a common characteristic of severely disabled readers is their confusion about what reading behavior is. Exposing them to an instructional scope and sequence that is not rigidly structured and controlled may add to their confusion. Secondly, there is a certain amount of security for the child in programs that are not eclectic because the materials and methods used throughout his remedial program become familiar to him. Finally, the likelihood of assigning tasks for which the pupil is not ready is greater in an eclectic approach because the teacher must build the instructional program as he proceeds with his teaching. Consequently, the chance for error in selecting appropriate materials and practices is greater in an eclectic approach than in an approach that consists of prescribed step-by-step procedures for the teacher to follow.

In the present chapter we will discuss selected, carefully delineated remedial reading approaches advocated for use with severely disabled readers. Since space does not permit a detailed description of all of the remedial approaches that have been carefully developed and widely advocated, we have selected those that seem most logical in their development and have reportedly been successful with more than a few seriously disabled readers. From our own experience and the experience of others, we know that an approach which is highly successful with one student may be in-effective with another student whose disability appears to result from essentially the same causal factors and who manifests nearly the same symptoms. Therefore, we recommend that remedial reading teachers know more than one specific approach and be ready to change methods when it becomes apparent that the approach currently being used is not succeeding. We caution against teachers' becoming so enamored of a particular approach that they fail to see or refuse to admit that a different approach might be used with better results for certain students.

Since entire books have been written to describe each of the different approaches we discuss in the present chapter, it is obvious that our descrip-tions will not be sufficient to train teachers in their implementation. There-fore references to sources that teachers may consult for the details they need have been included. Indeed, since these approaches are complex and some-what inflexible, we caution teachers against implementing any of them solely on the descriptions presented in this chapter.

Our readers will recognize that some of the approaches we describe are also used for instruction with able readers. In fact, some of them were designed for developmental, not remedial teaching. We believe that a major cause of reading failure is that students with a preferred mode of learning are exposed to approaches that are not suited to their particular combinations of strengths and weaknesses. For example, a student who has failed with an approach that in its initial stages demands much auditory discrimination and little visual memory might have been more successful in a program with a different sequence and different emphases. Since good remedial teaching is always accompanied by thorough diagnosis, there is good opportunity to match the method to the learner so that the greatest benefits are obtained. It is possible, then, that a pupil who learned little or nothing from one developmental program may in a remedial setting learn to read with a developmental program that makes different demands upon him.

LANGUAGE-EXPERIENCE APPROACH

The language-experience approach is an example of an approach that may be used with able as well as with severely disabled readers. From our own observations the language-experience approach is especially effective with children whose oral language development is retarded and with children who are indifferent about learning to read or who have strong negative attitudes toward reading. We have also observed that the language-experience approach is highly effective with secondary school disabled readers primarily because they dictate the material, so they do not perceive it as "babyish."

In his recent book Stauffer (1970) carefully describes the language-experience approach for teachers who wish to employ it. He says in the preface:

> The Language-Experience Approach as detailed in this text does take advantage of the wealth that children bring with them to school—linguistically, intellectually, socially, and culturally. By focusing on language as a means of communication, the transfer from oral language usage to written language is made functionally. Reading does become talk written down.

Regarding the use of language-experience with children who require special education he says:

> These children can talk, they have reactions to experiences, and they have ideas. In the privacy of a face-to-face confab, they talk. The delight they exhibit when they see 'their talk' being typed and when they can hold their own materials is indeed gratifying. Pride of authorship, of doing, of constructing verbally evokes deep-seated affective responses. (P. 247)

Major Assumptions

The language-experience approach relies heavily upon the pupil's oral language, which is better developed than his reading ability. Reading is conceptualized as essentially a thinking process rather than a translating or decoding process. Much importance is given to the child's having meaningful experiences with print so as to establish firmly the notion that print is a representation of oral language and that what can be said, can be written, and what can be written, can be read.

Proponents of language-experience methodology feel that using as reading material the pupil's dictated responses to a vivid experience will foster desired affective responses to reading. Stauffer (1970) describes the effect of this approach on children in special education classes: "These children showed special delight when they found a word in a magazine or book that they learned to recognize through a dictated and recorded account. The 'look, Mom, I can read' radiance is energizing as well as illuminating" (p. 247).

The language-experience approach also assumes that children will get powerful memory cues as they read material which they have recently dictated. As they read, they will in fact be recalling their ideas in the exact language they used to express them orally. When the child fails to recognize in print the words he has dictated, the teacher can stimulate correct responses by specific memory aids such as, "Do you remember where you told us your dog slept?" or "For what special occasion did you tell us you got your bike?"

Finally, the language-experience approach assumes that poor readers experience fewer failures reading their own ideas expressed in familiar vocabulary and sentence patterns than they experience when they must read less familiar ideas expressed in less familiar language. The satisfactions the poor reader receives from responding accurately to his own ideas in print are more rewarding than the satisfactions he might receive from getting new ideas with less facility. As a matter of fact the disabled reader needs the security that can come only from reading material completely within his immediate experiential background and expressed in his own language patterns.

Instructional Materials

From the preceding discussion it is apparent that the pupils' dictated stories, descriptions, and other commentary constitute the content of the reading material used in the language-experience approach. Since seriously disabled readers usually write with even greater difficulty, the material they dictate should be typed for them. We have found that asking pupils to write, type, or copy their own dictation almost always defeats the purposes of the language-experience approach. We have also found that some students perform best with material that is prepared on a primary typewriter.

The pupils' dictation is used as the basic instructional material, but other instructional materials are usually a part of the language-experience approach. Wide reading in functional and recreational materials is encouraged as soon as the child develops sufficient skills to read nondictated material in conjunction with dictated material. Art work and dramatics are often used effectively in conjunction with language-experience stories. And we have had much success with helping pupils tape-record radio plays, stories, descriptions, and other creative productions which they read and later play for an invited audience. The tape-recorded material can be given a professional touch by incorporating simple sound effects and background music. Reading to pupils from a variety of materials to provide information for projects is another good instructional practice to accompany a language-experience approach.

Implementation

The first step in implementing a language-experience approach is identifying or creating an experiential base from which to elicit student commentary. Even though certain pupils may have suitable background experiences, the teacher may wish to establish a common base for several students or a particularly vivid and meaningful experience for an individual student. Background experiences of many kinds can be established: visits to places of interest, television programs, movies, musical selections, visits with interesting people, observations of animals, and other experiences that are likely to evoke personal reactions.

When a satisfactory experiential base has been identified or provided, students are encouraged to tell a story, give an oral description, supply dialogue for a play or react orally in some other way. Some pupils need more structure and help than others in dictating a readable product. This is especially the case when the product is a radio play or some other creation that will become a presentation for a selected audience. We have observed that pupils do their best dictating and reading when they begin to take pride in the creation of a book of stories, an original play, a series of original television commercials, or other projects that are cooperatively planned with their teachers.

When pupils are reading the typed copy of their dictation, the teacher listens carefully and insists upon complete accuracy. Care must be taken to make sure that bright students do not repeat from memory rather than read their material. As instruction proceeds and pupils acquire a functional sight vocabulary, the teacher structures the dictating sessions so that high-utility words are included in the material to be read. Phonics and other word-attack skills are taught incidentally as instruction proceeds and as pupils indicate a readiness to derive generalizations from observing their oral language in print. Specific skill development exercises may be incorporated into the later stages of the language-experience approach; and, ultimately, pupils are transferred from their own material to library books, textbooks, magazines, newspapers, and the writing of other students. Care must be taken, however, to move children gradually from their own dictated material to reading material written by others. Care must also be taken to avoid giving pupils material written by others that contains too many words that have not been thoroughly learned from reading their own material or that cannot be analyzed effectively with the word-attack skills they have learned.

FERNALD APPROACH

Although the approach to remedial reading developed by Grace Fernald (1943) has been questioned by many remedial reading specialists, it is almost always included among descriptions of methods to be used with severely disabled readers. The Fernald approach incorporates language-experience and kinesthetic techniques in a multisensory approach that "bombards" the student with visual, auditory, kinesthetic, and tactile (VAKT) impressions. Because of the painstaking nature of the approach and the slow progress made by pupils with whom it is used, we recommend that it be employed as a total approach only with highly motivated seriously disabled readers who have not been improved by less demanding approaches. However, the tracing technique alone may be used effectively to help certain pupils learn high-utility words that prove to be particularly troublesome for them to learn as sight words.

Major Assumptions

The need for pupils to be motivated to read is basic to Fernald's approach. Therefore, from the beginning, pupils dictate their own material and are given concrete evidence of their progress. They must not be read to at home or at school until they have mastered normal reading ability. The child's ego is protected at all times, and he is not permitted to return to regular classroom work until he is clearly capable of accomplishing the work that will be required of him when he does return. The language experience aspect of this approach assures that students will be reading material at their interest and maturity level even though they are disabled readers. The knowledge that a child's speaking vocabulary is better developed than his reading vocabulary is of course basic to this aspect of Fernald's approach.

A multisensory approach is assumed to be more effective with disabled readers than an approach which relies heavily on one modality. Fernald places much stress on the need for the pupil to experience each word he is learning through various modalities. The child says the word, sees the word written by the teacher, traces the word with his finger, writes the word from memory, sees the word again in type, and reads the word aloud for the teacher.

The Fernald approach guards against breaking the reading process into components so small that reading becomes a mechanical act rather than a meaning-getting process. For example, the child is never encouraged to sound out word parts or copy words he has traced. Each word is learned as a whole and immediately placed in a context that is meaningful to the child.

A further assumption is that disabled readers will, through the Fernald approach, eventually develop the ability to make generalizations about words and thereby learn new words on the basis of their knowledge of the characteristics of previously learned words. This is perhaps the most basic and the most questionable assumption made by Fernald, because unless the child does indeed develop this ability, he can never become a functional reader of English. The task of using a multisensory approach to learn enough words to meet the reading demands imposed upon children in our society is obviously unreasonable. Making generalizations is essential if reading is to be used for school achievement and other purposes. The Fernald approach assumes that the ability to generalize will be learned inductively without the explicit teaching of phonic generalizations.

Instructional Materials

Until the pupil has acquired a sight vocabulary large enough to give him successful experiences with the writing of others he is limited to reading stories of his own composition. These stories are dictated by the pupil and incorporate words that he has indicated he would like to learn. The stories, then, may include words above the child's reading ability level but within the range of his speaking vocabulary. He reads them from typed copy before too long an interval between dictation and reading.

Eventually the child is given material that is not of his own composition to read. Words which he does not know are told to him to avoid an unsuccessful reading experience and to help him encounter the material as a total message from which he can derive meaning. Material is never read to the pupil, nor is he permitted to attack letters or syllables within words. Fernald wants the reading selection always to be perceived as a complete meaning-bearing entity.

Implementation

The remedial reading approach developed by Fernald consists of four stages which blend one into the other as the pupil improves his ability to learn words and read them in context.

Stage One

The teacher using the Fernald approach with a seriously disabled reader begins remedial instruction by eliciting from the pupil a word the pupil wants to learn. The elicited word is written or printed on a strip of paper by the teacher in crayon, large enough for the child to trace. The pupil is then instructed to trace the word, saying each syllable of the word as he traces it. Fernald emphasizes the need for direct finger contact with the word during the tracing process.

When the student thinks he knows the word well enough to write it from memory, the word is removed from his sight, and he reproduces it as a unit from memory. After the pupil has learned a few words, he is encouraged to compose a little story that incorporates the words. The teacher writes the story from dictation, teaches the pupil any words in the story he does not know, has the student write the story, and finally has the story typed to be read by the pupil the following day. Each new word that is learned is written on a card and placed in a word-file arranged in alphabetical order. The word file becomes a source for providing disabled readers with the repetition they need for mastering a sight vocabulary. It also aids in teaching the letters of the alphabet and basic dictionary skills.

Stage Two

Tracing the words to be learned is eliminated in the second stage of the Fernald approach. The basic approach remains the same. That is, the pupil learns the words he has dictated and will read in the context of stories of his own creation. When students arrive at stage two is an individual matter, but eventually the student is able to learn words by looking at them, saying them to himself, and writing them from memory. Again, the pupil never focuses upon individual letter sounds, but rather reproduces words as whole units. Long words are attacked in syllables. For example, the pupil would learn the word *magazine* by pronouncing each syllable as he writes it—mag–a–zine. Since the word he is learning is not before him as he writes, the pupil must work from a visual image. If his written product is incorrect, he must study the word carefully to obtain an accurate visual image to be recalled while he attempts to write it again from memory. Obviously, it is expected that during stage two the stories that are dictated become larger and more sophisticated to match the growing maturity of the student.

Stage Three

Stage three is begun when the pupil has progressed to the point where he no longer needs to write on a card each word he learns. He is able to look at a word, pronounce it, write it from memory, and retain it without word-card drill. During stage three the child usually is given material other than that of his own composition to read. The new words he learns are those he does not know in the material he is reading.

Stage Four

Stage four is the final stage in the Fernald approach and is arrived at when the pupil begins to learn new words by generalizing from his knowledge of the characteristics of previously learned words. These generalizations are learned inductively through progressively more exposure to written material. The student may be read to when he reaches stage four, but usually prefers to read for himself. He is encouraged to survey his reading material before he reads and to learn any unfamiliar words so that the author's message will not be interrupted. At this stage the pupil is generally able to learn unfamiliar words either by generalization or by having them pronounced for him and then meanings explained. When stage four is reached, the pupil is a reader who gains information and satisfaction from his reading experiences.

ORTON-GILLINGHAM-STILLMAN APPROACH

Considerable controversy surrounds the approach to teaching severely disabled readers developed by Gillingham and Stillman (1968) on the basis of the theoretical assumptions set forth by Orton (1937). Orton's neurological explanation for the cause of specific reading disability and the remedial program that was developed by Gillingham and Stillman on the basis of that explanation have been criticized by neurologists and by educators.

We believe the criticisms that come from both camps are valid and should be heeded. However, we also know that the approach which we shall subsequently refer to as the Gillingham approach is reportedly being used successfully, with modifications, to treat certain children with severe reading disorders who have not been helped by other approaches. Therefore, we shall describe the approach and urge that teachers use only those aspects which can be implemented practically and which do not violate what are generally regarded as good principles of motivation and instruction.

We think the Gillingham approach should be part of a remedial reading teacher's repertoire and, as is true of all remedial approaches, adapted for use with individuals on the basis of careful diagnosis of pupils' strengths and weaknesses. We also believe the Gillingham approach should be reserved for severely disabled readers for whom less painstaking approaches have been unproductive and who for one reason or another are willing to expend considerable time and energy to be able to read even a little.

Major Assumptions

The underlying assumptions of the Gillingham approach were formulated by Samuel Orton. The following description by his colleague and wife, June L. Orton (1967), explains his basic theoretical position:

> Orton approached reading as one stage of the child's language development, preceded by spoken language (hearing and speaking) and expressed in writing, which includes spelling. He looked upon language as an evolutionary human function associated with the development of a hierarchy of complex integrations in the nervous system and culminating in unilateral control by one of the two brain hemispheres (cerebral dominance). Retardation in acquiring reading suggested to him that there was some interference with this natural process of growth and development. He was impressed with a specific characteristic of reading impairment in the children he studied—the instability in recognition and recall of the orientation of letters and the order of letters in words, which he termed "strephosymbolia," meaning "twisted symbols." This to him indicated an intrinsic difficulty of a special nature in the association process. Further observations disclosed mixed right-and-left laterality in the motor patterns of many retarded readers with these reversed tendencies. Study of the physiology of the brain led to his formulation of the hypothesis of a comparable intermixture of control in the two hemispheres of the brain in those areas which subserve the visual or reading part of the language function and are normally active only in the dominant hemisphere. He postulated that the mirrored (antitropic) images of the two hemispheres might then conflict when the child attempted to build associations between letters and spoken words, producing confusions and orientation errors and a general delay in learning to read. Genetic considerations suggested a probable hereditary explanation of the opposing right-and-left tendencies, which under these conditions might result in a disturbance in the development of the language function. . . . (P. 122)

The major assumption underlying the instructional practices of the Gillingham approach is that children with the characteristics described by Orton profit most from a synthetic approach to reading that incorporates training in spelling and penmanship. The sounds the letters of the alphabet represent must be learned one at a time and blended to form words. The letters are seen, the sounds they represent heard, and they are written according to specified hand movements.

Another assumption is that certain disabled children require visual, auditory, and kinesthetic training to acquire reading skills. The following figure illustrates this "language triangle" as conceptualized by Gillingham and Stillman (1968, p. 40):

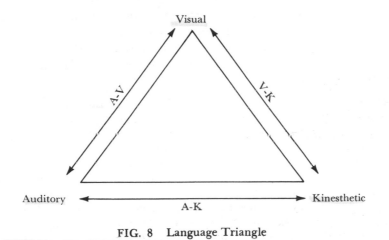

FIG. 8   Language Triangle

A final important assumption is that severely disabled readers require a teacher with special training and exemplary personal characteristics. The child's self-concept must be scrupulously cared for as instruction begins and as it proceeds. Not every teacher is capable of helping children with severe reading problems according to Gillingham and Stillman.

Instructional Materials

Specific instructional materials have been developed for use with the Gillingham method and are available from the same company that publishes the manual (1968). The materials include: Phonetic Drill Cards, Phonetic Words ("Jewel Case"), Syllable Concept cards, and Little Stories. These materials are keyed to the lessons outlined in the manual, and their use for the teaching of certain skills is indicated in the various chapters of the manual. The manual itself is essential for implementation of the program.

Implementation

The Gillingham Approach should not be implemented without careful study of the manual written by Gillingham and Stillman. Therefore, the discussion we give is to describe the basic techniques used and is not detailed enough to permit complete implementation of the approach. It should be noted that Gillingham recommends that the procedure she describes in detail be followed rigidly. She cautions that omitting any one of the sequential steps is to jeopardize the complete success of the procedure. However, the approach has reportedly been successful when used with modifications.

The pupil begins the approach with some explanation of the history and nature of the English language so as to put his problems with the language in proper perspective. He then learns three phonetic associations using instructional materials constructed to accompany the Gillingham manual. The three associations are described by Gillingham and Stillman (1968) as follows:

> *Association I.* This association consists of two parts—association of the visual symbol with the name of the letter, and association of the visual symbol with the sound of the letter: also the association of the feel of the child's speech organs in producing the name or sound of the letter as he hears himself say it. Association I is V-A and A-K. Part b. is the basis of oral reading.
>
> Part a. The card is exposed and the name of the letter spoken by the teacher and repeated by the pupil.
>
> Part b. As soon as the name has been really mastered, the sound is made by the teacher and repeated by the pupil. It is here that most emphasis must be placed if the case is primarily one of speech defect. The card is exposed, the implied question being, "What does this letter (or phonogram) say?", and the pupil gives its sound.
>
> *Association II.* The teacher makes the sound represented by the letter (or phonogram), the face of the card not being seen by the pupil, and says, "Tell me the name of the letter that has this sound." Sound to name is A-A, and is essentially oral spelling.
>
> *Association III.* The letter is carefully made by the teacher and then its form, orientation, etc., explained. It is then traced by the pupil over the teacher's lines, then copied, written from memory, and finally written again with eyes averted while the teacher watches closely. This association is V-K and K-V. In this work the teacher must keep the principles laid down in the Penmanship Chapter always in mind. Now, the teacher makes the sound, saying, "Write the letter that has this sound." This association is A-K and is the basis of written spelling. (P. 41)

Drill and repetition are stressed in the Gillingham approach. Gillingham and Stillman (1968) say: "From the first day the teacher should make a conscious effort to build up an effective drill technique. Not infrequently the time given to each card is double or triple that actually needed, and with less profitable result" (p. 44).

After ten letters are well known by all associations, the pupil begins his work with words by blending the sounds the letters represent. These words are available on small cards in a box referred to as the "Jewel Case." Eventually, the pupil can read and write any three-letter, perfectly phonetic word, and at that time such words are combined into sentences and stories (e.g., Fat Sam had *a* bat. Fat Sam at Bat. Fat Sam sat on *the* mat.) Irregular words needed to make sentences are told to the pupil before he attempts to pronounce them.

The pupil's instructional program progresses slowly. He learns to respond correctly to consonant blends, words with silent final "e", and he learns increasingly difficult phonetic word-attack skills. Spelling and writing skills are taught in conjunction with reading skills, with the blending of sounds being a major task.

The Gillingham approach is always used in place of, not in addition to, the pupil's regular classroom reading program. As a matter of fact, the child is not to do any reading, writing, or spelling except for his lessons with his remedial teacher. His other lessons must be read to him. According to Gillingham and Stillman the remedial sessions must be held daily for a minimum of two years to be effective and to avoid losing the gains made in the remedial program.

LINGUISTICS (C. C. FRIES)

A linguistic approach to reading instruction can mean many things depending upon which linguist is applying to reading instruction his interpretation of the best way to teach reading. We have taught some seriously disabled readers who made remarkable progress with the *Merrill Linguistic Readers* (Fries, Wilson, and Rudolph, 1966) program which is based upon the linguistic applications to reading made by Fries (1963). Therefore, we are including a description of that reading program in our discussion of specific remedial approaches.

Certain students appear to need the high degree of linguistic control built into the Fries approach. In addition, the concern of Fries for meaning and his emphasis upon comprehension of sentences adds a dimension to the program that helps disabled readers develop a concept of reading for meaning that is more difficult to attain with some other approaches that also exert rigid linguistic control.

Major Assumptions

The construction of the *Merrill Linguistic Readers* was based upon twelve principles which follow as they are stated in the teacher's edition of the first reader:

1. Learning to read begins with and builds upon the oral language "control" already achieved by the pupil—his mastery of the language that he uses when he speaks and that he understands when it is spoken. Oral language activities that are appropriate to the environmental factors and to the maturity of the group and that provide for growth at each level are thus regarded as a vital part of the approach.

2. The vocabulary and the grammatical structures presented in the reading materials must be within the oral experience of the child and must keep pace with the widening of that experience. The reading matter in the program must at all stages be such as to permit the pupil to identify the written words as the same words he knows very well when he hears them spoken.

3. The vocabulary presented must lead gradually to a thorough assimilation of the three major patterns that characterize the great body of English spellings. The spelling-pattern approach is built upon, and takes advantage of, the very high degree of regularity that exists, despite all assertions to the contrary, in the spelling of present-day English.

4. Emphasis on minimum contrasts in words that are otherwise similar in spelling (*mat—fat; mat—man; mat—met; mat—mate;* etc.) *if developed in carefully ordered succession,* is the most effective means of teaching word recognition. Through early and continued training in perceiving minimum contrasts, the pupil will develop the habit of paying close attention to the words he is reading and will in time attain a great degree of proficiency in word recognition.

5. Instant recognition and discrimination of the letters of the alphabet in any sequence whatsoever is an essential preparation for learning to read.

6. The introduction of a limited number of high-frequency words (sight words) that do not conform to the spelling patterns being developed at the time is vital to provide reading material that has normal sentence patterns. However, since the main emphasis should be on the "regular" spelling patterns being presented, the written form of such sight words should not be given special attention.

7. Knowledge of the major spelling patterns (and of inflectional endings) can be immediately applied by the pupil to the reading of innumerable other words formed in accordance with or incorporating or resembling those basic patterns. (This principle has been confirmed at every stage in the experimental use of the books. The word lists of the successive Readers in the present, formal edition reflect this fact.)

8. In the teaching of reading, there must be complete meaning responses by the child, not only to particular words but to those words in full sentences, and to those sentences in sequences of sentences. It is for this reason that the use of nonsense words should be avoided. Furthermore, because cumulative meaning is essential, the teaching procedures throughout the stories must be such as to take account of the different backgrounds and levels of maturity of the pupils. (It will be seen that the annotated editions of the Readers provide a second "track" for slower pupils.)

9. A continuing, known environment in the stories—representing ordinary settings and realistic experiences and characters—keeps the beginning reader from having to struggle to understand unfamiliar or fantastic concepts at the same time that he is learning to *do* reading. (In extensive classroom research, it has been found that pupils are so delighted with their own ability to read that they need nothing more to maintain their interest than such uncomplicated narratives *evidencing cumulative meaning* as now appear in the Readers.)

10. In order to focus the pupils' attention upon the reading materials themselves, pictures must be excluded from the basic series. Experience has consistently demonstrated that (a) pictures constitute a distracting element *in the process of learning to read,* and (b) because pictures furnish clues to meaning, they lead the pupils to *guess* at words rather than to *read* them. (Incidentally, the absence of pictures permits the release of highly individualized creativity when the pupils are encouraged to illustrate the stories, for they are not hampered by the interpretation of another "artist.")

11. Early practice in *writing* (first sentences, then stories), if guided so as to utilize the patterns and the sight words presented in the reading text, reinforces the child's grasp of the major spelling patterns and of the grammatical structures of standard English.

12. The teaching procedure must permit what amounts to a daily evaluation of reading progress, and the program must make provision for the testing and further development of each pupil's specific abilities to interpret, recall, organize, draw conclusions, and write independently. (Pp. 5–7)

Instructional Materials

The materials for the Fries linguistic approach include six readers for the primary grades and a skills book for each reader. Supplementary reading materials are suggested, but are not to be used until after the third reader has been mastered. The chalk board is used for initial presentation of words, initial presentation of words in sentences, review of words and sentences, presentation and solving of scrambled sentences, writing dictated words and sentences by pupils, writing original sentences by pupils, and word games.

Implementation

With the Fries linguistic approach letters are never taught in isolation, but in spelling patterns. The first spelling pattern learned by the pupil is "at." The teacher writes the word "cat" on the board, pronounces it, and spells it pointing to individual letters, uses it in a sentence, and has the pupil offer sentences of his own. The pupil eventually looks at the word, spells it, and pronounces it. Other words with the same spelling pattern, "fat," "Nat," are introduced and attention is called to the contrasts between the words. Words which do not conform to the spelling pattern being learned, but which are necessary to construct sentences (e.g., *is, a, the*) are taught as sight words and are not spelled out. They are circled to call attention to the fact that they are different from the pattern words which have minimal contrasts.

Sentences (e.g., "Nat is a cat.") are formed for the pupil to read silently and then orally. Much stress is placed upon expressive oral reading. Questions are asked about the sentences (e.g., "Who is Nat?") to insure reading for meaning. Stories are formed from the sentences (e.g., "Nat is a cat. Is Nat fat? Nat is fat. Nat is a fat cat.") and discussed.

When the "at" pattern is mastered, the "an" pattern is introduced, then "ap" pattern, and so on until the pupil masters all of the basic spelling patterns in the English language. Each new step builds upon patterns previously learned (e.g., mat—mate—meat).

To prevent children from relying upon picture clues no pictures are included in the materials. Much drill and repetition are used, and the primary motivational appeal is a sense of satisfaction in decoding the language properly and answering comprehension questions about the sentences that are read. When the six readers and the skills books have been successfully finished, the program is completed and the pupil supposedly has the basic reading skills mastered.

PROGRAMMED READING

We have observed programmed reading to be effective in helping pupils learn to read who have been almost completely unsuccessful with other approaches. The program developed by Sullivan (1966) is especially suitable for use with remedial readers because it includes placement tests that permit teachers to get pupils started within the sequence of the Sullivan materials at the exact point the learning process ceased. In addition, students who use the program proceed at their own pace and are evaluated frequently with progress tests.

Major Assumptions

The assumptions underlying the development of the *Sullivan Reading Program* are taken from the assumptions of programmed learning in general and from linguistic findings that urge rigid vocabulary control. Pupils move through a sequence of learning behaviors that build upon previously learned behaviors and differ very slightly in the tasks that are required from step to step. Immediate feedback is provided after the completion of each task so that the pupil is aware of his progress and can correct any errors he makes immediately. Vocabulary is controlled so that pupils encounter the regularities of English orthography before they are asked to decode irregularly spelled words. The program is based upon the basic assumption that reading is essentially a matter of making accurate letter-sound associations.

Instructional Materials

The *Sullivan Reading Program* includes placement tests, progress tests, programmed textbooks, and correlated readers. These materials are available at five ability levels: Series I, II, III, IV, and V. Series I is preceded by a Reading Readiness Program and a Readiness in Language Arts Program for pupils who need them. Each Series includes four programmed textbooks and a number of correlated readers for each textbook so that the pupil receives considerable practice in using the vocabulary he has just mastered in the corresponding programmed text. All of the materials make much use of pictures for clues to meaning and for motivational purposes.

Implementation

The nature and sequence of the program is shown by the following descriptions of each Series taken from the scope and sequence chart that outlines the program:

Series I starts with the short vowels and the most common consonants. With rare exceptions, each letter represents only one sound. Words are introduced in large, regular classes. The basic building blocks for a person learning to read English are 3-letter words of the pattern "consonant-short vowel-consonant." When the student is familiar with the sound values of the single consonants in such 3-letter words, digraphs, trigraphs, and consonant clusters are added both before and after the vowel to form longer and longer regular monosyllables. The sound-symbol relationships are introduced one by one. After its introduction each letter-sound relationship is used repeatedly until its decoding and encoding become absolutely automatic.

Series II introduces secondary sounds for the letters in clearly different linguistic environments. This Series is devoted largely to the study of new vowel classes with emphasis on the traditional long vowel classes formed by the vowel plus *e,* with or without an intervening consonant. It also studies synonyms and homonyms, and contains exercises in multiple meanings.

Series III concludes the study of the English monosyllable in Book 9. Two-syllable words are introduced in Book 10, and the rest of the series is devoted to their study. Homophones are studies in a series of drills, also regular comparatives of adjectives, words ending in *er,* and the suffix *ing.*

Series IV continues the analysis of two-syllable words, examining several word classes ending in *ing* including those which double the consonant before *ing* (plan*ning*), the superlative adjective suffix *est* (young*est*), and miscellaneous words ending in *est.* It also studies two-syllable words ending in *or, y, ly,* past participles ending in *en* (swoll*en*), the causative verb suffix *en* (straight*en*), adjectives ending in *en* (wood*en*), and words ending in a consonant sound plus *le* (gridd*le*).

Series V adds 744 new words to the student's vocabulary to make a total vocabulary of 3,463 words. Books 17, 18, and 19 continue the study of two-syllable words, introducing word classes according to the word endings. Book 20 introduces compound words belonging to various classes, grouped in terms of their first element or their last element, as well as miscellaneous compound nouns.

On the basis of placement test results each student is started in the textbook most suited to his needs. He responds to the tasks within that book and self-checks each response to determine whether or not he responded correctly. When he has completed the programmed textbook, he takes a progress test. The following illustrations taken from selected progress tests will show the nature and something of the sequence of the Sullivan Program:

Series I, book 1

picture of a pin	a pin a pit
picture of a cat	a can a cat
picture of a big pig	a big p—g
picture of Nan	Nan is n—t a man.

Series I, book 2

picture of a path	a bath a path
picture of a dish	a dish a fish
picture of a map	Is this a cap? Yes No
picture of sand in a hand	This is sand in my h—nd.

Series I, book 4

picture of a barn	This is a bar. barn.
picture of stork	I am a stork. storm.

Series II, book 5

picture of kite	Is this a kit or a kite?
picture of dog lifting paw	My dog can give me his paw. saw.

Series II, book 6

picture of white bus and gray truck	Which is white, the bus or the truck? _____ _____
picture of hoe	This is a hoe. toe.

Series III, book 9

picture of child praying	To kneel is to get down on your —nees.
picture of bread	This is a loaf of br——d.

Series III, book 12

picture of boy winking at girl	Al is w—nking at Jean.
picture of boy spading	Len is shading spading the earth for worms.

Series IV, book 12

picture of bird flying	This bird is ——apping its wings.
picture of hand cracking egg on frying pan	I am cr—cking this egg on the edge of the frying pan.

Series IV, book 16

picture of mouse eating cheese	This mouse is n—bbling at a piece of cheese.
picture of Ann falling in puddle	Ann slipped and fell in a mud p—ddle.

Series V, book 17

picture of hollow log	If a thing is empty in the middle, it is hollow. This is a _____ log.
picture of sandal	A ——ndal is a type of shoe.

Series V, book 20

picture of a bookcase

picture of girl in rain

There are six shelves of books in this ———— case.

A sudden heavy rain is called a cl——dburst.

The correlated readers also make much use of pictures and so far as the vocabulary constraints permit, contain stories pupils are likely to be interested in. Teachers are advised to have pupils read aloud as well as silently from the readers and to permit them to discuss the stories if the children want to.

Once pupils have learned how to progress on their own through the materials, the teacher's job is largely one of providing individual help and encouragement. Therefore, children who react badly to pupil-teacher interactions are able to finish the program with a minimum of personality clashes.

OTHER APPROACHES

Most teachers, we believe, will be able to help seriously disabled readers who appear to need instruction that is not eclectic with one of the approaches we have already discussed. The major task is to diagnose carefully and then to use diagnostic findings to select the approach most likely to help individual students become the best readers possible considering the strengths and weaknesses they bring to the remedial program.

A number of approaches other than those we have already discussed in the present chapter have been and are being developed by people interested in helping disabled readers. We shall discuss briefly some of those approaches to give readers of the present chapter a more complete picture of the work that is being done in the development of specific approaches that may help to prevent and to remedy severe reading disorders.

Color Phonics

The color phonics system was originated and is discussed by Bannatyne (1967) as a new technique for helping children with reading disabilities. According to Bannatyne, there are eleven criteria for an ideal remedial approach for "dyslexics," which he discusses as follows:

1. It has been demonstrated by many workers in the field over the last thirty years that the only successful technique for teaching dyslexics are those firmly founded on a phonetic basis. The logical phonetic structure of English, even if it is not perfect, seems to provide the dyslexic child with a memory reference basis which is more economical than the multitude of arbitrary sound-symbol associations used in nonphonetic methods of teaching reading.

2. The individual letters of the alphabet must be discrete units so that they can be arranged and rearranged in given order again and again; that is, each

letter must be printed on a tiny, individual card or plaque so that words can be spelled in sequence.

3. The somewhat irregular orthography of the English language must be further systematized so that the child is always able to identify a particular letter or combination of letters by referring to a logical cue. Replacing the irregular phonetic structure of the language with a regular one requires the child to transfer to the traditional orthography at a later date. As the dyslexic child finds it extremely difficult to memorize a set of sound-symbol associations, an additional set of symbols for the same sounds is scarcely likely to solve his problems.

4. The technique must allow the child to overlearn sound-symbol associations through a variety of stimuli and sensory pathways.

5. The technique should allow the child to work equally well when moving either from the printed to the sounded word or from the sounded to the printed word. Therefore, the letters with their logical cues will help the child both to spell words which he hears and to identify the phonetic structure of words which he sees in print.

6. The system should be usable in conjunction with any other technique which uses the traditional orthography as its basis.

7. It should be pupil-oriented rather than teacher-oriented. It should involve the pupil in active, manual, multi-sensory participation, rather than relying solely on the passive, visual approach which occurs in so much remedial reading and which has had so little success with dyslexic children.

8. Most of the systems for teaching dyslexic children rely on a formal, open-ended phonetics approach; because of their lack of finite definition in space, a practical goal cannot be presented to the children. The best system will enable the child to appreciate, understand, and accept the extent of the practical nature of the complete task ahead.

9. The technique should permit a feeling of increasing mastery, in the sense that the child must not only know from the outset his ultimate goal in terms of that material but must know also that each new step mastered brings the goal nearer by a well-defined amount.

10. The central idea of the technique must be equally applicable to the learning situation in all its steps. Whether the pupil be a seven-year-old dyslexic who is beginning to read or a poor speller at the university, the method should be of value to each in a variety of ways.

11. The child must become involved with and enjoy the materials with which he is working. Apart from this interest in the material for its own sake, the material itself should be sufficiently flexible and adaptable to allow for a variety of interesting approaches in each lesson. (P. 196)

The Color Phonics System is a synthetic approach to word analysis. Letters and letter combinations are printed on tiny cards which are arranged and rearranged to build words. Each card is distinctively colored to add an additional cue for identifying the various sounds the letters and letter combinations represent. On the back of all the consonant and colored vowels is a picture which represents the key word printed underneath, thereby providing students with an additional cue to the sounds of the letters. An elaborate system for coding the colors, letters, and pictures has been worked out so that they are mutually reinforcing. For example, the phoneme "ee" as sounded in "green" is printed in a green color and has as a picture a daub of green color with the key word "green." Other aspects of the coding system are considerably more complicated. The basis of the system is the correct sounding and blending of the letters and letter combinations to build words and finally sentences. Bannatyne says:

> . . . the need to reinforce the child's auditory sequencing processes means that child and teacher, particularly the child, must vocalize constantly. This applies not only to the careful sounding of the successive phonemes which make up a particular word, but also to the conversation which should proceed almost continuously between child and teacher. The pupil should be encouraged to think aloud at all times. (P. 198)

Initially the child with much help from the teacher composes the words and sentences he will read. During this initial stage he learns the color cues by rote. The child copies his work into a workbook. The tracing method suggested by Fernald (1943) may be used to help him learn certain difficult words. Eventually, the child becomes familiar with certain words that they need no longer be represented in color and vowel cards printed black on white are substituted for the color-cued cards. The transition to ordinary materials is made gradually as the students develop a suitable sight vocabulary and the self-confidence to move into uncolored materials.

Words in Color

Because the theoretical assumptions and basic methodology underlying the Color Phonics System and Words in Color are essentially the same, we shall not devote much space to Words in Color. Suffice it to say that color cues and synthesizing sounds are the two outstanding features of this approach. Gattegno and Hinman (1967), say:

> In Words in Color the use of inner criteria is constantly stressed, but there are also some devices used that help. First "p" is introduced and is colored brown when it is a sounded consonant, as in "pop." When "d" appears, "p" has been thoroughly practiced. To emphasize the distinction wanted, "I" is colored dark green. After "d" has been practiced for some time, "b" appears. However, because this procedure would make one watch only the color and not the shape, we revert to asking learners to watch the orientation of the shape and not the color by making the colors of "b" and "d" very close indeed. (P. 178)

A distinguishing characteristic of the Words in Color approach is called "visual dictation," which is a matter of the pupil's responding with the correct sound when color-coded letters are pointed to. For example, the letter "a" if pointed to would signal the student to make the sound learned for that letter. Pointing to *a*, two or three times would elicit the sound twice or three times. The word *pat* would be elicited by pointing at *p a t* in succession. Eventually by varying the speed of pointing, sentences such as "tip it up" can be sounded out and the student is supposedly on his way to successful reading.

A Neurological Impress Method

Heckelman (1969) reported good results with severely disabled readers from a pedagogical approach he termed the Neurological Impress Method. The approach Heckelman describes is simple in theory and in implementation. The basic theoretical assumption is that children can learn and have learned to read by following along and reading in unison with a good oral reader. The implementation of the approach, then, is to have the pupil read in unison with the teacher and slide his finger along the line of words being spoken so that the student's finger is always at the location of the word being spoken.

Before the sessions begin the pupil is told the nature and purpose of the instruction he will receive and some sentences or paragraphs are read in unison several times to establish a fluent, normal reading pattern for teacher and pupil. No attention is given to the materials themselves. The immediate objective is to cover as many pages of material without long pauses as the pupil is able to cover without becoming fatigued. At times the teacher's voice is louder and slightly faster than the child's voice. However, as the pupil becomes more capable of taking a leadership role in the oral reading, the teacher lowers his voice and lags slightly behind the pupil's reading. If the pupil begins to falter, the teacher increases the volume and speed of his reading to give the pupil the support he needs. At first the teacher accompanies the reading with a smooth, continuous motion of his index finger under the words being read. Later, the pupil uses his finger to accompany the reading. Pupils are told to "slide" across the words to the end of the page and to pretend they are sliding on ice. Pupils are also told not to concentrate on individual words, but rather to say the words as best they can without even thinking that they are reading. No concern is given to comprehension of the material that is read. The concern is entirely with the flow of the reading being done.

On the basis of his work with twenty-four students in grades seven to ten who were at least three years retarded in reading ability, Heckelman (1969) concluded the following: ". . . an oral Neurological Impress Reading Method was one method of breaking the "phonics-bound" condition which occurs in many children who have had intensive phonics and still have not learned to read fluently" (p. 281). Our own experience with the approach has been that certain disabled readers who seem to lack a proper concept of reading and who have serious phrasing problems are helped substantially by some work with the Neurological Impress Method. It is not an approach that is complete in itself as are some other approaches we have discussed previously in the present chapter.

The Progressive Choice Reading Program

The Progressive Choice Reading Program as developed by Woolman (1966) proceeds in three stages: Cycle I, Cycle II, and Cycle III. Because Woolman believes that complexity in a learning task may confuse children who have difficulty learning to read, he has broken the reading process into simple components which are learned in a carefully planned sequence. Essentially, the program is based upon discriminating differences among letter configurations, learning the sounds the letters and letter combinations represent, and blending the sounds accurately. However, the learning sequence and the tasks constructed by Woolman cause the program to be quite different from other basic programs that are phonics based.

The following discussion from the Teacher's Manual provides an overview of the program:

CYCLE I

In Cycle I all the letters of the alphabet except Q are presented in uppercase form. To learn to recognize, print and sound each letter, the child progresses through a series of five controlled steps, or learning levels:

1. *Audial Meaning Level.* The child hears words that he will ultimately read, and demonstrates that he understands their meaning in an oral context.

2. *Discrimination Level.* The child shows that he can distinguish differences between letter shapes and that he can print a particular letter shape used in words he has mastered at the Audial Meaning Level. A simple print style is used to facilitate the child's task of recognition and printing. The letter shapes are presented in a sequence that provides maximum discernibility; for example, an angular form, such as M, is followed by a circular form, such as O.

3. *Identification Level.* The child identifies letter shapes with letter sounds and demonstrates that he can print the shape of a letter when he hears its sound. Cycle I of *Lift-Off to Reading* is phonetically consistent—each letter is given a single sound. (All vowels in Cycle I are given the short sound only.)

4. *Compounding Level.* Using the letter shapes and letter sounds that he has learned, the child demonstrates his ability to print the correct letter sequence when he hears meaningless blended sounds, such as *omo, op, tos.*

5. *Visual Meaning Level.* The child reads and indicates by printed responses that he knows the meaning of the words he sees.

CYCLE II

When a child has demonstrated mastery of five learning levels for all uppercase letters (except Q), he is ready to move into Cycle II. In Cycle II all the letters of the alphabet are presented in lowercase form (and Q in both uppercase and lowercase). Again the child moves through the five learning levels, and learns to recognize sound, and prints the lowercase letters. Cycle II also includes study of twenty-six phonetically consistent compounds; of the alphabet as a sequence of letter names; of the effect of a final *e* on an internal vowel sound; and of several grammatical tools, including capitalization and punctuation.

CYCLE III

In Cycle III variant sounds for the letter shapes covered in Cycles I and II are introduced. The child studies words in which the same letter compounds have more than one sound. He also studies words in which the same sounds are represented by more than one combination of letter shapes. He is also taught to use the dictionary as a tool for vocabulary expansion. The goal of LIFT-OFF TO READING is reading for meaning, and in Cycle III must demonstrate comprehension of several stories. (Pp. iv, v)

Frostig-Delacato-Kephart Approaches

We have chosen to discuss the remedial approaches developed by Frostig (1964), Delacato (1959, 1963) and Kephart (1960) together and in less detail than we discussed other approaches for several reasons. First of all, they are representative of approaches that attempt to improve reading ability by treating aspects of physical development that are assumed to be basic to development in reading. Secondly, the research that has been done relative to their effectiveness in improving reading ability is contradictory and often not supportive of the programs. And finally, we believe that these three approaches are also representative of the approaches that are highly publicized and often implemented before they have been tested thoroughly enough to warrant their widespread use with remedial readers.

The Frostig Visual Perception Program

The Frostig tests and instructional materials are concerned with the development of visual perception. Certain disabled readers are assumed to be deficient in the ability to learn to read because they are lacking in basic visual perception skills. If these visual perception skills are strengthened through the proper training, the assumption is that a major obstacle to the student's reading development will be removed.

The *Developmental Test of Visual Perception* (Frostig, 1964) contains five subtests: (1) eye-motor coordination, (2) figure ground, (3) form constancy, (4) position in space, and (5) spatial relations. The Frostig-Horne (1964) instructional materials have been constructed to train pupils in the five areas included in the test as well as some other aspects of perceptual functioning.

The Delacato Approach

Delacato (1959, 1963) theorizes that incomplete neurological development is responsible for specific reading disability. Children who do not proceed normally through the various developmental stages of neurological development that are delineated by Delacato do not attain the condition of "neurological organization" and consequently experience great difficulty learning to read.

Before actual remedial reading instruction is begun the disabled child must receive a training program that consists of crawling exercises, posturing, and other physical manipulations that supposedly treat the brain itself. The exercises are described as neurological "patterning" and are prescribed on the basis of diagnosis that indicates the level or stage at which the normal neurological development has broken down. The various exercises the child must engage in are carefully planned to develop normal neurological processes and conditions. The establishment of cortical hemisphere dominance, for example, is an important aspect of the Delacato training.

When the preremedial treatment has resulted in complete neurological organization, remedial reading instruction is introduced. Interestingly, Delacato recommends that the pupil be introduced to reading by learning whole words from his experience and that phonics be reserved until late in the remedial program. Meaning is always stressed and considerable emphasis is placed upon the use of context clues to learn words and obtain meaning.

The Kephart Approach

Kephart (1960) does not attack severe reading problems by reading instruction, but instead attempts to develop the basic abilities upon which the reading process depends. The higher forms of behavior, he theorizes, develop out of and have their roots in motor learning. With training in the basic skills such as crawling, hopping, stretching, twisting, throwing, and lifting, certain weaknesses can be strengthened with a resulting improved performance in more complex activities such as reading. Kephart identified the following developmental areas to be of importance in school achievement: posture, laterality, directionality, body image, form perception, and spatial orientation. His program outlines specific diagnostic procedures and instructional practices for assessing and strengthening weaknesses in perceptual-motor skills development.

In this chapter we have attempted to give a reasonable picture of the different approaches that have been developed for use with seriously disabled readers. We have discussed some of the theoretical assumptions and the major instructional procedures for each of the various programs. Obviously, we had to select from the many different programs available those which we thought represented best the alternatives available to remedial teachers. We also had to make some decisions about which characteristics of the different programs we would discuss. Therefore, this chapter is intended to be an introduction to the many specific remedial reading approaches that have been developed. Teachers who want to implement any of the specific approaches will need to consult the references cited in the discussions.

At this time we know of no diagnostic instruments that will tell without error which approach will work best with which combination of strengths and weaknesses a given student might evidence. We believe, therefore, that the best approach for a particular disabled reader must often be determined by trial and error. We reject the notion that an approach which has been successful in a particular clinic or school setting with certain children will be successful in other environments with other teachers and pupils. An instructional approach cannot be considered apart from the unique personalities of those who use it and from the environments in which it is used. Consequently, we feel strongly that remedial reading teachers should be acquainted with a number of approaches to use with disabled readers and should regard what is indeed happening to a particular child's reading improvement more highly than what reportedly happened somewhere else. The proof of any approach lies in the effect it has on a particular child's reading ability.

Finally, we urge that this chapter be considered in conjunction with the ideas we presented in Chapter 6 relative to the development of a proper concept of reading and a positive attitude toward reading. All of the approaches described in the present chapter must be implemented in a way that will encourage the child to be a reader, not someone who has completed a systematized series of exercises without seeing the application of those exercises to functional and recreational materials.

THOUGHTS FOR DISCUSSION

"The remedial teacher must be resourceful. If, after a fair attempt to utilize one method, the pupil has not made adequate progress, the teacher must be willing to try something else. Adaptability to the pupil's needs is far more important than devotion to a particular plan of procedure." (Harris, 1970, p. 363)

"Despite its crucial importance, the work of the teacher should not be regarded as neural surgery nor as the manipulation of atomic materials. In teaching, a single technical misstep will seldom spell disaster. As a director of an age-old organic process, the teacher applies his important efforts in a more general fashion. He stimulates here, provides nutriment there, and confidently accepts one outcome and rejects another, often enjoying the enviable opportunity of being able to make up tomorrow for the things that were neglected today." (Stephens, 1967, p. 12)

"Fifty years of research covering reading and the remedial reader have produced a number of studies of why children who are seemingly internally or externally unimpaired fail to learn to read. One cannot read the reviews of this research in *The Encyclopedia of Educational Research* without being struck by the recurrence of the word 'inconclusive.' Do visual anomalies cause reading disability? The results are inconclusive. Do emotional problems cause reading disability? The results are inconclusive. Yet, the urgency of the problem continues to produce research designed to broaden the understanding of the problem. Seldom does a decade go by without a number of new theories being proposed on the basis of the latest research and the newest insights." (Kaluger and Kolson, 1969, p. 67)

"As to duration, a minimum of two years is the shortest training period from which we can anticipate any substantial or durable success. Many pupils who have shown gratifying progress, almost immediately find that their specific disability reasserts itself when the work has been dropped too soon, and wide reading and extensive themes are required prematurely." (Gillingham and Stillman, 1968, p. 23)

"There is no one single etiology for all learning disabilities. Rather, learning problems can be caused by any number of a multiplicity of factors, all of which may be highly inter-related. Unfortunately, all too often the child who is experiencing learning disorder is approached with a unitary orientation so that extremely important aspects of his unique learning problems may very well be ignored. The tendency of each professional discipline to view the entire problem 'through its own window of specialization' often obscures vital factors which may contribute to, or at least exacerbate, the basic difficulty. It is just as involved to conceive of one cure, one panacea, applied randomly to all types of learning disorders. Not every learning disabled youngster requires a special school, or psychotherapy, or kinesthetic techniques, or perceptual-motor training, or, for that matter, to regress to crawling along the floor!" (Abrams, 1970, p. 299)

REFERENCES

Abrams, J. C. Learning disabilities—a complex phenomenon. *The Reading Teacher,* 1969–1970, **23**, 299–304, 367.

Bannatyne, A. D. The color phonics system. In J. Money (Ed.), *The disabled reader.* Baltimore: Johns Hopkins Press, 1967, 193–214.

Delacato, C. H. *The treatment and prevention of reading problems.* Springfield, Ill.: Charles C Thomas, 1959.

Delacato, C. H. *The diagnosis and treatment of speech and reading problems,* Springfield, Ill.: Charles C Thomas, 1963.

Fernald, G. M. *Remedial techniques in basic school subjects.* New York: McGraw-Hill, 1943.

Fries, C. C. *Linguistics and reading.* New York: Holt, 1963.

Fries, C. C., Wilson, R. G., and Rudolph, M. K. *Merrill linguistic readers.* Columbus, Ohio: Charles E. Merrill, 1966.

Frostig, M., and Horne, D. *The Frostig program for the development of visual perception.* Chicago: Follett, 1964.

Frostig, M. *The Marianne Frostig developmental test of visual perception.* Palo Alto, Calif.: Consulting Psychologist, 1964.

Gattegno, C., and Hinman, D. Words in color. In J. Money (Ed.), *The disabled reader.* Baltimore: Johns Hopkins Press, 1967, 175–191.

Gillingham, A., and Stillman, B. *Remedial training for children with specific disability in reading, spelling and penmanship.* Cambridge, Mass.: Educators Publishing Service, 1968.

Harris, A. J. *How to increase reading ability.* (5th ed.) New York: David McKay, 1970.

Heckelman, R. G. A neurological impress method of reading instruction. *Academic Therapy,* Summer, 1969, **4** (4), 277–282.

Kaluger, G., and Kolson, C. J. *Reading and learning disabilities.* Columbus, Ohio: Charles E. Merrill, 1969.

Kephart, N. C. *The slow learner in the classroom.* Columbus, Ohio: Charles E. Merrill, 1960.

Orton, J. L. The Orton-Gillingham approach. In J. Money (Ed.), *The disabled reader.* Baltimore: Johns Hopkins Press, 1967, 119–145.

Orton, S. T. *Reading, writing and speech problems in children.* New York: Norton, 1937.

Stauffer, R. G. *The language-experience approach to the teaching of reading.* New York: Harper and Row, 1970.

Stephens, J. M. *The process of schooling.* New York: Holt, 1967.

Sullivan, M. W. *Sullivan reading program.* Palo Alto, Calif.: Behavioral Research Laboratories, 1966.

Woolman, M. *Lift-off to reading.* Chicago: Science Research Associates, 1966.

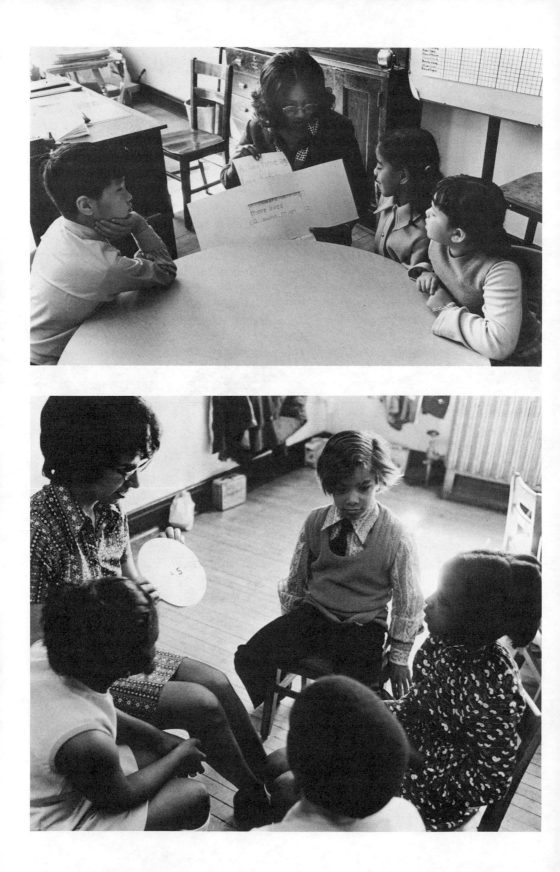

Chapter 10

Spelling[1]

When George Bernard Shaw died in 1950, he left a substantial sum of money to be spent for reforming the English spelling system. For this he is cherished at some time or another by nearly everyone who has tried to learn English spelling. He is especially cherished by everyone who has tried to teach English spelling. The idiosyncrasies of our orthography are indeed frustrating to both learner and teacher.

Frustrating though it may be, teaching children how to spell the English language is a definite responsibility of the American school. Our spelling system is part of our language, and it is important that people learn to use all dimensions of their language as effectively as they are able. Although the system may seem inconsistent and may be difficult to master, users are not permitted to take liberties with it. A word is either correctly or incorrectly spelled. And those who spell words incorrectly are judged by many as either uneducated or careless.

Many poor spellers are also poor in other language abilities. Therefore, corrective and remedial teachers often need to set priorities in regard to the sequencing and emphases of their instructional programs. We feel that for most corrective and remedial pupils spelling is low on the list of priorities. Consequently, we recommend that most poor spellers be given special help with their spelling in conjunction with other language arts instruction. In relatively rare instances a child who is good in reading, speaking, listening, and expressing ideas in writing may be extremely poor in spelling. If he has a sincere desire to improve his spelling, such a child will probably make rapid progress with intensive specific instruction, and he should be given that opportunity. But most poor spellers will ultimately profit more if spelling is taught within the context of broader skill areas. With this approach the more important abilities of reading, speaking, listening, and logical thinking can be emphasized and used as motivational forces to encourage poor spellers to improve their spelling so they will be better able to communicate their ideas in writing. In practice, this approach has students learning spelling rules and how to spell individual words as they

---

1. Much of the discussion in Chapter 10 is reprinted with permission from the September, 1970, issue of *The National Elementary Principal.*

need them to write sentences relative to interesting and meaningful reading, listening, and speaking experiences. This approach would not preclude small doses of intensive instruction to teach a particular generalization or particular word. The intensive instruction, however, would be given within the context of some meaningful writing experience. The assumption is that poor spellers have been exposed to a developmental program of spelling instruction and have probably developed negative attitudes toward spelling instruction. Therefore, it is important for teachers to be concerned with the affective as well as the cognitive responses of poor spellers to remedial spelling instruction.

Learning to spell is a tedious business, especially for pupils who have difficulties with the concept and mechanics of establishing sound-symbol relationships. Consequently, teachers of corrective and remedial spelling must be prepared to make spelling instruction as enjoyable as possible, to help pupils avoid extreme frustration, to praise them for small improvements, and to motivate them by keeping the utilitarian value of being a good speller clearly visible.

In the present chapter we discuss (1) the history of the English spelling system, (2) the nature of English spelling, (3) spelling in the language arts curriculum, (4) how children learn to spell, (5) survey, specific, and intensive levels of diagnosis for spelling, and (6) specific teaching procedures for corrective and remedial spelling instruction. We feel that to teach spelling effectively to students who have failed to learn in a developmental program the teacher must understand the phenomenon of English orthography and the processes necessary to master it, if indeed anyone ever does. We also feel that giving poor spellers insights into the history and nature of English spelling may be helpful to their achievement and to their self-concepts. Pupils who understand the unique history and characteristics of the English spelling system may feel less inadequate as learners because they have trouble learning a difficult system and may be helped to cope with the peculiar problems it presents. Our major objectives are similar to those expressed by Moffett (1968), "My recommendations aim to develop self-correction and self-diagnosis. Students take responsibility for spelling, but the teacher sets up processes that make this possible" (p. 93).

THE HISTORY OF ENGLISH SPELLING

Both the regularity and the irregularity of English spelling must be attributed to natural growth. The history of that growth reflects both the regularity and the irregularity that is characteristic of all cultural evolution. Our spelling system has resisted a completely logical development just as the different cultures through which it has evolved have resisted a completely logical development. And although Shaw would have it otherwise, it is likely that it will retain its present characteristics.

The English language spelling system got its start when our Anglo-Saxon ancestors began to write. In Anglo-Saxon times Latin was the vehicle for all education. What was worth knowing, it was felt, was recorded in the language of the Romans. Therefore, when Anglo-Saxons learned to read, they learned to read Latin, and when they learned to write, they understandably borrowed the spelling system of the Latin language.

The Latin learned by the Anglo-Saxons was largely alphabetic. That is, it was composed of graphemes (letters) that rather consistently represented phonemes (meaningful speech sounds). Consequently, the concept of grapheme-phoneme correspondence was attained by the Anglo-Saxons from their contact with Latin. This should not be construed to mean that the English language itself is derived from Latin. It does mean that the first writing system used to represent English was an alphabetic system.

The attempts of the Anglo-Saxons to use a modified Latin alphabet to record their own speech sounds reflect the variety of Anglo-Saxon dialects. They spelled as they spoke, but the same word in Anglo-Saxon might be spoken differently in different geographic regions. Therefore, the same word might appear in the writing of different men in quite different forms. So although there was a certain consistency in Anglo-Saxon (Old English), there were also some understandable inconsistencies.

The inconsistencies were increased by the effects of the Norman conquest of the Anglo-Saxons in 1066. As a result of this conquest the Norman or French culture was superimposed on the Anglo-Saxons. For a time the two languages with their different spelling systems coexisted; but eventually, like the French boy and the Anglo-Saxon girl, they married and became one. And each brought to the marriage its individual peculiarities, some of which persisted in spite of the merger. Baugh (1963) quotes William Caxton, a late fifteenth-century English author:

> And certaynly our langage now used varyeth ferre from that whiche was used and spoken whan I was borne. For we englysshe men ben borne under the domynacyon of the mone, whiche is never stedfaste, but every waverynge, wexynge one season, and waneth & dyscreaseth another season. And that comyn englysshe that is spoken in one shyre varyeth from a nother. In so moche that in my dayes happened that certayn marchauntes were in a shippe in tamyse, for to have sayled over the see into zelande, and for lacke of wynde, thei taryed atte forlond, and wente to lande for to refreshe them. And one of theym named Sheffelde, a mercer, cam in-to an hows and axed for mete; and specyally he axyd after eggys. And the goode wyf answerde, that she coude speke no frenshe. And the marchaunt was angry, for he also coude speke no frenshe, but wolde have hadde egges, and she understode hym not. And thenne at laste a nother sayd that he wolde have eyren. Then the good wyf sayd that she understod hym wel. Loo, what sholde a man in thyse dayse now wryte, egges or eyren? (P. 236)

One result of these inconsistencies in the language was the haphazard spelling practices observable in Middle English. Laird (1957) comments as follows:

Certainly some of the confusion is a confusion of dialects. Many Middle English scribes, like their Anglo-Saxon predecessors, had a sense of phonetic values in letters, and tried to spell a word the way they pronounced it. But many others seemed to have spelled with the greatest abandon. We constantly see the same word spelled in two ways in adjacent lines, and I recall once having noticed one word spelled four different ways in four consecutive lines of a Middle English manuscript. (P. 285)

Obviously, Middle English writers did not feel obliged to be consistent in their spelling. One man, Orm, is mentioned by Laird and other historians of the English language as an exception to this attitude toward spelling. However, like Shaw's, his zeal does not appear to have been very contagious, and his particular system was largely confined to his own written production.

Reformation is a part of man's nature, so it was natural that a movement would begin to reform those who would spell English according to the spirit rather than the law. Fries (1963), attributes most of the reform of English spelling to the development of printing. He says,

Under the influence of the printer, the ideal for spelling became "regularity" — that the "same" word be spelled always in the same way whenever it occurred. "Correctness" of spelling gradually came to mean uniformity, and the diversities in the practice of authors were eventually almost completely eliminated by the rules set up and applied by the editors and proofreaders. (P. 168)

Perhaps the printers, their editors, and proofreaders cried out for regularity in spelling for pragmatic reasons, or perhaps they were reflecting man's natural desire to order the disordered. At any rate, the license to spell as one pleased was revoked, and the demand for correctness became greater for spelling than for any other facet of the language arts. That demand has resisted numerous attempts to change the rigidity fixed by the early printers. And today children are still being rewarded in spelling bees for knowing that "psychology" begins with a *p* and not a *c* or an *s*. Those who do not must shamefacedly return to their seats.

It is unlikely that readers of the English language will ever permit writers to spell with the abandon that characterized Middle English composition. Therefore, anyone who wishes to communicate in writing will have to have the skills demanded by our orthography. The teacher who understands the history and nature of English spelling and how children learn to spell will be more successful with poor spellers than the teacher who dutifully puts students through the exercises recommended by a particular set of instructional materials. Pupils with learning disabilities will profit more from spelling instruction that is selected in terms of their individual strengths and weaknesses from the many available instructional materials and teaching methods. Because of our growing fund of knowledge about the learner, the learning process, and English orthography, corrective and remedial spelling instruction can be more productive than was possible at one time.

THE NATURE OF ENGLISH SPELLING

We pointed out earlier in this chapter that at one time in the history of English writing it was not unusual for authors to spell the same word in different ways. We pointed out, too, that this tendency toward inconsistency was halted, probably by the emergence of the printing industry. The form of a word at the time of the printers' decree against further change has remained the same in spite of attempts to regularize English orthography. Consequently, writers of the English language are faced with a somewhat irregular, but relatively fixed spelling system.

Until the English language was subjected to scientific investigation by scholars in the field of linguistics, it was generally assumed that irregularity was the predominant feature of English orthography. However, some scientific studies of English spelling have shown it to be more regular than was previously thought. The findings of these studies may be used to argue against the notion that there is little relationship between how a word is said and how it is spelled. Obviously, the position taken in regard to the degree of regularity of the system will determine the methodology used to teach the system. If, as was once thought, the principal characteristic of the system is irregularity, then teaching practices would logically emphasize the selection of words with high utility to be learned by drill and repetition. The form relationships of these words to other words would not be emphasized.

If, on the other hand, the system were thought to have enough regularity to merit the employment of generalizations (rules) to aid the speller, then the learning of these generalizations would become the object of teaching emphasis. Since even a cursory examination of English spelling will disclose both regularity and irregularity, it is apparent that both of these dimensions must be considered in any instructional program. However, the relative attention to be given to each dimension should be decided on the basis of scientific findings regarding the actual nature of the system.

In early research directed at improving spelling instruction the assumption was that English orthography was highly irregular. Therefore, researchers were mostly concerned with finding which words in the English language had the greatest utility for writers. Samples of writing were analyzed to determine which words appeared most frequently in the writing of school children at different grade levels. Since it would be impossible to teach all of the words in the English language, it seemed logical to select and teach those most likely to be needed by student writers. Dolch (1942) summarized the situation as follows:

> How many words does the school need to teach children to spell, and which are those words? The usual number presented by spelling books has been about 4,000, but when lists of twenty spellers were combined they included 13,641 different words in all. Various studies have shown, however, that most written material is made up of a small number of words, 1,000 words covering about 90 per cent of the total. (P. 21)

Currently, the research that is having major impact on spelling instruction is coming from the field of linguistics. In the light of the recent findings of linguistic research, it appears valid to conclude that the English spelling system is considerably more regular than it formerly was assumed to be. These latest findings argue strongly for the teaching of generalizations as the logical emphasis in the spelling program. Linguists present an illuminating picture of the alphabetic nature of the English language (e.g., the letters of the alphabet represent sounds of the language) and the systematic way in which these letters pattern in the English orthography. Chief among these linguistic scholars is Charles C. Fries. His delineation of the major spelling patterns in the English language serves as a rationale for the position of those who stress the regularity and the systematic nature of the English language. Fries (1963, pp. 171–181) outlines major sets of spelling patterns in English writing (e.g., bat, cat; bad, cad; span, spat). These patterns are not presented in detail here; however, we strongly urge teachers of spelling to study them as an illustration of the systematic nature of English spelling.

Whether or not the systematic characteristics of English spelling are significant enough to warrant the teaching of spelling generalizations has been a point of contention. Although the alphabetic and systematic characteristics of the language are generally acknowledged, the critical question for spelling instruction seems to be how consistently the phonemes of the language are spelled. In other words, how alphabetic and how systematic is English orthography?

Moore (1951) reported the work of Paul R. Hanna, who in 1950 investigated the consistency with which the 3,000 most frequently used words in children's writing were spelled. The results of his study showed that the phonemes of those 3,000 words are regularly represented by particular graphemes nearly 80 percent of the time. However, the 1950 study of Hanna was attacked by researchers who found less consistency than Hanna found and by critics who maintained that a 3,000 word sample was too limited to permit generalizations about the language. Consequently, in 1962, Hanna replicated his first study. For his second study Hanna subjected 17,000 words to computer analysis and found again that the orthography is far more consistent than it was once assumed to be. Hodges and Rudorf (1966) summarized the findings of Hanna's second study as follows:

> . . . the statistical examination made in the course of the study ascertained that the great majority of phonemes in spoken American-English are indeed consistently represented in writing when the main phonological factors underlying the orthography are taken into consideration: (1) position in syllables, (2) syllabic stress, and (3) internal constraints. (P. 31)

Internal constraints refers to the effect that surrounding phonemes have on a particular phoneme. For example, when the phoneme /f/ follows the phoneme /s/, it is always spelled "ph" (e.g., sphere, sphinx).

A subsequent study utilized the information regarding the effect of position, stress, and environment on phoneme-grapheme relationships and employed a computer program to find out how many of the 17,000 words could be spelled accurately by the use of oral-aural cues only. Hodges and Rudorf (1966) report, "Of the total number of words, 8,345 (49 percent) were spelled correctly. An additional 6,332 (37.2 percent) of the words were spelled with only one error, 1,941 (11.4 percent) with two errors, and 390 (2.3 percent) with three or more errors" (p. 32). This means that knowledge of even a few rules will help a writer of English spell a great many words. This seems especially significant in the light of studies which indicate that over one-half of English writing consists of a repetition of one hundred words and that four thousand words account for nearly 99 percent of the words used by English writers.

It should not be inferred from the evidence supporting the regularity of the English language that a good instructional spelling program is a matter of teaching children generalizations. Clymer (1963) has pointed out that teaching generalizations without care for the utility value of generalizations can be wasteful. He analyzed the utility value of forty-five phonic generalizations selected from the manuals accompanying four widely used sets of readers for the primary grades. The generalizations were tested against a list of approximately 2600 words. The list of words included all of the words introduced in the four sets of readers plus the words from the *Gates Reading Vocabulary for the Primary Grades.* A percent of utility was calculated by dividing the number of words pronounced as the generalization claimed by the total number of words to which the generalization could be expected to apply. Seventy-five percent was set as the minimum percent of utility for a generalization to be considered useful. Eighteen of the forty-five generalizations met the criteria for usefulness. The range for percent of utility was 0 to 100 percent. Obviously, no spelling generalization should be taught without careful assessment of the value that generalization is likely to have for the writer.

All available evidence regarding the nature of the English language indicates that an instructional spelling program must provide for both the regularity and the irregularity of English orthography. The evidence also indicates the need for materials and methodology that provide for both the regularity and the irregularity of the system. Spelling instruction can no longer be primarily a matter of memorizing the pecularities of selected words. Children should also learn the basic structural properties that underlie the spelling of many words. However, children should also be taught that generalizations about English spelling are not steadfast rules, and that for most generalizations they will encounter words that do not conform.

SPELLING IN THE LANGUAGE ARTS CURRICULUM

There is a distinct relationship between spelling and the arts of reading, writing, speaking, and listening; and practice in one of the arts often results in increased ability in spelling. Good readers, for example, learn to spell many words by seeing them in their reading, and writing words in a composition helps students to remember how they are spelled. Because reading is a decoding process and spelling is an encoding process, one is sometimes thought to be the reverse of the other. A comparison of spelling and reading shows, however, that the two are not exactly reverse processes. In its simplest form reading is indeed the translation of letters to their sound equivalents. But while readers do not attend to every letter in most words, spellers must. Consequently, spelling requires concentration on each letter of each word; reading does not. This distinction is clearly stated by Lefevre (1970):

> Although it is an active process in other ways, reading requires no "production" of letters, words and sentences at all; what reading requires is not pronouncing all the letters in every word, not naming all the words in list order, but recognition and comprehension of graphic representations of entire sentences taken as unitary meaning-bearing patterns. (P. 83)

Because of its natural relationship with the other language arts, spelling should be a part of the total language arts curriculum. Each of the other content area instructional programs should also teach spelling and reinforce what is taught elsewhere. But spelling needs a home, and that home is logically within the language arts curriculum. And within the language arts curriculum spelling needs its own instructional program. It is not enough to depend upon the transfer effects from reading and other language activities to develop spelling ability. The best way to teach spelling is in a systematic way with specific educational objectives for spelling. The ideal is to coordinate these objectives with other language arts objectives so that what happens in the classroom reflects the interrelatedness of all the language arts and the specific objectives of the spelling program. Pupils who share a field trip or some other experience may discuss their experience, write about it, and later read what they have written to their class. Spelling instruction may be incorporated into the child's writing activity and thereby capitalize upon the child's desire to express himself in writing. The wise teacher encourages the child to learn how to spell the words he needs to communicate his ideas in writing. In this way the spelling words he learns are derived from his personal language development and have immediate utility for him. He is likely to remember how to spell the words he learns in this way, and he is likely to learn inductively much about how particular English sounds are represented in writing. As we pointed out earlier, this approach does not preclude intensive and specific instruction in spelling per se, especially for some pupils. The approach does, however, emphasize that good spelling is a tool to be used for communication purposes and not an end in itself.

HOW CHILDREN LEARN TO SPELL

Attitudes and Motivation

Learning to spell is a matter of developing attitudes and understandings as well as memorizing the forms of individual words. Perhaps the most basic of these objectives is the development of positive attitudes toward learning to spell and toward spelling correctly. Classroom teachers at all academic levels know the frustration of teaching spelling to pupils who don't seem to care whether they spell correctly or not. Motivation and attitude development are as important to spelling as they are to any other area of curriculum. Many students are faulty spellers because they have not learned to be careful spellers. The wise teacher of spelling, then, will find some means of motivation and reward that stimulates children to learn to spell correctly and to practice what they learn.

There are many spelling games that teach pupils to attend to the distinguishing characteristics of words. For example, one game begins when a pupil supplies a one- or two-letter word such as *a*. The next pupil must add one letter to make a different word, such as *at*. The letters may be rearranged (tap), but one letter must be added each turn and that addition must result in an English word. The pupil who cannot continue the process when his turn comes, forfeits a point or receives some such penalty. A child can compete against himself or another child, or children can compete against each other in teams.

Providing time for pupils to write about their personal ideas or experiences will often result in their learning to spell new words. For motivational purposes, it is important for the teacher to teach the words the child wants to learn to complete his composition rather than teaching him teacher-selected words around which a composition must be written.

If the pupil understands that testing in spelling is done to guide learning and if the teacher understands that real improvement in spelling is not measured in terms of test scores but in the growth in ability to spell words correctly in daily writing, then evaluation of achievement in spelling can take on new meaning for both and become a powerful motivating device. One of the best ways to motivate a pupil is to have him keep a graph of his progress. A suggested method is to have the pupil keep a record of words misspelled in written composition on several occasions during the school year. Simply have the pupil count the spelling errors in the first 100 words of a composition and keep a record of progress throughout the school year.

Setting and achieving realistic goals is important to maintaining motivation. Four or five words mastered per week is sufficient for most disabled spellers. Pupils might keep a notebook or a card file where they can keep a record of the words they learn. The record serves to demonstrate progress and to permit systematic review.

A spelling folder may provide a motivating record of progress if it contains spelling tests and written work done at the first of the year and subsequent papers showing improvement. Some teachers have the pupil save only the best paper and/or test written each month.

Cognitive Processing

Positive attitudes are the necessary base from which spelling is learned. However, spelling is essentially a cognitive process. Hodges (1966) has conceptualized this process as follows:

> The act of spelling may also be described as one kind of information processing. Words to be spelled are assimilated through the sensory modes of hearing and vision, while the writing of them (the behavior which is sought) represents the results of many complex cognitive processes in which what the ears hear and the eyes see is reinforced by the haptical senses of touch and kinesthetics. Clearly, sensory and motor processes are a part of the act of spelling, but the intervening cognitive processes lie at the heart of effective spelling ability. (P. 38)

According to Hodges, the brain stores "programs" or plans to react in certain ways to certain situations. The presentation of a particular stimulus triggers the plan of action stored in the memory as the appropriate response to that stimulus. Programs stored through multisensory experiences are more likely to be triggered than programs stored through a single sense. Hodges says, ". . . a child who has learned to spell a word by the use of the senses of hearing, sight, and touch is in a good position to recall the spelling of that word when he needs it in his writing because any or all the sensory modes can elicit his memory of it" (p. 39). The following steps describe how a teacher might use a multisensory approach to teach a spelling word:

1. Read the word in a sentence to the children.
2. Write the sentence on the chalkboard.
3. Read the sentence orally again and underline the word as it is read.
4. Point to the word and have the children say aloud what it is.
5. Write the word in isolation.
6. Have the students trace the word in the air and say the name of each letter as they form it.
7. Have each student write the word on his paper.
8. Have the students construct sentences with the word in it and then read their sentences aloud.

Intellectual processes are at the heart of learning to spell. The learner must commit to memory the forms of irregular words for which no generalization can be formulated. He must also commit to memory the spelling generalizations which are judged to have the greatest utility for him. Before the sensori-motor processes can be employed to commit the word he hears in his mind to a graphic representation of that word, he must either (1) recall the exact form of the word from his visual memory, or (2) recall and apply a phoneme-grapheme correspondence generalization that fits the particular word he wants to write.

Inductive Approach

We pointed out earlier that words learned by a multisensory approach are likely to be recalled more readily and more accurately than words learned through a single sense. Probably the best way for corrective and remedial students to learn generalizations so that they can be recalled readily and applied accurately is inductively. All spelling generalizations rest on the concept of the regularity of the alphabetic nature of the language. Therefore, the first concept children must learn is that in the English language a certain letter or combination of letters may represent a particular sound heard in many different words. For example, the long *e* sound heard in the word *heat* is represented by the letters *ea* not only in the word *heat* but in other words as well (*seal, meat, bead, neat*). Like all spelling generalizations, this basic concept is probably learned best if it is learned inductively. Hanna, Hanna, Hodges, and Rudorf (1966) say,

> The instructional area most likely to be neglected in the spelling programs is that of pupil discovery of the behavior of phoneme-grapheme correspondences in his language and the rules and generalizations upon which the orthography is based. The inductive approach should be given the importance it deserves; and the teacher, rather than initiating the rule or principle to be learned, should encourage the pupil to extract it from close examination of words which illustrate the generalization being presented in a particular lesson. (P. 129)

The following procedure is presented as an illustration of how a teacher might use an inductive approach to teach the spelling generalization which states that "when the long *a* sound is the last sound in a word, the sound is usually represented by the letters *ay*":

1. Show the children a picture symbol of a word containing the letters *ay* in final position (*hay, tray, pray*).
2. Have the children say the word the picture represents.
3. Write the word on the chalkboard.
4. Have the children supply from their own speaking vocabularies words that have the same final sound (*ray, delay, relay, sleigh, today, Chevrolet, holiday*).
5. Ask the children to observe the spelling of words in which the final sound is long *a*.
6. Have the children verbalize the generalization they observe (when the long *a* sound comes last in a word, it is *usually* spelled *ay*).
7. Reinforce the generalization (the children might add the letters *ay* to the first letters they hear in picture symbols—picture of pig stimulates *p* + *ay* = pay).

Dictionary Training

An important aspect of every spelling program is training in dictionary usage. Pupils need to know how to use the dictionary for many purposes:

syllabication, accent, meaning, pronunciation, synonyms, homonyms, derivation, and root or base word. Most children learn how to use a dictionary with relative ease. Unfortunately, the development of positive attitudes toward using a dictionary is not so easily accomplished. The first condition to be met in a program that stresses the development of positive attitudes toward using a dictionary is to use dictionaries appropriate to the ages of the pupils using them. Children need children's dictionaries. These are now available for various academic levels, beginning with picture dictionaries for use in the primary grades. It is important that teachers give pupils meaningful and enjoyable dictionary activities and avoid uninteresting, repetitive tasks. Teaching the dictionary to small groups is one way to stimulate discussion about information found in the dictionary. Assigning short, interesting writing tasks and encouraging the use of dictionaries while writing emphasizes the idea that dictionaries are useful tools for writers. Dictionary games are good for letting pupils have fun with dictionaries while they are learning how to use them. One game requires children to name the kind of store they would shop in for certain items. The items supplied by the teacher have names likely to be unfamiliar to the students (dory, pyrotechnics, metronome, skewer, gypsum). This can take the form of a scavenger hunt with children competing as individuals or in teams to complete their dictionary shopping trip.

Instructional Materials

Although pupils may be taught spelling words, spelling generalizations, and dictionary usage within the context of all the instructional programs in the elementary school, spelling does require its own systematic instructional program. Instructional materials have been developed to help teachers teach spelling in sequential steps with specific objectives and materials for each ability level. Because of the importance of the materials used to the outcomes of the learning experience the materials should be selected by administrators and teachers with care. The following questions should be asked regarding all instructional materials for the spelling program:

1. Is spelling presented so that it is perceived by the child as a skill for communicating ideas in writing?

2. Have the spelling generalizations that are taught been selected and sequenced according to scientific observations regarding their utility value?

3. Have the words that are taught been selected and sequenced according to their suspected utility value for the children who will learn them?

4. Are the materials attractive and the exercises meaningful and motivating to the child for whom they are intended?

5. Are the materials designed to encourage the teacher to use the inductive approach to teaching generalizations?

6. Do the materials provide for using the multisensory approach for learning difficult, irregular words?

7. Do the materials provide for the many aspects of a spelling program (phoneme-grapheme relationships, structural forms, dictionary skills)?

Publishers of instructional spelling materials should be prepared to answer all of these questions for prospective buyers. And prospective buyers should be prepared to have a variety of materials available for students who have failed to learn with the materials and methods used in the regular developmental program. When one approach and certain materials fail to produce satisfactory results, other approaches and materials should be tried. Switching materials and/or approaches is usually more beneficial to corrective and remedial spellers than a more intensive application of the developmental program which was unsuccessful. The following list of published materials is illustrative of the materials being produced commercially.

Basic Programs

Power to Spell, by P. R. Hanna and others (Houghton Mifflin), series for grades 1–8. This series uses a few basic concepts to help pupils understand not only how our language is spelled but also why it is spelled the way it is.

Spellingtime Series, by G. Hildreth and others (Random House/Singer), series for grades 1–8. This series has materials at three different achievement levels for each grade to provide for average, above-average, and low-ability students.

Basic Goals in Spelling, by W. A. Kottmeyer and A. Claus (Webster Division/McGraw-Hill), series for grades 1–8. This series is designed to give children spelling power through word lists grouped according to like sound-symbol and structural patterns. Spelling generalizations are taught inductively.

Supplementary Materials

Key-Lab, by P. R. and J. S. Hanna (Houghton Mifflin). This laboratory of materials correlates directly with the first-grade text in *Power to Spell,* but can supplement any beginning spelling program.

Spelling Word Power Laboratory, by D. H. Parker (Science Research Associates). This laboratory is designed for grades 4–7 and contains learning wheels grouped into color-coded levels that match a student's level of spelling ability. Fundamental techniques of programmed learning are incorporated into the program.

Flash-X (Educational Developmental Laboratories). This tachistoscopic device is manually operated and gives a flash exposure to words printed on discs. Discs with words at various difficulty levels and blank discs for printing teacher-selected words are available.

Sounds We Use, Set I, Consonant Sounds (8 filmstrips)

Sounds We Use, Set II, Vowel Sounds (4 filmstrips, Ginn). These film-strips are closely correlated with the Ginn Basic Readers for the primary grades and are designed (1) to develop and reinforce the auditory and visual recognition of the sounds of letters, and (2) to review, practice, and apply these phonic skills.

My Word Book, by D. C. Rogers and others (Lyons and Carnahan), series of 8 books. This series could be used as a basic as well as a supplementary program. The program is arranged in three developmental learning stages: Primary, Intermediate, and Upper Grades. It relates spelling to the total language arts curriculum and furnishes a direct approach to sounds, structure and meaning.

Learning How to Use the Dictionary, by P. McEvoy (Macmillan). This is a programmed approach to teaching (1) the basic skills used in finding words in the dictionary, and (2) those skills needed for defining, spelling, and using words appropriately.

Basic Dictionary Skills, by R. A. Wakefield (Scott, Foresman). This program contains thirty-two exercises dealing with the use of the dictionary for spelling, pronunciation, inflected forms, definitions, etymologies, synonyms and usage. It is designed to augment the instructional material in the *Thorndike-Barnhart High School Dictionary.*

Games

Spelling Learning Games, by P. Lamb (Lyons and Carnahan), for grades 1–6. Kits A, B, C, D, E vary in difficulty and contain a number of games each.

Dolch Vowel Lotto, Consonant Lotto, and Group Sounding Game, by W. Dolch (Garrard). These games are designed to help children learn sounding.

DIAGNOSING STUDENTS' SPELLING NEEDS

Survey Level Evaluation

Many tests, both formal and informal, have been devised to help teachers diagnose pupils' spelling weaknesses. In general, the tests can be placed into three categories: (1) standardized survey-type tests, (2) standardized diagnostic-type tests; and (3) informal teacher-made survey- and diagnostic-type tests.

Some Standardized Survey Tests

The standardized tests have age and grade norms; they are objective, based on word counts and lists of general utility; and they enable progress to be measured accurately and readily. The disadvantages of the standardized tests are that they are general and not tailored for any specific group; the norms are based upon the performance of children other than those being tested; and finally, they do not take into account the needs and interests of the individual pupils. Survey tests do, however, help teachers screen their classes to discover which children are likely to need corrective or remedial instruction and should, therefore, be given further diagnosis.

The decision on which type of test to use is one that needs to be made by the teacher after consideration of the purpose for which he is testing. The test descriptions below are included to illustrate the variety of tests available and to aid the teacher in determining his choice of measuring instrument. Not all of the available survey-type tests are given, of course; others would undoubtedly serve the purpose equally well.

Iowa Tests of Basic Skills, by E. F. Lindquist and A. N. Hieronymus (Houghton Mifflin). Multilevel edition for grades 3–9. Three types of norms are offered: grade-equivalent norms, grade-percentile norms for individual pupils, and grade-percentile norms for school averages. A valuable feature is the inclusion of three sets of percentile grade norms to be used for testing done in the beginning, middle, or end of the school year. Provision is made for reporting results in profile form to both parents and teachers. Electronic and hand-scoring answer sheets are available.

Metropolitan Achievement Tests, by H. H. Bixler and others (Harcourt). Primary II for grade 2, Elementary for grades 3–4, Intermediate for grades 5–6, Advanced for grades 7–9. This is a well-established test that gives grade equivalents, percentile grade norms, and stanine scores which make subtests on all batteries comparable. Hand- and machine-scoring answer sheets are available.

Stanford Achievement Tests, by T. L. Kelley and others (Harcourt). Primary I level for grades 1.5–2.4, Primary II for grades 2.5–3.9, Intermediate I for grades 4.0–5.4, Intermediate II for grades 5.5–6.9, and Advanced for grades 7.0–9.9. Three forms are available and may be hand- or machine-scored. Grade scores, grade equivalents, stanines, and percentile ranks are given.

Comprehensive Tests of Basic Skills, by the staff of California Test Bureau (California Test Bureau). Four levels for use in Grades 2.5–12 with two forms at each level. Hand- and machine-scoring sheets are available.

Survey tests are of two types: the recall type, where the pupil must recall and write the word after hearing it said in isolation and used in a sentence; the recognition type, wherein the pupil selects the correctly spelled word from several choices. It is generally conceded that the recall type is more difficult but also more valid than the recognition type.

Ordinarily the results of survey-type spelling tests show as wide a range in spelling ability as the range in reading ability indicated by reading tests. When spelling retardation is based upon the difference between spelling age and mental age, the usual practice is to consider a discrepancy of more than one year as indication of a need for remedial work. A more realistic standard is set by one state (Oregon) in that the discrepancy assumed to indicate a need for remedial instruction varies with the grade level of the pupil; e.g.:

3rd and 4th grade	1.5 years below ability level
5th and 6th grade	2.0 years below ability level
7th and 8th grade	3.0 years below ability level

Informal Survey Measures

Several methods have been devised by classroom teachers to measure spelling ability at the survey level. Most common, of course, is the use of the routine weekly spelling test, which is a part of the developmental spelling program. Use of other informal measures is determined by the need, as felt by the classroom teacher, for additional information. If it is felt that more evidence is needed, the teacher might use a self-constructed measure such as an original composition assignment to examine a pupil's spelling in actual practice, or a test made up of vocabulary words from the back of the basic reader. The latter offers the advantage of testing children with words they have already encountered in their reading. Or the teacher might choose to administer one of the many informal diagnostic tests which have been devised for classroom use. An example of one such test, taken from the *Teacher's Manual* of the *Portland Speller,* follows:

A DIAGNOSTIC TEST*

A diagnostic test may help children to recognize special kinds of spelling errors they make. Use Form I initially, then compare errors made in weekly spelling lists and in daily writing. Follow with Form II to evaluate improvement.

Type of Error	Form I	Form II
1. ie and ei	weight, chief, deceive	neighbor, belief, receive
2. y to i when a suffix is added	earlier (early), lazily (lazy)	happiness (happy) easily (easy)
3. y to i in plurals and tenses	denies (deny)	skies (sky)
4. os and oes in plurals	radios (radio), Negroes (Negro)	solos (solo), tomatoes (tomato)
5. final e which makes preceding vowel long	fate (fat) cane (can)	bite (bit) hate (hat)

* From Teacher's Manual, *Portland Speller,* Portland (Oregon) Public Schools. Copyright 1956. Used with permission.

Type of Error	*Form I*	*Form II*
6. final e dropped when suffix is added	roving (rove) reciting (recite)	hiring (hire) stating (state)
7. final consonant doubled when suffix is added	letting (let) sitting (sit) supper (sup)	stepping (step) bigger (big) running (run)
8. ful, ness, some, as suffixes	handful, sadness, bothersome	cupful, kindness, lonesome
9. ea, oa, ay, ow, ee, oo, oi sounds	beach, float, say, show, seed, moon, spoil	each, soap, pay, slow, seed, soon, toil
10. omission of apostrophe in contractions	can't, I've, you're	don't, I'd, they're
11. addition of apostrophe when not needed	its, yours	ers, Johnsons
12. confusion from pronunciation	picture, accept, library	furniture, surprise, February
13. confusion of vowel sounds	get, catch	just, can

A similar informal group diagnostic spelling test was developed by Kottmeyer (1959, pp. 87–90) to meet the need for a short, general estimate of "grade" achievement in the St. Louis schools. The test comprises two lists of thirty-two words each. List 1 is for pupils whose placement is grade 2 or 3; list 2 is for pupils whose placement is above grade 3. The words were selected from second- and third-grade spelling vocabularies and they include the phonic elements that commonly occur in such vocabularies. Local grade level and percentile norms were established by administering the test to some 20,000 pupils in grades 1–6. Similar tests could be constructed by local school districts or, on a smaller scale, by individual teachers.

The chief advantage of an informal diagnostic spelling test is that the range can be more restricted than that of the typical spelling test in an achievement battery. Therefore, informal tests are likely to be very useful with poor spellers. And, when a poor speller is also a poor reader, informal tests can be devised to get at phonic elements that are necessary in both skill areas.

Specific Level of Diagnosis

The objective of specific diagnosis is a detailed analysis of a pupil's performance. Tests at this level are aimed at determining the specific strengths and weaknesses of small groups or, ideally, the specific capabilities of individual pupils. The purpose for testing is what finally separates the specific and survey level of diagnosis. In view of this, then, it should be apparent that the classroom teacher might conceivably use the Portland test or the Kottmeyer test, discussed above, at either the specific or the survey level of diagnosis. An entirely different set of outcomes and understandings may come from a test when it is administered and interpreted with individuals rather than large groups. The mechanics of tabulating specific results of survey tests can be an overwhelming task for a large group. But for a small group or an individual pupil, the tabulation can be not only specific but interesting and enlightening as well. Observation of individual reactions and responses, possible only in small-group or individual testing, can provide a teacher with insights that can be gained in no other way.

A Standardized Diagnostic Test

The formal test discussed below has been found helpful by remedial teachers for use in diagnosing specific spelling deficiencies.

Gates-Russell Diagnostic Tests, by A. I. Gates and D. H. Russell (Teachers College, Columbia University). This test measures many aspects of spelling: spelling words orally; word pronunciations; giving letter-for-letter sounds; spelling one or more syllables; reversals; method of word attack or word study; auditory discrimination; and a measure of the effectiveness of visual, auditory, kinesthetic, or combined methods of study. Performance in each of the subsections is given in grade-level scores, however no description of the normative population is given.

This is perhaps the most thorough of the diagnostic spelling tests. Provision is also made for recording handwriting speed and quality, vision test results, hearing, handedness, eyedness, and speech factors. The final work-up provides a more complete picture of a disabled speller than any other single device known to the authors.

Informal Diagnostic Measures

The *Phonics Knowledge Survey,* by D. Durkin and L. Meshover (Teachers College, Columbia University), might be used for specific diagnostic purposes with poor spellers. The survey comprises sixteen subtests, including Vowel Generalizations, Vowel Combinations, Digraphs, Consonant Blends, and Sounds of C and G. The utility value of some of the phonic generalizations tested is questionable, but the test does help the teacher identify some basic weaknesses that are characteristic of poor spellers.

A less structured but nonetheless effective diagnostic procedure has been suggested by Watson (1935, pp. 47–53). Her method is informal and could be used by any concerned classroom teacher. An adapted and supplemented diagnostic procedure based on Watson's approach is given below.

1. Administer a test of approximately 40 words to the entire class. The words can be from either an informal diagnostic test (e.g., the Portland test, described earlier) or any graded list. The words should be at grade level.

2. After scoring the test papers and tabulating the results select the lowest 20 percent of the papers for further investigation. (Note the movement from the survey to the specific level of diagnosis.)

3. Work with individual pupils. A realistic procedure is to have the student attempt to define all the words he has misspelled and to omit the ones that are not in his meaning vocabulary.

4. The pupil should then orally attempt to spell the remaining words for the teacher. This will give the teacher the opportunity to note phonic and syllabication difficulties, speech and/or hearing difficulties, etc. A fairly complete record of errors and difficulties should be made.

5. Ask the pupil to study the words missed for, say, 10 minutes. (This will depend on the number of words.) Observe his method of study and note the apparent efficiency of the method.

6. Collect and record IQ information, if available, in order to estimate the general ability of the pupil.

7. Evaluate the findings and draw conclusions as to the severity of the spelling disability.

8. Prepare a step-by-step plan for correcting the disability. The remedial plan should then be discussed with the pupil. His interest and cooperation should be secured, if possible, for unless he sees the need for and value of spelling improvement, the success of the plan is likely to be limited. Provision should be made for the pupil to see his progress and there should be agreement as to frequency and method of teacher check-ups.

The following are some additional sources for specific diagnostic information.

1. *Study of cumulative folders.* Records of past testing in all subjects, health information, records of vision and hearing checks, teachers' remarks, etc., can contribute a great deal to the teacher's understanding and evaluation of the disability.

2. *Observation and evaluation of daily work.* Spelling ability of the pupil in daily written work, study habits, capacity for self-direction, attitude toward academic tasks, and adequacy of pupil's social and emotional adjustment will also provide clues and insights into the problem.

3. *Miscellaneous sources of information.* Pupil responses in oral spelling can indicate phonic ability, slovenly speech, articulation problems, auditory perception, etc. Analysis of oral responses can enlighten the teacher. Conferences with the pupil often prove fruitful. Range of vocabulary and ability and willingness to use the dictionary are also indicative of instructional needs.

Many other possibilities and opportunities for collecting helpful information will occur to the teacher. It might be well at this point, however, to emphasize the fact that diagnosis should go only as far as it needs to go and no further. We have found that spelling is an area somewhat like handwriting in that diagnosis and remedial help can be relatively uncomplicated and straightforward. It is also worth noting that poor performance in spelling may spring from a generally negative attitude toward all academic tasks. If this is found to be the case, the teacher will find remedial teaching in spelling alone to be unproductive.

Intensive Diagnosis

The need for intensive diagnosis of spelling disability will rarely be indicated. But if remedial teaching based upon a thorough diagnosis at the specific level proves ineffective, the teacher may find it desirable to develop the diagnosis into a thorough case study. However, there will seldom be a need for intensive diagnosis in spelling only. Severe, deep-seated problems that result in poor spelling will almost always result in generally poor performance in the related skills of reading, listening, handwriting, and oral and written expression. Intensive diagnosis that seeks basic causes for learning problems will, therefore, necessarily be concerned with performance in the several skill areas.

The function of intensive diagnosis is to uncover underlying causes for learning difficulties. Information gathered by case study procedures is likely to be useful in clarifying the causes for specific spelling difficulties that were uncovered at the specific level of diagnosis. With such understandings, the remedial teacher is in a better position to plan a truly individualized instructional program, to establish a good pupil-teacher relationship, and, if necessary, to make referrals for other specialized examinations and/or treatment.

CORRECTIVE AND REMEDIAL TEACHING

Throughout this book we have cautioned teachers against adopting one approach to be used with all disabled learners. Although some categorization is possible and desirable when dealing with learning disabilities, the fact is that individualization of the instructional approach is the key to effective corrective and remedial teaching. In the following discussion we have developed some categories for different types of poor spellers and have suggested some instructional procedures to be used for students in the various categories. The categories we have established and the instructional practices we have assigned to each one are not mutually exclusive. A particular pupil may appear to fit into several categories better than into one. In some cases the approach suggested for students in one category may work better with certain pupils in another category. However, the experiences we and other teachers have gained by diagnosing and teaching poor spellers have enabled us to offer some reasonably valid categories and to suggest some teaching practices to help students in each of them. The following discussion of specific teaching practices for specific disabilities should not be considered apart from the more general discussion regarding how children learn to spell presented earlier in this chapter.

Careless Spellers

For a number of reasons some pupils are not sufficiently motivated toward being good spellers to cause them to avoid carelessness. Some careless spellers are good in other language skills and other careless spellers are also haphazard about their reading, sentence structure, handwriting, etc. Although many careless spellers are also careless readers, there are enough pupils who are good readers and careless spellers to subdivide our discussion of careless spellers.

The Careless Speller and Poor Reader

The vast majority of poor readers are also poor spellers and for a certain number of these students carelessness is the cause of poor performance in both skill areas. Reading ability is significantly more important than spelling ability for nearly everyone. Therefore, we recommend that the emphasis of a remedial program for careless readers who are also careless spellers should be upon reading improvement. Teachers will be better able to motivate students to attend to word configurations, to note generalizations, and to establish grapheme-phoneme relationships within the context of reading instruction rather than spelling instruction. Spelling instruction for these students should be incidental and should be offered to help students produce written commentary relative to their reading experiences. When their reading accuracy has improved, more specific and intensive spelling instruction may be given to them. We think it is a mistake to use spelling instruction as the basis of a remedial program for pupils who are poor readers as well as poor spellers.

The Careless Speller and Good Reader

In our teaching experience we have found a surprisingly large number of students who read well, but spell badly. For the most part these students work well with ideas and want to communicate their thoughts as quickly as possible without regard for correct spelling. Unfortunately, their poor spelling often causes them to make an impression that is unworthy of their ability. The primary teaching task with these students is to help them recognize the importance of correct spelling. As a rule, when these students decide they want to improve their spelling, they have relatively little difficulty doing so. Ordinarily, the teacher has to help them diagnose their errors and then has to do some straightforward teaching of words and rules that need to be learned. The writing assignments for these students should be meaningful to them and should be written to be read by a specified audience. Students who know that their purpose for writing is to communicate ideas to a particular audience are more likely to be concerned about spelling their messages correctly than students who are just writing to complete an assignment. The basic approach is to help these students understand that their ideas will be communicated more effectively if they spell correctly.

Reluctant Readers

Unfortunately, there are students who have learned the basic reading skills, but who for some reason or other do little or no voluntary reading. These students frequently have difficulty spelling words that are not spelled phonetically because they have not encountered the words in print and hence lack a visual image of them. Ultimately, the best corrective measure for the spelling of these students is more extensive reading. Obviously, this objective is often difficult to achieve. Therefore, teaching them how to use a dictionary and encouraging them to refer to it when in doubt about how to spell a particular word is probably the best way for them to improve their spelling until they can be persuaded to do more voluntary reading.

Students with Poor Auditory Discrimination

Experienced teachers and researchers have found significant differences in the auditory discrimination ability of good and poor spellers. It follows that if a pupil cannot hear the difference in, say, the short sound of *i* and *e,* his ability to spell correctly words containing these sounds will be impaired. The efficacy of teaching auditory discrimination to poor spellers has been pointed up in a study by Hudson and Toler (1949) in which disabled spellers in grades 4, 5, and 6 showed marked improvement after they had worked on auditory perception. Most authorities in reading have also emphasized the importance of teaching auditory discrimination to improve both reading and spelling ability. Durrell (1964) summarized the case for emphasis on auditory perception when he said:

> The auditory factor is not only the most important, but also the most seriously neglected subskill in beginning reading. The primary symbolic language is speech, and from this we transfer to print. If there are defects in the perception of the separate elements in the spoken word, there is little possibility of developing either good reading or good spelling, regardless of the method chosen. (P. 72)

Methods for improving auditory perception are varied. The authors have often seen a method suggested by Kottmeyer (1959, pp. 122-145)—wherein pictures are used in rhyming, matching, etc., and "key" pictures serve to help the pupil remember various letter sounds—used with success. Durrell (1964) appears to favor another approach:

"We avoid the teaching of word sounds by relating them to pictured objects; it seems more efficient to relate them to printed words high in imagery. This not only relates the sound element directly to the letter in a whole word, but it also enables the rapid learner to acquire a sight vocabulary while the slower learner is identifying the word sound." (P. 74)

Perhaps the best method lies somewhere between the Kottmeyer and the Durrell methods. Or, because the most appropriate method might vary from pupil to pupil, it would probably be profitable for a teacher to try both methods to determine which is best for an individual. Teachers should select the method or adaptation with which they are most comfortable and which appears to produce the best results for them.

Since auditory discrimination training is essentially the same for reading as for spelling, the materials and exercises discussed in Chapter 7 may be adapted to teach spelling. For example, exercises which require the pupil to pronounce printed words being used to teach particular phonic elements may be modified as follows:

1. Write the letter of the first sound in "jump."
2. Write the letter of the last sound you hear in "sat."
3. Write the first two letters you hear in "sleep."
4. Write the last two letters you hear in "lunch."

Auditory discrimination training for corrective and remedial spelling instruction should always be preceded by careful diagnosis, using formal or informal auditory discrimination measures (see Chapters 5 and 7). It is wasteful and boring for a child to be given an entire auditory discrimination training program when he is lacking the ability to discriminate only certain elements.

Students with Poor Visual Imagery

As we pointed out earlier in the present chapter, the English language is not entirely alphabetic. Because many words in the language are not spelled according to phonetic rules, spellers must rely upon visual memory to produce certain words. According to Hildreth (1955) one safe rule in teaching spelling is: "Emphasize visual imagery as well as sound if you want pupils to spell accurately and to learn readily" (p. 37). Nearly all formal spelling study methods advocated by commercial systems include a step that encourages the pupil to attend carefully to the form of the word. Visual imagery is also called into play when the pupil writes the word. However, for pupils who cannot visually recall a word after reasonable study, the teacher may need to encourage a more rigorous method, such as the kinesthetic approach advocated by Fernald.

The Fernald-Keller approach is a kinesthetic method that requires the child to (1) trace the word he wants to learn with his finger (actual fingertip contact with the word is deemed essential at first) until he can produce the word from memory, and (2) write the word in a sentence or a story. Students who progress with the Fernald-Keller approach eventually are able to eliminate the tracing stage and learn to spell the word by writing it out after looking at the written model. The time required for the elimination of the tracing stage reportedly varies greatly among children (for a more detailed discussion of the Fernald-Keller approach see Chapter 9).

Students with High Intelligence

Some pupils who are poor spellers, but who have high intelligence may profit from learning a few spelling generalizations that are likely to have high utility value for them. Some examples of helpful spelling generalizations for these students are the following:

1. Most nouns form their plurals by adding *s* to the singular; *es* is used when it makes the word easier to pronounce (e.g., dress, dresses).
2. Drop the final *e* before adding a suffix beginning with a vowel.
3. When the final *y* is preceded by a consonant, change the *y* to *i* before adding any suffix that does not begin with *i*.
4. *Q* is always followed by *u*.
5. *I* before *e* except after *c*, or when sounded as *a*, as in *neighbor* and *weigh*.

Two facts are important to remember regarding spelling rules. (1) Most disabled spellers cannot quickly recall rules when they are needed; therefore, it is not generally worthwhile to devote much time to teaching rules. (2) Words which are exceptions to the rule are generally easy to find. The teaching of spelling rules to students who are not intelligent enough to make generalizations readily or to students who are likely to be more confused than helped because of the exceptions they will almost certainly encounter should be avoided.

Students Troubled by Spelling "Demons"

Most pupils are plagued by a number of especially troublesome words that are sometimes referred to as spelling "demons." We have found that mnemonic devices help many pupils recall the correct spelling of such words and thereby save repeated trips to the dictionary. These devices are often interest builders as well as practical helps, and we recommend their use with corrective and remedial spellers. Obviously, mnemonic devices that are more trouble to learn and remember than learning the word itself or resorting to the dictionary should not be taught. The following list represents mnemonic aids that have reportedly helped pupils improve their spelling.

1. Station*er*y is pap*er*.
2. Is old *age* a tr*age*dy?
3. A *prof*essor is a *prof*.
4. Bad gram*mar* will *mar* your writing.
5. The *l's* are para*ll*el in this word.
6. Princi*ple* is a synonym for ru*le*.
7. A princi*pal* is a *pal*.
8. A good *secret*ary can keep a *secret*.
9. *Three e's* are buried in c*e*m*e*t*e*ry.
10. There is no word in English ending in *"full"* except the word full when it stands alone; e.g., thank*ful,* spoon*ful,* help*ful,* etc.
11. There is no word in English beginning with *"recco."* *Rec*ommend means to re (again) commend.
12. *All right* is the same as *all wrong*.

Students Who Lack Phonics Ability

The ability to make accurate and precise associations between the graphemes and the phonemes of regularly spelled words is necessary for correct spelling. Since spelling is a matter of encoding the individual sounds that make up words, students who are unable to transpose phonemes to letters obviously must learn to do this if they are to spell correctly.

A multisensory approach for teaching remedial spelling is described by Gillingham and Stillman (1968) who define spelling as, ". . . the translation of sounds into letter names (oral spelling) or into letter forms (written spelling)" (p. 52). The Gillingham and Stillman approach to remedial reading is described in Chapter 9 and incorporates their program for teaching spelling to severely disabled learners.

Gillingham and Stillman (1968) suggest that a few days after blending is started, the analysis of words into their component sounds should begin:

> Teacher: Listen. I am going to say a word very slowly: /map/, /m/–/a/–/p/, /m/–/a/–/p/, /m/–/a/–/p/. What sound did you hear first? . . . Yes, /m/ . . . What letter says /m/? . . . Yes, *m*. Find the *m* card and lay it on the table. What is the second sound? Listen. /m/–/a/–/p/. (P. 52)

The lesson proceeds until the child has heard and recognized all three phonemes in the word *map* and can see the word laid out before him with his letter cards. He is informed that what he sees is the way to spell *map* and told to write it. Gillingham and Stillman stress that after the word *map* has been written correctly, the following procedure should be followed precisely and without variation:

After the teacher pronounces /bat/:

Child repeats	Child names letters	Child writes naming each letter as he writes it	Child reads
/bat/	b–a–t	b–a–t	/bat/

Gillingham and Stillman describe their approach as follows:

> The sequence is echo speech, oral spelling, written spelling. The child hears his teacher's voice—auditory. He hears his own voice—auditory. He feels his own speech organs—kinesthetic. He hears the names of the letters—auditory. He sees the letters—visual. He feels his hand form the letters—kinesthetic . . . . Sometimes he should write with eyes averted to focus attention upon feeling the form followed by his hand. (P. 52)

Teachers who intend to use the Gillingham-Stillman system for remediating spelling disability will find the entire system presented in detail in their book.

SELECTING THE BEST REMEDIAL PROCEDURE

Remedial teaching must be implemented on the basis of the best diagnostic information available, and the teaching procedures employed should be those that are known to be most effective in strengthening the particular weakness that is discovered. Therefore, the spelling teacher should note carefully the nature of a child's spelling errors, attempt to find the particular knowledge lacked by the child, and proceed to teach the child what he needs to learn. The following schema illustrates how specific spelling errors can be traced to probable causes and how the suspected cause determines the instructional procedures to be used in strengthening the diagnosed weakness.

Spelling Errors	Probable Cause	Remedial Procedure
"bad" for "bat" "cown" for "clown"	poor auditory discrimination	Give practice in hearing likenesses and differences in words that are similar. Have the student look at a word as it is pronounced to hear all the sounds and see the letters that represent them. Play rhyming games.
"enuff" for "enough" "clim" for "climb" "krak" for "crack"	poor visual imagery	Expose words that are not entirely phonetic for short periods of time and have the child reproduce them in writing from memory. Have child trace words with his finger and write them from memory.

Spelling Errors	*Probable Cause*	*Remedial Procedure*
"comeing" for "coming" "happyly" for "happily" "flys" for "flies" "payed" for "paid"	pupil has not learned rules for formation of derivatives	Stress visual imagery. Teach generalizations of forming tenses and adding suffixes.
"form" for "from" "abel" for "able" "aminal" for "animal" "mazagine" for "magazine"	poor attention to letter sequence in certain words	Have pupil pronounce words carefully. Stress sequence of sounds and letters.
"there" for "their" "peception" for "perception" "sasifactry" for "satisfactory"	carelessness	Discuss the importance of good spelling for social and vocational purposes. Encourage careful proofreading of all writing.
"hires" for "horses" "bothry" for "brother" "meciline" for "medicine"	lack of phonics ability	Use a multisensory approach whereby the student sees the word, hears the word, says the word, spells the word orally, and copies the word.

Like other skill areas there are many approaches to the improvement of spelling ability, and the approach selected should be based on a careful diagnosis of the problem. A good remedial spelling program provides for the individual needs of the students who are referred for special help.

THOUGHTS FOR DISCUSSION

"I agree . . . that practice spelling books are a waste of time because pupils either memorize individual words, when rules of regularity could apply, or simply copy. I would not, however, advocate the . . . practice of having pupils keep notebooks of spelling rules." (Moffett, 1968, p. 92)

"It is a common practice among some teachers to count as misspelled those words which are illegible or badly written. Because of this, poor handwriting and poor spelling ability have been found to go hand in hand at least to a slight extent. Furthermore, there is a tendency on the part of poor spellers to write poorly in order to cover up as many of their misspellings as possible." (Blair, 1946, p. 274)

"Misspelling was once an upper class shibboleth; today it is a cardinal sin. The puritanical code of correct English dictates a stern insistence at all times on the correct spelling of all words, beginning with the first grade. Too often lists of mysterious words must be studied, completely out of context, with no immediate function for the child. In some classrooms, unhappy pupils are drilled on false, illogical and misleading rules or precepts by which they are apparently expected to spell words correctly by deduction." (Lefevre, 1970, p. 22)

"The relationship of phonemes to spelling is a subtle matter, since the sounds of 'words' in the flowing stream of speech vary considerably according to rate, stress, and their relationships to sounds going before and coming after them. It can also be argued, however, that for spelling purposes words are removed from the speech stream, which strongly delimits the effects of intonation, stress, and rate; but words pronounced in this artificial way should not be confused with their counterparts in normal speech." (Lefevre, 1970, p. 64)

"Some corroborative evidence as to the inability of certain children to hear the phonetic sounds of words correctly has been obtained in studies of children who were very poor at spelling. It is sometimes observed that children who have laboriously acquired the ability to read are still abnormally deficient in spelling." (Vernon, 1958, p. 61)

REFERENCES

Baugh, A. C. *A history of the English language.* (2nd ed.) New York: Appleton-Century-Crofts, 1963.

Blair, G. M. *Diagnostic and remedial teaching in secondary schools.* New York: Macmillan, 1946.

Clymer, T. The utility of phonic generalizations in the primary grades. *The Reading Teacher,* **16**, 1963, 252–258.

Dolch, E. W. *Better spelling.* Champaign, Ill.: Garrard, 1942.

Durrell, D. D. Learning factors in beginning reading. In W. G. Cutts (Ed.), *Teaching Young Children to Read.* Bulletin No. 19. Washington, D.C.: U.S. Department of Health, Education and Welfare, 1964.

Fernald, G. M. *Remedial techniques in basic school subjects.* New York: McGraw-Hill, 1943.

Fries, C. C. *Linguistics and reading.* New York: Holt, 1963.

Gillingham, A., and Stillman, B. W. *Remedial training for children with specific disability in reading, spelling, and penmanship.* Cambridge, Mass.: Educators Publishing Service, 1968.

Hanna, P. R., Hanna, J. S., Hodges, R. E., and Rudorf, E. H., Jr. *Phonemegrapheme correspondences as cues to spelling improvement.* U.S. Department of Health,

Education and Welfare. Washington, D.C.: Superintendent of Documents, U.S. Government Printing Office, 1966.

Hildreth, G. *Teaching spelling, A guide to principles and practices.* New York: Holt, 1955.

Hodges, R. E. The psychological bases of spelling. *Research on Handwriting and Spelling.* Champaign, Ill.: National Council of Teachers of English, 1966.

Hodges, R. E., and Rudorf, H. E. Searching linguistics for cues for the teaching of spelling. *Research on Handwriting and Spelling.* Champaign, Ill.: National Council of Teachers of English, 1966.

Hudson, J. S., and Toler, L. Instruction in auditory and visual discrimination as means of improving spelling. *Elementary School Journal, 49,* 1949, 466–469.

Kottmeyer, W. *Teacher's guide for remedial reading.* St. Louis: Webster, 1959.

Laird, C. *The miracle of language.* Greenwich, Conn.: Fawcett, 1957.

Lefevre, C. A. *Linguistics, English, and the language arts.* Boston: Allyn and Bacon, 1970.

Moffett, J. *A student-centered language arts curriculum, grades k-6: A handbook for teachers.* Boston: Houghton Mifflin, 1968.

Moore, J. T., Jr. Phonetic elements appearing in a three thousand word spelling vocabulary. Unpublished doctoral dissertation, Stanford University, 1951.

Vernon, M. D. *Backwardness in reading.* Cambridge, England: University of Cambridge Press, 1958.

Watson, A. E. *Experimental studies in the psychology and pedagogy of spelling.* (Contributions to Education, No. 638). New York: Bureau of Publications, Teachers College, Columbia University, 1935.

Chapter 11

Arithmetic

The broad goals of modern mathematics instruction, in behavioral terms, could be stated as follows:

The student will be able to:

1. demonstrate a knowledge of mathematical systems, symbols, and operations

2. use graphs, tables, and algebraic and trigonometric sentences to show the relationship between two sets of numbers and identify which of these relationships are mathematical functions

3. demonstrate a knowledge of the historical development of counting, measuring, and of mathematical symbols and systems

4. apply knowledge of mathematical symbols, systems, and operations to the solution of quantitative problems

5. demonstrate and use knowledge of the properties of geometric figures.

6. demonstrate and apply knowledge of logic symbols and operations to the solution of problems involving logical inferences

7. demonstrate knowledge of the mathematics of probability and apply it to the events of uncertainty

8. select and use support technology such as calculators, computers, and slide rules in the solution of mathematical problems and other problems (e.g., social behavior, environment, etc.) which require mathematical solutions

9. measure things which are quantitatively describable

It will occur to the reader that such goals, for the remedial pupil, are *more than somewhat* unrealistic. The goals of remedial arithmetic have not changed a great deal since they were stated by Kendall and Mirick (1915) over a half-century ago: "less academic and more practical; less abstract and more concrete; less an attainment and more a useful servant" (p. 165). These aims, together with the message humorously depicted below, form the rationale underlying the present chapter.

We realize, of course, that some purists and academicians might quarrel with this approach but almost universally, teachers of children with extreme learning problems will applaud it. In the discussion that follows, the reader will find: (*a*) some prevalent attitudes regarding remedial arithmetic, (*b*) causal factors in arithmetic disability, (*c*) diagnostic techniques, (*d*)

LAFF - A - DAY

11-11

"Here's your trouble, back here at 2 plus 2."

specific remedial techniques that have been found useful with children, and finally, a brief but useful bibliography which provides sources of additional help.

The subject of remedial arithmetic has received less attention in the area of remedial and corrective teaching than any of the other basic skill subjects. The reasons for this are not entirely clear for there are certainly sufficient numbers of children who have difficulty in mastering the subject. Some of the reasons advanced to explain this neglect are:

1. Both teachers and parents often feel that the subject is not as vital to academic success as the language arts. While mathematicians would probably not agree with this conclusion, and the writers are merely stating it, not defending it, it can be effectively argued. Almost every secondary school curriculum contains provisions for basic instruction in mathematics which consists of little or no more than fundamentals of basic arithmetic, known as "consumer mathematics" or some such euphemism. Once having completed this offering, students can, and are, quite easily programmed around mathematics for the remainder of their academic careers, especially if their plans are limited to junior college or a liberal arts major.

2. Until the present time, there have been no truly *remedial* math texts written although a few making such a claim have been marketed. Most mathematicians' idea of remedial instruction is presenting a seventh-grade youngster having trouble in mathematics with a fourth-grade text expecting it to provide the necessary learnings or to fill in the gaps in his knowledge. This practice is, of course, rarely successful for several reasons, chief of which is that if the pupil has not learned from the text the first time around, it is extremely unlikely that he will on the second try unless a different technique or approach is applied. Remedial education is rarely successful unless a great deal of attention is paid to diagnosis of the specific factors causing the learning problem and then to individualizing the program to meet those specific needs.

The philosophy, structure, and methodology of elementary mathematics has changed in recent years and will undoubtedly continue to change in the future. Exactly how these changes will affect the teaching of remedial math is impossible to assess at this time. It is safe to say, however, that numbers of children will continue to have problems mastering this inherently difficult subject. Insight into the structure and application of our number system will continue to be a prime objective; reasonable proficiency in arithmetic calculation and algebraic manipulation will always be essential to the study of mathematics. Such goals may seem rather idealistic to the teacher of disabled or slow learners whose immediate need is, typically, to overcome difficulty with basic computational skill. We shall, therefore, limit our discussion in the pages that follow to this all important task.

CORRELATES OF ARITHMETIC DISABILITY

The same physical, sensory, personal, social, and intellectual factors that influence learning ability in general affect learning in the specific area of arithmetic. The reader may wish to refer to Chapter 2 for a review of these factors. Two areas covered in that chapter—educational and motivational factors—deserve special emphasis here because of their relationship to learning problems in arithmetic.

Educational Factors

Several specific items within this category deserve special attention.

Inadequate Instruction. Many authorities have pointed out the fact that many elementary teachers are seriously lacking in professional preparation for teaching arithmetic. Teacher inadequacies are said to be due to both the lack of sufficient mathematics requirements in the teacher training institutions and the lack of adequate in-service upgrading of teachers engaged in teaching mathematics. The feeling is that teachers cannot very well teach a subject in which they are not adequately prepared. However, it should be pointed out in defense of the elementary classroom teacher that experts in almost every subject area tend to make the same charge. The implication is not that the charge is completely unfounded but rather that ever-increasing demands are being made for teacher-training-in-depth in all subjects. Any suggestions for solution of this problem are beyond the scope of this book.

Overemphasis on Drill and Memorization.   Repetitive practice that has little or no meaning for the pupil is almost certain to create distaste for arithmetic and to produce few understandings or concepts. A discovery method that leads the pupil to insights and generalizations is a much more educationally sound approach.

Lack of Social and Emotional Readiness.   As in beginning reading instruction, readiness is required for beginning instruction in arithmetic. Even though educators have sometimes neglected to profit from what they know about varying rates of development insofar as teaching reading is concerned, the situation in reading instruction is immeasurably better than in arithmetic instruction. Very little attention is paid to individual differences or varying stages of readiness in most arithmetic programs.

Insufficient Attention to the Vocabulary of Arithmetic.   Insufficient attention to the highly specialized vocabulary and jargon of arithmetic often leaves pupils groping for understanding. "Invert and divide," "cancel," "common denominator," "find the product," and more recently "set," "commutative," "binary," "proof," "bridging," "algorism," "function" are but a few of the hundreds of verbalisms that must be understood. (Suggestions for helping pupils with vocabulary as well as the reading skills required in arithmetic are offered in the section on remedial procedures.)

Motivational Factors

Success in all subjects in the school instructional program is largely dependent upon interest and motivation. While arithmetic is not usually the subject that suffers most from lack of interest, it is still a factor in underachievement in that area. In view of some of the factors already discussed, it is no less than remarkable that more pupils do not develop antagonistic feelings toward arithmetic. Teachers who are less than adequately prepared, who introduce pupils to the subject before they are physically or emotionally ready, who use drill indiscriminately and then add insult to injury by using words and terms that are not understood do little to build interest and motivation in arithmetic.

Another facet of this same problem is inherent in parental attitudes expressed in remarks at home such as, "I hated math when I was in school" or "Machines do all the arithmetic now—there is no need to know how to do it." Such attitudes, appalling but prevalent, can contribute to a pupil's loss of incentive to learn arithmetic.

DIAGNOSTIC TECHNIQUES IN ARITHMETIC

The three levels of diagnosis discussed earlier—survey, specific, and intensive—are applicable in arithmetic. As in the case of spelling, the first two levels are generally sufficient for all but the few pupils whose disability is so complicated that an intensive case study investigation of underlying causes is indicated.

Survey Level of Diagnosis

In Chapter 5, "Diagnosis in Reading," a tabulation of test results attained by an actual seventh-grade class was presented. The purpose there was to demonstrate how the scores could be used for diagnostic screening purposes in reading. The table included arithmetic and mental age information. The same table is reproduced here to illustrate how such an analysis can also be useful for survey diagnosis in arithmetic.

The reader will note that many of the points made in a reading-oriented analysis of the table can also be made in an arithmetic-oriented analysis. Some additional points are discussed here.

Noting the fact that the mean arithmetic age of 12 years 8 months is only one month less than the mean mental age of 12 years 9 months and that both are greater than the mean chronological age of 12 years 2 months might lead one to the erroneous conclusion that achievement in arithmetic is adequate. An examination of individual scores will not only show the fallaciousness of such an assumption but will also reveal other important points. These are best illustrated by considering cases individually.

Pupils 1 through 6—These pupils are the brightest in terms of MA, and all but two are at or close to their ability level in reading. In arithmetic, however, these pupils are one to three years behind their MA. This could indicate need for additional testing. With the exception of Pupil 6, they appear to be in need of corrective teaching designed to bring them closer to their potential. Pupil 6 appears to need more intensive remedial work in arithmetic.

Pupils 17, 25, and 32—These pupils appear at first glance to be over-achieving in arithmetic. In view of their apparent reading disability the teacher would want to investigate further. While arithmetic does not appear to be a problem, reading almost certainly is. The pupils may need another intelligence evaluation.

Other important data would be evident to the classroom teacher if the class were his. Standardized test scores cannot be used alone; they must be tempered with judgments based upon observation and experience. In general, however, it will be noted that seventeen pupils have arithmetic ages one year or more below their MA. This in itself indicates a need for further testing and exploration.

TABLE 3

Test Scores for Survey Diagnosis in Arithmetic

Pupil	Chrono-logical Age (CA)*	Mental Age (MA)*	Reading Age (RA)*	Arithmetic Age (AA)*	Difference Between MA and AA	Difference Between MA and RA
1	12.0	14.3	15.0	13.2	− 1.1	+ 0.9
2	11.11	15.0	15.0	13.2	− 1.10	—
3	12.5	16.1	15.0	14.8	− 1.5	− 1.1
4	12.2	14.9	15.0	13.9	− 1.0	+ 0.3
5	12.4	15.2	15.0	14.1	− 1.1	+ 0.2
6	12.0	17.1	15.0	14.2	− 2.11	− 2.1
7	12.0	14.8	15.0	14.5	− 0.3	+ 0.4
8	11.2	14.3	14.6	14.0	− 0.3	+ 0.3
9	12.1	14.8	14.6	13.7	− 1.1	− 0.2
10	11.9	16.7	14.6	14.5	− 2.2	− 2.1
11	11.6	14.0	13.9	13.9	− 0.3	− 0.3
12	12.3	13.7	13.4	14.2	+ 0.7	− 0.3
13	11.7	13.7	13.3	12.2	− 1.5	− 0.4
14	12.5	13.1	14.2	14.4	+ 1.3	+ 1.1
15	12.1	12.11	13.2	12.3	− 0.8	+ 0.3
16	11.7	12.3	12.6	13.0	+ 0.9	+ 0.3
17	11.11	12.0	12.6	14.4	+ 2.4	+ 0.6
18	12.1	11.4	12.4	12.1	+ 0.9	+ 1.0
19	12.3	11.8	12.3	12.5	+ 0.9	+ 0.7
20	12.9	12.0	11.6	11.4	− 0.8	− 0.6
21	11.7	11.7	11.3	12.3	+ 0.8	− 0.4
22	12.6	12.0	10.9	11.9	− 0.3	− 1.3
23	12.4	12.3	10.7	11.9	− 0.6	− 1.8
24	12.1	12.9	10.7	12.5	− 0.4	− 2.2
25	11.11	11.0	10.6	13.8	+ 2.8	− 0.6
26	12.6	10.8	10.4	11.1	+ 0.5	− 0.4
27	12.4	10.9	10.2	12.0	+ 1.3	− 0.7
28	12.2	10.8	10.1	10.7	− 0.1	− 0.7
29	12.0	10.6	9.9	10.6	—	− 0.9
30	13.3	10.5	9.9	11.2	+ 0.9	− 0.8
31	12.7	10.4	9.8	11.7	+ 1.3	− 0.8
32	13.2	10.6	9.5	12.8	+ 2.2	− 1.1
33	13.3	10.3	9.3	12.1	+ 1.10	− 1.0
34	12.1	9.7	9.2	11.0	+ 1.5	− 0.5
35	11.8	12.0	9.1	11.2	− 0.10	− 2.11
36	13.0	10.4	9.0	10.7	+ 0.3	− 1.4
Range	13.3–11.2	17.1–9.7	15.0–9.0	14.8–10.6		
Mean	12.2	12.9	12.8	12.8		

* All ages are in years and months.

Formal and informal diagnostic measures and techniques are presented below.

Formal Measures

At the survey level of diagnosis the task of evaluating group achievement and screening to locate pupils in need of remedial teaching can be expedited by any of a number of group achievement tests. The following list includes some representative achievement batteries with descriptions of the arithmetic subtest of each.

Iowa Test of Basic Skills (Houghton Mifflin), for grades 3–9. Hand, electrical, or electronic scoring is available. A spiral-bound, multilevel, reusable booklet is available. Grade norms and percentile norms for three times during the school year are available. Both teachers and pupils can have results in profile form.

California Achievement Test (California Test Bureau), for grades 1–14. The arithmetic section consists of four subsections on reasoning. The fundamental section covers all basic computational areas. Single booklet editions are available for arithmetic. Hand scoring for primary level and both machine and hand scoring for other levels. Grades and age equivalents and percentile grade norms are provided.

Coordinated Scales of Attainment (Educational Test Bureau), levels for grades 1–8. There are eight separate single-booklet editions. Levels 1 and 2 contain sections on Arithmetic Experience, Number Skills, Arithmetic Computation, and Arithmetic Problem Reasoning. Levels 3 through 8 contain only the latter two sections. Grade and age equivalent norms are provided

American School Achievement Tests (Public School Publishing Company), primary, intermediate, and advanced. There are three sections—numbers, arithmetic computation, and arithmetic problems. Self-marking answer booklets are provided. All batteries are supplied with grade and age norms.'

Metropolitan Achievement Tests (Harcourt), levels for first through ninth grade. These tests consist of concepts and skills sections for all levels, with problem solving and computation sections for grades 3 through 9. Stanine scores, grade equivalent, and percentile grade norms are provided. Both hand- and machine-scoring editions are available. Partial batteries can be obtained.

SRA Achievement Test (Science Research Associates), grades 1–9. Grade equivalent and percentile grade norms for first and second semesters are available. Hand scoring at all grade levels and machine scoring for intermediate grades and junior high school are available.

Stanford Achievement Tests (Harcourt), levels for grades 2–9. Sections on computation and reasoning are provided for all grade levels. Percentile norms by grades and modal-age norms are provided.

Informal Measures

Informal diagnosis at the survey level would consist largely of analysis of the routine work done by pupils in their day-to-day oral and written assignments. Classroom assignments are not geared primarily to reveal specific weaknesses; they are demonstrations of overall achievement in a subject. Thus, evaluations of regularly assigned work may reveal gaps in skill mastery difficult to determine from standardized group tests.

The following informal test, suggested for beginning sixth grade, could be useful in pointing up weaknesses in the basic computational skills. A teacher could easily increase or decrease the difficulty level depending upon the grade being tested. At the survey level, difficulty with any of the basic computations would be noted.

INFORMAL SURVEY TEST

Addition	300	37			
	60	24		234	123
	407	6	271	574	324
	2	19	389	261	451

Subtraction	765	751	7054	8004	90327
	−342	−608	−3595	−5637	−42827

Multiplication	36	44	721	483	802
	×10	×83	×346	×208	×357

Division	2)36	12)36	6)966	16)1081	13)8726

Other appropriate kinds of problems will occur to the teacher. An informal survey test should include several items of each kind so that a simple error will not be mistaken for a more fundamental difficulty.

Without a prohibitive amount of work, a teacher could chart the kinds of errors made by any given pupil. The great majority of errors would fall under one of the following headings:

Addition	*Subtraction*
errors in combinations	combinations
counting	counting
carrying	regrouping
faulty procedures	faulty procedures

Multiplication	*Division*
combinations	combinations
counting	counting
remainder difficulties	carrying
faulty procedures	faulty procedures

Specific Level of Diagnosis

Several of the tests and manuals cited at the survey level of diagnosis offer teaching and testing suggestions for the specific level of diagnosis.

These sources, together with the basic mathematic series used in the regular instructional program, provide the best and most appropriate help for the teacher faced with diagnosis at this level. Also, the remedial methods, workbooks, and remedial aids suggested later in the chapter can be used for this purpose. Rather than suggest inappropriate or outdated tests in this area, we advise consulting the resources mentioned above as a beginning. In some cases, because of the highly individualized problems encountered, the teacher may need to look further for help. The guidelines suggested below for selecting a diagnostic test should be considered:

1. Are the ages and grade levels of the pupils to be tested at or near the middle of the range covered by the test? (If the pupils to be tested are at the extreme ends of the range of the test, the results will not have as much diagnostic value.)

2. Does the test specifically cover aspects of math that are or have been taught in your school? (It would make little sense to test a pupil on the new developmental mathematics if he had never been exposed to that method.)

3. Is the test cumbersome to score, difficult to administer, or difficult to interpret? (Time and difficulty of administration may not be overriding factors, but difficulty in interpretation most likely would be.)

4. Is it published by a firm you've come to respect and trust? (Probably no test will be ideal in all respects; so often, in the final analysis, the teacher must rely on the professional reputation of the publisher.)

Teacher-Made Measures of Computation Ability

While teacher-made diagnostic tests may appear to be relatively easy to construct, the teacher must remember that the validity of the test depends a great deal upon how thoroughly the sampling problems cover all aspects and understandings involved in arriving at a correct answer. For instance, some tests that give one or two problems in each of the fundamental processes are labeled "diagnostic." Such tests are more properly called "inventories" or "screening" tests. As an example, in testing knowledge of basic addition facts that involve all digits from 0 to 9 in pairs, there are 100 possible combinations of digit arrangement. While it is unlikely that a pupil would need testing on every one, the teacher needs to know what the various possibilities are. This also applies to other and more involved areas of arithmetic.

Causes for pupil failure in arithmetic computation are usually very specific, so the task of determining where remedial work is needed may be fairly uncomplicated. Thus, teacher-made tests are likely to be extremely useful for they can be used to pinpoint a particular area of difficulty. A sample teacher-made test that identifies basic understandings in the area of decimals is given by way of example.

TEACHER-MADE DIAGNOSTIC TEST IN DECIMALS

Change to decimals:

½	⅞	³⁄₁₀	3	2¼
1⅘	5¹⁄₁₀	3⅙	⅛	2⅕

Rounding of decimals:

Is 31.6 closer to 31 or to 32?

Is $3.51 closer to $3.00 or is it closer to $4.00?

Is .49 closer to 1 or is it closer to 0?

Is 1.07 closer to 1.7 or is it closer to 1.0?

Round off and change to hundredths:

1. 3.626   ....
2. 123.320   ....
3. 54.910   ....
4. 231.999   ....
5. 103.545   ....

Write the decimals for:

Three-fourths ....

Seven-tenths ....

Thirteen-hundredths ....

Fifteen-thousandths ....

Two hundred ten-thousandths ....

Divide:

$$18\overline{)9.0} \qquad 36.2\overline{)293.26} \qquad 2.9\overline{)1137} \qquad 3.3\overline{)69.69} \qquad 3.20\overline{).5842}$$

Multiply:

.84	2.02	.76	.16	15
×.27	×13.4	×.08	× 22	×9.4

Subtract:

13 cents from $1.12   ....

5.4 from 6.9   ....

6.7 from 9.1   ....

334.28 from 374.78   ....

2.8 from 80.26   ....

Add:

31. + 3.10 + .062 + 41.038   ....

Arrange in order of increasing value:

.31   1.07   231.7   20.040   2.16

Convert to fractions:

.3 ....   .25 ....   .08 ....   .132 ....

While the test above samples a pupil's knowledge of many facets of computation with decimals, it is not as complete as some of the formal diagnostic measures. However, as previously emphasized, diagnosis should go only as far as is necessary; informal tests can be tailor-made to meet specific needs. Similar tests in other areas of fundamental computational skills can be readily devised by the interested teacher.

As we have said, specific diagnosis in the fundamental skills of arithmetic may not be as involved or complicated as specific diagnosis in a skill area like reading. Nevertheless, efforts at specific diagnosis always require a systematic, efficient approach. The following check list may be useful in systematizing the diagnostic approach to basic computational skills.

Diagnosis of Problem-Solving Ability

Diagnosis in the area of problem solving is much more difficult than in the area of computation. Adequate diagnostic tests have not been developed in the area of problem solving, probably because of the elusiveness of the component parts. It seems reasonable to suggest, however, that general intelligence is much more closely related to problem-solving ability than to computational ability.

The following check lists may help the remedial teacher to consider the several aspects involved in problem-solving ability.

1. Can the pupil read the problem?
2. If orally presented, can he listen effectively?
3. Can he determine what is wanted?
4. Can he select pertinent elements?
5. Can he discard irrelevant elements?
6. Can he relate one element to the other?
7. Can he select a proper computational process?
8. Can he organize a procedure?
9. Can he estimate an answer?
10. Can he check his answer?

DIAGNOSTIC CHECK LIST

	Needs Improve-ment	Adequate	Good	Above Grade Level	Excellent
Addition					
Whole numbers	....	....	....	....	....
Fractions	....	....	....	....	....
Decimals	....	....	....	....	....
Subtraction					
Whole numbers	....	....	....	....	....
Fractions	....	....	....	....	....
Decimals	....	....	....	....	....

	Needs Improvement	*Adequate*	*Good*	*Above Grade Level*	*Excellent*
Multiplication					
Whole numbers	....	....	....	....	....
Fractions	....	....	....	....	....
Decimals	....	....	....	....	....
Division					
Whole numbers	....	....	....	....	....
Fractions	....	....	....	....	....
Decimals	....	....	....	....	....
Vocabulary of arithmetic	....	....	....	....	....
Place value and zero	....	....	....	....	....
Mensuration	....	....	....	....	....
Graphs, scales, and charts	....	....	....	....	....
Roman numerals	....	....	....	....	....
Other	....	....	....	....	....
....	....	....	....	....	....

A word of caution should be interjected into any discussion of diagnostic techniques in problem solving. Some diagnostic tests profess to measure abilities and skills in problem solving by identifying such elements of problem solving as comprehension (as in reading), understanding what is given, understanding what is asked for, estimating the answer, and giving the correct answer. A study by Chase (1961, p. 282) suggests that such an approach may not be a good one to use in teaching or in diagnosing inadequacies in problem solving. Chase found that for the forty-two sixth-grade children he studied, measures of computational skill and fundamental knowledge were more successful in identifying good and poor problem solvers than was a diagnostic test based upon the elements outlined. In other words, the technique of using a formal-analysis approach does not appear to be the best means of identifying poor problem solvers. It cannot be relied upon to point up the causes for unsuccessful performance in solving arithmetic problems nor does it indicate the missing skills and/or abilities.

Intensive Level of Diagnosis

As in the other skill areas, it will seldom be necessary to move to the intensive level of diagnosis in order to work successfully with pupils disabled in arithmetic. But in cases where remedial teaching based upon specific diagnosis proves to be ineffectual, it will be useful to move to the intensive level of diagnosis to seek underlying causes for the learning problem. The case study procedure described in Chapter 4 can be adapted for purposes of intensive diagnosis in the area of arithmetic.

Seldom will a learning disability so severe that it requires intensive diagnosis be confined to the specific area of arithmetic. More commonly, the factors that are causing the problem in arithmetic will also be causing problems in other areas as well. At the survey and specific levels, diagnosis can fairly realistically be confined to a single skill area; at the intensive level it will usually be necessary to deal with multiple problems.

The point to be made here is that the majority of problems in arithmetic stem from computational difficulties. These can be dealt with at the specific level of diagnosis. More complicated problems are likely to be accompanied by deficiencies in the other skill areas. Then a case study that gets at underlying causes is in order.

REMEDIAL TEACHING IN ARITHMETIC

Before considering specific procedures for corrective and remedial teaching in arithmetic, several basic points need to be emphasized. No matter what method of correction is used, it is likely to be more successful if the teacher adheres to the following points.

Some Fundamentals

1. *Enlist the cooperation of the pupil.* It is often easier for a pupil to see the need for learning arithmetic than to see the need for learning some of the other basic skills. The remedial teacher should capitalize on this fact. It is also a good practice to explain to the pupil the nature of his difficulty and briefly review the steps needed to correct it. Care must be taken not to oververbalize, however. Actions speak more loudly than words. A pupil gains much more from *realizing* one success experience than he does from hearing about a half dozen he is *about* to have. Provide success experiences early.

2. *Use efficient remedial procedures.* The purpose of diagnosis is to point the way to efficient and effective remedial instruction. Remedial work that follows a definite plan is much more likely to be effective than a shotgun approach. Writing down short-term achievable goals is a good practice for the teacher and the pupil. This procedure also allows the remedial plan to be modified as frequently as necessary.

3. *Use proved methods and materials.* Most arithmetic disabilities can be traced to ineffective early teaching. Number operations must be made meaningful; both visual and manipulative material should be used before confronting the pupil with abstractions. Arithmetic is truly a sequential skill—new learnings cannot be attempted until all the previous steps have been mastered. In no other subject is the saying "first things first" quite so true.

4. *Investigate and correct related factors.* Despite the fact that most arithmetic failures result from ineffective teaching, some failures are the result of emotional, physical, or environmental factors. Teachers need to determine whether any of these factors are causal or contributory and take steps to correct those that can be corrected.

Specific Remedial Procedures

Because remedial teachers have found that most problems in arithmetic are due to deficiencies in basic computational skills, the discussion that follows will be concerned mainly with this area of teaching. The remedial teacher who needs a detailed, step-by-step remedial method should consult one or more of recommended references at the end of the chapter.

Addition

It is impossible for any pupil to progress very far or to experience a great deal of success in any phase of arithmetic without mastering the basic addition facts and developing the ability to recall the sum of any two one-figure numbers. While there are eighty-one separate facts involved in the span of $1 + 1 = 2$ to $9 + 9 = 18$, experience has shown that few pupils have difficulty with the 1's or with the doubles, that is $2 + 2 = 4, 3 + 3 = 6$, etc. This, then, leaves the fifty-six basic addition facts—which follow—to be mastered.

While the chart on page 291 presents the fifty-six addition facts most needed in remedial work, the teacher should also check to make sure the pupil knows the doubles. The teacher will find it profitable to use the chart as is or to add any of the doubles the pupil does not know. The important thing to remember is that mastery of the addition facts represents a first step in remedial teaching if the pupil cannot rapidly and accurately recite the correct answer to any of the combinations.

The addition facts were purposely shown without their sums lest they be presented to the pupil to be learned by rote. This would be a very poor remedial procedure. Pupils should not be told sums; they should discover them. Counting any manipulative material such as paste sticks, tongue depressors, chips, or similar items will provide a good opportunity to see how $7 + 4 = 11$, etc.

After the pupil has mastered the addition facts below, he is ready to begin the more difficult processes of addition, beginning with simple column addition with a total less than 10 and proceeding from there to higher decade addition. There are many methods prescribed by the specialists for teaching column addition—adding by endings without bridging, adding by endings with bridging, adding by regrouping (carrying), etc.

An examination of textbooks for teachers will reveal the fact that mathematicians are not agreed on one "best" method for teaching these

ADDITION FACTS

8	3	4	5	7	6	9	6
+2	+6	+7	+4	+3	+3	+6	+9
5	8	5	3	9	5	6	4
+9	+7	+2	+4	+5	+7	+4	+5
3	8	7	2	6	8	2	6
+2	+5	+6	+9	+5	+9	+4	+8
3	2	7	6	5	4	9	4
+5	+7	+5	+2	+8	+9	+3	+2
5	7	7	9	3	3	6	9
+3	+4	+8	+2	+7	+9	+4	+8
2	4	2	8	9	3	2	9
+8	+3	+3	+3	+7	+8	+6	+4
7	5	4	7	2	8	6	8
+9	+6	+8	+2	+5	+6	+7	+4

elements of addition. Perhaps a point made earlier in connection with remedial teaching deserves repeating here: The remedial teacher cannot be a slave to a *best* method if he does not thoroughly understand it or if he is not comfortable in teaching it. Any method that obtains good results when used aggressively and enthusiastically can be considered an "approved" method. It is also true however that poor results may stem from an approved method if it is not used aggressively and enthusiastically. Experienced remedial teachers know they often need to settle for less-than-ideal methods to get results with individual disabled learners. Remedial teachers would do well to remember that during this transitional period there may be more reason than ever to know and be able to use several methods—dependent upon the specific background experience of the pupils.

As previously indicated, one of the major causes of difficulty in arithmetic arises when the pupil does not thoroughly understand a given process. For example, a child can parrot "write down the 6 and carry the 2" in an addition problem without really knowing what he is saying or why he is saying it. A basic remedial technique is to take the pupil through each step of the operation by having him work the problem aloud and answer such questions as the following.

Problem	Questions
	1. What does the plus sign (+) mean?
47	2. Where do we begin to add, at the right-hand
54	column or the left-hand column? Why?
+48	3. Why do you think the numbers are written one
149	over the other?

Questions

4. The sum of the right-hand column is 19. What does the 1 mean? What does the 9 mean?
5. When we say "write down the 9 and carry the 1" what does it mean?
6. Could you come close to estimating the answer to this problem? How?
7. Is 149 a reasonable answer?
8. How would you check your answer?

If the pupil has merely learned a mechanical procedure for adding a column without understanding or insight, this technique will soon reveal that fact. Thus the remedial teacher can readily determine when a back-to-the-beginning approach is needed.

A summary point in regard to the addition facts is that it is upon this foundation that so much future skill depends; without skill in this basic area, success in other arithmetic skills is unlikely. Also, insofar as basic addition facts are concerned, the teacher should not shrink from providing ample practice until they are mastered. This latter statement does not conflict with the one made earlier regarding overemphasis on meaningless drill and memorization. A differentiation must be made between "drill without understanding" and practice with understanding.

Subtraction

The fact that the subtraction process is less complex than the other fundamental processes of arithmetic, except addition, of course, probably explains why pupils have considerably less difficulty in this area. There are basic subtraction facts, however, which pupils should practice until they can solve them rapidly and accurately. This group also consists of fifty-six facts because, as in addition, children seldom have difficulty with the facts where 1 is subtracted from a number or those where the remainder is 1. Doubles (e.g., $14 - 7 = 7$) also offer little difficulty to most pupils. This, then, leaves the group of fifty-six facts shown on page 293. In subtraction, the greatest single source of difficulty is in problems where a large digit must be subtracted from a small digit, as in the problem $\begin{array}{r} 84 \\ -\ 26 \end{array}$. The difficulty is due to a misunderstanding or lack of knowledge of place values, borrowing, etc. Because the concept of borrowing 10 from the 80 and adding it to the 4 is too abstract for some pupils, the remedial teacher needs to employ visual/manipulative material to demonstrate what takes place when one borrows. The pupil needs sufficient practice in this area to insure understanding, as this is a process common to many other computational operations as well. If the process of carrying was adequately taught in connection with higher decade addition, borrowing in subtraction should

SUBTRACTION FACTS

11	11	13	11	10	15	8	12
−2	−8	−5	−9	−4	−8	−3	−8
8	9	12	12	16	14	15	13
−6	−3	−7	−3	−7	−9	−9	−8
17	12	11	10	9	6	10	7
−8	−9	−5	−3	−6	−2	−7	−3
10	12	7	9	11	7	14	9
−8	−5	−4	−4	−7	−2	−5	−5
8	17	14	5	12	11	16	11
−5	−9	−8	−2	−4	−4	−9	−6
13	10	9	9	13	15	5	8
−6	−2	−7	−2	−9	−7	−3	−2
10	7	6	11	14	13	13	15
−6	−5	−4	−3	−6	−4	−7	−6

not present a problem. The pupil needs to see that this process is the reverse of carrying.

Multiplication

One of the first observations a teacher is likely to make about a pupil with an arithmetic disability is that "he doesn't know his multiplication tables." If a pupil does not know his basic multiplication facts, it follows that both multiplication and division will be impossible for him. In fact, so closely are the two processes related that it is now common practice to teach multiplication and division at the same time. Teachers have long been aware of how little understanding a pupil gains from rote learning of multiplication tables. It is not only more interesting for a pupil to learn multiplication facts for himself through the use of manipulative materials which will show him that three 3's are 9, two 4's are 8, etc., but there is also a much greater likelihood that he will retain what he learns.

As in the case of both addition and subtraction, if we eliminate the 1's and the facts whose multiplier is 2, we again have fifty-six multiplication facts with which remedial pupils are most likely to have difficulty. These are shown at the top of page 294. Not counting the doubles, each combination accounts for two multiplication facts (e.g., $7 \times 5 = 35$ and $5 \times 7 = 35$). Some economy in learning can be gained from learning these together. This will also help a pupil when he cannot readily think of one combination but knows the opposite form; but the ultimate aim, of course, is to learn each of them so well that there is no need to resort to this latter method. It should also be clear that in remedial teaching it is not necessary to stress the facts involving a 1 or a zero either as a multiplier or as the number to be multiplied (e.g., 0×4, 4×0, 4×1, 1×4) because such items have no social utility and tend only to confuse.

MULTIPLICATION FACTS

8	2	2	9	3	9	3	6
×4	×4	×8	×3	×7	×9	×3	×5
3	5	2	6	5	6	2	7
×6	×7	×3	×6	×5	×7	×5	×5
2	7	3	8	9	4	4	4
×6	×8	×8	×8	×7	×7	×6	×9
8	6	3	3	6	6	9	4
×9	×4	×4	×9	×8	×3	×4	×5
3	8	5	9	8	6	2	9
×5	×7	×3	×8	×5	×9	×9	×6
8	2	7	4	5	7	7	4
×3	×7	×7	×4	×9	×4	×9	×3
8	4	7	7	5	9	5	5
×6	×8	×6	×3	×4	×5	×8	×6

Again, as was mentioned in both the addition and subtraction sections, carrying is a basic concept that should be mastered at the addition stage of instruction; thus, it should present no great problem in multiplication. The pupil does need to understand, however, that he must multiply *before* he adds the carried number or it will change his answer. For example, a pupil who is confused sometimes wants to do a problem in this way:

$$
\begin{array}{cccc}
 & & & 24 \\
 & 24 & & \times 8 \\
 & \times 8 & \text{instead of} & \overline{32} \\
 & \overline{402} & & 160 \\
 & & & \overline{192}
\end{array}
$$

It will be apparent to the reader that the pupil added the carried 3 to the 2 *before* he multiplied. To make it clear to the pupil why he cannot do this, it might be necessary to write eight 24's in a column to show him how the eight 2's total sixteen 10's, and with the three 10's carried, he has a total of nineteen 10's.

Another problem that frequently occurs also illustrates a misunderstanding of the multiplication process:

$$
\begin{array}{r}
1428 \\
\times 323 \\
\hline
4284 \\
2856 \\
4284 \\
\hline
\end{array}
$$

Very few disabled learners know why the partial products of 2856 and 4284 are moved over one place. The remedial teacher can add a great deal to the pupil's understanding by explaining that we set the partial product of 2856 over one place because we are multiplying by 10's, which is one place over; likewise the partial product of 4284 results from multiplying by three 100's, so it needs to be moved to the third place. In all arithmetic procedures, multiplication or other, the pupil needs to understand why he does what he does; only through such understanding can he learn to do the operation well. Generally, anyone is more apt to like something that he understands and does well.

Division

Division is the fourth and the most difficult of the basic computational procedures that children must learn in order to achieve success in arithmetic. As was mentioned previously, there is an economy in teaching division and multiplication together because they are basically the same operation. This is not always possible, however, particularly with disabled learners. Some remedial teachers believe that teaching both operations at the same time may be responsible for some of the misunderstandings the remedial pupil has acquired. In other words, the practice of teaching both processes at once may simply be more than some children can handle. This, then, accounts for each operation being presented separately here. The judgment is the teacher's to make, on an individual basis, whether the pupil can absorb both operations at once or whether teaching each separately is wiser.

Again, if we remove the facts whose divisor is 1 and those whose quotient is 2, we are left with fifty-six basic division facts. Because of the difficulty many children have in learning division, it is essential that a remedial teacher use visual or manipulative devices to make the concepts clear. In some cases it will undoubtedly be necessary for the teacher to go back to

DIVISION FACTS

6)30	7)49	9)63	9)36	3)12	9)81	8)64	7)28
2)10	5)15	4)20	5)40	7)42	8)32	6)24	4)12
9)45	9)54	7)56	2)6	9)72	3)27	5)45	5)25
4)36	3)18	4)32	3)21	6)54	2)12	3)15	8)48
8)56	5)30	6)48	2)16	6)42	7)35	8)72	5)35
5)20	7)63	7)21	2)18	2)14	6)36	3)9	2)8
9)27	8)24	4)16	3)24	4)28	4)24	8)40	6)18

the beginning step of having the pupil make an array of dots on his paper, e.g.,

in order that he may "show and tell" the number of 2's in 6 and the number of 3's in 6; or the teacher may have to use markers or some such device to make it clear to the pupil exactly what is meant by division. An approach using practical examples may also be useful; an example follows.

Joe collects pictures of baseball players. He is pasting them in a scrapbook. He can get six pictures on a page. If he has eighteen pictures, how many pages of his scrapbook will he use?

The same kind of problem can be used when the teacher starts on problems with remainders.

A word of caution should be interjected here regarding "long" and "short" division. While neither of these terms needs to be used with children, the teacher should make sure to teach only long division. This is division wherein each step of the process is shown on the paper as illustrated:

$$\begin{array}{r} 4\ r1 \\ 6\overline{)25} \\ \underline{24} \\ 1 \end{array}$$

Experience has shown that children make fewer mistakes with a long division approach and the steps in the operation are more likely to be understood. Short division makes it necessary to "keep figures in your head," which may be overwhelming to an already confused pupil.

"Estimating the quotient" is sometimes a difficult thing to teach disabled learners. The pupil seems to have little difficulty in doing this if there is only a one-figure divisor, but he has a much more difficult time if he is confronted with a two-figure divisor. The rule, of course, is that if the second figure of the divisor is 5 or more, we round it off to the next multiple of 10; if the second figure of the divisor is less than 5, we round it off to the next lower multiple of 10. For example, in the problem below we see that 28 is closer to 30, so we would say "how many 3's are there in 21," not "how many 2's are there in 21." If the divisor were 24 or less, we would

$$
\begin{array}{r}
78 \\
28\overline{)2184} \\
196 \\
\hline
224 \\
224 \\
\hline
\end{array}
$$

have said, "how many 2's are there in 21" to estimate our first quotient figure. The pupil needs to understand, however, that there is no sure way accurately to estimate the correct quotient figures each time. There is a greater likelihood of getting it right, however, if he follows the above suggestion.

Fractions

Most misunderstandings regarding fractions are thought to be due to poor introductory instruction and insufficient use of visual/manipulative material. Use of such materials is usually desirable when beginning remedial work in this area of fundamentals. Only after the pupil demonstrates that he really knows what a fraction is should the teacher allow him to deal with fractions abstractly.

A word of caution regarding the teaching of formal definitions and the use of terms the pupil does not at first understand may be in order. Definitions developed by the pupil, though often cumbersome and ungrammatical, are much more meaningful than those found in texts. One of the best ways for a pupil to develop his own definitions is to have him work with concrete fractional parts of something. Tagboard, paper plates, measuring cups, blocks are only a few that come to mind; the possibilities are almost endless. After a pupil works with, for example, a paper plate that has been cut into fourths, it is easy for him to see that $\frac{2}{4} = \frac{1}{2}$, etc. After he has worked with this kind of material, he may derive a great deal of benefit and insight from making charts similar to the one shown below.

ONE							
½				½			
¼		¼		¼		¼	
⅛	⅛	⅛	⅛	⅛	⅛	⅛	⅛

After sufficient work with such devices, the teacher will be able to draw from the pupil certain important facts which he has discovered about fractions. Some of these, in the pupil's language, might be:

1. The bottom number of a fraction tells how many pieces that what we are talking about is divided into.
2. The top number of a fraction tells how many pieces we are talking about.
3. The bigger the bottom number is, the smaller the fraction is. (True only if the numerator doesn't change.)

While cumbersome, this kind of insight is what a pupil needs to really understand fractions.

The entire series of steps in teaching fractions is too detailed to be covered here. It might be helpful, however, to suggest the order of teaching the various fraction processes favored by many teachers. (Preference for this sequence may be because of the teacher's training. There is good reason to teach multiplication of fractions before attempting addition of them—it is easier. Addition of whole numbers is easier than multiplication of whole numbers and many teachers tend falsely to accept the same conclusion about fractions.)

1. adding like fractions
2. subtracting like fractions
3. adding unlike fractions
4. subtracting unlike fractions
5. multiplying a fraction by a whole number
6. multiplying a whole number by a fraction
7. multiplying a fraction by a fraction
8. cancellation
9. dividing a fraction by a whole number
10. dividing a whole number by a fraction
11. dividing a fraction by a fraction

By using manipulative materials, problems that can be drawn or diagrammed, proper sequence with ample practice, and review of each of the previous learnings, the remedial teacher will have little trouble in aiding the pupil to overcome his disability.

Decimals and Percentage

Generally speaking, pupils do not have as much difficulty in learning decimals as in some of the other fundamental processes. Adding and subtracting decimals is rarely a remedial concern (except that some pupils do "line them up" incorrectly in sums such as $3.5 + 8.64 + 9.352$). The major difficulty is in the pointing off of decimal places in division problems. Most remedial teachers have found that by following Fernald's (1943, p. 243) practice of allowing pupils to learn decimals through use of money, less difficulty is experienced in this area. Fernald felt strongly that difficulty in pointing off decimal places is due to confusion arising from verbalizations and rules. She found it most helpful to have a place where children could have access to many materials, such as "boxes of play money, jars of beans of various sorts, rulers, boxes of small sticks that have been fastened by the children into bundles of various sizes, and other objects that can be used by children to represent number situations." Remedial teachers will find such material useful.

If all of the various processes involving decimals are understood, there is every indication that percentage will not be difficult. Basically, the pupil needs to be comfortable with five kinds of percentage problems: (1) how to change numbers to percents; (2) how to change percents to numbers; (3) how to find the percent of a number; (4) how to find what percent one number is of another; and (5) how to find a number when a percent of it is known.

Brueckner and Grossnickle (1953) have stated that "the study of percent offers no new difficulty not found in work with decimals, except the language of percent" (p. 426). If a pupil has a thorough understanding of decimals, the computational work will present no hurdles. In introducing the terminology, however, it is advisable to let the pupil develop and arrive at his own definitions, however crude. They can be refined after the concept is mastered.

Most pupils have had some experience with percent even before it is formally introduced, which makes it easier to teach. Use of counting boards, discs, and other visual manipulative material helps to clarify the concepts. Newspaper ads dealing with sales have provided many a teacher with meaningful instructional material. Remedial teachers report little difficulty in correcting deficiencies in the area of percentage.

Workbooks, Programs, Materials

A complete listing of workbooks, programs, and materials would comprise a volume in itself. This, plus the fact that the literature is virtually devoid of any compilation or discussion of the relative merits of each, makes it impossible to present anything but a representative sampling of the more widely used materials. There are scores of others of equal value available; teachers would undoubtedly wish to see samples or examination copies before ordering any of the material listed.

Mathematics In Action, by E. Deans et al. (American Book). This is a basic mathematics program designed to meet the needs of average children and the special needs of the low achiever. The material proceeds at a more gradual pace than conventional texts, and mathematics skills are not dependent upon reading skill; considerable reliance is placed on pictures, diagrams, and cartoons to help the pupil follow the story of a mathematical concept. Very attractive format.

Elementary Arithmetic Series, by T. M. I. Grolier (distributed by Teaching Materials Corporation). This self-tutoring series of workbooks are for use with the Grolier Min/Max Teaching Machine. They can be used independently as workbooks using the programmed learning principle. They are written at a third-grade reading level. A separate activity book is included. The basic concepts of arithmetic are covered in over 2000 frames. The series is supposed to take twenty-five to thirty hours to complete. The low reading level and step-by-step program make this a remedial tool. Close supervision is needed for remedial pupils, however.

Structural Arithmetic, by C. Stern, M. B. Stern, T. S. Gould (Houghton Mifflin). Designed and successfully tested over many years, *Structural Arithmetic* is based on experimentation with brightly colored and highly durable blocks and groups of cubes that have the properties of numbers. Through experiences with the manipulative devices, pupils visualize abstract number concepts in concrete terms, discover number relationships, and actually work out general principles which they can readily apply to all computation. For each level, there is an unusually complete Teacher's Guide including detailed teaching suggestions, enrichment experiments, self-corrective materials, a testing program, and provisions for individual differences. A complete kit of materials with the Teacher's Guide is available for levels K-3. Also, Starter Sets containing only the basic materials can be purchased for Grades 1-3.

Merrill Mathematics Skilltapes, by F. T. Sganga (Charles E. Merrill). The program consists of forty cassette tapes color-coded with nine Student Study Booklets and a Teacher's Guide. It covers eleven major topics of basic computational skills: the base ten system of counting, addition, subtraction, multiplication, division of whole numbers; understanding of fractions; addition, subtraction, multiplication, and division of fractions; and decimals. Each cassette is a complete lesson on one part of a topic, each topic is presented in a logical, step-by-step order, beginning with fundamental ideas and building upon them. The package contains ten each of nine booklets and forty lessons on separate cassettes with fifteen to eighteen minutes playing time on each side of the cassette. The program provides approximately seventy-two instructional hours.

SRA *Visual Approach To Mathematics,* Grades 1-8 (Chicago, Science Research Associates). This program is a complete transparency program for basic elementary mathematics instruction. Containing hundreds of colorful acetate transparencies for use on an overhead projector, it is designed to complement and enrich a traditional or modern mathematics curriculum. The first three boxes, Levels 1 through 3, are appropriate for primary grades; the last three for intermediate and upper grades.

Programmed Math Series One, prepared by Sullivan Associates (McGraw-Hill). A series of eight paperback programmed texts with workbook, problem book, and placement and progress tests for each. A teacher's manual is available for the series. The program was designed for individualized instruction for the slow learner or the slow reader, or for the educationally disadvantaged.

Bucknell Mathematics Self-Study System I, edited by J. W. Moore and W. I. Smith (McGraw-Hill, Webster Division). System I consists of programmed instruction for average and below average junior and senior high school pupils. It contains six books each on fractions, decimals, and percentage, plus teacher's manuals, student progress forms, achievement awards, tests and directions for using the system. Paperback. Intended for the slow learner or disadvantaged.

Math Aids (Scott, Foresman). Supplementary materials that reinforce important mathematical ideas. Contains Arithmetic Readiness Cards, six sets of cards covering grouping, numeration system, addition basic facts, subtraction basic facts, multiplication basic facts, and division basic facts. A guidebook accompanies each set. Also *Arithmecubes,* sixteen colorful cubes used in games that help children learn number facts, develop mathematical concepts and skills. Cubes show numerals 0 through 9; signs for addition, subtraction, multiplication, division; symbols for "is equal to," "is not equal to," "is greater than," "is less than." Accompanying booklet gives directions for twenty-four games ranging from preschool through sixth-grade levels.

SELECTED ADDITIONAL READING

Below are listed some highly recommended sources of methods and ideas useful for coping with mathematical deficiencies in children with learning problems:

Academic Therapy (San Rafael, Calif.: Academic Therapy Publications). Particularly recommended is the Fall 1970 issue, Vol. VI, No. 1, the entire theme of which is "Building Number Skills in Learning Disabled Children." Especially helpful is the article by Ronald Horowitz, but many others are valuable as well.

Evaluating Pupil's Understanding of Arithmetic, by W. H. Dutton (Englewood, Cliffs, N.J.: Prentice-Hall, 1964). A very practical paperback that reviews the research, suggests evaluative techniques, and contains a rather complete bibliography.

Remedial Techniques in Basic School Subjects, by G. M. Fernald (New York: McGraw-Hill, 1943). This text is a classic in remedial education. Its major thrust is in the area of reading, but it also contains a pertinent section on teaching arithmetic to the slow learner or underachiever.

Preventing Failure in the Primary Grades, by S. Engelmann (Chicago: Science Research Associates, 1969). The major portion of the text deals with reading instruction, teaching, and management techniques for children who have very severe learning problems. Some 143 pages, however, are packed with suggestions for teaching arithmetic to the beginning and slow learning child. Engelmann presents a highly structured and detailed exposition of his topic. *Must* reading for the teacher of the severely disabled learner.

THOUGHTS FOR DISCUSSION

"The danger is great that the subject-matter approach to curriculum organization will be overemphasized. In fact, considerable evidence is available to show that emphasis upon a strictly 'mathematical approach', introduction of new forms of mathematics in many grades, and continued stress upon achievement measured by standardized tests have already begun to jeopardize some of the new programs." (Dutton, 1964, p. 101)

"Teachers and parents have been subjected to a barrage of cures. Traditional curriculum guides and recipe-lesson-plans have been supplanted by the 'new math,' and old wooden blocks have been renamed 'rods.' Rather than giving new answers many of these approaches are based on memorization and manipulation. One cannot assume that because a learner remembers mathematical manipulations in relation to concrete objects, such as rods, that he understands the underlying concepts." (Horowitz, 1970, p. 18)

"There are many kinds of faulty learnings and deficiencies in arithmetic, any one of which may contribute to a specific or general disability. Since these deficiencies will vary from child to child, it is not to be expected that there can be a uniform approach to the correction of learning difficulties in arithmetic for all children in a given class or grade. The corrective program must be adapted to the needs of each child from the standpoint of his characteristics and the nature of his disability." (Brueckner and Bond, 1955, p. 240)

"Arithmetic lessons are to be handled the same way as reading lessons. Work in small groups with the children for about twenty to thirty minutes a day. Work on a variety of tasks during this period, devoting perhaps five minutes to a counting operation, five minutes to the introduction of a new operation, five minutes to work on a more familiar operation, and ten minutes on worksheet problems." (Engelmann, 1969, p. 253)

REFERENCES

Brueckner, L. J., and Grossnickle, F. E. *Making arithmetic meaningful.* Philadelphia: John C. Winston, 1953.

Brueckner, L. J., and Bond, G. L. *The diagnosis and treatment of learning difficulties.* New York: Appleton-Century-Crofts, 1955.

Chase, C. I. Formal analysis as a diagnostic technique in arithmetic. *The Elementary School Journal,* 1961, **61**, 282–286.

Dutton, W. H. *Evaluating pupil's understanding of arithmetic.* Englewood Cliffs, N.J.: Prentice-Hall, 1964.

Engelmann, S. *Preventing failure in the primary grades.* Chicago: Science Research Associates, 1969.

Fernald, G. M. *Remedial techniques in basic skill subjects.* New York: McGraw-Hill, 1943.

Horowitz, R. *Academic Therapy.* Fall 1970, **VI** (1). San Rafael, Calif: Academic Therapy Publications.

Kendall, C. N., and Mirick, G. A. *How to teach the fundamental subjects.* Boston: Houghton Mifflin, 1915.

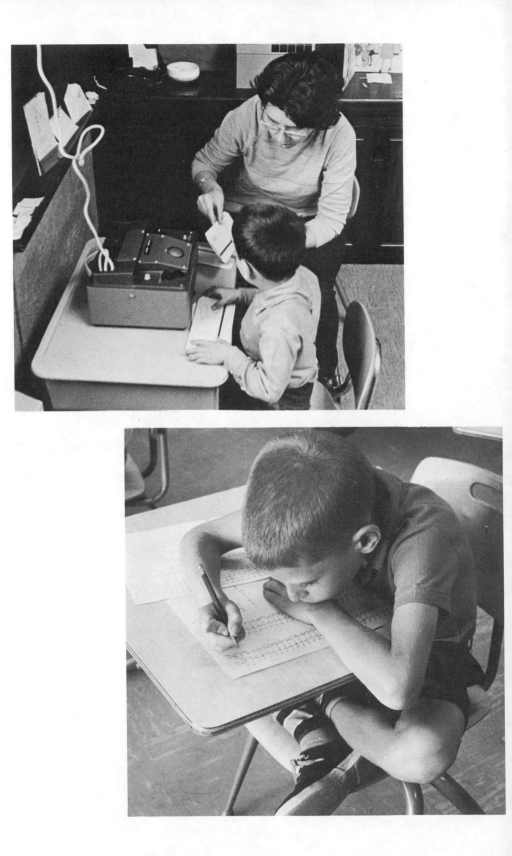

Chapter 12

Listening

Considerable research has been done in the area of listening. However, the overall quality and usefulness of that research is not impressive. Nor are we satisfied with the tests and instructional materials that have been developed to help pupils receive the instruction in listening they need. Most of all we are concerned about the extremely limited attention teachers at all academic levels are giving to listening. The fact that we need more research and better materials does not excuse the obvious neglect of listening instruction in classrooms. We believe the attention given to listening in regard to research, materials development, and classroom instruction must be significantly increased if the best interests of pupils are to be served, especially those of pupils who have deficiencies in other curriculum areas and who may need to rely upon listening for most of their information and much of their recreation. Chapter 12, then, is written to help corrective and remedial teachers make use of the research findings, materials, and instructional practices that are available and to encourage them to add to the existing resources for improving listening instruction.

In discussing curriculum areas other than listening we have emphasized the different levels of diagnosis that might accompany corrective and remedial teaching: survey, specific and intensive. Because of the nature of listening and the manifestations of poor listening ability, the concept of the three levels of diagnosis is difficult to apply. Therefore, in Chapter 12 we depart somewhat from our usual chapter format and do not discuss survey, specific, and intensive levels of diagnosis for poor listeners.

LISTENING IN THE SCHOOL CURRICULUM

The importance of having good listening skills for productive living cannot be overemphasized. Even a cursory observation of pupil and teacher classroom behavior will show that a large share of each school day is occupied with spoken interchange. Anderson (1965) says,

> No one questions the importance of listening as a means of learning for boys and girls. Paul Rankin's pioneering study showed that high school students in Detroit spent 30 per cent of the time they devote to language each day in speak-

ing, 16 per cent in reading, 9 per cent in writing and 45 per cent in listening. Dr. Miriam Wilt more recently found that elementary school children spent about 2½ hours of the five-hour school day in listening. (P. 80)

Rankin's study was reported in 1928 and Wilt's study in 1950. Considering the increased use of audio-visual instructional materials and the findings of more recent classroom interaction studies which show that teacher talk occupies a major share of the school day (Herman, 1967; Markgraf, 1957; Floyd, 1960) it seems reasonable to believe that listening is currently playing and will continue to play an important role in school learning. And it is obvious that for most people engaged in nonschool pursuits the demand for good listening ability is greater than the demand for ability in either reading, writing, or speaking. This is true of people's language activity whether they are using language for information-getting or recreational purposes. In the light of these observations, it is difficult to explain the incidental rather than concentrated attention given to listening training in the instructional programs of most schools.

Listening instruction is no less important in corrective and remedial instructional programs than it is in developmental instruction. Students experience difficulty in developing listening ability just as surely as they experience difficulty in other curriculum areas. When this happens, they need special help to bring their level of listening skills development more in line with their listening potential. Students with reading problems need especially to receive special training in listening. Unless they can compensate for their reading deficiencies by good listening skills and habits they will not be able to receive and process ideas for functional or recreational purposes. Students with weaknesses in skill areas other than reading also need good listening instruction. A good listener with weaknesses in arithmetic, handwriting, spelling or other skill areas may be more successful in personal relationships and in certain jobs than a poor listener who has better ability with these other skills. The point to be made here is that good listening is a quality to be prized in itself and should not be neglected in favor of skills deficiencies that are more apparent or that appear to be more critical to success in school.

LISTENING AND READING

Listening and reading are both receptive skills and as such have similar characteristics. Moffett (1968) presents a paradigm that is helpful in conceptualizing the nature of all discourse: "The elements of discourse are a first person, a second person, and a third person; a speaker, listener, and subject; informer, informed, and information; narrator, auditor, and story; transmitter, receiver, and message. The structure of discourse, and therefore the super-structure of English, is this set of relations among the three persons" (p. 10). Listening and reading are, of course, both on the receptive side of the paradigm. The message which is received has its origin elsewhere. One important inference to be taken from Moffett's paradigm is the interdependence among the speaker, the message, and the listener. Neither operates independently, but in the context of the totality of each communication situation. In this conceptualization, listening may be discussed as cognitive and affective behavior in response to an audible message and reading as cognitive and affective behavior in response to a printed message. The message exists not as an independent entity but as a reflection of the idiosyncratic nature of the sender at the time of transmission and as an interpretation influenced by the condition of the listener or reader at the time it is received. We are conceptualizing listening, then, as a complex process similar to reading. Horrworth (1966) has termed the receiving process "auding" which she defines as hearing, plus listening, plus cognizing. Horrworth's definition of auding as ". . . the gross process of listening to, recognizing and interpreting spoken symbols" (p. 856), is similar to our definition of listening in the present chapter. We have chosen to use the term *listening* rather than the term *auding* to maintain a consistent usage of terms throughout the book and, thereby, to avoid misunderstanding.

In the discussion that follows, we shall consider four components of listening development that corrective and remedial teachers ought to recognize as distinct but interdependent behaviors: (1) hearing, (2) discriminating words, (3) attending to ideas, and (4) developing specific listening skills. There are, of course, some similarities between the following discussion and the discussion of reading behaviors in Chapter 6. The similarity is intended, for it underscores the interrelationships between listening and reading and suggests some pedagogical practices that may be mutually beneficial to the development of competence in both areas.

Nevertheless, listening and reading are distinctively different in terms of the neurological development and the training needed to be successful with each. There is no guarantee that a good listener is neurologically able to become a good reader. Crosby and Liston (1969) say,

> All learning is a function of the brain—but different functions. Much of what a child (or any person) learns in or out of school involves a brain function which might be called comprehension. He understands the meaning of oral speech and of many signs, symbols, gestures and facial expressions by which meaning is conveyed. If he is not dyslexic and learns to read, he comprehends the meaning of printed words. . . . There is an area (or areas) of the brain which has the function of language comprehension. There is another area (or areas) whose function is reading. (P. 75)

Neurologically, then, some children may be equipped to comprehend oral language, but be unable to translate or decode printed language. In regard to the training function, it is obvious that good readers may or may not be good listeners and vice versa. Good listening skills are taught by using exercises in listening. They do not necessarily emerge as a by-product of reading instruction.

Another important difference between effective reading behavior and effective listening behavior is that required by the difference between the speaker's and the writer's language. Nichols and Stevens (1957) list eighteen specific differences taken from the research of Borchers (1936). As a professor of speech, Borchers studied the differences between written and oral style. The following eighteen rules or suggestions for oral language were devised to tell what "should be"; but since they are based upon Borchers' observations of speakers' production, they serve to delineate some basic differences between written and oral production:

1. In oral language there is a greater variety of sentence length than in written style.

2. There should be greater variety in sentence structure in oral style.

3. Sentences are less involved in structure in oral style.

4. Personal pronouns "I", "we", and "you" are more numerous in oral than written style

5. Oral style requires more careful adaptation to the speaker.

6. Oral style requires more careful adaptation to the audience.

7. Oral style requires more careful adaptation to the occasion.

8. Oral style requires more careful adaptation to the subject matter.

9. Fragmentary sentences may be used in oral style.

10. Slang may be used in oral style.

11. Contractions are used more often in oral style.

12. Oral style is more euphonious.

13. Indigenous language should be more predominant in oral style.

14. Repetition is more necessary in oral style.

15. Concrete words should be used more often in oral style.

16. Effusive style or copiousness is more predominant in oral style.

17. Vehement style is more predominant in oral style.

18. The rhythm of oral style is different from the rhythm of written style. (P. 57)

Nichols and Stevens conclude,

> Actually those eighteen statements are reasonably accurate observations of how people compose their language when they talk as opposed to when they write. They give a fairly good picture of what happens to our language as we talk "off the cuff"—which means: thinking, putting the thoughts into words and communicating them orally, all of which is accomplished almost simultaneously. (P. 58)

Borchers has provided evidence regarding differences between normal speech and writing. The relatively recent research regarding "compressed speech" is adding another dimension to the effect of the speaker's delivery on listening comprehension. Although the results of the investigations are not completely clear-cut, it appears that rate of delivery is a factor in listening comprehension and that by cutting words from an oral communication and speeding up the rate of delivery listening may be enhanced. Foulke (1968) found that speed of presentation did not appear to be a critical factor with rates of 250 to 300 words-per-minute, but college pupils' comprehension declined rapidly above that point. Woodcock and Clark (1968) reported that listening rates of 228 to 328 words-per-minute seem to be more efficient for both learning and retention than the normal rate of 178 words-per-minute. Students with lower IQ's performed best at the lower rate. Woodcock and Clark suggest that high-speed listening may be a good way for elementary school children to learn. Other researchers have reported the results of their work with speech compressed in various ways, but the applications of their work to the listening development of corrective and remedial students is not yet clear. It may be that listening can be a better way to learn than reading. However, until more is known about the effects of compressed speech on listening comprehension, corrective and remedial teachers will have to rely upon their knowledge of the typical, unaltered oral production of English speakers to help pupils respond differently to writing and speech.

DEVELOPING LISTENING ABILITY

Like other abilities, listening is developed best when attention is given to the specific components that comprise the total listening act. A haphazard rather than systematic approach to listening improvement will produce disappointing results. Teachers must determine which abilities, skills or habits are in need of improvement and then provide instruction focused upon strengthening diagnosed weaknesses.

Hearing

Hearing is discussed as a correlate of learning disability in Chapter 2. Certain points from that discussion are repeated with additional information in order to provide a comprehensive treatment of listening within the present chapter.

Hearing acuity, which is the physical ability to hear sounds, is basic to listening and differs from auditory discrimination in that the former is physiological and the latter is intellectual. Poor hearing acuity requires medical attention; poor auditory discrimination is the business of the school. This is an important distinction. The only responsibility of the school in the correction of poor auditory acuity is one of identification and referral for medical attention. Intensive diagnosis of hearing loss, then, is within the domain of the medical specialist rather than the domain of the teacher.

The responsibility for the identification and referral of students with poor auditory acuity should not be taken lightly. Most schools employ some systematic screening program to detect students with deficient hearing. Certainly this should be a regular part of every school's health services. The exact nature of the screening process should be worked out jointly between the school and local health officials. Most authorities favor the use of an audiometer to identify pupils who need a more intensive medical examination of their hearing. There are a number of excellent audiometers on the market that can be used efficiently and effectively in testing children's hearing. Two audiometers rated high for screening children with hearing disorders are Maico, Models MA 12 and MA 16 (Maico Hearing Instruments, Inc.); and Beltone, Models 10 C and 11 C (Beltone Electric Corp.). Essentially an audiometer measures sensitivity to sounds at different frequency and intensity levels. From the audiometer readings an audiologist is able to obtain an "audiogram" of an individual's hearing in terms of frequency and intensity. Figure 9 (p. 312) shows an audiogram for a child with normal hearing. Figure 10 (p. 312) shows an audiogram for a child with a *moderate* hearing loss in one ear. It should be noted from figure 9 that a hearing loss of less than 15 decibels is considered normal.

In addition to knowing the results of periodic audiometric testing, teachers should watch for other manifestations of hearing problems. As was pointed out in Chapter 2 these include earache, faulty pronunciation, tendency to favor one ear, breathing through the mouth, complaints of head noises or dizziness, unnatural pitch of voice, inattention or poor scholastic achievement, rubbing of ear, blank expression when directions are given. Children who present these symptoms should be promptly referred for appropriate medical diagnosis and treatment.

Some hearing deficiencies cannot be corrected sufficiently to enable the pupil to hear well enough for typical school conditions. In these cases special provisions must be made. It is often helpful to provide flexible seating arrangements which permit the pupil with a hearing loss to move about and be as near to whoever is speaking as possible. Consultation between the medical diagnostician and the teacher will be helpful in determining the best location for the student in terms of his particular hearing problem and the usual classroom interaction patterns. Of course, if the student's hearing loss is so great that modifying the classroom conditions is not sufficient to permit learning, the pupil should be considered for an educational program designed especially for the acoustically impaired.

Word Discrimination

Auditory discrimination, which is sometimes called auditory perception, is discussed in Chapter 7 in regard to its importance in word attack and in

Name_____

Date_____

Examiner_____

O = right ear

x = left ear

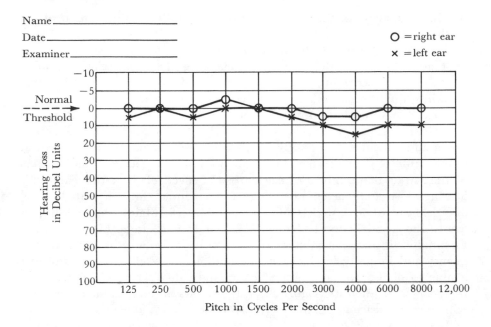

Pitch in Cycles Per Second

FIG. 9 Audiogram for Child with Normal Hearing

Name_____

Date_____

Examiner_____

O = right ear

x = left ear

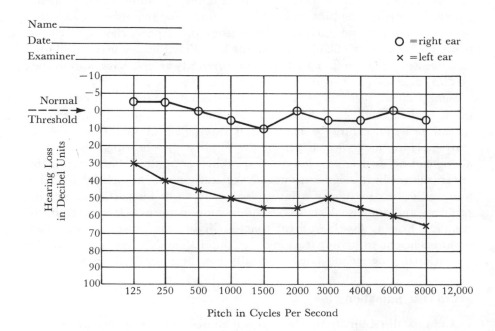

Pitch in Cycles Per Second

FIG. 10 Audiogram for Child with Moderate Hearing Loss in Left Ear

Chapter 10 in regard to its importance in spelling. Because the ability to discriminate sounds is basic to listening it is also given some attention in the present chapter. The focus here, however, is not upon discriminating the sounds of letters but rather upon distinguishing one word from another as they combine in sentence patterns. Users of a language tend to ignore the junctures or pauses in speaking that they carefully indicate by spacing in their writing. As a result some words tend to lose their distinctive auditory properties. For example, an invitation from one American to another American to eat lunch might sound something like the following:

> Cheet chet?
>
> No, chew?
>
> No, Squeet!

Relatively few pupils have serious difficulty distinguishing among words in sentence contexts; and nearly all, if not all, pupils discover that they have been hearing one or more words incorrectly for as long as they can remember. Two classic although perhaps contrived examples are the boy who was heard to recite, "Our Father Who are in heaven, Harold be Thy name" and his friend who always said, "Our Father Who aren't in heaven, hallowed by Thy name." Confusions of this kind are usually caused either by generally poor vocabulary development or by idiosyncratic reactions to a particular word in a particular context. Certainly pupils who are poor readers are more likely to confuse spoken words because they lack a visual image and must rely solely upon their auditory powers. Therefore, pupils who need corrective or remedial instruction are more likely to hear words incorrectly than students who are more facile with language.

Although the problem of confusing words that are heard with other words is not prevalent, corrective and remedial teachers can do much to prevent students with this difficulty from serious misconceptions and embarrassment. The difference between hearing, "I hardly agree with you" and "I heartily agree with you" is substantial. One of the writers recalls a tenth-grade pupil who had never discriminated the word *as* from *has*. In one assignment he wrote, "Has long has I have to go to school, I better make the best of it." A check with other teachers revealed that he consistently substituted "has" for "as" in his speech and in his writing. On some written assignments that had been returned to him, the error was noted in red pencil. However, he never knew why and didn't bother to ask. He apparently wrote and spoke what he heard.

Diagnosing Word Discrimination Problems

The concept of specific diagnosis does not apply to word discrimination problems. There is no way one could systematically test the myriad possibilities for mishearing words in the English language. However, careful observation of students' oral and written production will sometimes disclose words that have been heard incorrectly and are consequently being interpreted and used incorrectly. Given plenty of opportunities to speak and write, students will eventually misuse words that they have not heard correctly. The best diagnostic procedure, then, is to listen closely to students' speech and to read carefully what they write.

Correcting Word Discrimination Problems

How a teacher proceeds after having ascertained that a student is using incorrectly a word he apparently has misheard depends upon the individual student and the teacher's personal relationship with him. Most students are able to have this kind of error pointed out to them by their teacher without undue embarrassment and without interfering with the attainment of other instructional objectives. For other students it may be wiser not to test the pupil-teacher relationship or to risk the student's progress with other objectives by calling his attention to another error. Explaining the error is probably best done in private and should probably be accompanied by some assurance that most, if not all, people are subject to hearing and using words incorrectly. If the word has been improperly used by the student over a long period of time, he may need some practice exercises to help him establish a mental set for the correct usage. These exercises may be oral or written and consist mainly of structuring opportunities for the student to hear and reproduce correctly what he previously heard and reproduced incorrectly. The teacher might speak the word in various contexts. Writing the word in sentences may also impress the correct sound of a word upon the student. Of course, care should always be taken that the exercises do not become meaningless drill resembling penance more than learning.

Attending to Ideas

Listening is an active process and as such requires participation on the part of the listener. Demos and Grant (1966) list the following as listening errors that result in poor communication: (1) not paying attention, (2) thinking about how to respond while attempting to concentrate on what is being said, and (3) neglecting to ask questions when clarification is needed. They suggest two guiding principles for effective listening: (1) talk less, listen more and (2) listen as if you were going to be required to repeat verbatim whatever is being said.

Unlike reading, most listening experiences do not permit review. Lack of attention means irretrievable loss of the speaker's ideas. In addition, the distracting influences that surround most listening situations (e.g., extraneous noise, the speaker's mannerisms and appearance, the movements of other listeners, the reactions of other listeners, the obligation of an eventual response, etc.) require the listener to tune out distractions and tune in the speaker's ideas. Therefore, the primary responsibility of the teacher in teaching students to attend to spoken ideas is twofold: he must teach students to (1) ignore distractions and (2) focus on the speaker's "ideas."

Diagnosing Inattentive Listening

Since attention is a necessary prerequisite for communication between a speaker and a listener, any test that measures the exchange of ideas that occurs when spoken ideas are heard is also measuring listening attention. However, attention alone does not necessitate communication. A pupil may attend to a speaker without understanding what he is saying. Therefore, poor communication between a speaker and a listener may be caused by either faulty attention or faulty idea-processing. Consequently, it is good diagnostic procedure to determine pupils' ability to avoid distractions and focus on ideas apart from their ability to understand or process ideas.

Although any standardized auditory discrimination test (see Chapter 7) or any listening comprehension test (several are discussed later in the present chapter) may be used in the identification and diagnosis of causes for inattentive listening, we prefer informal measures. Standardized tests are administered under conditions quite different from the conditions of actual listening situations. Consequently, students' listening as measured by standardized tests may not be indicative of their listening in typical classroom learning situations. This is especially true of students with learning problems.

Careful observation of a pupil's behavior at times when he is being spoken to may tell the teacher much about his listening difficulties, but overt behavior is not always a good indicator of attention or inattention. We have not found that slouchy physical posture, playing with objects, or poor eye contact with the speaker are necessarily indicators of inattentive listening. We are not referring here, of course, to concentrated absorption in matters other than the speaker but rather the random or nonabsorbing behavior that many good listeners engage in while a person is speaking to them. As a matter of fact overt behavior while listening may reflect a person's cultural background more than his immediate state of attention. Hall (1969) says, "Basically, the informal rule for black culture goes somewhat as follows: If you are in a room with another person or in a context where he has ready access to you there are times when there is no need to go through the motions of showing him you are listening because that is automatically implied" (p. 380). He illustrates his point with the following anecdote:

> One of my black assistants, working as a draftsman, got into trouble with his engineer boss who wanted to tell him something. Following his own culture, my assistant continued working at his drafting table without looking up, thus giving the engineer no visible or audible sign that he was listening. The man finally said, "John! Are you paying attention to me?" At which point John looked up and said, "Of course." (P. 380)

The only valid way to assess a student's listening performance is to solicit a verbal response or some other kind of overt behavior from him that requires him to draw upon the speaker's message. Of course, the behavior solicited must not require a high-level cognitive processing of the ideas heard. The behavior should be a matter of following simple directions or repeating concrete ideas. And since the objective is to find out how well the student attends to ideas in typical school situations, the assessment should be done in various school situations, unannounced to the student. The following describe some situations in which students' listening attention can be observed under regular school conditions. Certainly the list is not exhaustive; creative teachers will be able to devise many more situations.

1. Give the class oral directions for an unfamiliar task and see which students do not follow them. For example, "Will everyone please put his arithmetic book and his social studies book on his desk. Put your arithmetic book on top of your social studies book so I can see only your arithmetic book as I walk down the aisle." Note which students do not comply and which seek a repetition from you or a classmate.

2. While engaged in individual social conservation or instruction, ask a student to repeat your last sentence in his own words.

3. Say something absurd in the course of talking to a class, small group or individual and note who does not react to the absurdity.

4. Use a nonsense word while giving directions to an individual and observe his reaction. For example, "Put the book on the framler when you finish."

5. Ask a question that calls for an obvious answer but is out of context in the present discussion. For example, "By the way, who can tell me what the day after tomorrow is? Those who can tell me, raise your hands."

6. Play a short, tape-recorded story and ask students to summarize the story in their own words when it is finished. Do not tell them beforehand that they will be asked to do this.

7. Play a musical selection, the title of which is obvious from the lyrics (e.g., "My Favorite Things" from *The Sound of Music*). Ask the students to write the obvious title of the selection when it is concluded.

8. After a short speech ask the students to (1) describe the speaker's appearance and mannerisms and (2) tell the major ideas he presented. Note which the students attended to more carefully.

9. Read a ballad, short story, or news article that moves to an obvious ending. Stop reading before the ending and ask students to supply the obvious ending. Do not tell them ahead of time that they will be asked to do this.

When implementing the suggestions above it is essential that the speaker be articulate and comprehensible. The point is to identify who listens inattentively in what situations, not to make attentive listening difficult. As a general rule, the difficulty level of the listening task should be about equal to the child's independent reading ability level; however, the listening ability of corrective and remedial readers generally exceeds their reading ability.

Correcting Inattentive Listening

Four factors figure prominently in inattentive listening: (1) poor motivation to hear the speaker's message, (2) too much teacher talk, (3) excessive noise and other distractions, and (4) lack of a mental set for anticipating the speaker's message. By careful attention to these four factors a teacher can help students become more attentive listeners.

Much of what students are asked to listen to each day is not of particular interest to them. In fact, weeks often pass in some classrooms without a break in what might be called routine oral communication. This is especially detrimental to students who are not generally motivated to do well in school or able to succeed at routine school tasks. Consequently, these students tend to develop poor listening habits. The job of the teacher is to plan high-interest listening experiences often enough to keep students alert to hearing ideas that are relevant to their needs and interests. Teachers should have adequate resources for giving students stimulating listening experiences throughout each school day. These resources include phonograph records, tape recordings, news articles, radio and television programs, people from the community, and the relatable experiences of other students. All of these resources may be used in conjunction with specific units of study or as diversions to break the daily routine of the classroom. Teachers have found that a liberal use of high-interest listening experiences each school day is of considerable help in overcoming the habit of giving poor attention to spoken communication.

Another reason students tune out speakers, especially teachers, is that they are talked at too much. Floyd (1960) investigated the communication process in elementary classrooms and found the teacher-pupil ratio of questions asked to be 95 to 5 and of words spoken 71 to 29. It is little wonder that students are not always attending to the teacher's voice. Teachers should strive to limit their own talk and give students more time to be reflective and to talk among themselves. Students can process just so many spoken ideas before becoming fatigued. If teachers limit the oral commentary in a classroom to matters of interest or import, students will learn to give their full attention to speakers.

Noise and other distractions have an influence on students' listening ability. Dawson and Zollinger (1957) suggest that for good listening the classroom atmosphere should be relaxed, comfortable and quiet. Most children can tolerate some noise and confusion in a classroom and still learn. However, there are limits to the distractions a speaker can successfully overcome even with students who have a good tolerance for distractions. Students with learning problems are usually more disturbed by noise and confusion than students without learning problems. Therefore, the corrective and remedial teacher should be especially careful to provide a listening environment with a minimum of noise and movement.

Perhaps the best instructional practice for correcting inattentive listening is teaching students to anticipate what the speaker will say. This on-going anticipation will result in the active participation of the listener in the communication process between himself and the speaker. Teachers can train students to develop a habit for predicting what the speaker will say. This is accomplished in much the same way that teachers train students to predict what they will learn from their reading. On the basis of a title or a preview students can jot down points they think the speaker or speakers will make. Or a game of "see if you know what comes next" played periodically between the teacher and the students help students develop the habit of anticipating a speaker's message. For this game the teacher reads all but the last sentence or two of a suitable paragraph and asks the students to finish the paragraph in their own words. Stories recorded on phonograph records and tapes are especially good for getting students to anticipate outcomes of a listening experience and to listen attentively to verify or change their predictions.

Developing Specific Listening Skills

The many different purposes for listening may be placed into two categories: (1) listening to get information and (2) listening for pleasure. Within each of these broad listening categories, many specific listening purposes may be identified and many different skills for achieving those purposes listed.

A discussion that attempted to give more than a selective treatment to the development of specific listening skills for different listening purposes would be a massive undertaking and certainly not within the limits of the present chapter. Therefore, we have chosen to discuss the following aspects of listening skills development because we feel they are the most important in corrective and remedial teaching: diagnosing skill weaknesses, teaching students to set listening purposes, to listen for main ideas and for details, to attend to sequential ordering, to detect relationships among ideas, and to listen critically.

In our discussions regarding the development of specific listening skills we have included suggestions for instructional materials and practices. Although we emphasize the use of materials that can be adapted to teach specific listening skills, we think teachers should be familiar with commercial programs that are designed expressly for teaching an array of listening skills. Because these programs contain lessons for improving a variety of listening skills, one or more of them is relevant to each of our discussions regarding the development of a particular listening skill. Listening programs of this kind are available from Scott, Foresman and Company ("Coordinated Communications Program"), Science Research Associates ("Listening Skills Program"), and Educational Developmental Laboratories ("Listen and Read" and "Listen and Think").

Diagnosing Specific Skill Weaknesses

Standardized tests are available for the assessment of listening ability and are helpful in diagnosing students' listening deficiencies. The Durrell Reading-Listening Series (Harcourt) contains group tests of listening (vocabulary and sentences) and is available for use at three levels: Primary, grades 1-3.5; Intermediate, grades 3.5-6; and Advanced, grades 7-9. The Brown-Carlsen Listening Comprehension Test (Harcourt) is suitable for use in grades 9-13 and contains five subtests: Immediate Recall, Following Directions, Recognizing Transitions, Recognizing Word Meanings, and Lecture Comprehension. The Sequential Tests of Educational Progress, or STEP (Educational Testing Service), which include tests of listening comprehension, are available at four levels: Level 4, grades 4-6; Level 3, grades 7-9; Level 2, grades 10-12; and Level 1, college. The Spache Diagnostic Reading Scales (California Test Bureau) contain a listening subtest that may be used as early as grade 1. Teachers who use these standardized listening tests should recognize that constructing and standardizing an accurate measure of listening ability is difficult because listening is so greatly influenced by the conditions of each listening situation. Standardized listening tests may be helpful in diagnosing listening ability, but they should always be accompanied by informal assessments which we believe can give teachers more accurate information regarding students' listening ability under typical classroom conditions.

Informal diagnostic listening tests may be used to find out how students listen for specific purposes and under different classroom conditions. The procedure is as simple as having students respond to questions that ask them to produce specified information that was given to them orally. They may be asked to trace a sequence of events, to state a cause-effect relationship, to recall certain details, etc. The listening situation upon which the test is constructed may be a conversation, a lecture, a debate, a tape recording, a panel discussion, an oral reading, etc. The important thing is that teachers find out which specific listening skills (e.g., listening for main idea, to recall a sequence, to detect relationships) need strengthening in which kinds of listening situations. It should not be assumed that a student who listens to a lecture effectively is necessarily a good listener in a group conversation or that a student who can recall details can necessarily detect the relationships among spoken ideas.

Most reading material can serve as test material for listening diagnosis. Several paragraphs from a textbook, a newspaper or magazine article, or a chapter from a novel may be used to test listening as long as the material is presented by a good oral reader. It should be remembered, however, that writers usually compose material to be read silently differently from material to be read orally. Therefore, good judgment must always be used when assessing listening ability by an oral reading of printed material. It should also be remembered when measuring listening comprehension with questions about printed material that has been read orally that readers have an advantage over listeners in that they control the rate of the input. On the other hand, listeners have an advantage over readers in that they have facial expressions, vocal intonations, and other paralanguage to aid their comprehension.

Learning to Set Listening Purpose

Setting purpose is as vital to effective listening as it is to effective reading. Above all, pupils should be taught to set purposes for listening according to the nature of the speaker's message and their particular informational needs or their particular recreational preferences. The listening skills to be employed, then, are determined by the listening purpose and may be stated in the same terms (e.g., listening for main ideas; listening to enjoy rhythm and rhyme).

Although it would seem that all pupils would intuitively vary their listening behavior according to the nature of the spoken content and their information needs or recreational preferences, such is not the case. Some pupils approach every listening experience with the same mind set. This "set" varies among pupils from focusing on details to gaining a general impression. Many students just "listen" without any plan for getting ideas.

An important step in teaching pupils to listen for specific purposes is to impress upon them that listening is probably their major means of getting information and is frequently used by them for recreational purposes. Although it would appear to be obvious, the important role of listening in pupils' lives is often not recognized by them. This is especially true of students with poor language development because so much attention is given to their reading, spelling, and composition deficiencies. Informal observations by one of the writers disclosed that pupils receiving remedial reading instruction almost always listed reading, spelling, and writing as problem areas for them, but almost never identified listening as a personal weakness. Yet correlational studies indicate that poor readers, writers, and spellers are likely also to be poor listeners. Cleland and Toussaint (1962) found that the STEP Listening Test showed a high positive correlation (.67) with the Gates Reading Survey—Form II and with the Durrell-Sullivan Reading Capacity Test (.70). And Loban (1969) says, "In American research the linkage between oral and written language has . . . been affirmed. Pupils ranking high in silent reading comprehension and in oral reading interpretation prove to use fewer short oral utterances, and those expert in silent reading show more verbal dexterity and flexibility with the syntax of spoken communications" (p. 102). Students who are poor listeners need to have the importance of listening pointed out to them and be shown that they can improve by being more "scientific" about how they listen. Students who are performing poorly in school may not realize how important good listening skills are in their daily lives. Some straightforward talk with them about the nature of listening and how listening skills can be improved may be necessary to motivate them to improve.

When pupils have a positive attitude toward improving their listening skills, it is a simple matter for them to attain the concept of listening for purpose. They may be asked to list the many different listening situations they participated in during a day or a week. Then they might compile a list of their reasons for being listeners in these situations. Noting which listening experiences might have been more productive if some prelistening purpose setting had been employed is a good exercise for teaching the importance of purpose setting. Finally, pupils should explicitly be given specific purposes for actual classroom listening experiences until they develop the ability to do this for themselves. For example, the teacher might introduce his oral reading of a social studies article as follows: "Your major purpose in listening to this article is to find the author's viewpoint on why slums continue to exist. Don't get bogged down on the statistics he presents, just listen to determine where he puts the blame for our current ghetto problems and what he suggests to improve conditions." Eventually, most students will develop a habit for purpose setting and will enter most listening situations with an appropriate listening plan.

Teaching Students to Listen for Main Ideas

From the barrage of words that comes his way from any given speaker, the listener must weigh and sort the information he receives to find the major ideas being communicated. The separation of main ideas from supporting ideas permits the listener to comprehend the speaker's message and to recall it more easily at a later time. Students who have not learned to extract main ideas from speech are often overly impressed with details and are likely to miss the speaker's intent altogether.

The following practices may be helpful in teaching students who attach the same importance to everything they hear to organize their listening around main ideas.

1. Have pupils listen to a recording of a Broadway musical (e.g., *Camelot, The Unsinkable Molly Brown, My Fair Lady*) and in their own words tell the idea that each song contributed to the entire production.

2. Prepare and deliver a short speech to pupils. Have them note gestures, facial expressions, movements, pauses, etc., that signal, "this is a main idea."

3. Prepare a short speech in which each main point is explicitly pointed out. For example, "My second main point is . . ." followed by supporting ideas. Have the pupils list the main ideas presented.

4. Deliver a series of oral paragraphs. Pause between paragraphs and ask pupils to title the paragraph they just heard. The paragraphs may or may not be related.

5. Have students listen to a serialized radio or television play and list the theme of each segment.

6. Read selections from a book of exercises designed to improve reading for main ideas and have pupils state the main ideas in their own words.

7. Arrange a symposium in which four or five speakers discuss a single aspect of a broad subject (e.g., why student participation is important in community projects; why teacher participation is important in community projects; why industry participation is important in community projects; why small business participation is important in community projects). Student listeners might be asked to suggest a title for the symposium and list the main point of each speaker.

8. Select a printed advertisement that has several outstanding characteristics (e.g., slogan, colors, composition). Describe the main features of the advertisement orally while students look, listen, and note major features discussed.

9. Select a poem that has one major idea. Read the poem while pupils listen for the main idea.

10. Have pupils listen to radio commercials and note the major idea or ideas being communicated.

11. Read selected newspaper or magazine advertisements aloud and have pupils state in one sentence the message of each advertisement.

Teaching Students to Listen for Details

Certain listening situations demand that the listener attend carefully to details. The haphazard manner in which many pupils follow detailed oral directions is testimony to the need for specific instruction in listening for details. The following practices have been found helpful in teaching students to develop the necessary skills for hearing and remembering details.

1. Construct and tape record imaginary conversations between people familiar to the pupils. Ask the students to discover who the speakers are on the basis of spoken clues. For example, listening carefully to details in the

conversation may disclose that two anonymous speakers are the coach of a particular professional football team and his quarterback. We have often found high school and college English classes, speech classes, debating students and drama groups willing to prepare and record this kind of material for corrective and remedial students.

2. Have each pupil add a word in the construction of logical sentences. For example the teacher begins the sentence by saying, "The pilot . . . ," one student adds a word and says, "The pilot who . . . ," another student says, "The pilot who wants . . ." and so on. The articles "a," "an," and "the" may be included with any added word. The game is over when the sentence is completed or no pupil can add another word and retain the logic of the sentence.

3. Construct different environmental settings on audio tape. For example, a library is suggested by pages turning, whispers, footsteps, a book dropping, shushing, etc. Sound effects records are helpful in preparing these tapes.

4. Have pupils listen to a mystery story in which the author has provided clues that are uncovered to solve a crime. Ask pupils to jot down clues as they are disclosed throughout the story.

5. On the basis of an oral description have pupils draw a character, building or scene.

6. Have speakers talk about why they did something or decided something. Student listeners should record the different reasons they offer.

7. Read a paragraph in a social studies book that describes social conditions in a particular location. Have pupils repeat as many specifics as they can recall.

8. After teaching students how different musical instruments sound, have them list which instruments they hear in *The Grand Canyon Suite* or some other piece.

9. Give individual students a number of items to collect (e.g., a blue pencil, a piece of paper with John's name on it, Sally's pen, the shoelace from Bob's left shoe). Have each student write a list of items for another student to collect. A variation on this activity is to give students an oral grocery list and send them on an imaginary shopping trip. When they "return," they can be asked to name each item as they unpack it.

10. Have students listen to a political speech or a presidential report and then discuss the presentation in detail.

11. Prepare and tape record a fictitious conversation and have students listen for clues which tell who is talking and when the conversation took place (e.g., a reporter interviewing a general after a well-known Civil War battle). We have found college and high school history students helpful in preparing these tapes.

Teaching Students to Attend to the Sequence of Ideas

The ability to recall in correct sequence ideas presented orally is important in every curriculum area as well as in daily living. The following exercises are intended to train students to listen in a way that facilitates the recall of ideas in a particular sequential order.

1. The teacher begins by saying, "We are going on a camping trip. We will need a tent." A student is asked to add another needed item and says, "We will need a tent and a . . . ." Other students add to the list after repeating in correct order each of the items previously named. Obviously, this exercise may be varied to suit the experiential backgrounds of the participating students.

2. Give students a series of directions that take them through a useful process in a logical, meaningful way (e.g., setting up equipment for a science experiment or performing a mathematical calculation in a prescribed manner). Let one student perform the sequence of operations while the class observes. We advise that whenever possible the directions given for this listening exercise be related to some curriculum objective and not involve students in meaningless or illogical operations.

3. Have students listen to a recording of a Broadway musical and, after listening, place the musical selections or scenes in the order in which they occurred.

4. Using a sound effects record, tape record a story of sounds (e.g., a fog horn, walking footsteps, a scream, a siren, screeching brakes, running footsteps, a police whistle, a gun shot, a falling body). Have students tell the story as it happened and in their own words.

5. Read a short mystery story to students and ask them to recall the order of the events that led to the unravelling of the mystery.

6. Give a lecture on some historical happening that can be described as a series of events leading to a particular happening (e.g., the signing of the Declaration of Independence). Ask students to list the order of occurrence after the lecture.

7. Have students listen to a radio or television newscast and relate the different stories in the order they were reported. Students might compare the different orderings presented by different reporters on different stations.

8. Have students listen to a sports event on the radio and then reconstruct the action in their own words as it happened.

9. Have students attend a meeting open to them and later report the progress of the meeting as it was conducted.

10. Invite a person from the community (e.g., a florist, a mechanic, a state patrolman) to describe the steps in some process required in his work. Have students enact the process after it has been described (e.g. a patrolman stopping a driver, asking for his driver's license, writing a ticket, filling out his report, appearing in court).

Teaching Students to Detect Relationships Among Ideas

The importance of comprehending relationships among spoken ideas cannot be overstated. Serious communication gaps result when listeners fail to note coordinate, subordinate, temporal, and cause-effect relationships. The following exercises are suggested for helping students perceive various relationships among spoken ideas.

1. Read articles describing conditions that resulted in particular social happenings (e.g., causes of the social protests of the 1960's). After the reading ask students to relate "why" certain occurrences happened as they did.

2. Explain the importance of attending to connecting words such as *because, however, consequently, and, but* and provide spoken illustrations of their importance to the speaker's meaning (e.g., "It is a beautiful day, and I am going"; "It is a beautiful day, but I am not going"; "Because it is a beautiful day, I am going").

3. Give students a list of connecting words (e.g., *since, because, consequently, and, but*) and have them select the best one to insert at a particular pause in a spoken sentence. For example, the teacher says, "I intended to buy it (pause) my money didn't arrive." Students supply the appropriate word or words from their list.

4. Give students a list of connecting words (e.g., *and, but, therefore, consequently*) and have them listen for those words in paragraphs read by the teacher. The teacher stops when one of the given words is reached and students finish the sentence (e.g., "He reached into his pocket, but . . ."). The remainder of the sentence supplied by the student is evaluated in terms of how it fits with the key word and the context of the entire paragraph.

5. Read sentences that contain two occurrences, one of which happened before the other (e.g., "We played ball after it stopped raining"), or both of which happened at the same time (e.g., "We played ball while it was raining"). Have the students tell the temporal order of the happenings. Samples of sentences like these are often found in workbooks for developing reading skills.

Teaching Students to be Critical Listeners

There is no doubt that some speakers have a persuasive way with words. The fact that people buy things they neither need nor want is evidence of the power of the spoken word as is the fact that historically people have followed politicians who led them into tragic situations. Students who have difficulty communicating their own ideas are especially in need of critical listening training because they may be so impressed by a speaker's language facility that they fail to question his intent and his logic. The following suggestions are recommended for helping corrective and remedial students develop critical listening skills.

1. Have students listen to persuasive speakers and ask two questions while they are listening: (1) What does the speaker want me to do? (2) If I do what he wants, will my best interests be served? Taped television and radio commercials are excellent materials for this activity. It is also good practice to have students write their own persuasive speeches and try them out on each other.

2. After listening to a persuasive speaker students may be asked to repeat as concisely as they can the essence of his message. Have them discuss (1) the message itself, (2) the speaker's purpose, (3) the speaker's experiential background, and (4) the appeal of the speaker's voice and language apart from his message.

3. Immediately after listening to a persuasive talk students may be asked to indicate their willingness or lack of willingness to do what the speaker suggested (some role playing is often necessary). A scale might be constructed upon which students are able to indicate the degree of their willingness (e.g., I definitely would; I think I would; I don't think I would; I definitely would not). Then students are asked to state briefly in writing (1) what the speaker urged them to do and (2) why he urged them to do it. After reflecting upon the message separated from the personal appeal of the speaker, the students respond again to the scaled choices and note changes in motivation. We have found that high school speech and English classes and college speech classes often have students prepare and present persuasive speeches. Frequently, these speeches are suitable for recording and using with corrective and remedial students.

4. Have students analyze the language used by speakers trying to persuade listeners. Have them note superlatives, exaggerations, and emotionally loaded words. Have the students suggest substitute language that might be a more accurate representation of an idea or a product.

5. Teach students some of the rudiments of debating and have them debate relevant issues.

6. Invite a salesman from the community to discuss honest salesmanship.

7. Invite a member of the police department to describe his experiences with confidence games and the speaking techniques of confidence men.

8. Give students several facts about some incident in the news. Have one-third of the class write an impartial radio broadcast of the incident; one-

third slant the facts one way; and the other one-third slant the facts another way. Human interest articles from newspapers are excellent sources for interesting incidents.

Providing Pleasurable Listening Activities

Students need opportunities to discover how pleasurable listening can be. Teachers should know their students' interests and provide them with listening experiences that match their present interests and foster new ones. We believe that when the objective of the teaching is to provide enjoyment, other objectives should not be actively sought. Undoubtedly, various listening skills will be strengthened as students enjoy a listening experience; however, they should be strengthened incidentally. Students should not be given prescriptions for listening or post-listening evaluations when the objective is enjoyment. The teacher's task is to know what his students are likely to enjoy and to provide it with no strings attached. The listening experience should be appealing enough to capture attention and stimulate learning with a minimum of pre- post-listening instruction. We are not saying that pre- and post-listening activities should be avoided altogether when enjoyment is the objective. Listening related activities that serve to heighten awareness and enjoyment should definitely be used. However, students should be permitted great freedom in how they listen and how they respond to speakers, plays, music, and other experiences presented primarily to be enjoyed.

We are not presenting a list of specific practices for providing pleasurable listening activities, since such a list would of necessity be incomplete, arbitrary, and soon outdated. Teachers are urged, however, to make use of the following: musical selections; recorded plays, poems, and stories; story telling and story reading; interesting speakers; live drama; debates, panel discussions, informal group discussions and symposiums. We especially recommend conversation before and after a shared listening experience since much of the enjoyment of an aesthetic experience lies in sharing it with another person.

There is no shortage of recorded materials available for use with corrective and remedial students. Teachers should consult librarians, instructional materials centers, and publishers' catalogs for suggestions. Phonograph records and tapes are becoming more and more numerous. For example, selected Newbery Award books have been recorded with appropriate music and sound effects (Newbery Award Records, Inc.), and the "Tell Me a Story" and "Sights and Sounds" programs (Random House/Singer) can be used to give children many hours of enjoyable listening.

Although commercially prepared materials are plentiful, teachers should not overlook themselves and their students as good resources. Students like to hear a story read or told by a good reader or speaker, and they enjoy informal oral communication with each other. Obviously, no one enjoys listening to a poor reader or speaker labor his way through a story, and this should be avoided. However, there are many opportunities for teachers to give students enjoyable listening experiences using the various human resources within the classroom.

Most teachers maintain a collection of favorite workbooks, kits, paperbacks, games, and other materials for improving students' reading ability. However, few teachers possess a comparable collection of tapes, phonograph records, written paragraphs, and other materials to improve students' listening ability. We would urge corrective and remedial teachers to be as enthusiastic about preparing and collecting developmental listening materials as they are about preparing and collecting developmental reading materials. Perhaps what is needed is a commitment to teaching listening that is as sincere as the commitment typically reserved for other areas of the curriculum.

THOUGHTS FOR DISCUSSION

"If you're guilty of faking attention while listening you deceive only yourself. . . . listening takes energy. The expenditure of this energy leaves the listener looking, not as though he were cast from concrete, but as a very much alive human being who is following the spoken word with interest." (Nichols and Stevens, 1957, p. 105)

"Memorizing facts is not the way to listen. When people talk they usually want you to understand their ideas. The facts are only useful for constructing the ideas. Grasping ideas is the skill on which the good listener concentrates. He bothers to remember facts only long enough to understand the ideas that are built from the facts. But then, almost miraculously, his grasping an idea will help the good listener to remember the supporting facts more effectively than does the person who goes after facts alone." (Nichols and Stevens, 1957, p. 106)

"No one can listen, observe, or speak effectively outside the scope of his accumulating experiences. What we do to lend vitality and meaning to the experiences of childhood substantially determines the success of our efforts to improve these three vital components of receptive and expressive communication." (Shane, Mulry, Redden, and Gillespie, 1963, p. 114)

"Teaching youngsters to recognize the gimmicks which commercial and political propagandists use is important but probably not enough. Propagandists generally prey upon human needs, and unless people understand their own needs it is likely that they will succumb to propagandistic pressures. Intensive training in propaganda analysis surely should help to fend off the pressures, but a study of human needs along with propaganda analysis should be at least doubly effective." (May, 1967, p. 152)

"Research studies reveal that listening is a factor in scholastic achievement, that poor listeners can be helped to improve their skills, that listening is subtly modified by attitudes toward the speaker, the situation, and the audience, that mass listening is modified by the social nature of the situation (the same listener responds variously to the same speech in different audience contexts), that poor listening with or without hearing impairment retards normal language development, and that listening is so important in business and industry that many large enterprises have offered to their employees (at all levels) training courses in listening." (Commission on the English Curriculum of the National Council of Teachers of English, 1956, p. 253)

"Parallel speaking and listening skills should be included in the same lesson. For example, listening for the main idea can be combined with a lesson on stating the main point." (Pronovost, 1959, p. 10)

"Although investigators have only begun to explore listening, recently called the master key to all the language arts, there is agreement on these assumptions: (1) There is an identifiable factor of listening comprehension. Moreover, it can be tested objectively. It is distinguishable from other language factors, such as reading and verbal mental ability. (2) The process of critical listening has been observed in children, even pre-school children, although it may be restricted by lack of knowledge and experience. (3) Hoping for natural growth in listening ability is not enough for our day and age. Just as systematic instruction is necessary in reading, so systematic instruction is necessary also in listening." (Lundsteen, 1964, p. 743)

REFERENCES

Anderson, P. L. *Language skills in elementary education.* New York: Macmillan, 1965.

Borchers, G. An approach to the problem of oral style. *Quarterly Journal of Speech,* February, 1936, **22**.

Cleland, D. L., and Toussaint, I. H. The interrelationships of reading, listening, arithmetic, computation and intelligence. *The Reading Teacher,* 1962, **15**, 228–231.

Commission on the English Curriculum of the National Council of Teachers of English. *The English language arts in secondary school.* New York: Appleton-Century-Crofts, 1956.

Crosby, R. M. N., and Liston, R. A. Dyslexia: What you can—and can't—do about it. *Grade Teacher,* February, 1969, 74–76.

Dawson, M., and Zollinger, M. Helping children to listen effectively. *Guiding Language Learning.* Yonkers, N. Y.: World Book, 1957, 160–192.

Demos, G., and Grant, B. Sharpening your communication skills. *Education,* February, 1966, 174–176.

Floyd, W. D. An analysis of the oral questioning activity in selected Colorado primary classrooms. Doctoral research study, Colorado State College, 1960. *Abstracts of Field Studies for the Degree of Doctor of Education,* 1961, **22,** 46–50. (Abstract)

Foulke, E. Listening comprehension as a function of word rate. *Journal of Communication,* September, 1968, **18,** 198–206.

Hall, E. T. Listening behavior: Some cultural differences. *Phi Delta Kappan,* March, 1969, 379–380.

Herman, W. L., Jr. The use of language arts in social studies lessons. *American Educational Research Journal,* March, 1967, **4,** 117–124.

Horrworth, G. L. Listening: A facet of oral learning. *Elementary English,* 1966, **43,** 856–864.

Loban, W. Oral language and learning. *Oral Language and Reading.* Champaign, Ill.: National Council of Teachers of English, 1969, 101–102.

Lundsteen, S. W. Teaching and testing critical listening in the fifth and sixth grades. *Elementary English,* November, 1964, **41,** 743–747.

Markgraf, B. R. An observational study ·determining the amount of time that students in the tenth and twelfth grades are expected to listen in the classroom. Master's thesis, University of Wisconsin, 1957. Annotated in S. Duker, *Listening Bibliography.* Metuchen, N. J.: Scarecrow Press, 1968.

May, F. B. *Teaching language as communication to children.* Columbus, Ohio: Charles E. Merrill, 1967.

Moffett, J. *Teaching the universe of discourse.* Boston: Houghton Mifflin, 1968.

Nichols, R. G., and Stevens, L. A. *Are you listening?* New York: McGraw-Hill, 1957.

Pronovost, W. *The teaching of speaking and listening in the elementary school.* New York: David McKay, 1959.

Shane, H. G., Mulry, J. G., Reddin, M. E., and Gillespie, M. C. *Improving language arts instruction in the elementary school.* Columbus, Ohio: Charles E. Merrill, 1963.

Woodcock, R. W., and Clark, C. R. Comprehension of a narrative passage by elementary school children as a function of listening rate, retention period, and I.Q. *Journal of Communication,* September, 1968, **18,** 259–271.

Chapter 13

Handwriting

More often than not difficulties in handwriting coexist with difficulties in reading and spelling. The most apparent reason for the relationship is that malfunctions in each area may spring from a common cause, like inadequate visual memory, inability or lack of readiness to handle visual symbols, or difficulties with sound-symbol relationships. But, perhaps at a more subtle level, difficulties in reading and/or spelling may be the cause for apparent difficulties in handwriting. A child who is failing in reading and spelling is apt to have negative feelings toward verbal activities in general, and these feelings may be manifested in careless, illegible handwriting. Illegibilities may result, too, from a kind of negative motivation brought about by a desire to hide misspellings. In certain instances, though, poor handwriting may have a more specific cause: a deeply rooted emotional problem may render a child agraphic, or a physical problem may obstruct the motor aspect of the handwriting act. Nevertheless, in our experience we have found that handwriting problems are much more frequently caused by perceptual and personality factors than by physiological and motor factors.

This chapter is divided into two major parts, the first dealing generally with approaches to teaching handwriting and the second dealing specifically with the diagnosis and treatment of handwriting problems. The intent is to establish a framework for considering corrective and remedial handwriting instruction by examining practices and programs and then to focus upon diagnostic and remedial procedures.

APPROACHES TO TEACHING HANDWRITING

Handwriting is, in many ways, the most concrete of the basic skills: handwriting samples can be physically measured and analyzed and they can be preserved and compared over a period of time. The end product is not so fleeting and evasive as a verbal response; nor is it so nebulous as a correct computation or the comprehension of a written passage. Yet, perhaps it is the very tangible nature of the handwriting product that makes for oversimplification and superficiality in dealing with skill development in handwriting. Historically, many instructional practices in handwriting have been based upon tradition rather than careful analysis of the task, and certain practices have been blatantly illogical.

Recent developments have, however, been encouraging. Handwriting is seen less as an art form and more as a tool for personal communication. Consequently, there is new emphasis upon methods and materials for teaching the skills needed to produce legible handwriting with reasonable efficiency (Otto and Andersen, 1969). Whether the changed perception of function in handwriting is accompanied by a deterioration in the quality of writing is open to some question. Logically, emphasis upon function could result in a more casual approach to formal instruction and to the correction of illegibilities. Enstrom (1964, 1965) feels that handwriting quality has indeed declined. Yet, as recently as 1961 Erlebacher and Herrick (1961) reported no appreciable difference in the quality of handwriting samples gathered in 1912 and in 1959. Of course a partial cause for such discrepancies is inherent in the fact that there is no standard operational definition of quality in handwriting. Some writers look almost exclusively for "readableness" while others look for a pleasing appearance as well.

Whatever the definition of quality, the fact is that handwriting is treated as a tool subject in most schools. By examining present practices and specific approaches to instruction we can point out what we feel are some salient features of sound instruction in handwriting as well as some persistent weaknesses.

Surveys of Practices

In a 1956 UNESCO report of an international survey on the teaching of reading and writing, the late William S. Gray (1956) noted that the nineteenth-century emphasis on form and quality in handwriting had given way, since the turn of the century, to a concern with the learner and his problem in expressing his meaning with acceptable standards of speed and quality. Thus, while handwriting has come to be seen more as a tool than as an art form, it is not seen as a purely mechanical act. Instead, handwriting is recognized as a highly personalized means of expression. Harris (1960) put it this way: "Handwriting is widely thought of not only as a tool but also as a means of individualized personal expression" (p. 616). The teacher of handwriting, then, ought to strike a balance in requiring reasonable legibility while tolerating personal idiosyncrasies in the handwriting product. Whether such a balance is indeed struck is not entirely clear from the available surveys of practices in teaching handwriting.

A state-wide survey reported by the Committee for Research in Handwriting in 1951 is still one of the most comprehensive surveys of practices available. The survey was replicated almost a decade later both in Wisconsin, where the original study was done, and nationally. The results, reported by Herrick and Okada (1963), showed that (*a*) national practices were not substantially different from practices in Wisconsin, and (b) there was no appreciable change in practices during the intervening decade. The main conclusions derived from the survey data follow.

1. Most Wisconsin elementary schools—like those in other states—teach both manuscript and cursive writing.

2. In most Wisconsin schools, instruction in handwriting is begun before the end of the first grade.

3. By the end of the first grade, most Wisconsin schools have children using handwriting as a tool.

4. The general Wisconsin practice is to shift from the teaching of manuscript to cursive writing in the year-and-a-half period preceding fourth grade. Practices 2, 3, and 4 parallel that of other states.

5. There is a great deal of variability in the number of practice periods per week devoted to specific handwriting practice. For grades 1–6, teachers appear to *prefer* five periods per week, however.

6. Average amount of time per week spent in handwriting practice also varies greatly. The Wisconsin pattern runs from 50 minutes for grades 1–3, to 40 minutes for grades 4–6, to 30 minutes for grades 7–8. (There is some reason to believe that this might be somewhat less time than the national average.)

7. Most Wisconsin handwriting teachers prefer short periods of handwriting instruction—usually 15–20 minutes.

8. In the majority of Wisconsin schools, teachers claim to draw content for handwriting practice from other current instructional activities, usually spelling.

Again, the Wisconsin results are generally representative of the results obtained nationally. Clearly, there is much variability from school to school in specific provisions made for handwriting instruction. The survey data also provide some information regarding factors emphasized and techniques used in teaching handwriting.

1. Wisconsin teachers place a good deal of emphasis upon legibility and letter formation in teaching handwriting. Slant, spacing, and body position follow, in that order. Speed is not stressed much, and then only in the upper grades.

2. Most schools pay some special attention to pupils having difficulty in learning to write, usually as a part of the regular program of handwriting instruction. (It should be pointed out here that little is known about the nature of this "special attention." There is a need to explore this problem carefully.)

3. Teachers pay considerable attention to the position of the feet, arms, wrist, and fingers; the paper; and the writing instrument. But they do not worry much about arm movement.

4. Some ways teachers help children learn to write: music, push-pulls, forming letters in the air.

5. Mastery of numerals is usually expected first, then small letters, and finally capital letters. Every pupil is expected to show some proficiency in all by the end of grade 3.

6. Right-handed children are given more adequate help than left-handed children in learning to write. That is, only two-thirds of the responding schools claimed to make provision for the left-handed writer.

Two additional facts revealed in the national survey were that (1) only 7 percent of the respondents claimed to have diagnostic or remedial programs in handwriting, and (2) very few respondents reported that they made any effort to help their pupils recognize their own errors or to develop a personal style of writing. Our position, discussed in detail elsewhere in this chapter, is that the most straightforward approach to correcting handwriting faults is through the identification and correction of each pupil's errors.

Some additional insight into practices in teaching handwriting can be derived from the report of a survey of practices advocated by commercial handwriting systems (Committee for Research in Basic Skills, 1960). The survey covered materials made available by the following companies:

COMMERCIAL SUPPLIERS OF INSTRUCTIONAL MATERIALS
ON HANDWRITING

American Book Company	A. N. Palmer Company
Beckley-Cardy Company	The Peterson System (Macmillan)
W. S. Benson & Company	Pitman Publishing Company
Bobbs-Merrill Company	Public School Publishing Company
The Economy Company	Scott, Foresman Company
I. Z. Hackman	Schmidt, Hall & McCreary Company
Harlow Publishing Corporation	E. C. Seale and Company
Harr Wagner Publishing Company	Steck Company
New Laurel Book Company	Zaner-Bloser Company
Noble & Noble Publishers, Inc.	

Taken together, the nineteen companies listed were supplying 95 percent of the instructional materials in handwriting used in the United States at the time of the survey. There is, of course, a close parallel between practices advocated by the commercial systems and the instructional practices within the schools. The following generalizations are derived from the survey data:

1. For the most part, the commercial systems are in agreement that *legibility* is the overall objective in handwriting instruction. Legibility is

commonly defined in operational terms: writing which is easily read and easily written is legible. The fact that there is no standard alphabet, however, bespeaks the fact that legibility has not been precisely defined.

2. Handwriting is generally regarded as a tool for communication; its role is one of function. Handwriting instruction is, therefore, closely correlated with instruction in reading, spelling, the language arts, and social studies. Some systems regard the meeting of standards of legibility and appearance in other instructional areas aside from the handwriting period as the true test of handwriting instruction.

3. There is some agreement on considerations for developing motor skills in handwriting. For example, movements of the arm rather than finger actions are desired to achieve fluent writing (reasonable speed); as arm movements are made, a rhythm in writing is developed. This approach, unfortunately, is not backed by research.

4. Systematic procedures for learning letter forms are proposed by some systems: seeing the letter or word, hearing it, tracing it in the air, etc. Again, there is little actual research which examines the perceptual aspects of learning to write.

5. There is general agreement that practice is necessary and practice should be purposeful; but the purposes for handwriting activity that are proposed are varied, ranging from the experience of the children (labeling, letter writing) to a particular stroke to be learned. The frequent practice of having pupils draw circles and practice vertical and horizontal strokes is supported by very little research evidence.

6. While the systems use handwriting scales in comparing the quality of the pupils' writing with standardized norms, much greater emphasis is placed upon students' self-evaluation of their own writing. The identification of specific errors defines the kinds of practice which are needed. (This finding is not in line with the surveys of practice, where little claim is made to helping pupils identify and correct their own errors.)

7. There is general recognition that pupils' abilities in writing will cover a wide range; there is no expectation of a uniform degree of skill in the classroom. Lesson plans are based upon group and individual instruction.

8. The fundamental principles of good writing are the same for all grades. But in the upper elementary grades there is a tendency to use the handwriting period for remedial purposes—that is, diagnosing and correcting handwriting defects that have been revealed in pupils' daily work. Pupils are helped to become more proficient in identifying general and specific inaccuracies of letter forms, slant, size, spacing, and quality of alignment of writing.

The commercial systems surveyed are, then, in general accord on a number of matters. Perhaps it is noteworthy, too, that the practices advocated by the commercial systems tend to be more nearly in accord with sound sensible procedures than some of the actual practices reported. Finally, Petty (1964) has legitimately pointed out that the several systems show considerable divergence in their letter form models, in the sequence in which letters are introduced, and in certain recommended teaching practices.

A related study of letter forms—upper- and lower-case, manuscript and cursive—advocated by the nineteen commercial systems was reported by Herrick and Otto (1961). The letter form models provided by each system were photographed and reduced to a common size. This reproduction of letter forms permits a straightforward comparison of the various models given by the several systems. As an example, models of the letter M advocated by representative systems are given in figure 11.

The letter form study clearly shows that there is no general agreement regarding the shapes and strokes. But whether the differences are significant in terms of efficiency of production is still not known. Three questions posed in the report of the study continue to await answers.

> 1. When connected writing employing different systems is compared, are there significant differences in (a) legibility, (b) aesthetic appeal, (c) efficiency of reproduction?
> 2. To what extent does the use of one or another system facilitate or retard (a) the development of handwriting skill, (b) transition from manuscript to cursive writing?
> 3. Is it possible for judges to categorize children's handwriting samples by systems used in instructional practice? If the answer is affirmative, how closely does adult writing approximate the model used in school training? (P. 25)

If the answers were known, we would have reasons for choosing among the various forms; or, at least, we would *know* that the variation in letter forms advocated is not a significant factor in the teaching and learning of handwriting.

Transition from Manuscript to Cursive Writing

The national survey of practices in handwriting by Herrick and Okada (1963) showed that most children are first taught manuscript writing and then required to make a transition to cursive writing, usually sometime between the beginning of second and the end of third grade. While the introduction of manuscript writing in the schools is relatively recent, dating back to the 1920's, the practice seems both sensible and defensible. Hildreth (1963a), for example, pointed out the interrelatedness of manuscript writing and early reading and suggested that the two areas ought to be mutually reinforcing. And Herrick (1960) suggested that the straight lines, circles, and spacing of manuscript writing are more in line with young children's motor and eye-hand-arm coordination than are the strokes and formations in cursive writing. Otto and Andersen (1969) summed up the current state of affairs thus: "The question now is not whether manuscript writing ought to be taught, for it is in fact taught, but whether, and, if so, when, the transition to cursive writing should be made" (p. 574).

FIG. 11 Selected Letter Forms from the *Letter Form Models* Comparison Study

a. Upper-Case Cursive

b. Lower-Case Cursive

c. Upper-Case Manuscript

d. Lower-Case Manuscript

The question of *whether* cursive writing *ought to be* taught is one that seems to have a straightforward, albeit virtually totally ignored, answer. After reviewing the relevant research, both Harris (1960) and Andersen (1966) concluded that there is little evidence to recommend the change to cursive writing. Manuscript writing seems to meet the needs of adults in terms of both speed and legibility. Both Templin (1960) and Hildreth (1963b) have argued that the transition to cursive writing is both unnecessary and wasteful. Templin made the telling point that in other skill areas early learnings are broadened and reinforced, not replaced! Smith (1970) suggested, too, that for newly literate adults the transition is likely to be time consuming and confusing and totally unnecessary. Nevertheless, for the foreseeable future the transition to cursive writing is likely to continue. The tradition of cursive writing is strong.

The only existing research evidence relevant to the question of *when* the transition should be made seems to suggest that the time of transition is of little consequence. Otto and Rarick (1969) studied the effect of four different transition times—ranging from early second to late third grade—upon subsequent performance in handwriting, spelling, and reading and concluded that when the transition is made is less important than what is offered in the instructional program.

Our personal feeling is that cursive writing has little, other than tradition, to recommend it. We are, however, reconciled to the fact that it is likely to be with us for a long time. Nevertheless, there is no good reason for burdening children with learning problems with a transition to a writing style that is likely to be confusing and frustrating. Our recommendation for children who have severe problems in communication skill areas is that the transition not be made or, at least, that it be indefinitely deferred.

Assessing Quality of Writing

In handwriting as in other basic skill areas, the diagnostic process begins at the survey level: pupils who are operating below a certain level of performance are identified so that their problem can be more specifically diagnosed and remedial teaching provided. Unfortunately, screening criteria are not likely to be so clear in handwriting as in, say, reading. Classroom teachers, parents, employers—the many people who are concerned with the end product—may not agree upon the criteria or minimum standards because they place different emphases upon the importance of speed, legibility, and beauty or character. For functional purposes, of course, both speed and legibility are important and the relative emphasis necessarily shifts from one activity to another. However, speed can easily be quantified and criterion levels can be established for different purposes. But with legibility the problem of quantification is much more complex. Because the problem is a persistent one and because it demands at least an arbitrary solution by each teacher of handwriting, it merits careful consideration.

Quality and Legibility in Writing

The scope of the problem could be narrowed greatly if it were possible to reach agreement that in handwriting *quality* and *legibility* are synonymous. When the handwriting product was valued more for its aesthetic appeal than for its function, such agreement would have been out of the question. But even now, with the trend away from art form and toward communication tool, judgments of the legibility of a handwriting sample continue to be confounded by something more than strict "readableness." There are two aspects involved: (1) it is difficult for a judge to keep a single factor (e.g., "readableness") clearly in mind as he evaluates a sample of handwriting, and (2) a single objective measure, such as the speed with which samples of handwriting can be read, fails to distinguish between samples that are clearly different in general merit. That is, regarding the latter, beyond a certain level of legibility, speed of reading would remain constant but judges could continue to make reliable judgments of overall quality.

To say that *quality* is *legibility*, then, is to evade the issue. To separate the "readableness" of a handwriting sample from the impression made by its total appearance seems to be, if not impossible, quite undesirable. Quality in handwriting is a global concept that cannot readily be described in concrete, quantifiable terms. Researchers who have grappled with the problem have produced a variety of scales to be used in assessing quality.

Handwriting Scales

Herrick and Erlebacher (1963) have described the development of scales for assessing quality in handwriting in considerable detail; other reviews of the development of handwriting scales are given by Harris (1960), Andersen (1966), and Otto and Andersen (1969). Some of the scales and the problems encountered in their development are discussed here.

The first handwriting scale, *The Thorndike Scale for Handwriting* (Teachers College Press), was developed by E. L. Thorndike. The scale includes handwriting at fifteen different quality levels, ranging from very poor, barely legible writing to beautifully formed writing of a quality that might serve as a model in a penmanship manual. The single fifteen-sample scale is intended for use at all grade levels. In developing the scale, subjects were asked to "write as you usually do" to produce samples and the samples were then judged as to degree of goodness or poorness on the basis of "general merit." The criterion of "general merit" as a basis for judging quality of handwriting by implication includes some consideration of beauty or pleasing quality as well as absolute clarity and uniformity of line and form.

In 1912 a scale developed by Ayres (1912) appeared; and in 1915 the "Gettysburg Edition," so called because it employs lines from Lincoln's "'Gettysburg Address," was published. Like the Thorndike, it is a composite scale, designed for use in grades 2 through 8. The scale includes samples from eight quality levels. To rate a specimen of handwriting, a teacher must decide which of the eight scaled quality levels the specimen is most nearly like. In developing his scale, Ayres questioned Thorndike's use of "general merit" as the criterion for judging the quality of writing. He felt that hand-writing is produced in order that another person might read it and, therefore, he used the criterion of readability, which was measured by the median reading speed of ten judges reading a given sample. In other words, the longer it took the judges to read handwriting samples the poorer the hand-writing and the lower the scale value.

The criterion of readability as the basis for determining the quality of handwriting seems logically defensible. However, there is evidence (Erle-bacher and Herrick, 1961) that the "average reading speed" criterion dis-criminates better among poor handwriting samples than among good samples. It appears that as quality decreases and approaches the poor end of the scale, readers find it necessary to read more and more slowly in order to decipher what has been written. However, after quality has become reasonably good there seems to be no significant increase in the speed at which samples are read despite clear differences in "general merit." The readability criterion, then, is inadequate for purposes of taking in a wide range of quality that goes from poor to excellent. Yet if we can agree that handwriting is a tool and nothing more, the readability criterion is adequate. It appears that, after a certain point, increases in quality no longer enhance legibility or ease of reading but simply improve the general appearance—the aesthetic appeal—of handwriting specimens. Those who accept hand-writing simply as a tool would be unconcerned about differences in general merit that go beyond the level of maximum readability.

Scales developed by Freeman (1915; 1959) in 1915 and revised in 1959 demonstrate still other concerns of scale builders. (The revised Freeman scale is available from the Zaner-Bloser Company.) Freeman felt the revision was needed because the Ayres and the Thorndike are composite scales—that is, there is but one set of specimens for use at all grade levels—yet at different grade levels handwriting varies greatly in size, style, and quality; and the only recently devised scale for instructional use in a modern style of writing used specimens from only one community. The revised scale was devised to meet the following specifications: (1) a series of scales, one at each grade level from 1 through 8; (2) national in scope—specimens from throughout the nation were considered in building the scale; (3) each specimen rated on the basis of general merit, with the primary emphasis upon legibility and form; and (4) scale specimens selected to show balance in all elements of form—spacing, alignment, letter formation, and uniformity in size and slant. The scale consists of five quality levels at each grade level; scales for grades 1 and 2 are written manuscript style and scales for grades 3 through 8 are in cursive style.

Like Freeman, West (1926) developed grade-level scales rather than a single composite scale. The scales, which were revised in 1957 (West, 1957), include a speed criterion as well as a quality-legibility criterion. The seven quality levels of each grade-level scale range from the poorest sample with slowest speed to the best sample of fastest speed. While the attempt to consider both speed and legibility is sensible, the problem is that there is not a direct relationship between them. Instead, "as speed increases beyond a certain point, legibility or quality decreases" (Herrick and Erlebacher, 1963, p. 213). We shall return to this point in the discussion of remedial procedures.

The scales devised by Freeman, Ayres, and West are the most widely used for purposes of rating the quality of writing produced by school children (Herrick and Okada, 1963). Yet there is lack of agreement among the scales upon such important points as whether a scale should be a composite or broken down by grade level and precisely what should be considered in selecting standards of quality. All four of the scales discussed are fairly crude; that is, the various levels of quality represented on the scales are separated by rather wide gaps. This makes it reasonably easy to place specimens on the scale for rating purposes, but precludes making the fine distinctions between specimens that would be most useful for instructional purposes. If, for example, it were possible to measure day-to-day improvement and to set goals for improvement, the instructional values of scales would be much enhanced. As it is, the pupil is usually confronted with models that differ considerably from his own writing; it would be more realistic to show him where he is and how he might move from there to a little better.

The groundwork for developing scales that provide small-step intervals and make provision for considering the size and slant of specimens to be rated has been laid (Herrick and Erlebacher, 1963). "Slant" refers to the tilt of letter forms. Left-handed writers, for example, tend often to give their letter forms an extreme back slant that detracts from their legibility. Inconsistent slant makes for extreme illegibility. Cursive letter forms generally have a slight forward slant. The sample in figure 12 has a moderate

FIG. 12   Handwriting Sample with Moderate Back Slant

back slant. The use of a small interval scale adapted for size and slant permits finer rankings of samples than the gross scales. Herrick and Erlebacher (1963) have given specifications for constructing such scales.

The basic point to be made about standards of legibility and the assessment of legibility through the use of scales is that the decision rests with the local school, or in absence of curriculum policy, with the individual teacher. Any one of the three scales described could serve, once a minimum standard has been set, as a screening device for locating pupils who need help with their handwriting. When such a minimum standard has been agreed upon, whether a pupil meets the standard becomes a fairly straightforward decision. As we have pointed out, the difficulty is in reaching agreement upon what will be accepted as the minimum standard.

Some Specific Approaches

As a tool for communication, handwriting is a means for recording and conveying thoughts: the emphasis is upon *what* a pupil writes. In handwriting *instruction,* however, the emphasis is necessarily upon *how* a pupil writes: the main concern is the legibility and efficient production of written symbols. Only after the handwriting act has become automatic can handwriting assume its proper role as an efficient tool for expressing ideas. The *how* and the *what* of handwriting are in phase when pupils' writing is sufficiently rapid and legible to meet their needs in all instructional areas.

Here we shall consider three specific approaches to developmental instruction in handwriting. The intent is not to probe deeply into the issues of scope and sequence. The reader who is interested can examine the materials offered by the commercial suppliers listed on page 334 or the report of the survey of these systems (Committee for Research in Basic Skills, 1960) to get an overview of widely used materials and approaches. The approaches selected for consideration here represent relatively recent developments, and in our opinion each is conducive to effective corrective and remedial teaching.

A Perceptual-Motor Approach

In a series of recent articles in *Elementary English,* Furner (1969a, 1969b, 1970) described a program of handwriting instruction in which the perceptual-motor nature of learning is emphasized. Her main point, which has the support of logic and data from a field test, is that instruction in handwriting should "build perception of letters and their formation as a guide for motor practice, rather than emphasizing only the motor aspect . . ." (Furner, 1970, p. 68). A closely related point is that copying and tracing techniques do not build the required perceptual abilities; therefore, stress must be placed upon (*a*) accurate perception of letter forms, (*b*) the general features of handwriting, and (*c*) appropriate procedures to permit the pupil to compare his writing to models of desired writing in order to make plans for improvement. Such an emphasis is, of course, completely appropriate in the corrective-remedial teaching of handwriting.

The following points summarize Furner's specific instructional recommendations. They are designed to "assist teachers in improving current programs which place primary emphasis on the motor aspect of handwriting skill . . ." (Furner, 1970, p. 68).

1. Involve pupils in establishing a purpose for each lesson.

2. Provide many guided exposures to the formation of letters, e.g., focus attention upon different aspects of the formational process in subsequent trials, in order to assist the child in building a mental image of the letter form.

3. Encourage a mental as well as a motor response from each child during the writing process, e.g., have the child describe the process as he writes or have him visualize or write a letter as another child describes it. This procedure makes use of multisensory stimulation.

4. Stress self-correction by emphasizing comparison and improvement rather than writing many samples. Practice in sustained writing to develop speed and stamina should be given in sessions other than those devoted to developing the perceptual aspects of writing.

5. Provide consistent letter form models. (The teacher's writing should conform to the style adapted by the school.)

6. Keep expectations regarding quantity of writing consistent with what children can realistically produce. (Furner, for example, found that the average first grader can write only 16–17 letters per minute. This amounts to only about 30 words in ten minutes.)

7. Limit the use of unsupervised writing or copywork. Prolonged writing periods not monitored by the teacher are apt to be detrimental to both the perceptual and the motor aspects of writing.

Taken together, Furner's recommendations put deserved stress upon the perceptual aspect of handwriting. Note that the approach does not prescribe the letter form models to be used; the intent is not to teach specific forms but to insure the forms chosen be thoroughly learned and efficiently produced.

A Programmed Approach

The approach developed in the *Handwriting with Write and See* (Lyons and Carnahan) materials appears at first to be quite different from that advocated by Furner; but careful examination shows that while specific techniques differ, the intent—to develop perceptual as well as motor skills—is the same.

The *Write and See* program represents a definitive and, in our opinion, a highly successful attempt to embody sound learning principles (see Chapter 3) in a comprehensive approach to handwriting instruction. One salient feature of the program is the special pen and paper: when a child forms a letter correctly the pen writes gray; but when he is wrong, it writes yellow. Thus, the child has immediate *knowledge of the success* of his writing effort, immediate *reinforcement* of a correct response, and, presumably, *motivation* derived from the challenge of continuing to produce gray lines. A second feature is that the material is programmed: at first only very simple responses are required and progress is made through a progression of very small steps, so the child is almost always able to do what is asked of him. And finally, the perceptual aspect is given stress in that the child learns to judge samples for legibility, to analyze them for sources of illegibility, and to take a critical attitude toward his own writing.

The program includes eight books: Book 1; Book 2; Book 2 Manuscript-Cursive; Book 3; Book 3 Manuscript-Cursive; Book 4; Book 5; Book 6. The transition from manuscript to cursive writing can be made at either second- or third-grade level by using the appropriate alternate book at the level chosen. Individual teachers may decide whether they wish to permit pupils to proceed through the program at their own pace or to use the books at grade level. In a corrective-remedial situation the teacher is free to break into the sequence at any appropriate point.

In the teacher's guidebooks for the system a brief definition of each of five critical visual-motor skills and suggestions for remedial help to improve each skill are given. They are:

1. Visual-Motor Coordination—the ability to coordinate visual movements with movements of the body.
Remediation: fine motor activities.

2. Figure-Ground Perception—the ability to focus on an object accurately in relation to background stimuli.
Remediation: activities developing the ability to focus on a relevant image without confusing it with other stimuli.

3. Perceptual Constancy—the ability to perceive the unchanging properties of an object, despite the variability of images seen by the eyes.
Remediation: activities developing the ability to recognize forms regardless of size, color, or position.

4. Position in Space—the ability to perceive the spatial position of an object in relation to the viewer.
Remediation: activities developing spatial position, such as up, down, across, over, under, in, out, left, right, top, bottom. (Children who tend to do "mirror writing" need extensive drill here.)

5. Spatial Relationships—the ability to perceive two or more objects in relation to each other and to the viewer.
Remediation: exercises developing the ability to see any number of different parts in relation to each other.

Each of the exercise books in the program offers activities designed to develop these visual-motor skills. There is reason to believe that development of the skills will pay off not only in handwriting but in reading as well, particularly with children who experience modest difficulties in perceptual-motor orientation. Children with severe difficulties will, of course, need more intensive help.

We feel that the *Write and See* materials can be used with profit in corrective-remedial teaching. The skillfully designed, step-by-step instructional sequence is made to order. Furthermore, the uniqueness of the special pen and paper is likely to appeal to the flagging interest of the child with handwriting problems.

An Individualized-Diagnostic Approach

Tagatz, Otto, Klausmeier, Goodwin, and Cook (1968) reported the results of a study designed to determine the effects of three different approaches to handwriting instruction in grades three and four. The study was conducted by the instructional staff of Giese School in Racine, Wisconsin. Very briefly, the three approaches were:

1. *Formal Group Approach.* The instructional plans outlined in the commercial material adopted by the school were followed. In grade three the Peterson Directed Handwriting materials (Macmillan), *Adventures in Handwriting* series, were used; and the *Correlated Handwriting Series* (Zaner Bloser) was used in grade four.

2. *Formal-Individualized Approach.* The procedure here was to follow the sequence of instruction outlined in *Penskills II, An Individualized Handwriting Skills Program* (Science Research Associates). The program was individualized in that it permitted pupils to proceed at their own pace and, within the limits of the materials provided, to focus upon their own problems. It was a "formal" program in that the instructional materials were prescribed and restricted to the contents of the *Penskills II* kit.

3. *Individualized-Diagnostic Approach.* With this approach there was no systematic use of commercially prepared materials. The procedure followed was similar to that outlined in the latter part of this chapter: individuals were assisted and encouraged to recognize errors and malformations in their own writing and to work specifically on the elimination of personal difficulties. In general, an attempt was made to help each pupil focus on a limited number of his own problems at the beginning of an instructional sequence, and then he was permitted to practice while doing writing of his own choosing. All pupils were encouraged to develop the habit of continuously evaluating their own handwriting, e.g., once each week they wrote a standard sentence which they evaluated in terms of a normative scale.

The individualized approaches were clearly superior to the formal group approach; and the individualized-diagnostic approach was superior at grade three, but not at grade four.

The main point here is that the individualized-diagnostic approach described in this chapter has merit, too, in the regular developmental application. Aspects of the Furner and of the *Write and See* approaches could, of course, very readily and very profitably be integrated into the individualized-diagnostic approach.

DIAGNOSIS AND REMEDIATION

To be effective, an instructional program in handwriting ought to stress, as an integral part of the total developmental program, means for helping individual children learn how to evaluate and improve their personal writing; therefore, the essentials of diagnosis and remediation should be found in the regular program. Here, however, we shall be concerned with the identification and treatment of relatively severe problems that require individualized corrective-remedial teaching.

Survey Diagnosis

The main purpose of diagnosis at the survey level is to identify pupils with problems. In the area of handwriting this purpose is served by speed norms, some means for rating the legibility of samples, and familiarity with some of the basic problems in handwriting.

Speed Norms

Frank N. Freeman (1954), who was for years a leading authority on handwriting, suggested speed norms for grades two through eight in 1954. Speed is expressed in letters produced per minute in the schema that follows:

Grade	II	III	IV	V	VI	VII	VIII
Speed	30	40	50	60	67	74	80

According to Freeman, the speeds given for the several grade levels are averages demonstrated in research studies of children's writing speed. Speed of writing is extremely flexible, and normally speed can be increased from habitual rates without sacrificing reasonable legibility. Speed norms, such as those presented, are best conceived simply as a rule of thumb; they are best employed as a means for locating pupils whose speed is substantially below the norm. When teachers seek to collect specimens of writing for speed analysis, they should direct pupils to "write as well and as rapidly as you can" since these directions are the most commonly employed in research studies from which the norms are derived. Directions directly affect performance, and such directions as "write as fast as you can" or "write as you normally do" would result in samples different from those produced with the directions suggested above.

More recently, Groff (1961) suggested that some of the earlier speed norms were based upon data gathered under questionable conditions. He gathered data from 4,834 middle-grade pupils and compared his findings with those reported earlier by Ayres (1917). The data are summarized in Table 4.

TABLE 4

			Percent of Pupils			
Letters		Grade		Grade		Grade
Per	4	4	5	5	6	6
Minute	*Ayres*	*Groff* (N = 1563)	*Ayres*	*Groff* (N = 1522)	*Ayres*	*Groff* (N = 1749)
10–19	Not re-ported	6.8	1	3.8		1.5
20–29		25.4	2	13.5	2	5.5
30–39		31.5	5	31.5	3	18.4
40–49		21.3	12	26.0	8	27.1
50–59		9.9	20	12.6	14	21.2
60–69		3.6	22	7.0	19	12.9
70–79		.8	19	3.2	21	7.9
80–89		.3	12	.8	16	3.6
90–99		.1	5	.4	10	.9
100–109			2	.4	5	.8
110–119					2	.4
	M = 55	M = 35.06	M = 64	M = 40.65	M = 71	M = 49.65

Groff's speeds are considerably slower than those reported by Freeman or Ayres. We feel that Groff's data were indeed gathered under more realistic conditions and that they are, therefore, considerably more credible. Although the Ayres and Freeman norms are still widely used, we recommend that they be taken with a grain of salt. Such a procedure will save both teachers and pupils from needless frustration and fatigue.

Remedial teachers must, of course, be concerned about their pupils' writing speed, because unless writing is reasonably fluent it cannot function efficiently as a tool in regular schoolwork. "If handwriting must be painstakingly drawn to be legible, the demands of the task are likely to inhibit expression through writing" (Otto and Koenke, 1969, p. 233).

Legibility Ratings

Freeman (1954) also suggested legibility norms for grades 2 through 8. The norms, given in the schema that follows, are based upon the *Ayres Scale* ratings of handwriting samples of pupils from 46 cities. According to Freeman, the pupils in the sample were representative of pupils who have been exposed to "typical" methods of teaching handwriting.

Grade	II	III	IV	V	VI	VII	VIII
Rating	30	40	50	60	67	74	80

The *Ayres Scale* is but one of several that have been used widely to assess quality in handwriting. As noted in the preceding section, scales developed by Freeman and West continue to be used.

Like speed norms, legibility norms are best conceived as rule-of-thumb guidelines for locating pupils whose performance deviates substantially from the local average. What is needed, then, is local agreement upon minimum standards of speed and legibility. When local standards have been established, the purpose of survey diagnosis is to locate pupils whose performance falls short of the standard.

In addition to the legibility rating scales already discussed, at least two others are readily available. The *California Achievement Tests Complete Battery* (California Test Bureau) includes a handwriting subtest and both scales and norms are provided. *Penskills II, An Individualized Handwriting Skills Program* (Science Research Associates) includes scales for assessing the legibility of handwriting samples from pupils at various grade levels. Many of the publishers of commercial materials include scales—either one of the popular scales already described or one of their own making—in the total package provided.

In day-to-day teaching the regular use of scales may prove to be unwieldy. A solution to the problem was suggested in the report of a study by Otto, Askov, and Cooper (1967). The complete text of that brief report is given here because it makes both the rationale and the pragmatic approach to scaling handwriting samples quite clear.

LEGIBILITY RATINGS FOR HANDWRITING SAMPLES: A PRAGMATIC APPROACH

Rating pupils' handwriting samples for legibility at fairly frequent intervals can yield information useful in motivating pupils and in establishing a basis for corrective teaching. Yet, in practice the awkwardness of using the typical legibility rating scales probably prevents most teachers from making such assessments very often. The notion underlying this study was that once teachers have established a set of criteria for making legibility judgments by using scales, they should be able to make reasonably reliable judgments even when the formal use of scales is discontinued.

Handwriting samples were obtained by having 240 fourth and sixth grade pupils write a paragraph containing two sentences which include all the letters in the alphabet and which are the standard sentences for the California and Wisconsin scales, respectively: "The quick brown fox just came over to greet the lazy poodle" and "The quick brown fox jumps over the lazy dog." Thus, there were two standard sentence samples from each pupil. Three judges independently rated the samples for legibility, First, the California scale, a 7-point scale that is provided as a part of the *California Achievement Test* battery (Tiegs and Clark, 1957), and the Wisconsin scale, a 7-point scale devised for the present study by procedures outlined by Herrick and Erlebacher (cf. Herrick, 1961, pp. 207–231), were used to assign a legibility rating to the appropriate sample from each pupil. Then the judges assigned a legibility rating of 1 to 7 to each sample without using a scale.

Inter-judge reliability coefficients (Pearsonian) were .77, .72 and .69 with the California scale and .85, .80 and .74 with the Wisconsin scale; the between-scales correlation was .79. When ratings were made without scales, the inter-judge coefficients were .79, .91, and .85 with the California sentence samples and .72, .74 and .86 for the Wisconsin sentence samples; the between-samples *r* was .82. The judges did about as well, then, without the scales as with them, and there was no loss in the reliability of the ratings for individuals when the scales were not used. When each judge's ratings of the California sample sentences with and without the scale were correlated, the *r*s were .77, .83, and .76; with the Wisconsin sentences *r*s were .76, .85 and .73.

These results indicate there was no significant loss in the magnitude of judges' reliability ratings when the use of scales was discontinued. The implication appears to be that, given a background of experience in making such judgments, teachers do not need to use scales to make reliable judgments regarding the legibility of pupils' handwriting. Further research is needed to determine optimum procedures for establishing criteria for judging. Meanwhile, a preliminary period of scale-based judging appears to be useful.

Remedial teachers will find that they can use existing scales to help pupils perceive improvement in their personal handwriting as well as to do the survey screening required to identify problems. They can use the procedure described by Otto, Askov, and Cooper (1967) to make interim judgments regarding pupils' progress.

Basic Problems in Handwriting

Screening at the survey level should focus upon three basic kinds of problems:

1. *Handwriting is of generally poor quality.* Whatever the reason, the pupil is unable to produce handwriting that meets minimum legibility standards.

2. *Handwriting is acceptable when the pupil sets his own pace, but deteriorates under pressure to write more rapidly.* The pupil is unable to apply his handwriting skill to meet even normal classroom demands for speed.

3. *Handwriting is habitually produced at an extremely slow rate.* Quality may meet legibility standards, but speed of production is below minimum standards.

Diagnostic screening can be geared to locating pupils who are experiencing any of these types of difficulty. Once a pupil with difficulty has been identified, it is the purpose of specific diagnosis to examine more fully the exact nature of the difficulty. If, for example, a child is found to have general difficulty in producing legible handwriting, the task in specific diagnosis is to determine the causes for illegibility, such as extreme backhand, inconsistent spacing or size, inadequately formed letters, etc. The task in diagnostic screening is simply to locate pupils who are not able to produce handwriting with sufficient efficiency to meet minimum standards of speed and quality for their personal daily needs.

To do an adequate job of diagnostic screening it is usually necessary to gather handwriting samples for that particular purpose. It is possible to get only a limited amount of information regarding a student's handwriting from examination of his themes and other written work. Sometimes legible handwriting is produced only at the cost of such a slow rate that the total handwriting act is grossly inefficient. On the other hand, writing of generally poor quality may indicate nothing more than lack of motivation; pupils whose writing is poor due to carelessness often can produce acceptable handwriting if they want to do so.

It is desirable, then, to get samples of pupils' writing under reasonably controlled conditions. Builders of handwriting scales typically instruct their subjects to "write as you usually do" when they seek samples of writing. However, for purposes of diagnostic screening there is a need for samples of "best" handwriting and "fastest" handwriting as well as "usual" handwriting. With such samples, the teacher is able to see how the pupil writes when there is no time pressure and he is actually trying to produce good writing, when he is writing in his usual manner, and when pressure is applied to write fast. There is general agreement that the material used in producing written specimens should: contain a vocabulary that is familiar to the writer so there will be no difficulty with spelling or pause due to lack of comprehension; contain most or, preferably, all the letters of the alphabet; and be copied or memorized by the writer. A sentence that meets the requirements and has been used frequently is "The quick brown fox jumps over the lazy dog."

When the sentence to be written has been selected, the procedure for obtaining specimens of "usual," "best," and "fastest" writing is quite simple.

First, the pupils should be able to see the sentence, say "The quick brown fox jumps over the lazy dog," on the board and to read it over several times in order to become familiar with it.

Then the teacher can give the instructions for the "usual" sample: "Write the sentence five (more or less, depending upon pupil's age level) times. Try to write as you usually do." A two- or three-minute sample of writing should be obtained; of course the number of times children can write the sentence in that amount of time will vary greatly. It should be clear, too, that this should be but one kind of sample of "usual" writing. The prime source of examples of "usual" writing is the writing produced to meet day-to-day needs.

After a period of relaxation, the teacher can give the instructions for the "best" sample: "Now I want to see how well you can write. Take all the time you need and write the sentence three times in your very best handwriting."

After another period of relaxation, the teacher can give the instructions for the "fastest" sample: "Now I want to see how fast you can write. I am going to give you three minutes to write the sentence as many times as you can. Write as fast as you can and I will tell you when to stop."

When the three controlled samples have been obtained, the teacher has a basis for comparing handwriting produced under differing conditions. Scales and norms such as those described earlier make it possible to determine whether the samples meet the minimum standards that have been adopted at the local level. Inspection of the "usual," "best," and "fastest" samples makes it possible for the teacher to identify those pupils who are unable to meet minimum standards of speed and/or legibility and those whose quality of writing deteriorates markedly under speed pressure. Pupils so identified can then be scheduled for specific diagnosis of their difficulties. It will be found that some pupils who typically produce handwriting of inferior quality are able to produce "best" handwriting that is clearly acceptable. Normally, such children are not remedial cases and every attempt should be made to deal with them, especially by helping them to build motivation to write better, in the regular writing period and in other situations demanding written work.

Specific Diagnosis and Remedial Teaching

Once pupils with inadequate writing skills have been located, diagnosis moves to the specific level, where the focus is upon immediate causes for the poor performance and corrective-remedial instruction is provided as needed. Here we shall consider sources of handwriting difficulties, special problems of the left-handed writer, specific approaches to correcting specific difficulties, and the need for establishing realistic levels of aspiration.

Remedial teaching in handwriting must be individualized to be effective. Typical penmanship drills are of virtually no value as a remedial device. The pupil who is deficient in handwriting needs help in recognizing his individual weaknesses and a plan for overcoming them. Effective teaching of remedial handwriting, then, combines specific diagnosis with individualized teaching. The aim of the remedial teaching is to help the pupil to become independent in evaluating and improving his own writing.

Sources of Difficulty in Handwriting

Gertrude Hildreth (1936) made a very succinct summary of the sources of difficulty in handwriting in the first edition of her book, *Learning the 3 R's*. Her statement has been a guide for many subsequent discussions and it serves as a basis for the present discussion.

Deficiencies in handwriting may be associated with a wide range of factors. In general, they fall into two main groups: factors that are inherent in the writer, and factors that arise from inadequacies of the instructional program.

Under factors inherent in the writer, Hildreth lists the following (the comments in brackets are ours):

a. Inaptitude for learning motor and language skills. [Sometimes this may be due to lack of readiness.]

b. Unstable and erratic temperament.

c. Disinclination to practice. [No doubt the often observed indifference to minimum standards of neatness and legibility is closely related to *b* and *c.*]

d. Difficulty in retaining visual impressions. [It appears that two aspects may be involved here: faculty perception—which may be due to visual defects or other perceptual deficiencies or both—and faulty imagery. In either case the pupil's ability accurately to recall letter form models is impaired and the result is inefficient reproduction of letter forms in handwriting.]

e. Left-handedness and ambidexterity. [Left-handedness will be discussed later. It appears that the awkward positions often assumed by left-handers contribute more to poor writing than left-handedness per se. Ambidexterity, however, may indicate the presence of directional confusion due to a lack of either left or right dominance.]

f. Defective vision necessitating glasses, especially for astigmatism.

g. Paralytic, spastic, crippled conditions.

Under factors arising from inadequacies in the instructional program, the following are listed by Hildreth:

a. Too early, forced instruction. [This is, of course, the opposite side of the coin to readiness, which is an individual factor.]

b. Complete lack of supervision.

c. Uniform, undifferentiated group drills. [Included here would be such things as slavish devotion to a highly formalized system of handwriting instruction, refusal to recognize and provide for individual differences, and lack of provision of adjusted goals that are suitable for and attainable by individual pupils.]

d. Practice of error. [Lack of diagnosis and remediation as an integral part of the total instructional program is implied here. An adequate instructional program provides for constant diagnosis to uncover and correct errors as they arise.]

e. Inappropriate writing materials, pencils, pens, paper.

f. Incorrect position of paper. [This is an especially important factor for the left-handed writer and will be discussed later.]

g. Transition from one style of writing to another. [Poorly planned transition from manuscript to cursive writing can seriously interfere with the development of handwriting skill.]

h. Neglect of writing practice in high school.

All of the above factors should be considered when an attempt is made to uncover the causes of handwriting difficulties and to outline a plan of remedial teaching. It should also be kept in mind that poor handwriting may be closely related to difficulties in other basic skill areas. A child who is severely disabled in reading, for example, may also be poor in handwriting. The common difficulty may be that the child has failed to learn to differentiate letter forms efficiently, with the result that he can neither decipher nor produce written symbols with much success. Lack of success in reading, too, may give rise to strong negative feelings toward everything connected with reading and the manipulation of visual symbols. It can also be observed that some pupils actively attempt to hide their spelling errors behind a facade of illegible handwriting. In some cases such interrelationships among skill deficiencies will be uncovered only by intensive, case study diagnosis.

The Left-Handed Writer

The child who is left-handed or who has not yet firmly established handedness when handwriting instruction begins needs individualized help as badly as any child who has been identified as a remedial case. As Freeman (1954) has pointed out, in the past it was often tacitly assumed that all children were right-handed and left-handers were left to shift for themselves. Left to their own devices many of them developed an awkward, hooked writing position because they attempted to place their paper in the normal position for right-handers. At the present time, we have every reason to believe that left-handedness is a natural and inherited trait of a small minority of children. With a minimum of individualized instruction, they can learn to write comfortably and well. Since the best way of keeping left-handers from becoming remedial cases is to provide special instruction early, we shall present a rationale for left-handed writing here, despite the fact that it is not strictly a remedial technique.

There is general agreement that a child who shows a strong preference for left-handed writing should be permitted to use his left hand. Occasionally, however, children in the early primary grades will appear to have no clear preference for either hand, and they may tend to change hands from time to time. Again, the present consensus is that such children may be encouraged to use their right hand with no ill effects; better still, they should be encouraged to make a choice. Both informal tests, such as observation of choice of hand in varied activities, and formal tests, such as the *Harris Tests of Lateral Dominance, Revised* (Psychological Corporation), may be useful to the teacher as he attempts to round out his understanding of a child's true hand preference.

Once a child has been clearly identified as being left-handed, he may need some assurance that left-handedness is quite normal. However, he should be helped to understand that being left-handed makes it necessary to do some things a bit differently and that, in handwriting, instructions intended for right-handers cannot be followed. If proper movement and a comfortable position are to be allowed, seating is of great importance: the left-hander should be given a left-hand arm chair or be seated at the outside at a work table. Insofar as it is possible, handwriting instruction to both left- and right-handers in a single group should be avoided and left-handed children should be seated together in order to prevent their emulating the movements and positions of right-handed pupils.

Proper position is of prime importance to the left-handed writer and it differs in some important respects from the proper position for right-handers. A fairly long pencil should be held loosely between the thumb and index finger, resting just below the first joint of the middle finger. The pencil should be gripped about an inch from the tip; this will permit the writer to see what he has written. The upper part of the pencil should rest in the cleft formed by the thumb and index finger. All of the grip fingers should be curved slightly, with the weight of the hand resting squarely on the outside of the hand and the outside of the little finger. The eraser of the pencil will then point directly at the left shoulder. If, however, the left-hander persists in pointing the eraser away from the left shoulder—in a somewhat vertical position—the paper should be canted so the bottom is somewhat left of vertical. "Hooking" the hand is a natural tendency and it should be anticipated. The hooking can be controlled quite effectively by helping the pupil to find the proper amount of slant for his paper. Normally, when the left-hander's paper is slanted opposite to the right-handed position the left-hander is able to assume a natural, "unhooked" and comfortable writing position.

In manuscript writing, where the strokes are primarily vertical and straight lines, both right- and left-handed pupils are probably best advised to place the paper squarely in front of them. In cursive writing, the paper should be canted to the left or right, depending upon hand preference. A certain amount of backslant is natural in the left-hander's writing, and a moderate back slant should be permitted in cursive writing. Extreme back slant, however, tends to be illegible, so the tendency must be controlled. In some cases it is advisable to defer the transition from manuscript to cursive writing for the left-hander; sometimes it may be desirable to permit him to remain with manuscript writing indefinitely. As always, the teacher needs to exercise judgment based upon careful observations of pupil behavior.

Again, insofar as it is possible, the teacher should attempt to show the left-handed child what to do rather than merely tell him. A good point to keep in mind is the fact that while the right-hander *pulls* his pen across the page, the left-hander *pushes*. The most natural tendency for the left-hander would be to write from right to left, which would result in mirror writing. A right-handed teacher needs to expend some energy, both physical and psychological, if he hopes to understand and to help the left-handed pupil. Finally, it is interesting to note the results of a study by Smith and Reed (1959). They found no support for the notion that left-handers necessarily write more slowly than right-handers. To the contrary, they found that neither handedness nor sex affected the performance of handwriting tasks as much as did the schools from which the subjects for their study were drawn. More recently, Groff (1963) also reported no difference in the writing rate of left- and right-handed pupils in grades four through six.

Some left-handers will show up in the upper grades as remedial cases because they never received proper early instruction and have, therefore, developed an extreme back slant, a hooked writing position, or other faulty characteristics. Sometimes adaptations in position can be fairly easily made with resultant improvement in handwriting quality. It is unrealistic, however, to expect that all—or even a majority—of left-handers in the upper grades will be readily able to make major adaptations in their handwriting position: this involves a good deal of unlearning and relearning. Instead, it may be necessary to accept less-than-ideal positions and to work at improving the formation of letters and other factors that enhance legibility.

Correcting Specific Difficulties

In handwriting it is usually possible to pinpoint very precisely the causes for illegibilities; when this has been done remedial teaching can be directed toward the removal of the causes. Hunnicutt and Iverson (1958) have stated it well: "Generalized teaching of writing as a whole to children as a total class is much less efficient than pinpointed teaching" (p. 264). Research studies have been very useful in helping to focus attention upon the common causes of illegibility and faulty letter formations. Two studies in particular have emerged as classics in the field, and they will serve as the basis for our discussion of specific diagnosis and remedial help where the primary problem is lack of quality in handwriting. Overcoming inadequacies in speed of writing will be discussed separately.

An early study by Newland (1932) demonstrates the encouraging fact that a very few types or errors account for a great proportion of the illegibilities in handwriting. Newland examined handwriting samples of 2,381 people, ranging from elementary school age to adult; 24 judges read the samples and recorded each time that "they encountered something in their reading of the specimens which made them stop and look a second time at what they were reading in order to determine what the writer meant." In all, 42,284 specific illegibilities were recorded and these included 499 different forms of illegibilities. Yet, a very small number of frequently appearing forms of illegibilities accounted for 50 percent of all illegibilities at all levels studied: elementary, high school, and adult. Table 5 (p. 356) makes this point explicitly clear.

Newland also grouped the different illegibilities by common types of errors in the writing process. The grouping is summarized in Table 6. By using the most common types of errors as a basis for diagnosis and subsequent remedial help, the remedial teacher can focus upon a relatively small number of faulty habits out of the large number of possibilities. It is interesting to note that such often-lamented practices as Types 21, 22, and 23 (see Table 6, p. 357) cause virtually no illegibility problems.

TABLE 5

The most frequent forms of illegibilities accounting for approximately
50 percent of all illegibilities among lower-case letters, their frequencies, and the
percentages they contributed to all illegibilities

	Elementary			*High School*			*Adult*			*Total*	
Fr.	Percent	Form	Fr.	Percent	Form	Fr.	Percent	Form	Fr.	Percent	Form
145	11	*e* closed*	373	11	*e* closed	882	18	*e* closed	473	15	*e* closed
81	6	*d* like *cl*	265	8	*t* like *l*	363	7	*n* like *u*	155	5	*n* like *u*
56	4	*a* like *o*	152	5	*a* like *u*	216	4	*d* like *cl*	148	5	*d* like *cl*
47	3	*a* like *u*	146	4	*d* like *cl*	200	4	*i,* no dot	131	4	*t* like *l*
45	3	*a* like *ci*	120	4	*r* like *i*	188	4	*a* like *o*	114	4	*r* like *i*
42	3	*t,* cross above	94	3	*i,* no dot	185	4	*r* like *i*	111	4	*i,* no dot
41	3	*r* like *i*	91	3	*o* like *a*	182	4	*t,* cross above	103	3	*a* like *o*
36	3	*b* like *li*	84	3	*h* like *li*	151	3	*k* like *li*	102	3	*a* like *u*
35	3	*t* like *l*	63	2	*r* like *s*	148	3	*t,* cross right	93	3	*t,* cross above
35	3	*i,* no dot	55	2	*t,* cross right		51		88	3	*h* like *li*
34	2	*r* like half *n*	53	2	*r* like half *n*				68	2	*b* like *li*
33	2	*o* like *a*	52	2	*t,* too short					51	
30	2	*h* like *li*	50	2	*n* like *u*						
27	2	*n* like *u*	50	2	*d* like *cl*						
	50			53							

| (14 of 279 forms) | (14 of 264 forms) | (9 of 220 forms) | (1 of 498 forms) |

*This means that "*e* closed" occurred 145 times in every 100,000 running letters written at the elementary level and
accounted for 11 percent of all illegibilities at that level.

A later study by Quant (1946) supplements the Newland study. Quant
set out to determine what effect, if any, irregularities in each of the following characteristics have upon the legibility of handwriting: letter formation,
spacing, alignment, slant, and quality of line. The characteristics named are
those which are commonly stressed in handwriting programs in the belief
that they reflect quality in handwriting. Quant produced a number of
handwriting specimens which contained various types of irregularities in
the five characteristics; and degree of legibility was measured by the rate
and accuracy with which thirty-five adults could read the specimens while
their eye movements were being photographed.

On the basis of eye-movement photographs the following conclusions
were warranted:

1. The most important factor in determining the legibility of handwriting
is good letter formation.

2. To a lesser degree, the compactness of handwriting affects its legibility
as measured by eye-movement photography. That is, the reduction of spacing
between letters and words tends to decrease the number of fixations required
to read the shortened line and, thus, it can be read more quickly than
"normal" writing or writing with longer spacing between letters and words.
Further study is probably needed to determine how much compactness makes
for optimum readability.

TABLE 6

Analysis of letter malformations

Type	Percentages Contributed			
	Elementary	High School	Adult	Total
1 Failure to close letters (*a, b, f, g, j, k, o, p, q, s, y, z*)	24	20	16	18
2 Top loops closed (*l* like *t, e* like *i*)	13	14	20	18
3 Looping nonlooped strokes (*i* like *e*)	12	27	12	16
4 Using straight up-strokes rather than rounded strokes (*n* like *u, c* like *i, h* like *li*)	11	10	15	13
5 End stroke difficulty (not brought up, not brought down, not left horizontal)	11	6	9	9
6 Difficulty crossing *t*	5	5	9	7
7 Difficulty dotting *i*	3	5	5	5
8 Top short (*b, d, f, h, k, l, t*)	6	7	3	5
9 Letters too small	4	5	4	4
10 Closing *c, h, r, u, v, w, y*	4	3	3	3
11 Part of letter omitted	4	4	3	3
12 Up-stroke too long	2	3	1	2
13 Letters too large	2	1	—*	1
14 Beginning stroke off line	—	3	1	1
15 Bottom short (*f, g, j, q, y, z*)	2	1	—	1
16 Using rounded up-strokes instead of straight ones (*i* like *e, u* like *ee*)	—	1	2	1
17 Down-loop turned incorrectly	1	1	1	1
18 Excessive flourishes	—	1	1	1
19 Part added to letter	—	—	1	1
20 Down-stroke too long	1	1	—	—
21 Up-loop turned incorrectly	—	—	—	—
22 Down-loop closed	—	—	—	—
23 Printing	—	—	—	—
24 Palmer *r*	2	1	—	—
25 Unrecognizably recorded	2	1	3	3
26 Unclassified	10	9	9	9

*The dashes represent frequencies which accounted for less than one-half of one percent of the total.

3. Evenness of alignment was found to be not important in legibility.

4. The regularity of slant was found to be significant; when slant is irregular, legibility is decreased.

5. Findings regarding the influence of weight of line (fine or heavy) upon legibility were inconclusive, although there was some evidence that a light increased the average number of words that could be read per fixation.

The results of Quant's study have clear implications regarding factors to be stressed in remedial teaching that is designed to increase legibility.

Teachers who want a more formalized method of making a diagnostic inventory of specific difficulties in legibility may find one or more of these diagnostic handwriting charts useful: *Minneapolis Self-Corrective Hand-writing Charts* (Farnham Printing and Stationery), the *Freeman Chart for Diagnosing Faults in Handwriting* (Houghton Mifflin), the *Pressey Chart for Diagnosis of Illegibilities in Handwriting* (Public School Publishing), and the *West Chart for Diagnosing Elements of Handwriting* (Public School Publishing). For most practical purposes, however, the Newland and Quant studies will provide all the guidance that is needed.

Lewis and Lewis (1965) have reported a study of errors in the formation of manuscript letters by first-grade children. Their study does for manuscript writing what the Newland and Quant studies have done for cursive writing. The following findings from the Lewis and Lewis study can serve to focus both diagnostic and remedial efforts in the early, pretransition grades.

1. The most frequent type of error was *incorrect size*. While the error was distributed among all letters, it was more frequent with the descenders, *p, q, y, q* and *j,* than with other forms.

2. The letter forms most frequently *reversed* were *N, d, q,* and *y.*

3. *Partial omission* occurred most frequently in *m, U,* and *I.*

4. *Additions* were most frequently with *q, C, k, m,* and *y.*

5. *Incorrect relationship of parts* was generally common, occurring most frequently with *k, R, M,* and *m.*

6. *Incorrect placement relative to line* was a common error with descenders and a less frequent error with the other letters.

7. The letter forms most frequently *misshaped* were *j, G,* and *J.*

8. In general, errors were most frequent in letter forms in which curves and vertical lines merge—*J, U, f, h, j, m, n, r, u;* errors were least frequent in in letter forms construed of vertical lines or horizontal and vertical lines—*E, F, H, I, L, T, i, l, t.*

Remedial help to improve speed, too, can be relatively uncomplicated and straightforward. To be efficient, handwriting must become "autom-atized," as Freeman (1954) put it. That is, the writer must become so skilled at the mechanics of writing that he need pay little attention to the how of writing. Only when a pupil has mastered the mechanics of producing handwriting is he ready to increase his speed. A pupil who typically produces handwriting slowly and laboriously, then, should be helped first to master the mechanics of handwriting. Once this has been done, most students respond well to a routine whereby their rate of writing is determined and compared to their grade norm, subsequent practice sessions are devoted to the gradual increase of speed, and increases are duly noted and praised. A few pupils appear to benefit from some sort of pacing, such as counting of strokes by the teacher.

To sum up, it should be clear that for most pupils remedial teaching in handwriting can be an uncomplicated process of helping them to remove specific causes of illegibilities and/or to increase their speed of writing. There seems to be little need for the generalized drills or esoteric practice routines that are sometimes suggested

Selected Instructional Materials

Many of the commercial handwriting systems already mentioned include remedial guidelines and materials that may be useful for specific purposes. Here we shall describe some supplementary materials that we have found to be particularly useful.

Alphabet 68 (Numark Educational Systems) is characterized by its publisher as "a new basic approach to modern handwriting." Designed as an ungraded approach for use in grades 3 through 12, it is recommended for use as (a) an introduction to cursive writing for beginners, (b) a refresher course for older pupils, or (c) a remedial program for pupils with problems. The basic and, to us, appealing feature of the *Alphabet 68* approach is that it introduces simplified letters in a stroke-by-stroke sequence; only after pupils become thoroughly familiar with the simple forms are the "traditional" letter forms introduced. The approach, which is presented in an attractive sixty-eight-page booklet, is built on the assumptions that schools have less time to devote to formal penmanship and that only a practical self-help procedure will help keep pupils interested. The procedures suggested make sense and they should prove to be useful to corrective-remedial teachers.

The Peterson Handwriting System (Macmillan) has introduced a sixty-four-page booklet titled *Improve Your Handwriting for Job Success,* with a foreword by Jackie Robinson. The booklet is addressed to older youth and adults and it stresses, in addition to the hard-sell motivational aspect, (a) proper position in writing, (b) proper grip of the writing instrument, and (c) the use of a "colorgraph" in teaching manuscript and cursive letter forms. The latter employs the color red in introducing new writing strokes and shows the sequence of strokes involved in producing each letter form. Applications of writing skills are provided for with blank forms that are important to adults: a social security application, employment forms, IRS exemption forms, etc. The booklet should be quite useful with upper grade and high school students.

In some cases a tracing, rather than copying, technique will prove to be useful. *Trac-a-bit* (Zaner Bloser) is a series of charts—both manuscript and cursive are available—on which the pupil traces model letter forms with a grease pencil. The charts are plastic coated, so they are reuseable. Space is also provided for the pupil to practice free-hand writing directly under the model that he traces first. In general, pupils who experience great difficulty in reproducing letter form models will profit from an opportunity to trace the letter forms as they are introduced.

Finally, two films, *Handwriting for Beginners: Manuscript* and *Improve Your Handwriting* (Coronet Films) may prove useful for motivational purposes. The first uses a fantasy story format to build motivation and to introduce good writing practice to beginners in the first and second grades. The latter stresses the importance of speed, clarity, and attractiveness in writing for junior and senior high school students.

Level of Aspiration

In order to improve their handwriting not only do pupils need to be motivated by seeing a need for improvement but they must also have a realistic perception of how they do in fact write and how they would like to write. Harris, Herrick, and Rarick (1961) found that fourth to sixth graders who served as subjects in a study had fairly stable aspirational models: they knew how they would like to write. But few of them could effectively arrange handwriting specimens in order of ease of reading (legibility); and they had great difficulty in rating their own handwriting samples, which were produced under different conditions and were clearly different in quality. The study points up the fact that middle-grade pupils may have great difficulty in modifying their writing to approximate aspired-to models; they would not know whether they are moving toward or away from the desired forms.

Clearly, some instructional effort needs to be expended in developing and encouraging the use of aspirational (how I would *like* to write) and normative (how I *do* write) models. Furner (1969a) has pointed out that this can be done, at least in part, by stressing the perceptual as well as the motor aspects of writing. Children who are aware of relatively small differences in letter forms are likely to be able to respond effectively to differences. They are likely, too, to be able to find and correct flaws that make for illegibilities. Pupils will benefit also from working with handwriting scales such as those provided in the *Penskills II* kit (Science Research Associates): pupils can match their writing to a given scaled sample and then move toward writing that approximates the next step on the scale. Much teacher guidance will, of course, be required at the early stages.

Intensive Diagnosis and Treatment

In some few cases, where pupils fail to respond to carefully planned remedial teaching, it may be desirable to probe more deeply. A formal case study, through which underlying causes for the handwriting difficulty are sought, can be undertaken. Such factors as these should be checked out: attempts to change handedness, difficulty with beginning instruction in handwriting, muscular and perceptual efficiency and functioning, general physical condition, presence of extreme nervousness, and emotional problems. Furthermore, the possible relationship of the handwriting disability to disability in one or more of the other basic skills should be considered. We have already mentioned the fact that performance in the several basic skill areas may be closely interrelated. If, for example, handwriting difficulties arise from a generally negative attitude toward language functions that is rooted in difficulties with reading and spelling as well as handwriting, then remedial help with handwriting alone is not likely to be successful. The information gathered in making a case study will help teachers to understand the writer and his problems. When the teacher understands the problems involved, he is in a position to be better able to devise a program of instruction designed to overcome the problems.

Callewaert (1963) has described a modified method of gripping the writing instrument that remedial teachers may find appropriate for use by certain pupils with a fairly severe problem in writing. The grip is recommended specifically to reduce muscle tension and fatigue in clinical cases of *hyperkenesia,* or writer's cramp. When the modified grip is employed, the shaft of the writing instrument is placed between the middle and index fingers— rather than between the thumb and index fingers as in the traditional grip— and the barrel is gripped with those fingers and the thumb. In writing, the wrist is canted more sharply than with the traditional grip. A brief tryout will demonstrate that the modified grip does indeed make it difficult to "choke" the pencil or to apply excessive pressure to the paper. The grip is easily mastered by normal writers to the point where writing speed and legibility are essentially similar to that achieved with the traditional grip (Otto, Armstrong, and Koepke, 1966). The grip is, according to Callewaert, particulary effective when combined with a flowing, rounded style of cursive writing.

THOUGHTS FOR DISCUSSION

"Because the tangible product (handwriting) has always been superseded by the content it conveys, and, more recently, because mechanical means for writing have been discovered, formal study of handwriting per se has often been bypassed. It is so common, so ordinary that the study of its history and development has been neglected." (Otto and Andersen, 1969, p. 570)

"The current status of research in spelling and handwriting is reflected in the continuing low level of interest and activity on the part of educators." (Horn, 1967, p. 168)

"The excellence of writing may be considered from the standpoint of either the writer or the reader. From the one point of view we consider the economy of production and from the other, economy in recognition." (Freeman, 1914, p. 118)

"The goal of handwriting instruction is to develop a tool of communication which can be used by a child or an adult to meet expressive needs with maximum efficiency in terms of legibility and speed and minimum effort in terms of time spent, concentration required, or physical effort expended." (Furner, 1970, p. 61)

"For whatever reason or combination of reasons, young adults write as they wish to write or as they find it convenient to write, regardless of the emphases on form and style through which they labored as children, and their handwriting will change still further as they grow to old age." (Strickland, 1969, p. 378)

"A great deal of time has been wasted on class drill in the past which might better have been spent on more library reading or other enriching experiences. Proof of this lies in the fact that the quality of writing done by high school and college students who had daily drill periods for handwriting in the elementary school is little or no better than the quality of writing of those who did not have such drill." (Strickland, 1969, p. 381)

". . . it is probably expedient for adults (in Adult Basic Education classes) to master both styles (manuscript and cursive) simultaneously, or at least very early in the sequence of their emerging literacy." (Otto and Ford, 1967, p. 139)

REFERENCES

Andersen, D. Handwriting research: movement and quality. In T. A. Horn (Ed.), *Research on handwriting and spelling*. Champaign, Ill.: National Council of Teachers of English, 1966, 9–17.

Ayres, L. P. *A scale for measuring the quality of handwriting in school children.* New York: Russell Sage Foundation, 1912.

Ayres, L. P. *Measuring scale for handwriting.* New York: Russell Sage Foundation, 1917.

Callewaert, H. For easy and legible handwriting. In V. E. Herrick (Ed.), *New horizons for research in handwriting*. Madison, Wis.: University of Wisconsin Press, 1963, 39–52.

Committee for Research in Basic Skills. *Comparison of practices in handwriting advocated by nineteen commercial systems of handwriting instruction.* Madison, Wis.: School of Education, University of Wisconsin, 1960.

Committee for Research in Handwriting. *Handwriting in Wisconsin: A survey of elementary school practices.* Madison, Wis.: School of Education, University of Wisconsin, 1951.

Enstrom, E. A. Decline of handwriting. *Elementary School Journal*, 1965, **66**, 22–27.

Enstrom, E. A. Print-handwriting today. *Elementary English*, 1964, **41**, 846–850.

Erlebacher, A., and Herrick, V. E. Quality of handwriting today and yesterday. *Elementary School Journal*, 1961, **62**, 89–93.

Freeman, F. N. *The teaching of handwriting.* Boston: Houghton Mifflin, 1914.

Freeman, F. N. An analytical scale for judging handwriting. *Elementary School Journal,* 1915, **15**, 432–441.

Freeman, F. N. Teaching handwriting. *What research says to the teacher.* Bulletin No. 4. Washington, D.C.: National Education Association, 1954.

Freeman, F. N. A new handwriting scale. *Elementary School Journal,* 1959, **59**, 218–221.

Furner, B. A. The perceptual-motor nature of learning in handwriting. *Elementary English,* 1969, **46**, 886–894. (a)

Furner, B. A. Recommended instructional procedures in a method emphasizing the perceptual-motor nature of learning in handwriting. *Elementary English,* 1969, **46**, 1021–1030. (b)

Furner, B. A. An analysis of the effectiveness of a program of instruction emphasizing the perceptual-motor nature of learning in handwriting. *Elementary English,* 1970, **47**, 61–69.

Gray, W. S. The teaching of reading and writing: An international survey. UNESCO, Monographs on Fundamental Education X. Chicago: Scott, Foresman, 1956.

Groff, P. J. Who writes faster: *Education,* 1963, **83**, 367–369.

Groff, P. J. New speeds in handwriting. *Elementary* English, 1961, **38**, 564–565. (Also in W. Otto and K. Koenke (Eds.), *Remedial teaching: Research and comment.* Boston: Houghton Mifflin, 1969)

Harris, T. L. Handwriting. In C. W. Harris (Ed.), *Encyclopedia of educational research.* (3rd ed.) New York: Macmillan, 1960.

Harris, T. L., Herrick, V. E., and Rarick, G. L. *Perception of symbols in skill learning by mentally retarded, gifted and normal children.* Project SAE 6436 extended to Project SAE 7135, U.S. Office of Health, Education and Welfare. Madison, Wis.: School of Education, University of Wisconsin, 1961.

Herrick, V. E. Handwriting and children's writing. *Elementary English,* 1960, **37**, 248–258.

Herrick, V. E. (Ed.), *New horizons for research in handwriting.* Madison, Wis.: University of Wisconsin Press, 1961.

Herrick, V. E., and Erlebacher, A. The evaluation of legibility in handwriting. In V. E. Herrick (Ed.), *New horizons for research in handwriting.* Madison, Wis.: University of Wisconsin Press, 1963, 207–236.

Herrick, V. E., and Okada, N. The present scene: practices in the teaching of handwriting in the U.S.—1960. In V. E. Herrick (Ed.), *New horizons for research in handwriting.* Madison, Wis.: University of Wisconsin Press, 1963, 17–38.

Herrick, V. E., and Otto, W. *Letter form models advocated by commercial handwriting systems.* Madison, Wis.: School of Education, University of Wisconsin, 1961.

Hildreth, G. *Learning the three r's.* Minneapolis: Educational Publishers, 1936.

Hildreth, G. Early writing as an aid to reading. *Elementary English,* 1963, **40,** 15-20. (a)

Hildreth, G. Simplified handwriting for today. *Journal of Educational Research,* 1963, **56,** 330–333. (b)

Horn, T. D. Handwriting and spelling. *Review of Educational Research,* 1967, **37,** 168–177.

Hunnicutt, G. W., and Iverson, W. J. (Eds.) *Research in the three r's.* New York: Harper and Row, 1958.

Lewis, E. R., and Lewis, H. P. An analysis of errors in the formation of manuscript letters by first-grade children. *American Educational Journal,* 1965, **2,** 25–35. (Also in W. Otto and K. Koenke (Eds.), *Remedial teaching: Research and comment.* Boston: Houghton Mifflin, 1969.)

Newland, T. E. An analytical study of the development of illegibilities in handwriting from the lower grades to adulthood. *Journal of Educational Research,* 1932, **26,** 249–258. (Also in W. Otto and K. Koenke (Eds.), *Remedial teaching: Research and comment.* Boston: Houghton Mifflin, 1969)

Otto, W., and Andersen, D. W. Handwriting. In R. L. Ebel and V. H. Noll (Eds.), *Encyclopedia of educational research.* (4th ed.) New York: Macmillan, 1969.

Otto, W., Askov, E., and Cooper, C. Legibility ratings for handwriting samples: A pragmatic approach. *Perceptual and Motor Skills,* 1967, **25,** 638. (Also in W. Otto and K. Koenke (Eds.), *Remedial teaching: Research and comment.* Boston: Houghton Mifflin, 1969.)

Otto, W., and Ford, D. H. *Teaching adults to read.* Boston: Houghton Mifflin, 1967.

Otto, W., and Koenke, K. *Remedial teaching: Research and comment.* Boston: Houghton Mifflin, 1969.

Otto, W., and Rarick, G. L. Effect of time of transition from manuscript to cursive writing upon subsequent performance in handwriting, reading and spelling. *Journal of Educational Research,* 1969, **62,** 211–216.

Otto, W., Rarick, G. L., Armstrong, J., and Koepke, M. Evaluation of a modified grip in handwriting. *Perceptual and Motor Skills,* 1966, **22,** 310.

Petty, W. T. Handwriting and spelling: Their current status in the language arts curriculum. *Elementary English,* 1964, **41,** 839–845, 959.

Quant, L. Factors affecting the legibility of handwriting. *Journal of Experimental Education,* 1946, **14,** 297–316. (Also in W. Otto and K. Koenke (Eds.), *Remedial teaching: Research and comment.* Boston: Houghton Mifflin, 1969.)

Smith, A. C., and Reed, F. G. An experimental investigation of the relative speeds of left- and right-handed writers. *Journal of Genetic Psychology,* 1959, **94,** 67–76.

Smith, E. H. *Literacy education for adolescents and adults.* San Francisco: Boyd and Fraser, 1970.

Strickland, R. G. Language arts in the elementary school. (3rd ed.) Lexington: D. C. Heath, 1969.

Tagatz, G. E., Otto, W., Klausmeier, H. J., Goodwin, W. L., and Cook, D. M. Effect of three methods of instruction upon the handwriting performance of third- and fourth-graders. *American Educational Research Journal,* 1968, **5,** 81–90. (Also in W. Otto and K. Koenke (Eds.), *Remedial teaching: Research and comment.* Boston: Houghton Mifflin, 1969.)

Templin, E. Research and comment: Handwriting, the neglected R. *Elementary English,* 1960, **37,** 386–389.

Tiegs, E. W., and Clark, W. W. *California achievement tests, elementary.* Monterey, Calif.: California Test Bureau, 1957.

West, P. V. *Handwriting: Elements of diagnosis and judgment of handwriting* and *Chart for diagnosing elements in handwriting* Bloomington, Ill.: Public School Publishing, 1926.

West, P. V. *Manual for the American handwriting scale.* New York: A. N. Palmer, 1957.

Chapter 14

Oral and Written Expression

We have advocated an integrated approach to language arts instruction throughout this book. Our rationale for favoring this approach is that reading, writing, speaking, and listening are all language processes; and when they are developed simultaneously, they are mutually reinforcing. In addition, activity in one of the language arts may serve as a stimulus to motivate activity in another of the arts. A good story, for example, may spark the desire to talk or write about one of the characters or the outcome of the plot. Our discussion of instructional approaches for improving the speaking and writing ability of students who are weak in these two skills, therefore, will emphasize the need for carefully planned reading and listening experiences to motivate students to communicate their ideas and feelings orally and in writing.

For several reasons we will not discuss different levels of diagnosis in this chapter as we did in the chapters devoted to other skill areas. First, standardized instruments for diagnosing speaking and writing deficiencies are often based on language standards more contrived than real and generally do not give more information than informal assessments. Secondly, the basic causes of speaking and writing deficiencies are closely related to the basic causes of reading and listening deficiencies, and diagnosis at the intensive level would be concerned with essentially the same causal factors for problems in all four areas. And finally, the remedial approaches we advocate emphasize the strengthening of specific skills in a context of overall language growth rather than as isolated components. Improvement in oral and written expression is effected best by exposure to good models and personal interactions in situations arranged to facilitate inductive learning and to nurture general language development. Therefore, we feel that a delineation of different procedures for different levels of diagnosing speaking and writing disabilities would not be practical and might be misleading.

Although we are not delineating different levels of diagnosis for speaking and writing, we do favor careful observations of pupils' total language development to ascertain the instructional practices likely to be most beneficial to their speaking and writing development at any given time. These observations, however, should always consider above all the effectiveness of a pupil's communication in terms of his purpose, his message, and his audience in specific situations. In other words, the diagnostic information obtained by asking a pupil to punctuate certain types of sentences, compose a paragraph around a topic sentence, identify parts of speech, or present a three-minute persuasive speech to the class may be more misleading than helpful in assessing his actual speaking and writing abilities and needs. The difference between performing the component tasks that comprise speech and writing and communicating effectively in various contexts is considerable.

In addition, we recommend that all diagnoses of the writing and speaking deficiencies of students who express their ideas poorly be conducted in a highly personal way and that comparing a disabled student's performance to a standardized scale be avoided. In taking this stand we are assuming that corrective and remedial teachers have enough background in language and language development to operate from the highly individual and personal base that language development demands and that they do not need to rely upon or aim their instructional programs at group standards or norms. The information provided in this chapter and some further study of the references cited within the chapter should be sufficient to give corrective and remedial teachers the background they need. Our discussion of students with speaking deficiencies does not include children who have problems with the production of sounds. This is a matter for speech therapists and is outside the scope of the present chapter.

LEARNING AND USING THE ENGLISH LANGUAGE

All language is basically oral and functions in a systematic way for communication purposes. Writing systems derive from the need for people to record their oral communication. The English language accordingly comprises systems or rules for oral and written communication among people who have learned to respond in a predictable way to signals transmitted by fellow users of their language. For example, a reader of English could be expected to bring home the family meal if he complied with the following written request: "Would you please stop at the store on your way home and pick up the groceries I ordered?" Or, "I ordered the groceries. Would you please stop at the store on your way home and pick them up." On the other hand, dinner would be in jeopardy if the following were written: "up the home ordered pick I stop groceries would please you the at your store way on and." If the message were given orally to a forgetful husband the word *please* might be stressed to insure delivery and to chide him for past memory lapses. Or the voice might be perceptibly lowered on the word *please* for the same effect. However, if the word *home* were emphasized the husband would be urged not to secure the groceries on his way to work, perhaps because ice cream was one of the commodities ordered. The point is that the English language in both its oral and written forms is flexible, but only to a degree. Beyond certain limits communication is impaired.

Native speakers of a language learn the basic systems of their tongue without formal instruction. The purpose of remedial instruction in speaking and writing for native users of the language is not to teach them their language as if it were foreign to them, but rather to help them improve their communication within the constraints imposed by the systems of their language which they already know.

Language Development

Language must be learned. The infant who is deprived of language models will emit sounds from his physiological apparatus but will not refine those sounds into intelligible language. Language development, then, is dependent upon verbal interaction. Gleason (1969) says,

> Considering how much there is to learn, it is amazing how quickly children learn to speak. During their first year, babies spend much time listening to adults talk. They also make all sorts of strange sounds. Since babies do not know ahead of time what language they are going to grow up speaking, it is not surprising that they come equipped and ready to learn any of the world's languages. . . . In an English speaking community, the baby begins to utter English sound syllables with English-sounding intonation. (P. 16)

Each individual has the potential to learn his language rapidly and effectively. Loban (1963) found that when children enter kindergarten their speech closely approximates the speech of adults in their communities. They have internalized the rules of their grammar and can produce questions, descriptions, and narratives that are easily understood by their culture group. In addition, they are naturally eager to use their language to communicate their experiences to others unless this natural inclination has been stifled. Smith, Goodman, and Meredith (1970) say,

> The individual has the potential for extremely rapid and widespread language extension, but this is not to say the growth cannot be blocked, slowed, inhibited, or distorted. . . . If the expanding of his world through language is discouraged in the classroom and in the home, the child will take it to the playground and the street—although he may run the risk of cutting himself off from the most highly civilized aspects of his culture for the sake of vitality. . . . *A child's language development can be stunted whether he lives in a restricted ghetto, in a protected suburb, or in an isolated farm community.* (P. 8)

Corrective and remedial teachers are concerned with students whose language development has been stifled either during the preschool years or after they have begun their school learning. Students whose expressive powers have been stifled have stopped communicating in situations that would extend their language development; and they have, therefore, withdrawn from interactions with effective language users. The primary task facing the teacher of students who are deficient in oral and written expression is to reopen the developmental process by exposing them to good models and by motivating them to interact in natural language situations in which the objective is to communicate ideas and feelings effectively. To accomplish this task the child with poor speaking and writing ability must be motivated to move from his present stage of development to more refined stages without fear or embarrassment that he will be "incorrect" along the way. Lefevre (1970) says, "If dialect change is to be effected, each individual speaker must first volunteer to make the change himself. No captive audience in an American classroom, no captive people in a conquered land, have ever been forced to change their language without their consent; language change must be motivated, because it cannot be forced" (p. 9).

Dialectal Differences

The once widely held idea that there is a standard or correct English language toward which all users of the language should strive is no longer accepted. Effective communication occurs among speakers of a particular dialect although their grammar and usage do not conform to the grammar and usage of speakers of a different dialect. Currently, linguists are urging teachers to accept the reality of language differences without identifying one dialect as being superior to all others for communication purposes. The difference between "See can he go" is as natural and communicative to some listeners as "See if he can go" is to other listeners. The issue is not one of communication but of social acceptability by the greater English-speaking community. Smith, Goodman, and Meredith (1970) say,

> Perhaps the greatest handicap to more effective language programs in the schools has been the mistaken assumption that language that deviates from the standard (however defined) is bad, sloppy, or ineffective. . . . Children who do not speak high-status American English have language that has been adequate to their needs up to the time of school beginning. That same language continues to be an effective means of communication in the child's daily life, outside of school. This effectiveness is increased and the dialect is reinforced through contact with adults and peers in the subculture group. The teacher may say that "I done it" is wrong, but the subculture says over and over again to the child that "I done it" is right. It is only when the child comes into increasing contact with other subcultures and the general culture that his language may become less inadequate for his changing needs. (P. 49)

As the child removes himself, then, from his particular subculture, he must learn the dialect of his new group or suffer social disapproval. He learns this new dialect most effectively by increasingly frequent verbal exchanges with members of his new culture group. The deductive teaching of rules for "correct" oral and written expression has not proved effective in changing the language patterns of users of divergent dialects to patterns that are more acceptable for educated speakers of English.

Levels of Acceptability

The effective user of a language is able to vary his speech and writing according to different audiences and different communication situations. The vocabulary, syntax, and intonation a teacher uses to register a complaint at a faculty meeting is likely to be far different from the language she uses to complain to her family about the lack of cooperation she receives in keeping the house clean. A quick note written to a friend to suggest a golf game does not and should not look like a memo from the superintendent to all teaching staff. Social norms that regulate verbal interchange in various situations do exist, and speakers and writers must abide by them or suffer social censure.

Teachers must realize that giving a child the power to vary his language for different social settings is not a simple matter of correcting his "mistakes." Smith, Goodman, and Meredith (1970) say,

> When a child enters school he brings to it five or six years of language and experience. Because his world, prior to entering school, has been largely confined to his family, his home, and his immediate neighborhood, both his language and experience are heavily rooted in his subculture. The language he speaks is his mother's tongue. No matter what other language learning he achieves in his lifetime, the first one is most deeply rooted. (P. 48)

The first function of the school is to accept each child's language as a basic personal characteristic and then to introduce the child slowly and without trauma to more socially acceptable language for expressing his experiences. Children who are made ashamed of their speech and writing will avoid expressing themselves; when this happens, pupils who are in need of the most speaking and writing experiences in school will receive the least. Lefevre (1970) says,

> Anyone who attacks or appears to attack an individual's dialect is immediately understood to be attacking the person himself, attacking him and his very way of life; this is doubly true if the attacker is a teacher, a powerful official who may represent an alien, even a threatening way of life. A teacher who peremptorily undertakes to alter deeply ingrained language habits can inflict irreparable damage. . . . The student's natural dialect, unchanged, can be his immediate bridge to the skills of literacy; the teacher should not bewilder him in his initial approach to literacy by attempting to force him to learn a new dialect as a prerequisite. (P. 8)

We discuss different levels of usage and ways of helping children acquire acceptable levels of usage later in this chapter.

SPEAKING AND WRITING

Some Similarities

Projection.   Speaking and writing are both projector skills. As such they have some similar characteristics. For example, both require the formulation of a message in the mind of the speaker or writer; the transmission of that message using words, gestures, intonation, or punctuation; an anticipated audience; and a purpose for sending the message. Moffett (1968b) says,

> Within the relation of the speaker to his listener lie all the issues by which we have recently enlarged the meaning of "rhetoric"—what A wishes to do by speaking of such and such a subject to B. Within the relation of the speaker to his subject lie all the issues of the abstractive process—how the speaker has symbolically processed certain raw phenomena. But of course these two relations are in turn related: "what" and "what for" are factors of each other. As with all trinities, the relations of persons is a unity—somebody—talking-to—somebody—about something. (P. 10)

Thinking. Speaking and writing both are activities that require and improve thinking. Adler (1940) says, "Thinking usually tends to express itself overtly in language. One tends to verbalize ideas, questions, difficulties, judgements that occur in the course of thinking" (p. 111). Most people have experienced the clarification of a thought that occurs when telling it to someone else. Teachers who proclaim that they "didn't really understand it until they taught it" are giving testimony to speaking as a sharpener of thought. About writing, Burack (1965) says, "We ask our students to write because writing makes them think. . . . Writing is ultimately an exercise in logic. . . . For some of our students writing will mean the freeing of the intellect. For some it will be the disciplining of that intellect" (p. 505).

Evaluating Thinking. Speaking and writing may both be used to aid in the evaluation of pupils' thinking. Teachers who include private conferences in their evaluation programs are often amazed at the shallowness of some pupils' learning as evidenced by their inability to discuss subjects they have supposedly mastered. In some instances students are found who have completely misinterpreted certain subject matter or accepted an opinion as a fact. Essay tests, if evaluated carefully, are often helpful to the teacher who wants to find out how much his pupils really know.

Some Differences

Speaking precedes writing as a developmental ability and for most people retains its advantage in helping them express themselves. The importance of speech over writing for communication purposes cannot be questioned. With rare exception, people use speaking more than writing in their daily activities.

Intonation. The speaker of English has communication "aids" not available to the writer of English. The English intonation system permits speakers to express meanings through variations of rate, stress, and juncture that the punctuation system does not make possible. Many linguists refer to the use of tone of voice or intonation to communicate meaning as "paralanguage." The writer of English must rely upon his reader's sense of English intonations and write with a style that prompts his reader to supply the intonation patterns for which English has no definite graphic symbols. Lefevre (1970) describes the process as follows:

> Just as the speaker imparts a stress-timed rhythm to his speech, so does the writer impart a corresponding rhythm to the graphic counterparts of speech; stress-timed rhythm is inherent in the English language, both spoken and written. The reader picks up the writer's rhythm by an empathy parallel with that of the auditor and the speaker; that is, the reader identifies with the writer (as speaker) and empathizes with the muscular stress-pulse beat of the language patterns written down by the writer. In short, the reader responds to the rhythm of written and printed language in the same way as the auditor responds to the rhythm of spoken language; the rhythm of written English may indeed be stronger and more regular, because the composing process allows for painstaking construction and revision of wording. (P. 231)

The writer, then, must compose his message so that his reader will have adequate cues to the intonation intended.

Kinesics. Kinesics is the name given to the bodily movements that accompany oral discourse. Hand gestures, shoulder shrugs, finger pointing, head nodding, and other overt behaviors that accompany a speaker's delivery all help him to get his ideas across. The fact that many complex ideas can be communicated through pantomime without any recourse to words is testimony to the communicative power of bodily movement. In combination with the spoken word bodily movement is a highly effective and indeed natural way to communicate. It is a communication aid not available to writers.

Audience Feedback. A speaker is guided as he talks by the signals he receives from his audience. Raised eyebrows, smiles, frowns, questions, grunts of approval or disapproval, all cue him to clarify, repeat, emphasize, or de-emphasize his words. As a matter of fact, speakers of English have developed definite language patterns which are used to give other speakers immediate feedback (e.g., "uh-huh," "you don't say," "really," "I see," "Well I'll be."). Essentially, these say, "I'm listening and I understand," or, "I don't understand," "I approve," or "I don't approve what you are saying." The good speaker is alert to these signals and uses them as guidelines to help him convey his message according to his intended purpose. The writer, of course, does not receive immediate feedback from his audience. He must wait an indeterminate period of time before he knows the effect of his words. It is not uncommon for writers to find that readers have misinterpreted their meaning and have been confused or misinformed rather than enlightened. The intent of many written messages is misperceived because the author has not had the advantage of knowing the effect his words are having on his readers. He cannot immediately correct a faulty interpretation but must rely upon his writing skill to maintain a clear communication. When his writing skill fails to make his message clear he must suffer the results of misinterpretation. And unless he is given some feedback from his audience he will be unable to correct the misinterpretation and improve his future writing.

Time Element. Speakers must formulate their thoughts and express them much more rapidly than writers. A person writing a message usually has time for reflection before putting his ideas on paper, and, he has the additional advantage of reading his written product and revising it until it is satisfactory to him. Once a word is spoken to a listener an impression is made. A poorly chosen word or intonation pattern often has a lasting effect regardless of the speaker's assurance that "What I meant to say . . ." was something different from what he in fact said. Good writers keep a dictionary and other references nearby to help them choose their words wisely and check their facts. Speakers are usually extemporizing and must rely completely upon their background experience for the content of their messages and their intuitive sense of the language for their pronunciation and phrasing.

Development of the Message. In most communication situations speech is a give-and-take affair. A lecturer or public speaker may organize his talk and deliver it from start to finish without interruption. Most speaking situations, however, require the speaker to develop his message as he delivers it and to field questions and respond to comments and other reactions relative to his statements as he makes them. Consequently, speakers are diverted from their intended delivery by interruptions that writers never experience.

Handwriting and Spelling. The writer of English must have control of the English handwriting and spelling systems. This imposes a burden upon writers that is not shared by speakers. Putting ideas down on paper is especially difficult for students who have concomitant difficulties with handwriting and spelling.

IMPROVING SPEAKING AND WRITING ABILITY

From our discussion of the similarities and differences that exist between speaking and writing it follows that certain instructional practices may be employed to improve ability in both language arts and also that other instructional practices may be employed for each separately. In the remainder of this chapter we (1) discuss some guidelines for teaching that seem equally applicable to improving both speaking and writing ability, (2) suggest some specific instructional activities for improving pupils' speaking ability, and (3) suggest some specific instructional activities for improving pupils' writing ability. As is true of corrective and remedial teaching in other curriculum areas, the instructional materials and practices used to improve speaking and writing ability are generally not greatly different from those used in a regular developmental program.

Guidelines for Improving Speaking and Writing

Underlying all speaking and writing instruction for students who need extra attention given to their development in these two arts are the following guidelines.

1. Help students to see the value of improving their speaking and writing skills. Desire to improve is essential to communication improvement, and establishing this desire is the first and often the most difficult teaching task. Teachers who "force" instruction after their best efforts to motivate pupils have failed might more profitably focus their instructional efforts on an area of development for which the student is motivationally "ready" to receive instruction.

2. Recognize individual needs and aspirations regarding speaking and writing ability. Motivational appeals and instructional exercises must be varied to be relevant to pupils' unique personal characteristics. Writing "thank-you" notes and engaging in a business telephone call may or may not be meaningful exercises depending upon the individual pupil concerned. The sensitivity of the teacher to his pupils' perceptions of their communications needs is a vital element in improving their speaking and writing ability. A careful diagnosis of a student's habits, interests, and background experience is necessary to make decisions regarding the instructional program best suited to his needs.

3. Begin instruction at the pupil's current level of development. This, of course, demands a careful assessment of each child's abilities. A pupil who is having difficulty asking a question in class or talking in a conference with his teacher cannot be expected to engage in a debate or symposium successfully. Speaking and writing situations occur at various levels of sophistication. Teachers should avoid frustrating pupils' efforts by making unrealistic demands of them. The length of the speaking or writing task must be very carefully considered before it is assigned to pupils for whom self-expression is difficult.

4. Provide plenty of opportunities for practice. We learn to speak by speaking and to write by writing. Activities must be planned for pupils to be primarily participators, not spectators. Students modify their speech and writing more as a result of the feedback they receive from listeners and readers than from being told how to speak and write.. Obviously, pupils' speech and writing benefit from some exposure to effective speakers and writers, and listeners and readers are necessary components of a speaking and writing instructional program. However, most emphasis should be given to actual involvement in speaking and writing activities. Units of study that require students to talk for three minutes and listen to the speeches of their thirty classmates for ninety minutes should be avoided even if each student criticizes the speeches of the others.

5. Establish instructional objectives for the improvement of specific skills as well as for general language development. While it is true that general language development is basic to the improvement of specific skills, some pupils with generally good language development need special help with certain abilities. For example, a child who communicates well orally on the

playground may experience considerable difficulty answering questions in class. Or a pupil who writes interesting creative stories may be unable to write a factual report or summarize a chapter in a social studies book. The key to establishing instructional objectives for specific speaking and writing skills is careful diagnosis. Close observation of a pupil's oral and written expression under a variety of circumstances will disclose his particular strengths and weaknesses. Instruction should then be focused upon strengthening within a meaningful communication situation the weaknesses that have been identified.

6. Stress the quality of each spoken and written product in terms of the effectiveness of the desired communication. On this point we disagree somewhat with writers who advocate an emphasis on quantity of production rather than quality. Fader and Shaevitz (1966), for example, report as successful a project that had low-ability pupils writing journals that were evaluated only according to the quantity of written production. Teachers did not read the journals unless specifically requested by the pupils to do so, and copying from other printed material to satisfy the assigned number of pages was not prohibited. Certainly, children must speak and write if improvement is to be effected. However, for most pupils who need special help we feel that promoting quantity of production without careful attention to the effectiveness of the desired communication is needlessly postponing the focus on how well the pupil is able to transmit his ideas to others. We are not recommending that the mechanics of speech and writing (e.g., enunciation, usage, punctuation, capitalization) be major concerns, but we are suggesting that the effectiveness of the pupil's communication in terms of his purpose should be evaluated for all pupils except those with extremely retarded language development.

In our own attempts and in our observations of other teachers' attempts to improve the speaking and writing of students with deficiencies in these two areas, we have often been disappointed. Too many times we have observed teachers and pupils engage in activities designed to improve speaking and writing ability that have not paid off. In fact, we have often received the impression that pupils' communicative powers have been more stifled than improved by well-intentioned instruction. We have become especially aware of the negative effects of certain instructional practices on students' attitudes toward the tasks they were assigned and their desire for further instruction. All in all, our assessments of instructional programs for correcting oral and written expression have generally not been positive.

What appeared to be lacking in much of the teaching we did and observed was a good apportionment of attention to the various components of the instructional process. Certain components have typically been overemphasized; and others, perhaps the more important, have been neglected. For example, in typical speech units more of each pupil's time is spent evaluating the performance of others than in preparing and delivering his own message. In writing activities teachers typically spend more time correcting the errors of "finished" products than they do preparing and helping their pupils to write worthwhile papers. Unfortunately, too much of the coaching is done after the game has been played and too much has been assumed of pupils regarding their readiness to communicate.

A helpful conceptual model of the basic components of the teaching-learning interaction process may be constructed from the studies of Bellack (1965) regarding classroom discourse. He investigated the verbal interchange occurring in classrooms and reported the following:

> Examination of the transcripts of classroom discussions suggested that the verbal actions which characterize the verbal interplay of students and teachers could be classified in four major categories. We labeled these basic verbal actions *pedagogical moves* and classified them in terms of the pedagogical functions they perform in classroom discourse:
>
> *Structuring.* Structuring moves serve the pedagogical functions of focusing attention on subject matter or classroom procedures and launching interaction between students and teachers. They set the context for subsequent behavior or performance. For example, teachers frequently begin a class period with a structuring move in which they focus attention on the topic or problem to be discussed during that session.
>
> *Soliciting.* Moves in this category are designed to elicit a verbal response, encourage persons addressed to attend to something, or elicit a physical response. All questions are solicitations, as are commands, imperatives and requests.
>
> *Responding.* These moves bear a reciprocal relationship to soliciting moves and occur only in relation to them. Their pedagogical function is to fulfill the expectation of soliciting moves. Thus, students' answers to teachers' questions are classified as responding moves.
>
> *Reacting.* These moves are occasioned by a structuring, soliciting, responding, or another reacting move, but are not directly elicited by them. Pedagogically, these moves serve to shape or mold classroom discussion by accepting, rejecting, modifying or expanding what has been said previously. (P. 104)

The four "pedagogical moves" identified by Bellack might be represented as follows:

Teacher	*Student*
Structures ————————————————→	
Solicits ————————————————→	
←———————————————— Responds	
Reacts ————————————————→	

Although this model may be used to discuss the instructional process in any curriculum area, it serves our discussion of remedial speaking and writing instruction particularly well.

According to our model the teacher assumes major responsibility for structuring the learning situation, soliciting student behavior (in this case speech and writing), and reacting to the spoken or written product. In corrective and remedial instruction these three activities must be more carefully planned and implemented than in developmental instruction. In good corrective and remedial teaching these three components are used to support the pupil who needs more support than most pupils to communicate well orally or in writing.

Structuring

Structuring the learning situation is perhaps the most important aspect of improving pupils' oral and written expression. Unless the atmosphere of the classroom and the psychological readiness of the pupil are such that the pupil desires to express himself and does not feel threatened by the possible consequences of his expression, no real learning will occur. Speaking and writing are very personal behaviors, and too much anxiety or too little motivation to communicate will interfere with their effectiveness. Therefore, teachers must take the time to (1) assure the student that he will in some way be rewarded for his efforts and (2) help him find something within his experience that he feels is worthwhile communicating to his audience. Our observation has been that teachers generally move to the soliciting stage of the pedagogical process before the classroom atmosphere and the pupils have been adequately structured. The inadequate attention given to structuring the learning situation is in our opinion a major reason so many pupils fail to communicate their ideas well. They are asked to express themselves in an environment they perceive to be threatening and when they have nothing they particularly want to say. Structuring the learning situation for pupils who have experienced failure in their past efforts at communication requires patience and sensitivity to pupils' experiences and their perceptions of those experiences. One teacher working in a remedial teaching situation with two fourth-grade girls required nearly five weeks of daily meetings to bring her students to a point of readiness to discuss a story with enthusiasm and clarity. For five weeks the teacher talked very informally with them, played games with them, shared background experiences with them, and gradually built their self-concepts, trust, and knowledge. When the story to be discussed was finally read together, the girls participated in an oral discussion vigorously and displayed a level of intelligence that they had not exhibited in previous classroom discussions.

Soliciting

Soliciting oral and written responses from a pupil who has difficulty expressing himself requires a good knowledge of the pupil's present level of development and the particular instructional objective being sought. That is, the solicited behavior should be a reasonable expectation for the pupil and should be directed at giving him a successful experience with a particular kind of verbal behavior (e.g., expressing his feelings about a picture, asking a question, summarizing an essay). We have been more successful in helping certain students communicate their ideas when our solicitations have specified clearly the dimensions of the task. For example, supplying some pupil with the first sentence of a paragraph and asking them to add three more sentences has produced better results than asking them to "Write a paragraph." Other pupils, on the other hand, perform better when the solicitation is less constraining. The point is that neither approach is necessarily "better," but certain approaches work better for some pupils than for others. All solicitations, however, should be free of ambiguity. The student needs to know the nature of the product he is constructing so that he has working guidelines and criteria for evaluation. And again we emphasize that components of oral and written expression should not be given isolated drill, but rather should be placed in a learning context that gives primary attention to overall growth.

Too many solicitations, we feel, are not carefully considered before they are given in terms of their effect on the pupils who receive them. We heard one teacher, for example, ask pupils to describe their favorite room at home. It should have been obvious that these particular children probably had never considered the characteristic of any room in their homes, didn't have a "favorite" room, and didn't know what "describe" meant. "Tell me what you notice about the room we are in now" would have been a better solicitation for these children. Solicitations that are not carefully thought out and verbalized before they are presented to children who have speaking and writing deficiencies are rarely productive of quality responses.

Reacting

Although we have indicated in our model of pedagogical moves that the reacting process is the responsibility of the teacher, we believe that the reactions of fellow pupils to oral and written communications are often more beneficial to improving pupils' expression.

Moffett (1968b) attributes language learning to the reactions we receive from others. He says, "Learning to use language . . . requires the particular feedback of human response, because it is to other people that we direct speech. The fact that one writes by oneself does not at all diminish the need for response, since one writes for others" (p. 191). Clearly, the reacting process is essential to the improvement of oral and written expression. Regarding written products Moffett (1968b.) says,

> Clearly, the *quality* of feedback is the key. Who is this audience to be, and how can it provide a response informed enough to coach in all the necessary ways? How is it possible for every member of a class of thirty to get an adequate amount of response? Classmates are a natural audience. Young people are most interested in writing for their peers. Many teachers besides myself have discovered that students write much better when they write for each other. (P. 193)

Care must be taken, however, that pupils with communication problems do not become victims of unkind and unproductive peer evaluations. Some pupils need the considered reaction of a sensitive teacher for a long period of time before they are ready for give-and-take sessions with other students.

Since reactions to speech and writing are indeed powerful instructors, the teacher should bend every effort to use them wisely. A thoughtless reaction to a pupil's communication efforts could cause him to avoid expressing his ideas in the classroom and thereby have a negative effect on his learning regardless of the intent of the reaction.

Too often, teachers have urged pupils to share their "ideas" and then attacked their mechanics of expression. When this happens, students soon learn that *what* they say or write is not nearly so important as *how* they say or write it. Consequently, instructional programs lose the most important focus in communication improvement, the transmission of ideas from person to person. The result is often a series of artificial exercises that culminate in critical reactions to posture, gestures, missing commas, run-on sentences, or other mechanical matters. Reactions to the mechanics of expression should be given only to help a pupil strengthen a communication that he feels needs strengthening. Recently, one of these writers observed three fifth-grade boys writing an original play to be tape-recorded as part of a remedial reading summer program. After listening to their first recording one of the boys said, "How can I make 'Look at the moon man coming toward us' sound like I'm more afraid." Another of the boys suggested, "Look! A moon man! He's coming toward us!" delivered with increasing volume and definite pauses. The script was changed accordingly and delivered much more convincingly by the first boy at the next recording session.

Too much reaction to a pupil's response may reduce or negate the benefits of feedback. While it is tempting to comment upon "just one thing more" the tolerance for feedback is low among pupils who are anxious about their performance and want assurance of success. Teachers who settle for slight gains with each communication effort are likely to be more successful than teachers who administer massive treatment following each response.

Grammar and Usage

An important distinction for teachers of language improvement to make is that between grammer and usage. The former refers to the systematic structure, the syntax of a particular language; the latter term is concerned with the correctness or appropriateness of the alternatives selected by the user within that grammar. Bostain (1968) illustrates the difference clearly:

> The organization of the noises is the grammar of the language. A "grammatical" mistake in this view is an "organizational" mistake. The speaker produces non-native noises and arrangements like "I am here since six months." People . . . in their native tongue . . . almost never make organizational mistakes. . . . In

English, one of the grammar patterns we like puts "always" in front of a verb (except the verb "to be"; we like to put "always" after "to be"). So I would say, "We always drink tea," "I always smoke a pipe," but "I'm always there." . . . A German is likely to say, "I smoke always a pipe." When you tell him, "We don't say that," he comes back with, "Ach, I forget always your crazy grammar!" He's making a grammatical mistake. . . . Now let's take another look at "Chicago ain't 300 miles due west of St. Louis" in terms of the . . . kind of mistake. Just what kind of mistake is it? The error lies in choosing the wrong alternative. When you choose "ain't" you haven't made a grammatical mistake, for the sentence is organized perfectly. But you chose that kind of a negative particle that has unfortunate social consequences in polite company. You've made a "social" mistake. (P. 244)

Almost everybody gets control of the grammar of his native language before he is six years old. If this were not true, he could not make himself understood. Gleason (1969) says,

In the year and a half that intervenes between his first two-word utterance at eighteen months and his third birthday, the child learns all the essentials of English grammar. By the age of thirty-six months many children can produce all of the major English sentence types up to about ten words in length. And by the time a child enters school, his knowledge of English is so vast and complex that no one has yet been able to program the most sophisticated computer to turn out the sentences that any five-year-old can produce with ease and assurance. (P. 16)

Goodman (1967) says, "The child comes to school with great control over his language. He derives meaning from a rapid stream of speech by responding to certain built-in cue systems such as pattern, inflectional changes, key function words, and intonations" (p. 214). The child uses these "built-in cue systems" for projection as well as reception purposes.

Levels of Usage

Because a child has control of English grammar, it does not necessarily follow that his use of language, that is, the selections he makes from the alternatives available within his grammar, are adequate for his communication needs. Smith, Goodman, and Meredith (1970) say,

During their school years, the language of children becomes fully grammatical within the norms of their own dialect. Not only do they gain control over the structure of the language, but in a sense, the latent structure of language gains control over the language of the child. As the child fully internalizes the structure of the language, the structure of language determines the precise patterns and choice of words of his speech. All this increases his effectiveness in communication. But a wide range of language is acceptable by adult standards. Some language is more effective, interesting, precise, or euphonious than other language that is equally correct. (P. 168)

By the time children leave the elementary school they should be comfortable with and habitually use good colloquial speech. This level of usage is the standard informal level; it is the ordinary, comfortable usage of the teacher in the classroom and of people of culture and education in their more informal moments. Beyond this level are levels appropriate for speaking with strangers or for public speaking that should be developed at a later stage when polishing is appropriate. It should be understood, too, that written expression may often be more formal—thus, at a higher level of usage—than oral expression. Appropriate levels of usage, then, vary from one situation to another.

We shall briefly describe five levels of usage: They are the five levels most commonly described in the literature: (1) the illiterate level, (2) the homely level, (3) standard English, informal level, (4) standard English, formal level, and (5) the literary level.

The Illiterate Level

The language forms at the illiterate level are common in the speech of the uneducated; they appear in literature only to characterize the speech of people who are illiterate or uncultured (e.g., *growed, knowed;* he *done;* didn't have *no; youse; them* books; they *was;* I *ain't;* have *went*). Language use at this level is not acceptable classroom usage and should be corrected.

The Homely Level

Usage at the homely level is different from standard English, yet not completely illiterate. Included here would be some of the forms common in local or regional dialects and the usage patterns of children from, for example, rural areas where, despite some claim to literacy, the models provided by adults are not standard English (e.g., confusion in the forms of *lie* and *lay, sit* and *set, rise* and *raise;* she *don't;* John, *he* . . .; *haven't hardly;* I *want out;* light-*complected; like* for *as; right* for *very*—a *right* nice day; *to home* for *at home*). Rejection of such forms in the classroom may cause pupils to feel personal rejection, for too abrupt a change in language could cause them to feel cut off from the people from whom they learned the language. A better procedure would be to bring about a gradual change by providing models of standard usage and by helping children to notice and to value the more standard forms.

Standard English, Informal Level

Standard, informal English is the level discussed earlier, the level of colloquial speech among educated people. The language forms included at this level are commonly used by cultured people for informal, conversational purposes; but they are generally excluded from formal public speaking and conversation with strangers and from formal social correspondence and careful writing. As we have said, standard informal English should be the language of the classroom and the goal for elementary pupils.

Under the direction of Robert C. Pooley a committee of Wisconsin educators developed a sequential growth curriculum in English language arts for kindergarten through grade twelve (Pooley et al., 1967). The committee selected a list of language forms to guide teachers in their attempts to help students establish the "classroom dialect." The list (p. 305) follows:

A transition from all "baby-talk" and "cute" expressions

The acceptable uses in speech and writing of *I, me, him, her, she, they,* and *them* (Accepted: *it's me.*)

The appropriate uses of *is, are, was, were* with respect to number and tense

Standard past tenses of common irregular verbs such as *saw, gave, took, brought, stuck,* etc.

Elimination of the double negative: we don't have no apples, etc.

Elimination of analogical forms: *ain't, hisn, hern, ourn, hisself, theirselves,* etc.

Appropriate use of possessive pronouns: *my, mine, his, hers, theirs, ours*

Mastery of the distinction between *its,* possessive pronoun, and *it's, it is,* the contraction. (This applies only to written English.)

Elimination of *this here* and *that there*

Approved use of personal pronouns in compound constructions: as subject (Mary and I), as object (Mary and me), as object of preposition (to Mary and me)

Attention to number agreement with the phrases *there is, there are, there was, there were*

Elimination of *he don't, she don't, it don't*

Elimination of *learn* for *teach, leave* for *let*

Avoidance of pleonastic subjects: *my brother he; my mother she; that fellow he*

Sensing the distinction between *good* as adjective and *well* as adverb, e.g., he spoke *well*

The committee also eliminated the following taboos of the past (p. 305):

Any distinction between *shall* and *will*

Any reference to the split infinitive

Elimination of *like* as a conjunction

Objection to "He is one of those boys who *is*"

Objection to the reason . . . is because . . .

Objection to *myself* as a polite substitute for *me* as in "I understand you will meet Mrs. Jones and myself at the station."

Objection to the phrase "different than"

To help students who use language at the illiterate level develop the classroom dialect, teachers must continually expose them to good models and involve them in language arts activities that give them practice in using more acceptable forms. Some suggested activities are listening to good readers and speakers (see Chapter 12), play reading and acting, writing with teacher help, choral reading, and plenty of informal discussions with persons who use informal, standard English.

Standard English, Formal Level

When people move to the more formal level of standard English usage, they pay closer attention to (1) the tone of the words they use, (2) agreement in number, tense, and case, and (3) word order of modifiers and sentence elements. The public speech and formal writing of educated people are at the standard formal level. Most high school and some elementary pupils should be able to speak and to write at this level when the occasion demands formal usage, but they should also feel free to use the informal level when it is appropriate (i.e., for friendly letters and conversation, informal essays, narratives, etc.). Overzealous teachers who demand standard formal usage for all classroom conversation and writing are not likely to accomplish much because the model will be rejected as too "bookish" for many occasions. Pupils need to be able to recognize the characteristics of both the formal and informal levels and to sense the appropriate time to move from one level to the other.

Pooley (1946) makes the point that the formal level of usage is characterized more by restraint and care than by any particular expressions, but the following are among the examples he lists as "quite typical of the formal standard level: I *shall* be glad to help. . . . *Neither* of the party *was* injured . . . . Here are three *whom* we had omitted from the list" (p. 22).

The Literary Level

At the literary level, the aim is not simply to communicate but to achieve beauty. Language at this level surpasses the demands of ordinary communication and becomes an art form with rhythm, symmetry, and balance. Lincoln's "Gettysburg Address" is often cited as an example; his use of the language goes far beyond the clarity of expression that is the aim of standard English. Obviously the fluent use of language at the literary level is attainable only by a few gifted students and teachers. For most pupils, and for most adults, writing at this level will remain not a model that we can hope to duplicate but a thing of beauty that we can study and appreciate.

Correctness in modern English usage is relative—there are *levels of usage* rather than a *single standard of usage*. The educated person is able to choose the level that is appropriate for each situation in which he must express himself orally or in writing. To do this he must be sensitive to the language requirements of various situations and he must be comfortable with the usage patterns at each level. As Pooley (1933) put it in an early statement that was incorporated in the 1935 curriculum study of the National Council of Teachers of English and that has been widely quoted since then: "Good English is that form of speech which is appropriate to the purpose of the speaker, true to the language as it is, and comfortable to speaker and listener. It is the product of custom, neither cramped by rule nor freed from all restraint; it is never fixed, but changes with the organic life of the language" (p. 155).

Improving pupils' powers of expression, then, is not, as was once commonly thought, a matter of teaching them grammar. As a matter of fact, numerous studies have found that studying grammar has no salutary effect on speaking and writing ability. Smith, Goodman, and Meredith (1970, p. 157) cite research findings that disprove among others the following beliefs: (1) ability to cite grammatical rules improves grammar in written expression; (2) grammar instruction is the best approach to teaching sentence structure; (3) school grammar is the best approach to teaching punctuation; (4) when children cite grammatical rules, they apply them; and (5) knowledge of school grammar reduces errors in usage. They conclude, "School grammar instruction is ineffective" (p. 159). Lefevre (1970) says, "we cannot remind ourselves too often that no research supports the common fallacy that teaching any kind of formal grammar 'as such' improves performance in the arts and skills of literacy" (p. 163).

The most sensible approach for improving oral and written expression in regard to grammar and usage, then, is to (1) provide the student with good models of oral and written communication, (2) give him opportunities to experiment with the many alternatives available to him for expressing his ideas, and (3) help him to evaluate the effectiveness of the various alternatives in terms of different communication purposes and different audiences.

FOCUSING ON ORAL EXPRESSION

We pointed out earlier in this chapter that most people rely more upon the spoken word than the written word to communicate their ideas. In the light of this, it would seem that school curriculums would give the development of effective oral expression more systematic attention than the development of written expression. Such is not the case, however. Except for units of study or classes in which public speaking techniques are taught, the improvement of oral expression is generally not given an instructional emphasis. This situation is indeed unfortunate, for many students do not receive good models and opportunities for oral expression in their family situations. The competition these deprived students receive in school from students with exemplary home experiences is often so overwhelming that they withdraw from classroom interactions and express themselves in school only when the teacher "draws them out," which is infrequently. Obviously, the academic growth of these nonparticipators suffers, and eventually many are in need of remedial instruction.

Because most schools do not have remedial programs for improving oral expression, the improvement of oral expression for students with deficiencies should be an integral part of classroom instruction and remedial reading programs. If teachers are alert to the many possibilities for providing opportunities to develop speaking skills in all areas of the curriculum, students can receive the special help they need in situations more meaningful than short-term, contrived units of study which seldom achieve their stated objectives.

We are reiterating our position that improving oral expression is for the most part more a matter of total language growth than a matter of identifying specific weaknesses and focusing attention on them. The latter approach, we feel, often results in the assignment of exercises that ask students to talk about things for which they feel little enthusiasm in contrived situations. In addition, we feel that an approach which identifies specific deficiencies in oral expression and then singles them out for attention may make students overly aware of the mechanics of oral expression and may in the long run result in their being more concerned with the form of their expression than the content. We are also advocating an inductive approach to the improvement of oral expression because we have seen too many students who were taught deductively the speaking skills they were lacking lose their desire and willingness to express themselves in the classroom. Lefevre (1970) says,

> So far as possible, the student should experience his English lessons directly, through "inductive processes of discovery," and then express his experience in his own language; conversely, he should never be asked to memorize definitions and other purely verbal formulations that lie outside his experience. Thus, teachers try to realize an overall aim: the student's learning should be "concrete" and "operational," rather than verbal and abstract. This method avoids the serious pitfall of verbalism, a curse of our schools. The student's language learning in school should parallel his early childhood method of learning to speak his native tongue—playfully, through delighted experiences of discovery—through repeated "exposure" to language forms and patterns, by creative "imitation" and "manipulation," and by personal trial and error, with kindly (and not too much) correction from adults. (P. 75)

This does not mean, however, that remedial instruction should not be aimed at specific objectives for each child. Specific objectives are necessary, but they should be sought within the context of actual communication situations which incorporate the refinement of other language arts skills at the same time.

Identifying Pupils Who Need Special Help

The identification of pupils who need special help in their speaking development is not difficult. Two questions should be applied to all pupils, and the answers will determine which children are good candidates for special instruction: (1) Is the quality or quantity of his oral production preventing him from effective participation in speaking situations he encounters frequently? and (2) Is the quality or quantity of his oral production below the level expected in terms of his general mental development? Obviously, pupils whose general mental development is higher than is reflected in their oral expression and who are having difficulty communicating in normal situations are good candidates for special help.

Loban (1966), in a longitudinal study of 338 children, collected and analyzed speech samples at intervals between kindergarten and twelfth grade. His findings concerning the prevalent speech problems of his subjects through ninth grade may be used to alert teachers to the kinds of oral expression problems to expect of children who need special help. He found that most difficulties of children not handicapped by social dialect fell into five categories (p. 47): (1) inconsistency in the use of tense, (2) careless omission of words (excluding omission of auxiliaries), (3) lack of syntactic clarity (ambiguous placement of words, phrases, and clauses; awkward and incoherent arrangements of expression), (4) confusing use of pronouns, and (5) trouble with agreement of subject and verb when using "there is," "there are," "there was," and "there were." The difficulties he found among children speaking a social dialect fell into ten categories in the following order of frequency (p. 49): (1) lack of agreement of subject and verb, third person singular (other than the forms of the verb "to be"), (2) omission of auxiliary verbs (especially those formed with the verb "to be"), (3) inconsistency in the use of tense, (4) nonstandard use of verb forms, (5) lack of agreement of subject and verb while using forms of the verb "to be," (6) careless omission of words (excluding omission of auxiliaries), (7) nonstandard use of pronouns, (8) nonstandard use of noun forms, (9) double negatives, and (10) omission of the verb "to be."

From Loban's study it would appear that the oral expression problems of most children (1) can be identified by teachers through careful observation of children's language in various speaking situations, (2) are relatively fewer in kind than might generally be thought, and (3) indicate that even children with difficulties have the basic structural or operational characteristic of the grammar mastered.

Diagnosing the Problem of Pupils Who Need Special Help

We feel that teachers are able to identify pupils' speaking weaknesses by listening to them talk in a variety of situations. We feel too that pupils who are seriously disabled in oral expression are likely to be seriously disabled in reading also, and if intensive diagnosis is done in relation to the reading problem, the information obtained should be utilized to help plan the remedial speech program as well.

We recommend that teachers write short descriptions of the way students who need special help express themselves. For example:

Bob speaks in a monotone even when he is relating something that he is obviously excited about.

Betty never finishes telling a story without starting two or three more.

Peter starts to ask a question before he has thought out what he wants to know.

Virginia talks so rapidly that her listeners can't tell where one idea stops and another begins.

Randy hangs his head and mumbles when he answers questions, but not when he initiates a conversation.

Winston refuses to talk in the classroom, but communicates freely with his own circle of friends out of class.

Buddy can never find the word he wants to express what he has in mind, so he just says, "Aw, I don't know," or "You know what I mean," and stops.

Most teachers are able to describe pupils' oral expression problems accurately to suggest ways to structure meaningful group speaking situations and solicit the kinds of responses that promote the needed reactions. We are opposed to check lists of speaking deficiencies because they are too impersonal and give the impression that the components of oral expression can be improved as separate entities. Describing the actual behavior of their pupils will give teachers a better understanding of the problems they are trying to correct and, it is to be hoped, some ideas for the instructional activities needed to correct them. There is no substitute in corrective and remedial instruction in the language arts for a sensitive and creative teacher who understands the basic principles of language arts instruction and who can plan instructional activities that meet the individual needs of pupils with communication weaknesses.

Sample Instructional Activities

An essential ingredient in all instructional activities that are designed to improve oral expression is the sincere desire on the part of the student to say something. Teachers must be especially careful to structure speaking situations that are meaningful to the participating students. Regarding the selection of topics for students to talk about, Moffett (1968a) says, "The topics should be of the greatest possible interest to children whether they come from the children or the teacher. This means 'emotional involvement' " (p. 61). Teachers must first of all, then, know the interests of their pupils well.

Besides planning speech improvement activities around pupil interests teachers must also be careful to structure situations that facilitate pupil-pupil interactions as well as pupil-teacher interactions. To improve their speech pupils must talk a great deal. Small doses of conversation or responses that are short or infrequent will not suffice. If teachers are the only reactors to pupils' responses, pupils will not have sufficient opportunities to respond and receive feedback. Therefore, pupils must interact with each other if they are to get the necessary practice.

The following activities are illustrative of the approach we recommend to improve the oral expression of pupils who are weak in this ability. With some modification all of the following have been used effectively either by ourselves or by teachers whom we have observed. With all of the activities much care was taken to select interesting subjects to talk about and to stimulate as much student participtaion as possible.

Activity 1

Each pupil in a fourth-grade class was assigned to a discussion group with four other pupils. Pupils who needed corrective instruction were distributed among the groups, and at least one good reader was assigned to each group. The activity for each discussion group was somewhat different to strengthen the specific weaknesses of the student in the group who needed special help. The best reader in each discussion group was given a copy of a poem that had been read but not discussed by the top reading group that morning. The students were told that each student with a copy of the poem would read it aloud to his group and re-read it as often as his group desired. The following assignments were then given to the groups:

Group 1—Each student will tell the group one question he would like to ask the author of the poem and tell the group how he thinks the author would answer it.

Group 2—Each member of the group will tell what kind of picture he would draw to appear with the poem in a textbook.

Group 3—The group will write a short television commercial for the poem to persuade other fourth graders to read it. The members of the group will take turns reading the commercial.

Group 4—Each student will describe the pictures he saw in his mind as certain parts of the poem were read.

Group 5—Each student will tell why he would or would not include this poem in a reading book for fourth graders.

The teacher moved from group to group as the discussion progressed and asked certain students from the groups to present their contributions to the whole class when the class came together again as a whole. The following day the teacher informed the students of several unacceptable language forms he had heard in the group discussions held the previous day and asked the class to supply alternate forms more acceptable for classroom use.

Activity 2

Four seventh-grade boys in a remedial reading class became interested in space travel. With their teacher they read and discussed newspaper accounts, magazine articles, and short stories about space travel. At the suggestion of the teacher they agreed to write and tape-record a dramatic account of a trip to a fictitious planet. After some discussion each boy selected the part he would play in the production. Each line of dialogue was suggested by the boys and written down by the teacher after the acceptability of the language forms used for the purpose and the audience had been discussed. Eventually sound effects were included, and the production developed into a radio program with commercials, station identification breaks, and weather reports included. When the recording was completed, the boys played their tape for classes throughout the school and told how they had planned, written, and recorded their program.

Activity 3

After appropriate readiness instruction had been given, a class of thirty sixth graders was divided into groups of three. Each group was given a message to communicate by way of creative dramatics (e.g., parents don't always understand their children's problems; telling lies can get you into trouble; experience is a good teacher). Each student was then given a particular role to play (e.g., a father who gets excited and shouts when he thinks his children are doing something wrong; a girl who asks too many questions; a teacher who likes to help her pupils when they are in trouble). The students with oral expression problems were given roles to help them correct their weaknesses. The students in each group discussed the setting for their play and decided upon a story line. After several practice runs, the groups acted out their plays for each other.

Activity 4

A remedial reading teacher tape-recorded some carefully selected and sequenced excerpts from a sound effects record (e.g., children playing, a cat meowing, a dog barking, a window breaking, a baby crying). She asked her third-grade pupils to listen to the sounds and tell a story about what happened. Some of the stories were typed by the teacher and read into a tape recorder by the children who created them.

Activity 5

A class of fifteen remedial readers at the junior high school level were assigned to interview each other to discover any interesting facts about themselves that the others might not know. After the interviews each student told what he had learned about the person he had interviewed. Following each oral biographical sketch, questions were asked, personal experiences were related, and some informal conversation ensued. Ultimately, "guess who" biographical sketches were written and included in a class publication that was distributed to other students.

FOCUSING ON WRITTEN EXPRESSION

For most people, the ability to express themselves in writing is needed most during the time they are in school. Teachers at all academic levels assign themes, reports, and various projects that require students to put their ideas down on paper. A successful school experience depends in large measure upon the ability to produce a comprehensible written communication.

Although it is easier for people to avoid written self-expression after they leave school than when they are in school, most people can run their lives more efficiently if they are able to write letters, leave notes, jot down ideas for later consideration, inform an employer of some matter in writing, and satisfy any number of demands upon them that are best satisfied through writing. Therefore, giving students who have unusual difficulty learning to express themselves in writing special instruction remains an important responsibility of the school in spite of the growing utilization of dictating machines and tape recorders.

Handwriting and spelling ability are of course related to written expression. But since we have discussed those two curriculum areas in Chapter 13 and Chapter 10 respectively, we shall not discuss them in this chapter. Obviously, students who have handwriting and spelling well in hand are better able than students who do not to deal with the other aspects of writing that we shall discuss: punctuation, capitalization, sentence structure, and paragraph development. However, students with persistent handwriting and spelling weaknesses should not be deprived of remedial instruction and practice in the mechanics and rhetoric of written composition if they need additional help to improve those abilities also. Instruction may be integrated and attention given to all of these abilities.

Five principles are basic to the approach we advocate for improving writing ability: (1) writing is basically a thinking process and must be conceptualized as such by students and teachers—an idea poorly clarified in the mind of the writer will also be unclear on paper; (2) writing is always done for a particular purpose and a particular audience both of which the writer should be aware of at all times; (3) desire to commit an idea to writing is basic to writing improvement; (4) development in writing can proceed only on a base of oral language development; (5) frequent practice and audience feedback are essential to the improvement of written composition. Teachers who are unsuccessful in their attempts to improve student writing usually fail because adequate attention has not been given to one or more of the above principles.

Punctuation and Capitalization

In improving pupils' writing teachers should give considerably less attention to punctuation and capitalization than to sentence and paragraph development. The latter are more basic to the coherence and clarity of pupils' writing than the former. If a pupil's sentences and paragraphs are well constructed, punctuation and capitalization can be taught in a straightforward way by correcting them within his compositions in a spirit of improving the quality of his communication. Pooley et al. (1967) say,

> Since punctuation is an important aid in translating thought to written expression, it is best taught as an integral part of written communication. Punctuation affects and often determines meaning, for example, "Call me Mary," and "Call me, Mary." Along with this kind of illustration, it would be worthwhile to point out to students some of the more common means by which punctuation signals or determines sentence structure. Teaching methods emphasizing the meaning function of punctuation will have more effect than prescribing rules. (P. 225)

They also say, "It must be stated that there is no universally accepted method of punctuation. In general the trend is toward more open punctuation. The students may be helped by one simple statement: your punctuation is basically sound if it helps the reader understand your ideas" (p. 225). They conclude, "In teaching punctuation, the teacher will always remember that the current theory emphasizes the few items necessary for good communication, rather than an elaborate system" (p. 226). This is an especially important guideline for teachers who are instructing pupils who find it difficult to construct written sentences and paragraphs. Too much emphasis upon the English punctuation system per se will certainly interfere with the more basic developmental needs of pupils with poor writing ability. The same may be said of capitalization.

Sentence Writing

Perhaps the basic element in a remedial program for written expression is helping pupils develop a "sentence sense." In other words pupils must be helped to recognize the different syntactical patterns available to them for expressing their ideas. Lefevre (1970) says, "Sentence comprehension—sentence sense—is the beginning of reading comprehension as well as of the ability to write compositions" (p. 83). Regarding the preferred approach to developing a sentence sense he says,

> It is not helpful to insist, as some teachers still do, that every sentence must have a subject and a predicate, and must also "express a complete thought." Rather

than attempt to lay down an abstract verbal prescription that means little or nothing to the learner, it is preferable to allow him, over a generous period of time, to develop his own inductive definition of "sentence" by associating the term with varied examples of sentences with common components. (P. 168)

Any instructional program for the improvement of writing should include large doses of easy and absorbing reading. Pupils cannot be expected to produce good sentences of their own unless they experience good sentences in the writing of others. We are not advocating that pupils analyze composition models. We are suggesting that they develop a sense of English sentence constructions by reading material at their independent reading level (see Chapter 5).

Children often notice their own faulty sentence constructions when they read what they have written orally to an attentive audience. Therefore, having pupils read what they have written to their intended audience is good procedure. Sometimes this amounts to tape-recording original stories, plays, or other projects of the kind we describe as illustrative activities later in this chapter.

Some pupils need considerable help from the teacher while they are engaged in the process of writing. If the object of the writing is to produce a meaningful communication, most severely disabled pupils appreciate and learn from a cooperative effort between themselves and the teacher. This "team" approach also has merit because it eliminates the embarrassment and frustration of submitting a product that is ridden with errors.

Pupils need opportunities to play with sentence building in an atmosphere that encourages experimentation without the fear of poor grades. From his comparisons of the language used by elementary school children low in general language proficiency and elementary school children high in general language proficiency Loban (1963) concluded,

> Not basic sentence pattern but what is done to achieve flexibility within pattern proves to be a measure of proficiency with language at this level . . . pupils need many opportunities to grapple with their own thought in situations where they have someone to whom they wish to communicate successfully. Instruction can best aid the pupils' expression when individuals or small groups with similar problems are helped to see how their own expression can be improved. This instruction would take the form of identifying elements which strengthen or weaken communication, increase or lower precision of thought, clarify or blur meanings. (P. 88)

Strickland (1963) says,

> The run-on sentences characteristic of many children and the choppy or incomplete sentences of others are evidence of need for help in putting ideas together into well-knit and logical sentence schemes. A teacher might pick up from time to time a sentence or some ideas used by a child and encourage the group to find ways to express those ideas in better form. Children might write the kernel sentences on slips of paper, write their individual responses to such questions as what, when, why, where, or how, attach them to the kernel in a

variety of ways and read their sentences aloud for the reaction of the group. The tests for a good sentence would be, "Does it make sense?" "Does it say what you mean?" "Does it sound right?" (P. 170)

Pupils need to have practice improving the clarity of their written sentences by rearranging grammatical elements, deleting grammatical elements, substituting grammatical elements, and adding grammatical elements. For example, the pupil who writes, "We watched a television show. It was circus acts. The clowns were best. So were the elephants." might be asked the following questions to guide him toward writing more mature sentences:

1. Can you put your first two sentences together?

2. Can you tell in your new sentence who watched the circus acts with you?

3. Can you also tell in your new sentence "when" you watched the show?

4. Can you put your last two sentences together?

5. Can you tell in your new sentence exactly who liked the clowns and elephants best?

6. Can you also tell in your new sentence why *you* liked the clowns and elephants best?

The objective in this kind of activity is to give pupils experiences with the different possibilities for improving their communication by transforming their sentence patterns. Teachers will find many of the references at the end of this chapter helpful in providing more information about English sentences and how to teach pupils to improve their own sentences by transforming them in various ways.

Paragraph Writing

For most people, learning to write unified, coherent paragraphs is a lifelong process. Therefore, teachers should not be too distressed when they find many if not most of their pupils having difficulty in this regard. However, certain children have more difficulty organizing their ideas into paragraphs than others and may be helped when they are given instruction in addition to that given them in the regular classroom instructional program.

Some pupils have not learned to categorize or classify ideas. These students need some basic instruction in putting related ideas together. For example, they might be asked to sort twelve sentences into three piles, one dealing with birds, one with automobiles, and one with school activities.

Some pupils know which ideas belong together, but they are unable to put them in a logical sequence. These students are sometimes helped by the experience of arranging written sentences in different sequences (e.g., what happened first to what happened last, or most important happening to least important happening).

Most pupils profit more from organizing their own writing than from organizing sentences that are given to them by the teacher. A major problem for many pupils is connecting the ideas within and between paragraphs. Many compositions can be strengthened considerably by the careful use of transitional words and word groups at the beginning of sentences (e.g., Another . . .; Finally . . .; In addition to . . .; Because of what I just said . . .). Teachers should watch for opportunities to help pupils learn the importance of using transitional words and word groups to help them put their compositions together.

Perhaps the most important concept for students to attain relative to paragraph development is that written communication is essentially a matter of making assertions and elaborating upon them. Although it is not necessary or even desirable that every paragraph have a "topic" sentence, every paragraph does make an assertion of some kind or contain a number of unified ideas relative to a particular assertion. For example, an assertion may be made in one paragraph and elaborated upon (qualified, clarified, supported) in following paragraphs. Or the paragraphs containing the elaboration may precede the paragraph containing the actual assertion. The point is that paragraphs are units of thought relative to assertions of ideas. By conversing with pupils about the message they wish to communicate and their intended audience teachers can give them some valuable insights into paragraph development specifically and communication generally.

Identifying Pupils Who Need Special Help

Pupils who need special help in writing can readily be spotted by the quality of the written products they submit in response to classroom writing assignments. Recently, one of the authors collected three short writing samples from each of 450 fourth graders. The assignments asked the students to respond in prescribed ways to the content of short reading selections. A cursory examination of the written products from any one class revealed which students were consistently unable to express themselves adequately in writing.

The classroom teacher, then, is able to identify pupils with special problems within the context of the regular instructional program and without the use of a standardized instrument. By assigning writing tasks and evaluating pupils' best efforts to satisfy them, the classroom teacher can assess the writing ability of all his pupils and select for special instruction those whose performance is significantly below the level of their suspected potential. We have observed that classroom teachers are capable of using this approach without any special training and that their findings are especially valid because they reflect the teacher's knowledge of the actual writing tasks the students will be assigned.

Diagnosing the Problems of Pupils Who Need Special Help

Our recommended approach for diagnosing the problems of pupils who have been selected for special help in written expression is the same as the approach we favor for diagnosing oral expression. Brief written descriptions of a pupil's writing needs based on the teacher's examination of several writing samples serve as a diagnostic record and help the teacher focus instruction upon specific weaknesses. We do not feel that teachers require a list of writing faults to check the pupils' writing against. Teachers are educated users of the English language and will certainly recognize weaknesses that are significant enough to require remedial instruction. Verbalizing the pupil's specific weaknesses helps the teacher become more keenly aware of the exact nature of the problem.

The following descriptions are illustrative of diagnostic statements based upon the teacher's examination of several writing samples collected from each pupil.

Sarah has interesting things to say, and she presents her ideas in good sequential order. However, her sentences are short, choppy, and monotonous. She needs some instruction in coordinating, subordinating, and embedding ideas in a sentence. She also needs help in selecting the proper conjunction to express her ideas when she combines them.

Stanley has no sentence sense. He runs his sentences together without any feeling for where one idea ends and another begins. It appears that he puts in a comma whenever he thinks it's about time to use one. He uses a period only at the conclusion of his entire message.

Ken has no concept of paragraph unity. Each sentence in a paragraph may be totally unrelated to his other sentences in that paragraph. He never develops an idea logically. He does indent after five or six sentences, but his indentations do not represent a new assertion or a change in the focus of his elaboration of an assertion.

Joanne uses too many modifiers when she writes. She often strings several modifiers together. Yesterday she wrote, "My cute, new baby kitten is furry and quite black and very, very naughty sometimes."

Fred changes tense when he describes an action. In telling about a fight on the playground he wrote, "He was lots bigger than Billy so he hits him right on the top of his head." Fred also tends to omit words when he writes.

The descriptions should not list every fault found in each pupil's writing but should rather describe one or two weaknesses that the teacher intends to emphasize in his remedial work with the pupil. As the remedial instruction proceeds and weaknesses are strengthened, new descriptions should be written. Teachers should not try to correct every problem at once.

Sample Instructional Activities

The following are brief descriptions of activities which we and other teachers have found helpful in improving the writing ability of pupils who needed special help. They illustrate the approach we advocate for remedial writing instruction.

Activity 1

A class of fifteen ninth graders with poor writing ability was motivated to write and tape-record a program to accompany a series of colored slides. The slides were lent to the class by the agriculture teacher who photographed rural scenes as a hobby. Since most of the pupils in the class were from the same rural area, the colored slides were especially appealing to them. The class was divided into four groups, and each group was given a number of slides taken during a particular season of the year. The teacher prepared an introductory statement which explained the purpose of the program to an anticipated audience, and each pupil was assigned to write short passages to accompany the showing of the slides he selected to write about. Each pupil could describe the scene in his own words or describe his thoughts and feelings as he viewed the scene. Ultimately, pupils incorporated passages from poetry and background music into their production, wrote transitions to combine the work of the various groups, edited the script, recorded the program, and presented it to the entire student body at an assembly program. The teacher guided the pupils through all stages of the production, but all final decisions regarding what was recorded were made by student committees.

Activity 2

The teacher of an eighth-grade language arts class assumed the role of editor for the production of a class magazine to be sold to raise funds for starting a paperback library. Assignments were made to individual students according to their ability, needs, and interests. For example, a girl who had difficulty with paragraph construction was assigned to write an article describing the outstanding features of different articles of clothing in the new fashions for women. The teacher discussed the pupils' writing with them on an individual basis, and small groups of students were formed to react to each other's writing.

Activity 3

A sixth-grade class was given some biographical information about living authors of children's literature. Each pupil selected an author who appealed to him and read one of his books. He then composed a letter to his author communicating his personal reaction to the book. Pupils read each other's letters in small groups and made suggestions for improving the quality of the letters. Eventually the letters were mailed, and many pupils received personal replies from the authors to whom they had written. Most of the pupils were eager to read some of the books their classmates had read and asked if they could write letters in class to other authors whose books they had read.

Activity 4

Four fourth-grade boys in a remedial reading class were each given the title of a short reading selection taken from one of the *Science Research Associates Reading Laboratories* (Science Research Associates) and asked to write what they thought the selection would be about. The students read their predictions to each other and discussed the reasons for their predictions. Then the students read the actual selections and discussed them.

Activity 5

A teacher of three fifth-grade girls in a remedial reading class read the girls a story up to the exciting end and asked the girls collectively to write the ending. When the girls' ending was written, the teacher finished reading the story and the merits of both endings were discussed.

Teachers who know their pupils well will be able to structure meaningful activities that are tailor-made for their particular needs and interests. The importance of creative and relevant activities for students who have difficulty communicating their ideas and feelings cannot be overemphasized.

THOUGHTS FOR DISCUSSION

"If by teaching writing we mean teaching students to recognize the parts of speech and different sentence patterns, it seems safe to predict that the instruction will have little if any positive effect on their reading. On the other hand, if we teach writing as a thinking process, emphasizing logic and rhetoric and providing ample opportunity for constructing communicative sentences and paragraphs, reading ability will probably be improved." (Otto and Smith, 1970, p. 100)

"It may be considered trite to say that one must begin where the learner is. However, this point is really the crux of the matter from an instructional standpoint if one is to adhere to the basic principle that learning can proceed only from the known. There is no other place to begin with a child than where he is, with what he knows. To begin elsewhere is to expect him to build a structure with no foundation. Planning corrective instruction must begin with evaluation of what the child has to bring to the learning situation." (Johnson, 1967, p. 65)

"At age five or six the child goes to school. The school now shares the home's continuing responsibility for his language development. If the home has done its job well, the school's role is usually uncomplicated. But if a course of failure has been established, much insight and skill will be needed for alteration. . . . The culturally disadvantaged child often finds that the language patterns of his home are unacceptable to the school and that his usual ways of communicating are ineffective. And he finds that books are written about people he has never seen using language patterns he has never heard." (Frost, 1967, p. 10)

"Many teachers still have the seemingly logical view that children cannot express written thought until they have mastered basic literacy skills. 'I can't let them write stories yet,' said one second-grade teacher, 'they don't know how to spell.' Such a view if applied to speech-thought would mean that children could not be permitted to express themselves in oral language until they had fully mastered all the phonology of adult speech as well as all the intricacies of its structure; they would be confined to a vocabulary that accorded with adult meanings. This view, of course, is absurd." (Smith, Goodman, and Meredith, 1970, p. 234)

"The teacher of English and the language arts cannot know too much about the English language and the grammar available today. But that same teacher can all too easily attempt to teach too much of this knowledge directly in the classroom. It is not an objective of English teaching to make grammarians of the students. It can be cogently argued that 'direct teaching of grammar as formal subject matter—to be mastered for its own sake as a discipline—should be limited to a specific course or courses offered in high school, or to specific units of instruction possibly in junior high school." (Lefevre, 1970, p. 70)

REFERENCES

Adler, M. J. *How to read a book.* New York: Simon and Schuster, 1940.

Bellack, A. A. The language of the classroom: Meanings communicated in high school teaching. In J. B. Macdonald and R. R. Leeper (Eds.), *Theories of instruction.* Washington, D.C.: Association for Supervision and Curriculum Development, 1965, 100–113.

Bostain, J. C. The dream world of English grammar. *Readings in the language arts* (2nd ed.) New York: Macmillan, 1968, 242–246.

Burack, B. Composition: Why? what? how? *English Journal,* 1965, **54**, 504–506.

Fader, D. N., and Shaevitz, M. H. *Hooked on books.* New York: Berkley Publishing, 1966.

Frost, J. L. Language development in children. *Issues and innovations in the teaching of reading.* Glenview, Ill.: Scott, Foresman, 1967, 3–19.

Gleason, J. R. Language development in early childhood. *Oral Language and Reading*. Champaign, Ill.: National Council of Teachers of English, 1969, 15–29.

Goodman, K. S. The linguistics of reading. *Issues and innovations in the teaching of reading*. Glenview, Ill.: Scott, Foresman, 1967, 209–216.

Johnson, M. S. Basic considerations in corrective instruction. *Corrective reading in the elementary classroom*. Newark, Del.: International Reading Association, 1967, 61–72.

Lefevre, C. A. *Linguistics, English, and the language arts*. Boston: Allyn and Bacon, 1970.

Loban, W. D. *The language of elementary school children*. Champaign, Ill.: National Council of Teachers of English, 1963.

Loban, W. D. Problems in oral language. Champaign, Ill.: National Council of Teachers of English, 1966.

Moffett, J. *A student-centered language arts curriculum, grades k-13: A handbook for teachers*. Boston: Houghton Mifflin, 1968. (a)

Moffett, J. *Teaching the universe of discourse*. Boston: Houghton Mifflin, 1968. (b)

Otto, W., and Smith, R. J. *Administering the school reading program*. Boston: Houghton Mifflin, 1970.

Pooley, R. C. *Grammar and usage in textbooks on English*. Madison, Wis.: University of Wisconsin Press, 1933.

Pooley, R. C. Teaching English usage. National Council of Teachers of English Monograph No. 16. New York: Appleton-Century-Croft, 1946.

Pooley, R. C., et al. *English language arts in Wisconsin*. Madison, Wis.: Department of Public Instruction, 1967.

Smith, E. B., Goodman, K. S., and Meredith, R. *Language and thinking in the elementary school*. New York: Holt, 1970.

Strickland, R. G. Implications of research in linguistics for elementary teaching. *Elementary English*, 1963, **40**, 168–171.

Chapter 15

The Teacher and Remedial Teaching

Early in this book we made the point that good corrective and remedial teaching is not very different from good developmental teaching: the goal is to help pupils approach the limits of their ability to achieve. Likewise the desirable personal characteristics of the effective remedial teacher are not very different from those of the effective classroom teacher. Yet, another point made earlier is also relevant here: Because the disabled learner must overcome greater obstacles of previous failure and frustration than the adequate learner, his need for instruction that is thoughtfully conceived and sensitively executed is greater. Therefore the teacher who accepts responsibility for corrective and remedial teaching ought to have certain training and personal attributes that will permit him to deal effectively with special problems.

In *Animal Farm*, all of George Orwell's animals were equal; but some were "more equal than others." Perhaps what we are suggesting here is that if all teachers are equal, then corrective and remedial teachers ought to be more equal. They should be more skilled in diagnosis, more aware of their pupils' personal needs, more proficient in teaching, and better able to understand their pupils' problems. To some extent, these qualities can be acquired through training and experience; but the teacher's point of view is equally important. In the pages that follow we shall consider the development of a point of view as well as the development of specialized skills.

The assumption implicit throughout this book is that good corrective and remedial teaching is good teaching at its best. The purpose in Chapter 15 is to focus specifically upon the role and function of the teacher in good corrective and remedial teaching. Some points regarding the facilitation of learning are made first. Then the matter of who can most appropriately assume responsibility for corrective and remedial teaching is considered, and special programs and specialized personnel for dealing with learning disabilities are presented. And finally two points of view are examined.

FACILITATION OF LEARNING

We have, particularly in Chapter 3 but in most of the other chapters as well, addressed ourselves to the methodology—the how-to-do-it—of corrective and remedial teaching. This is, we feel, as it must be, for in order to focus instruction teachers must have a clear perception of the task and how to tackle it. Unfortunately, such an emphasis may appear to stress the *manipulation* of pupils rather than the *participation* of each individual pupil as attempts are made to overcome learning problems. This, of course, is not our intent. In another discussion, where a distinction was drawn between viewing pupils as *individuals* and as *persons,* two of the present authors said, "The individual may be assessed in terms of his reading skill development, categorized according to his strengths and weaknesses, and taught according to his own characteristics; but the person must remain unclassified, free to strive and to attain according to his own efforts and hopes" (Otto and Smith, 1970, p. 6). Our position here is the same.

Some Assumptions

Carl Rogers (1969, Chapter 7) has listed what he calls "principles or hypotheses" relevant to learning and its facilitation. Viewed as a set of assumptions they can be extremely relevant to the concerns of corrective and remedial teachers for they focus upon the personal aspect of learning. Remedial teachers need to be as sensitive to the personal aspect of learning as they are aware of the methodology of instruction. In the list that follows the italicized assumptions are from Rogers; the comments are ours.

1. *Human beings have a natural potentiality for learning.* Rogers' main point is that human beings are curious and eager to learn unless or until their enthusiasm is blunted by unsatisfactory learning experiences. The fact is, of course, that most disabled learners have had many unsatisfactory learning experiences and their enthusiasm for learning, at least the kind of learning that typically takes place in a school context, has indeed been blunted. The teacher's main responsibility in working with disabled learners is to see that conditions are such that each learner's potential and desire for learning is released. This is not likely to happen unless the teacher demonstrates his belief in the first assumption.

2. *Significant learning takes place when the subject matter is perceived by the student as having relevance for his own purposes.* Phonics generalizations, sight words, multiplication facts, legible letter forms—all of these will be learned most efficiently by a pupil who sees their relevance for his own purposes. Successful corrective and remedial teachers are able to be most helpful because they make it a point to discover (*a*) what subject matter is most relevant for an individual pupil at a given point in time, and (*b*) what can be done to demonstrate the relevance of subject matter as it is presented.

3. *Learning which involves a change in self organization—in the perception of oneself—is threatening and tends to be resisted.* Iscoe (1964) was talking to this point when he discussed the logical dilemma of the bright, underachieving child. Otto (1965) summarized the dilemma:

> If a bright child who has been doing unsatisfactory work begins, for any of a great number of reasons, to do acceptable work his parents and/or teachers are

likely to tell him that they knew all along that he could do it if he would **only** try harder. In effect, the child's new success earns him not praise for doing well now but criticism for having done badly before. Thus, the horns of the dilemma are: (a) to continue to do well and be blamed, and (b) to go back to underachieving and be blamed. (P. 333)

Teachers who recognize the possibility of such a dilemma or others like it are in a position to help children to resolve them.

4. *Those learnings which are threatening to the self are more easily perceived and assimilated when external threats are at a minimum.*

5. *When threat to the self is low, experience can be perceived in different fashion and learning can proceed.* The fourth and fifth assumptions are closely related. Together they underscore the need to remove external pressures and all potential sources of ridicule or scorn from the remedial teaching situation. The disabled learner almost always has good reason for feeling threatened and inadequate, so any further demonstration of his deficiencies *is not* needed. Understanding, support, success experiences, and help with devising means for self-evaluation *are* needed.

6. *Much significant learning is acquired through doing.* Any teacher who has seen the spurt in learning that usually accompanies introduction of a driver's manual as the basic text with teen-age readers needs no further evidence that this assumption is sound.

7. *Learning is facilitated when the student participates responsibly in the learning process.*

8. *Self-initiated learning which involves the whole person of the learner— feelings as well as intellect—is the most lasting and pervasive.*

9. *Independence, creativity, self-reliance are all facilitated when self-criticism and self-evaluation are basic and evaluation by others is of secondary importance.*

10. *The most socially useful learning in the modern world is the learning of the process of learning, a continuing openness to experience and incorporation into oneself of the process of change.* The last four assumptions have a single theme. They call for the involvement of the learner in his own learning. They underscore the need on the part of remedial teachers for a positive perception of each disabled learner's potential for progress through total participation, self-assessment, and self-direction. The facilitation of learning ultimately is inherent in the learner.

Rogers' main assumption, the one that is implicit in all the others, is that human beings will learn, that they have a "natural potentiality for learning." But if this is so, and we think it is, then what is the function of corrective and remedial teaching? Frieder (1970) suggested an answer in a discussion of the teacher's role as motivator:

All children learn; the issue is whether or not we can teach children what we want them to know. There are a number of prerequisites to solving this problem: We must, for example, decide what it is exactly, that we want children to learn; which children already know it; how we can teach it to the rest; and how we will know when they have learned it. In fact, there are so many areas of concern in the field of education, and they overlap so widely, that one of the first necessities in attempting to solve the problem of teaching children what we want them to know is developing an organized approach to the problem. (P. 28)

The issue in corrective and remedial teaching is similar: how we can help disabled learners focus on what they need to know; and the prerequisites to solving the problem are also similar: we must identify critical objectives, determine which have and which have not been attained, and decide how to pursue the latter and when they have been reached. As we see it, then, the function of corrective and remedial teaching is to facilitate learning by providing an organized approach.

A Framework for Organizing Instruction

A framework for organizing instruction to facilitate learning is suggested here. While the present focus is upon corrective and remedial teaching, the approach is, of course, equally appropriate for use in developmental teaching. The reader may wish to refer again to the discussion of behaviorally stated objectives in Chapter 3. The context there is different, but discussion of objectives and their function is relevant here.

Our suggested framework for organizing corrective and remedial instruction includes the following: identification of essential content, statement of objectives, assessment of skill development, identification of appropriate teaching/learning activities, and evaluation.

Essential Content

The most basic task in corrective and remedial teaching is to identify content which is considered, at least in the local setting, to be essential to academic success. Unless and until this is done there can be no straightforward approach to remediation; instead, remedial efforts will tend to lack focus and to be dispersed, shotgun style, at the discretion of each remedial teacher. Yet the fact is that up to the present time efforts to specify essential content have been rare and not very definitive except in the basic skill areas, where essential content amounts mainly to essential skills. In the context of the present book, where the focus is upon the several basic skill areas, specification of essential *skills* is generally adequate; but further efforts toward identifying essential *content* will be required before much can be said about remedial efforts outside the basic skill areas.

Even when the focus is limited to the basic skill areas, we are not suggesting that the essential skills identified in any area must have universal support. Opinions about what is essential are likely to differ for the foreseeable future. What we are suggesting is that remedial teachers ought to be satisfied that they have a clear notion of what *they feel* are the essential skills in any area, with, it is hoped, consensual support at the local level. If there is at least local agreement on essential skills, then the identification of pupils' skill deficiencies and focused remedial teaching can proceed in a reasonably straightforward manner.

A statement of essential skills in reading is given by Otto and Askov (1970). Their suggestion is that the statement be adapted as needed to be acceptable locally, but the statement does amount to a starting place. Similar statements for reading and for the other skill areas can be found, probably most readily in state or local curriculum guides. They must, of course, be used with discretion for they vary greatly in quality.

Objectives

Once essential skills have been identified, the next step is to specify objectives in behavioral terms for each skill. As pointed out in Chapter 3, a meaningfully stated objective (1) *identifies* and *describes* behaviors considered appropriate to a desired outcome, and (2) may specify the conditions under which the behavior is expected to occur. Objectives that are so stated permit reasonably straightforward decisions regarding (1) experiences that are most likely to produce the desired behaviors, (2) situations in which the behaviors are appropriate, and (3) the success or failure of the approach designed to produce the behavior. Thus, in corrective and remedial teaching, adequately stated objectives specify the criterion behaviors related to each essential skill. That is, performance that will be accepted as evidence of specific skill mastery is described in terms of overt behaviors.

At this point it should be clear that objectives that are related to essential skills should indeed specify *mastery levels* for performance. Each pupil should be expected to attain mastery—e.g., 80 percent or better of test items related to the objective—of each objective. A pupil's performance, then, is assessed with regard to an *absolute* or *criterion* referent—i.e., the objective— rather than a *relative* referent—i.e., the performance of his peers. Mastery learning is gaining solid support in all areas (Bloom, 1968; Bruner, 1960; Carroll, 1963; Mayo, 1970), but we feel it is imperative in the basic skill areas, where the foundations are laid for all subsequent learning.

Assessment

Adequately stated objectives serve to define essential skills in terms of observable behaviors. They permit examination of the skill development status of individuals in order to determine their strengths and weaknesses. This examination of specific skill development can proceed through the use of formal, paper-and-pencil tests or informal observations of relevant behaviors. In either case, the objective serves to specify the relevant behaviors and permits the teacher to determine which skills have or have not been mastered.

Instruction

Corrective and remedial instruction, then, depends on objectives and assessment: the teacher knows what constitutes adequate performance with regard to specific skills; and he determines the current skill development status of individuals. He then devises appropriate instruction to meet individual pupils' needs for specific skill development. In practice, this means that the teacher selects from the array of instructional materials and activities that are available those that appear to be most appropriate for a given pupil in a given situation at a given point in time.

This is the place at which a sensitive teacher must assume major responsibility. At the present time virtually no definitive knowledge has been generated regarding the systematic matching of pupils and instruction. Frieder (1970) put it well, although in somewhat different terms: "Many alternatives are currently available to the prescriber in the areas of media and strategies; but despite the advances in diagnosis and instruction, research has provided little concrete information about the prescriber's task—putting diagnosis and instruction together to reach objectives" (p. 29). Thus the task of working out the details of instruction rests squarely with the teacher. Yet, while there will always be a number of ways to pursue a given objective, well-stated objectives will, at the very least, specify goals of instruction

We doubt that research-based knowledge relative to the systematic matching of pupils and materials/methods is forthcoming in the foreseeable future. The point here is that teachers will need to continue to make judgments regarding the instruction of individual pupils. Such judgments will best be made by sensitive teachers with clear perceptions of pupils' needs, explicit objectives, and knowledge of a wide range of methods and materials. In facilitation of learning, particularly in corrective and remedial situations, there is no substitute for a good teacher.

Evaluation

Evaluation is necessary in the present framework for it provides a check on all of the other components. In the area of reading, for example, the pay-off from identification of essential skills, statement of objectives, assessment of individual's specific skill development, and focused instruction is functional reading ability, the ability to cope with the reading tasks encountered both in and out of school. If the desired end product is not forthcoming, then there is reason to examine each of the components to determine where the process breaks down.

One specific example of the framework for organizing instruction that is described above in general terms is the Wisconsin Design for Reading Skill Development (Otto and Askov, 1970). Components of the Design include an outline of essential skills, behaviorally stated objectives related to the skills, assessment exercises for each skill, and a resource file of materials and activities related to the skills.

RESPONSIBILITY FOR REMEDIAL READING

Any consideration of the attributes and functions of corrective and remedial teachers would be incomplete without specific consideration of where the responsibility for working with disabled learners resides. All too often there seems to be an implicit assumption on the part of many teachers that disabled learners and remedial teaching are the sole responsibility of "specialists"—remedial teachers, school psychologists, etc. While there is no questioning the fact that various specialists have vital roles to play in any school's remedial teaching program, it should be quite clear that there never will be an adequate supply of specialists to meet all needs for corrective and remedial teaching. Coordinated efforts on the part of administrators, specialists, and classroom teachers are required. But ultimately the responsibility for corrective and remedial teaching almost always rests with, or at least comes back to, the classroom teacher. Until a disabled learner becomes able to function with reasonable efficiency in a regular classroom, remedial teaching has not fulfilled its promise. The classroom teacher must of necessity play a critical role in the attainment of this goal.

Rappaport and McNary (1970) have spoken to the point:

Teachers of children with learning disorders know from experience how much a child's emotional blowups or other maladaptive attempts to cope with learning situations can interfere with academic progress. Frequently the child's academic progress is contingent upon how well such blowups are handled (Redl, 1966). Even when the child has psychotherapy the psychotherapist works with the child at best for only a relatively few hours of the week. Moreover, the therapist usually is not available to help the child work through the many blowups that occur within the classroom. Therefore, whether it is formally acknowledged or not, in public education the teacher plays the major role in the rehabilitation of children with learning disorders. (P. 76)

The example given by Rappaport and McNary has to do specifically with cases of emotional instability, but the point is quite explicit. Specialized help outside the classroom ordinarily accounts only for a small fraction of a child's total school time. The rest of the time the responsibility for providing meaningful learning experiences rests with the classroom teacher. To accomplish this, Rappaport and McNary have pointed out that teachers need backup support:

To assist in the development of the whole child is a stressfull obligation. Therefore, from an administrative standpoint, the school's organization should be designated to provide the teacher with backup support by a psychotherapist, a parent counselor, a physician, a nurse, and educational specialists (such as in the area of reading, adaptive physical education, etc.). When the teacher does not have backup support, and, as is too often the case, when additionally the teacher does not have facility with the required teaching skills, he or she can be expected to be overwhelmed with classroom chaos and personal stress. Under such conditions, the teacher can be expected not to foster the child's growth, but instead to undermine it, or at best to perform a holding action. (P. 77)

The obvious need on the part of classroom teachers, then, is reasonable comfort in the role of teacher, command of requisite teaching skills, and time—on an everyday schedule—to communicate with the specialists who may be involved. The first two needs can only be met by the teacher himself. This book and others like it can, we hope, provide some assistance. The latter need, though, is the responsibility of school administrators. The responsibility for establishing a physical setup that is conducive to good teaching is theirs. Administrators who attempt to turn over all responsibility for corrective and remedial teaching to specialists and/or teachers are derelict in their own responsibility as line officers in the school organization.

Stephens (1967) has suggested a promising approach to recognizing the facts of life regarding school staffing and to making systematic provision for children with learning problems. He suggests three levels of professional teachers: (1) the basic teacher, whose training is minimal and whose expected tenure as a teacher is brief, (2) the experienced, career teacher, who is well trained and acts as leader of a team of basic teachers, and (3) the remedial specialist, who is highly trained in the techniques of diagnosis and remediation and who is called in to deal with learning problems as they arise. While the Stephens plan continues to set regular classroom teachers and remedial specialists apart, which we find somewhat objectionable, Stephens would reply that to expect all teachers to be able to cope with all problems is as unreasonable as to expect all mothers to be qualified pediatricians. His point is not unreasonable.

In fact we have already suggested that corrective teaching is best done entirely within the regular classroom program, whereas strictly remedial teaching, which is confined to substantially disabled learners, is usually most realistically handled as a supplement to the classroom program. Thus, we do not deny the need for specialists. Our point is that specialists can do only part of the job, that the job of dealing with disabled learners requires a team approach, and that the classroom teacher must always be an active member of the team. To offer a homely analogy, the classroom teacher is like the pitcher on a baseball team. So long as he does his job flawlessly, he can carry on with little support. But he must feel reassured to know that he has seven specialists in back of him when he needs them.

SPECIAL PROGRAMS AND SPECIALIZED PREPARATION

The need for formal training in corrective and remedial teaching is dependent in part upon the goals of the individual. A teacher may decide to seek additional training either to become more proficient in dealing with pupils who need corrective or remedial help within the classroom or to become a full-time remedial specialist. The teacher who is interested only in developing personal skills can pay less attention to formal training. For purposes of self-directed study the present book and many of the references cited at the ends of chapters should be useful. The person who expects to become a specialist must, however, meet certification requirements in many states. Unfortunately it is difficult to generalize about certification requirements because specific specialty areas and types of preparation required vary widely from state to state. We shall, therefore, present some specific examples; the reader should check with the proper offices in his own state regarding specialty areas and certification requirements.

State of Georgia Program for Exceptional Children

To cite the example of a single state, the Georgia Department of Education has a Program for Exceptional Children that ". . . provides consultative services to public school systems interested in providing appropriate educational programs for children who deviate intellectually, physically, communicatively, or emotionally so markedly from what is considered normal growth and development that they cannot receive maximum benefit from participation in a regular school program" (Georgia Department of Education, 1969, p. 2). The specific programs described demonstrate the range of specialty areas offered in one state. Obviously some of the areas have more specific focus on learning problems as we have defined them than others, but virtually every area would have some concern with or could make some contribution to corrective and remedial teaching.

1. *Program for the Emotionally Disturbed.*   (The program is for persons who are unable "to maintain a set adjustment to" everyday surroundings. One specific expectation in establishing a program is that provision be made *for the student to return to the regular classroom whenever practicable.* This, we feel, is a desirable expectation that ought always to be made explicit. The need for involving the classroom teacher is quite clear.)

2. *Program for the Hearing Impaired.*   (The basic aim of the program is to provide the required special help in establishing and developing communication and language skills while providing opportunities for association with hearing peers.)

3. *Program of Hospital/Home Instruction.*   (The program is for persons confined to their home or a hospital due to a diagnosed, noncommunicable physical condition. Each child enrolled in the program is maintained *on his regular classroom teacher's register* and the special teacher works closely with the classroom teacher.)

4. *Program for Mentally Retarded-Educable.*

5. *Program for Mentally Retarded-Trainable.*   (Strictly speaking, we would not ordinarily consider candidates for either of these programs prospects for remedial teaching. They would benefit more from contact with *adapted* than with *remedial* programs of instruction.)

6. *Program for the Multi-Handicapped.* (The multi-handicapped are those individuals who have two or more *physical* problems severe enough to interfere with their receiving all or a part of their education in a regular classroom. The school curriculum is modified on an individual basis, depending on the personal handicap, and the physical setup is modified as needed.)

7. *Program for the Speech Impaired.* (The correction of grammatical errors and reading difficulties is specifically excluded from this program. The need for cooperative effort by appropriate specialists and classroom teacher is apparent where speech impairment and learning disability co-exist.)

8. *Program for the Visually Impaired.* (The program is for the *functionally blind,* the *legally blind,* and the *partially sighted,* as defined in the *Regulations and Procedures.*)

9. *Program for Special Learning Disabilities.* (The program is for children with "a disorder in one or more of the basic psychological processes involved in understanding or in using spoken or written languages." Again, an explicit expectation in establishing the program is that provision will be made for returning children to the regular classroom as soon as they are "able to make constructive use of regular classroom instruction.")

Certification in each area requires recommendation from an approved college or university stating that the candidate has completed a planned program of preparation.

Oregon Requirements for Certification

The Oregon State Department of Education has established certification requirements for the area of *extreme learning problems exclusive of mental retardation.* Remedial reading teachers and general remedial teachers are expected to hold the certificate. Requirements for the certificate are:

A. Basic Norm (four-year)
1. Standard general elementary norm.
2. Recommendations by the college or university in which the special education preparation was completed.
3. 24 quarter hours of preparation in special education in a college or university approved by the State Board of Education to prepare special education teachers, such preparation to include:
   Education or psychology of the exceptional child (a survey course)
   Intelligence testing (a clinical course)
   Behavioral problems in children
   Diagnostic and remedial techniques in basic school subjects (exclusive of reading)
   Diagnostic and remedial techniques in reading (a clinical course)
   An advanced course in reading instruction
   Clinical practice in reading, some of which shall be in a supervised setting in the public schools.

B. Standard norm (five-year)

    1. 42 quarter hours of preparation in special education, including the 24 quarter hours required for the four-year norm plus an additional 18 quarter hours distributed in the following areas: the mentally retarded child; intelligence testing, a clinical course; speech pathology—articulation defects, retarded speech, and emotional speech problems; audiology; advanced preparation in the education of children with extreme learning problems (a clinical course), to include principles of counselling applicable to work with parents and information relative to use of social agencies in the state.

    2. All requirements for the basic four-year norm.

Standards Proposed by the IRA

The Committee on Professional Standards of the International Reading Association has suggested minimum standards for the professional training of reading specialists. The standards are not specifically for remedial specialists; but the training suggested would be generally appropriate for remedial reading teachers, especially if the options elected were additional courses in diagnostic techniques and remedial practicum. Remedial teaching in the several basic skill areas would, of course, call for additional preparation and/or experience in each area. The minimum standards are:

    I. A minimum of three years of successful teaching and/or clinical experience.

    II. A Master's Degree or its equivalent of a Bachelor's Degree plus 30 graduate semester hours in reading and related areas as listed below:

        A. A minimum of 12 semester hours in graduate-level reading courses with at least one course in 1 and 2, and 3 or 4:

            1. *Foundations or survey of reading*—a basic course whose content is related exclusively to reading instruction or the psychology of reading. Such a course ordinarily would be the first in a sequence of reading courses.

            2. *Diagnosis and correction of reading disabilities*—the content of this course or courses includes the following: causes of reading disabilities; observation and interview procedures; diagnostic instruments; standard and informal tests; report writing; materials and methods of instruction.

            3. *Clinical or laboratory practicum in reading*—a clinical or laboratory experience which might be an integral part of a course or courses in the diagnosis and correction of reading disabilities. Students diagnose and treat reading disability cases under supervision.

            4. *Supervision and curriculum in reading*—a study of selected curricula and the planning of a sound school curriculum in reading; an understanding of the functions and duties of the reading supervisor or consultant and the effective ways of implementing them.

        B. At least one graduate-level course in each of the following content areas:

            1. *Measurement and/or evaluation*—a course which includes one or more of the following: principles and practices of test construction and the selection, administration, scoring, and interpretation of group stan-

dardized tests; nature, theory, function, and use of individual intelligence tests; theory, function, and use of tests of personality.

2. *Child and/or adolescent psychology or development*—a course which stresses how children and/or adolescents mature and develop with emphasis upon school activities and their relation to normal, healthy development.

3. *Personality and/or mental hygiene*—a course which includes one or more of the following: the nature, development and patterns of personality and methods of change; personality theories and their contritions to understanding the dynamics of personality; integration of psychological knowledge and principles and their relation to mental health; etiological factors, differential diagnosis, and methods used in the correction of behavior problems.

4. *Educational psychology*—a course which includes one or more of the following: study of behavior, development, school environment, conditions for learning, and methods of assessment; theories of learning and their implication for classroom practices.

C. The remainder of the semester hours in reading and/or related areas. Courses recommended might include one or more of the following:
Literature for children and/or adolescents;
Organization and supervision of reading programs;
Research and the literature in reading;
Foundations of education;
Principles of guidance;
Nature of language;
Communications;
Speech and hearing;
Exceptional child;
or any additional courses under II *A* and II *B*.

Wisconsin License Requirements

The Wisconsin State Department of Public Instruction has outlined minimum requirements for a teacher's license in remedial reading. Again, additional courses would be desirable for teachers who plan to do remedial teaching in the basic skill areas other than reading. The following is from the 1961 statement of certification standards for the state of Wisconsin:

Remedial reading. A Wisconsin teacher's license based upon a degree is required. In addition 12 special semester credits must be obtained. Courses in remedial reading and in a remedial reading clinic are required. The remaining credits may be chosen from adolescent literature, children's literature, techniques of improving developmental reading, and techniques of teaching the mentally handicapped. Three years of teaching experience are a prerequisite to obtaining the license.

The Reading Certification Committee of the Wisconsin State Reading Association has recommended requirements more nearly in line with the recommendations of the International Reading Association. As stated above, the requirement is clearly minimal; but there are those who would argue that the function of a certifying agency is indeed to establish minimums, not optimums. We would tend to support a minimal statement because such a statement permits flexibility in planning graduate programs that are sensitive to personal needs and the needs of local schools. Quantity has never been a good substitute for quality.

Personal Preparation

In practice, much of the corrective and remedial teaching in our schools is done by regular classroom teachers in the absence of any formal program of remedial instruction. Typically the teaching is done by teachers and encouraged by administrators who are sensitive to the needs and problems of their pupils. Such efforts should not be curtailed by slavish insistence upon formal training. Statements of standards and certification requirements should not serve as barriers but as guides to teachers who are seeking greater competence. There is no questioning the fact that effective diagnostic and remedial teaching demands specialized knowledge and skills; but it is a fact, too, that the successful classroom teacher already has much of this knowledge and many of these skills. Carl Rogers (1951) had this to say regarding the training of psychotherapists: "Training in psychotherapy exists in varying degrees. If the orientation is in the direction of a permissive and noncoercive therapy, then some training is better than none, more training is better than some" (p. 442). Training for remedial teaching, too, exists in varying degrees.

As we have already suggested, a good remedial teacher is likely to be not very different from an exceptionally good teacher. Lipson (1970) has listed some attributes that teachers ought to have or be attempting to acquire. The list can serve as a guide to any teacher who is seeking self-improvement. All of the attributes listed are desirable ones for remedial teachers. College or university courses could be selected for the contribution they are likely to make in developing any or all of the attributes.

1. The teacher should be an intellectual model for students.

2. The teacher should have attitudes, opinions and emotions which help, rather than inhibit, the students' learning.

3. The teacher should be able to determine the appropriateness of student behavior, and arrange proper contingencies for behaviors.

4. The teacher should be able to employ a complex and varied system of allocating resources.

5. The teacher should be a selective knowledge source both of knowledge regarding instructional strategies and information of direct use to the student.

6. The teacher must be able to collect, organize and interpret data, using the data as bases for decision making.

7. The teacher should be able to plan an educational program which will assist each student's career development. (P. 10)

A National Effort toward Personnel Development

Certain recommendations of the Secretary's (HEW) National Advisory Committee on Dyslexia and Related Reading Disorders (1969) are particularly relevant here because they lay the groundwork for a national effort to develop the manpower and resources required for a sustained attack on reading problems. While the recommendations are confined to the skill area of reading, implications for the several basic skill areas are clear. The recommendations that follow are quoted from the Committee's report (pp. 16–20); our comments are enclosed in brackets.

1. Review all current programs of the Federal Government related to reading in order to effect greater coordination and integration of these programs. These should be strengthened and extended as necessary to formulate a program plan which will spell out comprehensive objectives for Federal effort in relation to reading and develop a system of program analysis that embraces the scientific and professional elements essential to analyzing the use of public resources for reading improvement.

2. Provide grant or contract funds to develop model classroom programs to be used as a basis for stimulating research on and evaluation of reading instruction. These classrooms will study procedures, materials, aptitude and achievement measures, conditions for motivation, and teacher behaviors. These classrooms must, in turn, serve as observational models for training teachers in association with a program of teacher preparation.

3. Maintain continuous evaluation of instructional materials and procedures. Where evaluation through controlled research yields evidence of instructional effectiveness, these materials and procedures should be recommended for publication and wide dissemination.

4. Develop demonstration programs for professional preparation in reading instruction and remediation. These programs and their curricula should incorporate the results of scientific study and involve procedures which have been evaluated scientifically, tested in the classroom, and found effective for reading instruction and remediation.

5. Provide grant or contract funds for studies to determine the role, effectiveness, and training of volunteer and paraprofessional personnel in the field of reading instruction and remediation.

6. Provide grant or contract funds for preschool language and other programs that enhance reading development in order to construct and validate instructional procedures and materials to be used by agencies, schools, and parents. [We see a need for a note of caution here. In the past, attempts to discover exemplary procedures and materials have not been very successful. Perhaps the main problem is that, implicitly at least, the attempts have been directed to the discovery of THE BEST procedures and materials. The fact, of course, is that there are many "best" procedures and materials, depending upon such variables as the teacher, the pupil, and the situation. Future efforts ought to focus upon the discovery of guidelines, not ultimate answers.]

7. Provide grant or contract funds to construct and validate measures which constitute standards of literacy and reading skills. [Note that all of the literacy skills—writing, spelling, etc.—are included. This is important, for there is more to true literacy than reading.]

8. Request the Secretary of Labor to conduct studies which will establish the minimum level of reading skills needed for effective performance in benchmark occupations under specified conditions. [This recommendation was partly put into operation by the HEW-targeted research in reading effort, which was implemented in the fall of 1970.]

9. Provide grant or contract funds for research on the unique educational needs and vocational possibilities of persons with severe reading disorders. [Implicit in this recommendation is recognition of the fact that all cases of reading disability will never be "cured." A worthwhile first step toward the solution of any problem is the acceptance of reality.]

10. Provide a focal point for receiving and giving significance to recommendations by concerned professional organizations in the field of reading with respect to standards for reading teachers, clinicians, consultants, and supervisors.

11. Seek specific appropriations to provide fellowships, institutes, and short-term intensive training projects in the prevention and remediation of reading disorders for general classroom teachers, teachers of reading, reading supervisors, reading clinicians, and reading researchers.

Support the conduct of workshops on a national level involving educators and disciplines other than the field of education. These workshops will seek to determine desirable prerequisites for teaching elementary reading, explore the methods whereby these requisites can best be met, and disseminate the findings of these workshops to institutions concerned with teacher training.

13. Support the conduct of workshops in the health and education professions involved in diagnosis and treatment of reading disorders. These workshops will be established in consultation with universities and professional organizations concerned with training of personnel. Such workshops will evaluate current practices for exposing personnel in health and education fields to the nature of the reading process and of reading disorders, and they will formulate approaches for extending and improving these practices. [Taken together Recommendations 11, 12, and 13 call for both pre-service and in-service training. We feel that both kinds are required at all levels to insure competence and to promote professionalism.]

14. Seek to apply the Federal Government's classification standards for difficult teaching assignments (under the Civil Service Position Classification Plan) to include positions for teaching persons with reading disorders and for teaching reading to children in school grades one and two, and to make adjustments in the qualification standards accordingly.

15. Encourage states and Federal agencies to conduct a review of requirements for certification and teacher training and to consider incentives for special training in reading instruction for first and second grade teachers. [The focus on first- and second-grade teachers shows the emphasis placed upon early detection and correction of problems before they deteriorate into severe disabilities. We feel that such an emphasis is desirable in all the basic skill areas and that coordinated team efforts will help to insure that no single skill area is promoted at the expense of the others.]

16. Encourage states to include in the category warranting special training, certification, and incentives the teachers of bilingual children, teachers of children of migrant workers, and teachers of reading in inner city areas.

17. Encourage public interest in the support of community resources for the prevention, diagnosis, and treatment of reading disorders, development of programs to provide information on sources of professional services, support of professional organizations in expanding services, and provision of a focal point for obtaining and using volunteer services in meeting the needs of persons with reading disorders.

The recommendations clearly call for the involvement of classroom teachers, without denying the continued need for specialists. While individuals will agree or disagree with certain specific recommendations, they serve, at the very least, as a starting point for badly needed efforts to coordinate federal, state, and local activities. There are clear implications for special programs and for specialized preparation to cope with real and potential learning disabilities.

TWO POINTS OF VIEW

In the remaining pages of this chapter we shall examine two points of view that might be adopted by teachers who take responsibility for corrective and remedial teaching. But it should be clear at the outset that we are talking more about focus than about two mutually exclusive approaches: In what we have called a counseling point of view the focus is on the *individual;* whereas, with the social factors viewpoint the focus is on the *environment.* Of course, every individual grows up in an environment, and it would be as absurd to ignore the latter as the former. But in recent years we have seen so much emphasis placed upon the environment that we feel individuals may be getting lost. The reader can make his own decision regarding the validity of the points we make in the pages that follow.

A Counseling Point of View*

All disabled learners are not emotionally maladjusted nor are all emotionally maladjusted pupils disabled learners. Yet success in the basic skills— especially reading—is an essential step in normal development, for failure precludes the sequential acquisition of the higher level academic skills and learnings. Failure in the basic school subjects, then, is likely to interfere with adequate adjustment. To attempt to decide whether an individual pupil's learning problems were caused by emotional problems or vice versa is less important than to recognize the probability that many learning disabilities will be accompanied by varying degrees of emotional maladjustment.

*Robert C. Fredericks, Counselor at Portland (Oregon) Community College, is responsible for much of the discussion of the counseling point of view.

Many children with severe emotional maladjustments need intensive psychotherapy before they can respond to remedial teaching; every attempt should be made to secure competent professional help in such cases. But in the majority of cases it is up to the remedial teacher to deal with emotional problems along with learning problems. Mastery of diagnostic and remedial techniques provides the teacher with a means for outlining a plan of instruction, but success in remedial teaching is often as dependent upon meeting emotional needs as upon meeting instructional needs. This does not mean that remedial teachers must be highly trained counselors, but it does mean that teachers who can establish relationships that communicate acceptance and understanding with their pupils are more likely to be successful than those who depend entirely upon the manipulation of diagnostic and remedial techniques. ". . . the facilitation of significant learning rests upon certain attitudinal qualities which exist in the personal *relationship* between the facilitator and the learner." (Rogers, 1968, p. 5)

Successful remedial teachers have more than a collection of techniques; they have a way of working with children. From our observations, it appears that their success is often based upon an ability to establish relationships with their pupils. Although they may not be formally trained as counselors, they have what we shall call a counseling point of view, for the relationships that they establish are essentially counseling relationships. In the pages that follow we shall very briefly describe the basic elements of the counseling relationship and discuss some applications of a counseling point of view. We feel that a remedial teacher who has a basic understanding of the function of counseling and the counseling relationship and who utilizes some of the common techniques of counseling is in a position to work more effectively with disabled learners.

Function of Counseling

Because counseling is a complex process it is difficult to state what it is or what it does very concisely. It has been said, admittedly rather vaguely, that the function of counseling is to unchain the giant that resides within every individual; but counseling does not tamper with the giant. Perhaps counseling is best conceived as a positive expanding process. The purpose is not to bring about a complete personality change but, rather, to make changes and modifications of attitudes. Counseling stresses the positive growth of the individual toward greater self-understanding, self-reliance, and self-respect, which can help him to work through his own problems and to make his own decisions. Thus, counseling enables an individual to help himself.

Counseling Relationships

The foundation of the counseling process is the relationship established between the counselor and the client. (We shall use the terms "counselor" and "client" in discussing the counseling relationship. In the present context, "remedial teacher" and "pupil" would be equally appropriate.) The counseling relationship has certain characteristics that are similar to the interactions between close friends and relatives, but it is different in that two conditions are present that are not generally found in other relationships: It is structured in a psychological framework and the client is always positively accepted by the counselor. The details of establishing and maintaining the relationship vary widely—from play therapy with young children to directive and nondirective approaches with adults—but good relationships have certain characteristics in common. Again, because of the complexity of the counseling process—which is due in no small part to the fact that a number of things must happen concurrently—it is difficult to focus upon basic characteristics one at a time; but we shall do so for discussion purposes.

One of the characteristics of the counseling relationship, *uniqueness,* is paradoxical: While certain general statements can be made about the relationship, each relationship is unique because individuals are unique. Thus, a counselor must know and understand himself, have a generally positive feeling toward human beings, and be flexible enough to adopt basic counseling techniques to the particular needs of each client. The paradox is not a new one for teachers who know from experience that what works with one child does not necessarily work with another.

The counseling relationship also contains the paradox of *objective thoughts* and *emotional feelings.* A counselor must maintain an intricate balance between these two diverse positions. In order to apply the scientific principles of human behavior to what the client is presenting, the counselor must remain, to a degree, removed or detached from the remarks. He must not react to them personally. However, he must, at the same time, be emotionally involved with the client so as to communicate that he is sensitive to and aware of the feelings the client is expressing. This also enables the client to remain emotionally involved. If the counselor becomes too detached, he takes on the characteristics of a computer; but if he becomes too emotionally involved, he loses his objectivity and starts reacting personally. Thus, the counselor must strive to be both emotionally involved in and objectively detached from the counseling situation. This simultaneous dual role makes counseling both an art and a science.

The counseling relationship must also be *real;* it must be genuine, sincere, and honest. People carrying on conversations in everyday life mask their true feelings with small talk; but if such a facade is maintained in the counseling relationship, then conversation instead of counseling takes place. But a counselor cannot merely say, "I am interested in you"; he must show it by his behavior.

Rogers (1968, pp. 7–8) has cited an extremely credible example of *realness* in a teacher-pupil relationship. Barbara Shiel, a sixth-grade teacher, gave her pupils much responsible freedom but she continued to feel frustrated by chaos in the art room. This, in Miss Shiel's (1966) own words, is what happened.

> I find it (still) maddening to live with the mess—with a capital M! No one seems to care but me. Finally, one day I told the children . . . that I am a neat, orderly person by nature and that the mess was driving me to distraction. Did they have a solution? It was suggested that they could have volunteers to clean up . . . I said it didn't seem fair to me to have the same people clean up all the time for others—but it *would* solve it for me. "Well some people *like* to clean," they replied. So that's the way it is.

And that, indeed, is the way it ought to be!

Beginning counselors are sometimes unable to differentiate between a friendly relationship and a warm relationship. Being friendly is nothing more than a superficial aspect of a warm relationship; a big smile, a slap on the back, or a friendly remark are trite ways to convey warmth. The client is able to see through such actions as readily as a used-car buyer is able to see through the actions of the friendly salesman. A counselor—by his behavior, his manners, his facial expressions, his awareness, his consideration for the client—is able to transmit an atmosphere of warmth. Most of the successful remedial teachers we have seen have mastered the art of establishing warm, real relationships with their pupils.

Another important characteristic of the counseling relationship is *acceptance* of the individual by the counselor. To accept is to value an individual for his characteristics of infinite worth and dignity, to place extreme value on a human being for having an inner self, for being unique, for producing original thoughts and ideas. The counselor's acceptance tells the client that he is valued for his unique self and that he has the qualities necessary for positive development; thus, the client is better able to accept himself.

Sympathy is not a part of acceptance. A counselor who expresses sympathy is saying, "I agree with your suffering—you must feel awful—let me help you." Sympathy teaches the client to be dependent; instead of learning to operate independently, he learns to rely on the counselor. A counselor must feel *with* his client, which is empathy, not *for* a client, which is sympathy. Remedial teachers who do not guard against dependent relationships may find that children who have learned to function effectively during remedial sessions cannot do so when they return to the classroom.

Nor is judgment a part of acceptance. A counselor must completely accept the client; to judge is to express like or dislike, to present a personal evaluation of good or bad. Nonjudgmental acceptance is necessary if the client is to feel safe and free enough to express himself honestly and fully. In an accepting atmosphere the client gains a deep sense of freedom, which is seldom found in other interpersonal relationships; he is then able to drop his defenses and to experience being his true self.

(It should be interjected here that remedial teachers who have agreed that they can and should function as counselors up to this point often feel that they cannot realistically implement nonjudgmental acceptance. Their feeling is that because they are primarily tutors they must make judgments about a child's work; work that is incorrect or inferior cannot be accepted as equal to work that is correct and superior. Certainly this is a legitimate observation. It must be clear, however, that in an already paradoxical relationship the remedial teacher who operates with a counseling point of view must cope with still another paradox. The roles of teacher and counselor may at times seem to be at odds. The point to be made here is that a remedial teacher can continue to accept a child as a person even when it is necessary to evaluate his academic performance. Acceptance supersedes judgment. We shall return to this point later.)

A final characteristic of the counseling relationship is *understanding.* It follows acceptance and makes acceptance meaningful. To understand a client means to appreciate, by a process of intellectual thought and sensitive feelings, the significance of his remarks. To truly understand a client is to perceive his private world through his frame of reference, to see things as he sees them. This is a difficult task, for the counselor must leave his world and enter the world of the client. In making the transition the counselor leaves behind his ideas, perceptions, values, and feelings and bridges the gap to the thoughts and feelings of the client. At this stage the counselor is not outside looking in but rather inside seeing the meanings that the client gives to the experiences of his life.

Techniques

Listed below are some basic techniques of counseling that can be adapted by remedial teachers; brief explanations are given. The techniques are simply fragments that must be skillfully combined to make up an integrated whole which is more than the sum of the parts; and, because the techniques are general in nature, their use depends upon the individual and the situation. As he attempts to implement the techniques, the remedial teacher must keep in mind his paradoxical role as tutor-counselor. The suggested techniques are useful in building interpersonal relationships, but adaptations must be made to fit the teaching situation as well.

1. Drop the authoritative teacher role. Be an interested human being.
2. Communicate by transmitting attitudes and feelings. Do this by being real; it is more effective than simply to use words.
3. Arrange the physical setting so as to be close to the pupil. Do not sit behind the desk, but rather share the desk by having the pupil sit at the side. This is a technique that good remedial teachers have long applied.

4. Talk only about one-third of the time when the pupil discusses his problems. This gives him the opportunity to do most of the talking and shows that you are interested.

5. Ask questions that cannot be answered with yes or no. Instead of saying, "Do you like to read?" say, "What do you dislike about reading?" Or, instead of "Do you get along with your mother?" say, "Tell me about your mother."

6. Ask questions using the declarative tone of voice. Otherwise you may sound like an interrogator.

7. Do not interrupt the pupil when he is talking. This communicates that what he has to say is important. However, if he digresses from the subject, focus him back on the subject by saying, "How does this apply to the subject we started talking about?" or "What does this mean to you?"

8. Give the pupil silence in which to think. Realize that there will be periods of silence during which the pupil is thinking. This may take practice, for in normal conversation silence produces a feeling of awkwardness.

9. Move the focus from intellectual thought to emotional feelings when feelings are being discussed. Ask such questions as, "What does this mean to you?" and "How did you feel about that?" (See the following three techniques.)

10. Observe and interpret nonverbal clues. Notice when the pupil moves his body or cries or drums his fingers. It is important to understand the relationship between his nonverbal clues and the subject being discussed.

11. Be alert to notice a change in the rate of speech, a change in the volume of speech, or a change in the pitch or tone of the voice. Such changes may indicate that there are emotional feelings connected with the subject being discussed and that the subject needs further exploration.

12. Point out what is currently happening. Say, "I notice your eyes are moist. What kinds of feelings do you have?"

13. Use brief remarks. Do not confuse the pupil with long, complicated questions or comments.

14. Pause before talking. The pupil may wish to make additional remarks; a pause of a few seconds enables him to continue.

15. Don't give lectures on ways to behave. Ask the pupil to suggest alternatives and let him make the decision. Help him to examine the consequences of his alternatives. Information, possibilities, and alternatives may be presented, but only for his consideration. There is a big difference between telling a person what to do and suggesting alternatives.

16. Avoid talking about yourself and your experiences. Do not use "I" and avoid personal ancedotes. Focus on the pupil and *his* problems.

17. Clarify and interpret what the pupil is saying. Use such remarks as, "It seems to you that your mother wants you to go to college." At other times, make a summarizing remark. But make these brief interpretations *after* the pupil has presented his ideas.

18. Do not be alarmed at remarks made by the pupil. Instead focus on the reason behind what was said or done.

19. Do not reassure the pupil that things will be all right. This will be recognized as superficial. Look for ways to demonstrate change and progress.

20. Do not make false promises. Instead communicate a feeling for the pupil and a desire to see and understand his problem; but do not appear to be overly concerned or to assume his problem.

21. Do not make moralistic judgments. Instead focus on what is behind the pupil's behavior; ask yourself, "What is there about this person that causes him to behave in this manner?" As a remedial teacher, do not blame the student for his failures; try to understand why he has failed.

22. Avoid undue flattery and praise. Instead focus on why the student asks for an undue amount of praise. If a pupil constantly asks such questions as "Do you like this dress?" say, "Yes, but why do you ask?" or "Do *you* like it?"

23. Do not reject the pupil through your remarks or nonverbal clues, but instead attempt to accept him. Try not to show impatience; do not threaten or argue; guard against any act that might appear to belittle.

24. Refer "more serious" cases. A more explicit definition of "more serious" cases cannot be given here. The remedial teacher must sense his own limitations and seek additional help when he seriously questions his own competence.

We suggest the above techniques as a means whereby a remedial teacher can implement a counseling point of view without denying the paradoxical nature of his roles as tutor and "counselor." Children who are underachievers are not simply problem learners; they are learners with problems, many of which are emotional as well as academic. We feel that to adopt a counseling point of view is not to usurp the role of a professional counselor, but to be pragmatic in seeking a way of becoming a more effective remedial teacher.

Applications with Pupils

A counseling point of view can be extremely beneficial to a remedial teacher's efforts in working with children. A warm, positive, accepting relationship created by the teacher can enable a pupil to be more receptive to remedial teaching. As a student who has met defeat and failure in one or more school subjects experiences the teacher's positive attitudes of acceptance and understanding, the foundation for improvement is laid. Then, when remedial work is geared to the unique needs of the student, the stage is set for him to experience success, perhaps for the first time in his school experience. Motivation is created as the remedial teacher is able to give honest, genuine compliments, praise, and encouragement. This, in turn, produces a greater degree of self-confidence, additional educational goals, and forward movement. Just as failure tends to beget failure so, too, can success beget success.

The remedial teacher should understand that the acceptance and understanding inherent in a counseling relationship do not necessarily imply that he must use a permissive approach with all pupils. There is, for example, no incompatibility between the counseling point of view and the highly structured learning situation needed by some hyperactive children. Even a Marine Corps drill instructor could be warm, accepting, and understanding—if he should happen to be so inclined—without sacrificing any of the rigors of boot camp.

A counseling point of view can be useful, too, as the remedial teacher attempts to deal with the disturbances that may be causing or contributing to a learning disability.

For example, if a student has a physical symptom such as poor hearing, headaches, or frequent upset stomach, the teacher can ask questions like, "How do you sleep at night?" or "What kinds of pain do you have?" Such questions may aid in focusing upon the student's physical health; but, equally important, they serve the function of communicating to the student that the teacher is interested in him as a person. The teacher can also secure information that may lead to a referral for a medical examination.

Or, a disabled learner may frequently cause disturbances in the classroom. To get at causes for the misbehavior, the remedial teacher should not talk about his own personal experiences or give advice but, instead, listen to the situation as presented by the pupil. It may become apparent that the student's behavior is following a recognizable pattern because he does not know an appropriate way to behave. If this is so, the teacher can say, "Is there any other way you might act?" and give the student a chance to come up with alternatives. If he has no ideas the teacher should make no direct suggestions but, instead, ask him questions along the lines of, "Could you follow this course of action?" or "What might happen if you acted this way?" By presenting additional and more appropriate forms of behavior the remedial teacher may lead the pupil to try to learn other ways of behaving. Changed behavior can reduce the conflicts in a disabled learner's life and enable him to concentrate more upon his school work and upon the remedial teaching.

Finally, a student may have personal problems that cause him to feel depressed, rejected, fearful, or guilty. Again, the remedial teacher should listen to the student describe his feelings and the events which bring about the feelings, ask questions, and make clarifying statements, such as, "If I understand you correctly, you are having some difficulty with your father," or, "How do you feel about your father doing this to you?" Thus, an attempt is made to enter into the private world of the student in order to see his situation from his frame of reference. Then, as the student relates to the teacher and talks out his feelings, the emotional level is reduced and the student is better able accurately to perceive the world around him. When he is freed from concentrating primarily on his emotional problems, he is more able to respond to remedial teaching.

Instead of merely "treating" a learning problem and occasionally inquiring later as to the reason for the disability, a remedial teacher with a counseling point of view can often facilitate a long-term solution to the learning problem. The counseling relationship can help to reduce or eliminate a student's reluctance to learn; then the specific remedial program can insure success and accomplishment; and finally the praise and confidence of the teacher can be instrumental in promoting motivation and further growth. The counseling point of view, then, combines with the effective teaching of skills to result in optimum learning.

Applications with Parents

Parents, too, will generally respond in a favorable manner when they encounter a warm, sincere, honest, accepting, and understanding atmosphere. A teacher should recognize the fact that many parents are reluctant to visit school. They may, for example, feel inferior to an "educated" teacher; or they may be afraid that the teacher will criticize their method of raising children. When parents are apprehensive, their defenses are raised. A counseling point of view can help the teacher to help parents feel more at ease and drop their defenses.

At times parents come to a conference with feelings of hostility and antagonism toward a school policy, the administration, or the teachers. It is very easy for a teacher in this situation to react by defending the school and attacking the parents. However, to argue with a parent tends to be extremely unproductive, for each party simply defends his position. Then the major purpose of the conference—to help the child—is lost. A preferable procedure would be to let the angry parents express their negative feelings while the teacher neither agrees nor disagrees, attacks nor defends a position. After a period of time, the parents' anxiety may be reduced and then a successful conference can be conducted.

As parents express negative feelings the teacher can take an active part by using some of the following questions and remarks:

"If I understand correctly, you seem to have strong feelings about. . . ."
"How do you account for these feelings?"
"What is your understanding of. . . ?"
"How do you help Clyde study at home?"
"What did you say when he brought home his last report card?"
"What you are describing happened in the first grade. How might we help Clyde now?"
"What do you see ahead for your child?"

"This is the information we have about your child. How realistic does your goal seem?"

It is important to notice that the remarks above do not give in or surrender, nor do they attack. On the other hand, a neutral attitude is not maintained, for the teacher shows his interest by asking clarifying questions. Thus, the counseling point of view is utilized.

Two additional points need to be made. First, a conference can create a feeling of frustration if the teacher makes suggestions which the parent cannot completely understand or carry out. When parents fail, they feel frustrated and they transmit their anxiety to the child. As a result, the child is exposed to additional pressure; and, instead of helping the child, the teacher and the parents have compounded the problem. If suggestions are given to parents, they should be specific, concrete, and practicable. Second, in interacting with parents, or at a later time, with students, a teacher should never reveal information which was received in confidence. Individuals will not be open with a teacher if they have reason to suspect that their remarks will not be kept in confidence.

A parent conference should conclude on a positive note. The parents should feel that they have gained additional information, received new insights, and expressed their reactions and feelings. Occasionally, it may be desirable to suggest additional conferences. Successful implementation of a counseling point of view should help parents to consider conferences as valuable and meaningful; when this is so, they will feel free to return whenever additional conferences seem desirable.

Application for the Teacher

A remedial teacher must submit to careful self-scrutiny before he can adopt a counseling point of view and make it an operative part of his personal orientation. What a person *is* dictates what he *does*. Thus, the rational thoughts, emotional feelings, beliefs, and self-awareness of a remedial teacher determine his actions, attitudes, methods, and—ultimately—his results. The function of self-scrutiny is to help a person to examine himself in order to increase his self-awareness; for only when a person knows who and what he is can he hope to establish significant relationships with others in any predictable manner. Through self-examination a person can begin to discover the false fronts, the masks, the facades he employs in his day-to-day interactions. He may discover, too, that he often reacts as he *feels he should* instead of as he *feels he wants to react*. When a person gets to know himself—to see his "real self"—he is in a position to change and to develop in a positive way.

Self-examination that leads to change requires courage; it may cause apprehension, discouragement, and pain; it may require giving up complacency and comfort. But change is challenging and ultimately worthwhile.

The teacher who knows himself and is comfortable with change does not teach the same lesson for thirty years, nor is his life dull, narrow, shallow, constant.

The following sets of questions are suggested as guides to introspection. The first set deals with a specific incident in which a teacher has experienced disturbing emotional feelings.

1. What did Clyde say and do? How did he react? What feelings and attitudes did he transmit to me?
2. How did I behave? What did I say and do as I observed Clyde's reactions?
3. What caused *me* to react as I did? What was I feeling inside?
4. What did I wish to accomplish? Did I succeed?
5. Would I want to change my behavior if a similar incident came up in the future? If so, how?
6. What does looking at my behavior in this incident tell me about myself?

The second set of questions is more general.

1. How much have I changed in the past several years?
2. Do I have many "right" answers? If so, how come?
3. How safe do I really need to be?
4. How do I feel about change?
5. In what small area could I begin to change? What would it take on my part?

The capacity for change resides in each individual, but without self-awareness change is unlikely. If the procedures in a chemistry experiment are not changed, the results of each replication of the experiment will be the same. Similarly, the teacher whose inappropriate behavior leads to undesirable results will continue to get the same undesirable results until he changes his behavior. But when he becomes aware of his behavior pattern and, consequently, able to vary his approach, then the results will be different. The future does not have to be the same as the past. Self-awareness can lead to change, improvement, growth, and greater satisfaction. The teacher who is comfortable with change is one who can apply a counseling approach in his teaching because it is a part of his life.

To Sum Up

An understanding of the function of counseling, the creation of the counseling relationship, and the application of basic techniques can become an integral part of the general attitudes and techniques of the remedial teacher. However, it should be clear that every attempt was made to keep the present discussion (a) general in nature—not limited to any school or philosophy of counseling—and (b) pragmatic. Obviously there is much more to counseling. However, our purpose is not to transform remedial teachers into counselors but to borrow some useful concepts and techniques from counseling. Many teachers perceive counseling as something reserved entirely for specially trained personnel, like counselors, psychologists, and psychiatrists; as complex in nature, somewhat mystical, and far beyond their scope or ability; and as having negative or harmful results if performed to any degree by them. These perceptions are false, and the desirability of a more broadly accepted counseling point of view is becoming more widely recognized. In 1961 an important aspect of a proposed national mental health program was the concept that untrained or partially trained persons such as clergymen, family physicians, teachers, probation officers, sheriffs, scoutmasters, public welfare workers, and others can acquire the additional skill of mental health counselors through short courses and consultation on the job. (Joint Commission on Mental Illness and Health, 1961.) Such programs have been implemented with good results.

By projecting a counseling point of view, remedial teachers can contribute to more positive learning situations by creating rewarding interpersonal relationships. Rogers (1961) was speaking of such relationships when he wrote, "As I think back over a number of teachers who have facilitated my own learning, it seems to me each one has this quality of being a real person. I wonder if your memory is the same. If so, perhaps it is less important that a teacher cover the allotted amount of curriculum, or use the most approved audiovisual devices, than that he be congruent, real, in his relations to his students" (p. 287).

A Social Factors Viewpoint

We shall be frank in stating that we see a counseling viewpoint, with its focus on the individual, as potentially much more fruitful than a social factors viewpoint, with its focus on the environment or on groups, e.g., the "disadvantaged," the "culturally different." We feel that this is generally so, but we feel even more strongly that it is so with reference to disabled learners.

Compensatory Education

A social factors viewpoint, as we see it, results in stress upon *compensatory education*, that is educational efforts designed to overcome "deficits," operationally defined as deviations from norms derived from studies of "normal" populations. The "deficits" presumably account for dysfunctions in educational performance among members of such deviant groups. Up to the present time, however, efforts to provide compensatory education have not yielded results that are even promising. Gordon (1970) has pointed out the fact that despite the numerous programs tested and the vast amounts of money spent, positive findings have been rare. And in the cases where positive findings have been reported,

> . . . it is difficult, if not impossible to identify or separate treatment effects responsible for the result from general Hawthorne effects (brought about by possible impact of a changed situation) or from Rosenthal effects (the result of the impact of changed expectations). (P. 9)

Limiting Factors

Writing in an issue of the *Review of Educational Research* devoted to the education of socially disadvantaged children, Gordon (1970) also pointed out several conceptual and methodological problems involved in attempts to get at (*a*) special problems of the "disadvantaged" and/or (*b*) the impact of compensatory education programs. His points, which are quoted below, tend to underscore what we feel are the basic fallacies in a social factors viewpoint. Our comments are enclosed in brackets.

> 1. With rare exceptions the available research relating to the disadvantaged treats the target population as if it were a homogeneous group despite the mounting evidence that heterogeneity within the several subgroups so designated may be a more crucial problem in educational planning. [How, in the face of everything we know from the study of individual psychology, certain researchers and writers can continue in their attempts to characterize "the disadvantaged" is a mystery that surpasses understanding. But even when the focus is upon smaller, more clearly defined subgroups the results may be disappointing. If we are truly interested in individuals, then we had best focus on individuals.]
> 2. Similarly there appears to be a search for generic treatments or the one solution to the neglect of multiple solutions, individualization or the matching of treatment to certain characteristics. [We have already commented on the futility of the search for a BEST method. All efforts to date have failed and they will continue to fail unless we devise some way to mass-produce identical individuals.]
> 3. Studies in this area tend to depend excessively on quantitative measures and static variables to the neglect of the process variables and the qualitative analysis of the behaviors, circumstances and conditions studied. [Objective test scores and group characteristics are almost bound to take precedence when the focus is upon groups instead of individuals.]
> 4. Too much research is directed at relationships between single variables despite increasing awareness that there are few if any phenomena which can be adequately explained on the basis of the interaction between only two variables. [In remedial teaching most of the people who claim to have pat answers or sure-fire methods have fixated on a single variable, e.g., perceptual-motor functioning, phonics knowledge. We need to devise more and better guidelines and management systems to assist teachers in taking stock of multiple variables as they make instructional decisions and establish interpersonal relationships.]

5. Particularly in the study of disadvantaged populations, investigators suffer from the tendency to view characteristics which differ from some presumed norm as negative and consider any correlation between these negative characteristics and learning dysfunction as culpable. [Through proper diagnosis we can discover individuals' strengths as well as their weaknesses; then we should make use of the strengths to overcome the weaknesses.]

6. Educational research has been dominated by concern with hypothesis testing or verification to the neglect of investigation based on careful and systematic observation; this rather than theory testing is the immediate goal. [What we need to do is to concern ourselves more with the basic problems of teaching and learning and with the application of solutions to those problems in helping individuals toward optimal development.] (Pp. 11–12)

A Final Word

S. Alan Cohen (1969) has written an excellent book entitled *Teach Them All to Read* and subtitled *Theory, Methods and Materials for Teaching the Disadvantaged*. The book is replete with sensible, practical suggestions for teaching the disadvantaged; but the author has the following to say about his personal point of view: ". . . readers seeking dramatically new methods for teaching reading may be disappointed in this book. Many of the methods and materials that work well with disadvantaged children are not as new as they are intensive, thorough, sequential, and of very high quality. Because there are more similarities than differences between disadvantaged and advantaged children, the basic principles of teaching can apply to both" (p. 11). Indeed! And there are likely to be more likenesses than differences between any two groups of reasonable size.

The differences of consequence in effective teaching are individual differences. Children with learning problems have personal, individual problems. Their problems are best dealt with on an individual basis.

THOUGHTS FOR DISCUSSION

"We all discourage one another more than we encourage; we all are much better prepared to discourage." (Dinkmeyer and Dreikurs, 1963, p. 37)

"My belief that the choice of beginning reading methods is important does not lessen in any way my conviction about the importance of good teaching. Indeed, as we learn more about the teaching of beginning reading, we may find that a poor method in the hands of a good teacher produces better results than a good method in the hands of a poor teacher. But . . . good teachers are constantly searching for good methods." (Chall, 1967, pp. 308–309)

"It is my contention that tomorrow's educator, whether the humblest kindergarten teacher, or the president of a great university, must know, at the deepest personal level, the stance he takes in life. Unless he has true convictions as to how his values are arrived at, what sort of an individual he hopes will emerge from his educational organization, whether he is manipulating human robots, or dealing with free individual persons, and what kind of a relationship he is striving to build with these persons, he will have failed not only his profession, but his culture." (Rogers, 1969, pp. 217–218)

"Where there is the necessary technical skill to move mountains, there is no need for the faith to move mountains." (Hoffer, 1955, p. 12)

"We probably have a greater love for those we support than those who support us. Our vanity carries more weight than our self interest." (Hoffer, 1955, p. 12)

"The attitude of standing in the other's shoes, of viewing the world through the student's eyes, is almost unheard of in the classroom. One can listen to thousands of ordinary classroom interactions without coming across one instance of clearly communicated, sensitively accurate, empathic understanding. But it has a tremendously releasing effect when it occurs." (Rogers, 1968, p. 13)

"One of the givens in special education is that occasional failure with students is inevitable. The teacher who objectively asks why a particular approach has failed and then goes about revising it is in a far better position to assist disturbed children than one who views it largely as a personal defeat." (Hewitt, 1968, p. 67)

"We envisage . . . a third level of professionalization. This level consists of the remedial specialist who is called in when any child fails to respond to the treatment provided by the basic teacher under the direction of a career teacher. Such a specialist has at his disposal a great deal of knowledge. He is skilled in the more elaborate techniques of diagnosis. He can provide or direct remedial treatment. The members of this group must be highly trained and carefully selected. Obviously they must be well paid." (Stephens, 1967, p. 139)

"It is impossible to expect teachers to understand behavior of children who are 'different' unless they are allowed to come in contact with contemporary thought about race and intelligence, culture and behavior." (Nickerson, 1966, pp. 93–94)

REFERENCES

Bloom, B. S. Learning for mastery. *Evaluation Comment*, 1968, **1** (2).

Bruner, J. S. *The process of education.* Cambridge, Mass.: Harvard University Press, 1960.

Carroll, J. B. A model of school learning. *Teachers College Record*, 1963, **64**, 723–733.

Chall, J. *Learning to read: The great debate.* New York: McGraw-Hill, 1967.

Cohen, S. A. *Teach them all to read.* New York: Random House, 1969.

Dinkmeyer, D., and Dreikurs, R. *Encouraging children to learn: The encouragement process.* Englewood Cliffs, N. J.: Prentice-Hall, 1963.

Frieder, B. Motivator: Least developed of teacher roles. *Educational Technology,* 1970, **10**, 28–36.

Georgia Department of Education. *Regulations and procedures, program for exceptional children.* Atlanta: Author, 1969.

Gordon, E. W. Education for socially disadvantaged children: Introduction. *Review of Educational Research,* 1970, **40**, 1–12.

Hewitt, F. M. *The emotionally disturbed child in the classroom.* Boston: Allyn and Bacon, 1968.

Hoffer, E. *The passionate state of mind.* New York: Harper and Row, 1955.

Iscoe, I. "I told you so": The logical dilemma of the bright underachieving child. *Psychology in the Schools,* 1964, **1**, 282–284.

Joint Commission on Mental Illness and Health. *Action for mental health.* New York: Basic Books, 1961.

Lipson, J. I. Job description for a teacher in a new school. *Educational Technology,* 1970, **10**, 7–12.

Mayo, S. T. Mastery learning and mastery testing. *Measurement in Education,* 1970, **1** (3).

Nickerson, N. *Education for alienation.* Englewood Cliffs, N.J. Prentice-Hall, 1966.

Orwell, G. *Animal farm: A fairy story.* New York, Harcourt, 1946.

Otto, W. Yes, Virginia, there is an achievement dilemma. *Psychology in the Schools,* 1965, **2**, 329–333.

Otto, W., and Askov, E. *The Wisconsin design for reading skill development: Rationale and guidelines.* Minneapolis: National Computer Systems, 1970.

Otto, W., and Smith, R. J. *Administering the school reading program.* Boston: Houghton Mifflin, 1970.

Rappaport, S. R., and McNary, S. R. Teacher effectiveness for children with learning disorders. *Journal of Learning Disabilities,* 1970, **3**, 75–83.

Redl, F. *When we deal with children.* New York: Free Press, 1966.

Rogers, C. R. *Client centered therapy.* Boston: Houghton Mifflin, 1951.

Rogers, C. R. *On becoming a person.* Boston: Houghton Mifflin, 1961.

Rogers, C. R. *The international relationship in the facilitation of learning.* Columbus, Ohio: Charles E. Merrill, 1968.

Rogers, C. R. *Freedom to learn.* Columbus, Ohio: Charles E. Merrill, 1969.

Secretary's (HEW) National Advisory Committee on Dyslexia and Related Reading Disorders. Reading disorders in the United States. Washington, D.C.: Department of Health, Education and Welfare, 1969.

Shiel, B. J. Evaluation: A self-directed curriculum, 1965. Mimeo, 1966.

Stephens, J. J. *The process of schooling.* New York: Holt, 1967.

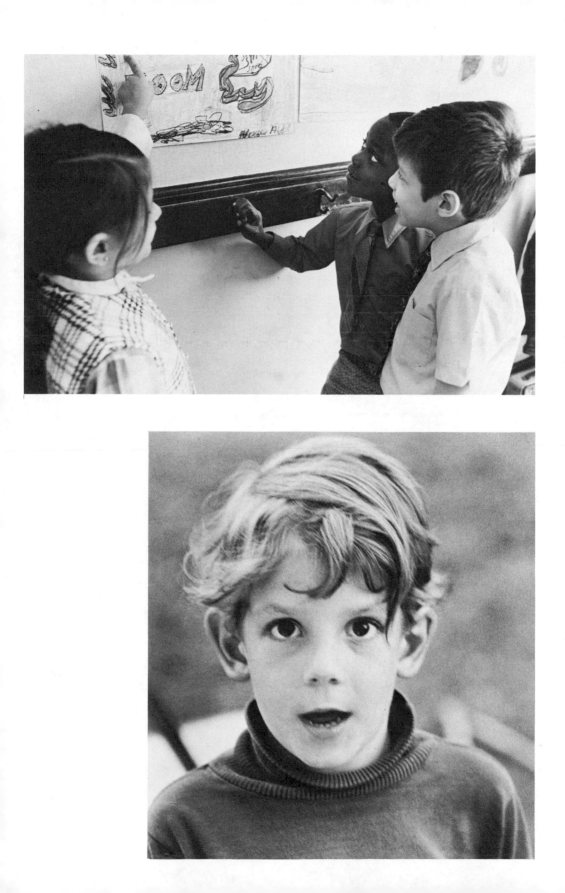

Suppliers of Tests and Teaching Materials

Academic Therapy Publications
1539 4th Street
San Rafael, California 94901

American Book Company
55 Fifth Avenue
New York, New York 10023

American Guidance Service, Inc.
Circle Pines, Minnesota 55014

American Optical Company
Southbridge, Massachusetts 01550

Baush and Lomo
Rochester, New York 14602

Beckley Cardy Company
1900 No. Narragansett Ave.
Chicago, Illinois 60639

Baltone Electric Corporation
Specialized Instruments Division
4201 West Victoria
Chicago, Illinois 60647

Benefic Press Publications
10300 West Roosevelt Road
Westchester, Illinois 60153

W. S. Benson & Company
109 East Fifth Street
Box 1866
Austin, Texas 78767

Bobbs-Merrill Company
4300 West 62nd Street
Indianapolis, Indiana 46268

Milton Bradley Company
74 Park Street
Springfield, Massachusetts 01102

California Test Bureau
Division of McGraw-Hill Book Company
Del Monte Research Park
Monterey, California 93940

Columbia University Teachers College
Bureau of Publications
(See Teachers College Press)

Committee on Diagnostic Reading Tests
Mountain Home, North Carolina 28758

Coronet Instructional Films
65 East South Water Street
Chicago, Illinois 60601

Economy Company
1901 North Walnut Avenue
Oklahoma City, Oklahoma 73105

Educational Development Laboratories
Division of McGraw-Hill Book Company
75 Prospect
Huntington, New York 11743

Educational Guidelines Company
P. O. Box 25308
Oklahoma City, Oklahoma 73125

Educational Testing Service
Princeton, New Jersey 08540

Educational Test Bureau
Educational Publishers, Inc.
120 Washington Avenue Southeast
Minneapolis, Minnesota 55414

ERIC Document Reproduction Service
The National Cash Register Company
4936 Fairmount Avenue
Bethesda, Maryland 20014

ERIC/CRIER
200 Pine Hall
School of Education
Indiana University
Bloomington, Indiana 47401

Field Educational Publications, Inc.
609 Mission Street
San Francisco, California 94105

Follett Educational Corporation
1010 West Washington Blvd.
Chicago, Illinois 60607

Garrard Press
510 North Hickory Street
Champaign, Illinois 61820

Ginn and Company
Waltham, Massachusetts 02154

Grolier Educational Corporation
845 Third Avenue
New York, New York 10022

I. Z. Hackman
Route 3
Elizabethtown, Pennsylvania 17022

Harlow Publishing Company
532-536 Northwest Second Street
Oklahoma City, Oklahoma 73102

Harr Wagner Publishing Company
(See Field Educational Publ.)

Harcourt, Brace and Jovanovich
757 3rd Avenue
New York, New York 10017

Houghton Mifflin Company
110 Tremont Street
Boston, Massachusetts 02107

Institute for Personality and Aptitude
    Testing
1602-04 Coronado Drive
Champaign, Illinois 61820

V. B. Lippincott Company
East Washington Square
Philadelphia, Pennsylvania 19105

Keystone View Company
Meadville, Pennsylvania 16335

Lyons and Carnahan
Educational Division
407 East 25th Street
Chicago, Illinois 60616

Macmillan Company
866 3rd Avenue
New York, New York 10022

Maico Hearing Instruments, Inc.
7375 Bush Lake Road
Minneapolis, Minnesota 55435

McCormick-Mathers Publishing Co., Inc.
1440 East English Street
Wichita, Kansas 67201

McGraw-Hill Book Company
330 West 42nd Street
New York, New York 10036

Charles E. Merrill Publishing Company
1300 Alum Creek Drive
Columbus, Ohio 43216

Mills Center
1512 East Broward Avenue
Fort Lauderdale, Florida 33310

National Computer Systems, Inc.
4401 West 76th Street
Minneapolis, Minnesota 55435

New Laurel Book Company
2249 South Calumet Avenue
Chicago, Illinois 60616

Newberry Award Records, Inc.
A Division of Miller-Brody Productions,
    Inc.
342 Madison Avenue
New York, New York 10017

Noble & Noble Publishers, Inc.
750 3rd Avenue
New York, New York 10017

Numark Educational Systems
Forest Hills, New York 11375

Open Court Publishing Company
1307-7th Street
LaSalle, Illinois 61301

A. N. Palmer Company
902 South Wabash
Chicago, Illinois 60605

Pitman Publishing Corporation
20 East 46th Street
New York, New York 10017

The Peterson System
(See Macmillan Company)

Pioneer Printing Company
Bellingham, Washington 98225

Prentice Hall, Inc.
Englewood Cliffs, New Jersey 07632

Psychological Corporation
304 East 45th Street
New York, New York 10017

Psychological Test Specialists
Box 1404
Missoula, Montana 59801

Public School Publishing Company
204 West Mulberry Street
Bloomington, Illinois 61701

Random House, Inc.
501 Madison Avenue
New York, New York 10022

Random House
Singer School Division
259 East Erie Street
Chicago, Illinois 60611

Readers Digest Educational Service
Pleasantville, New York 10057

Schmidt, Hall and McCreary Company
Parlo Avenue at 6th Street
Minneapolis, Minnesota 55415

Science Research Associates
259 East Erie Street
Chicago, Illinois 60607

Scott, Foresman & Company
1900 East Lake Avenue
Glenview, Illinois 60025

E. C. Scale Company
1053 East 54th Street
Indianapolis, Indiana 46220

L. W. Singer Company, Inc.
(See Random House/Singer School Div.)

Slossen Educational Publications
140 Pine Street
East Aurora, New York 14052

Steck-Vaughn Company
P. O. Box 2028
Austin, Texas 78710

Teachers College Press
Columbia University
525 West 120th Street
New York, New York 10027

Teachers Publishing Corporation
23 Leroy Avenue
Darien, Connecticut 06820

Titmus Optical Company, Inc.
Petersburg, Virginia 23803

University of Illinois Press
Urbana, Illinois 61801

U. Weston Walsh
Portland, Maine 04104

George Wahr Publishing Company
316 South State Street
Ann Arbor, Michigan 48106

Webster Division
McGraw-Hill Book Company
Manchester Road
Manchester, Missouri 63011

Webster Publishing Company
(See Webster Division,
McGraw-Hill Book Co.)

Wepman, Joseph M. (Auditory
    Discrimination Test)
950 East 59th Street
Chicago, Illinois 60607

Zaner-Bloser Company
613 North Park Street
Columbus, Ohio 43215

Index

Photo Credits